# TWO THOUSAND YEARS OF MISSIONS BEFORE CAREY

# TWO THOUSAND YEARS OF MISSIONS BEFORE CAREY

**BASED UPON AND EMBODYING MANY OF THE EARLIEST EXTANT ACCOUNTS**

**LEMUEL CALL BARNES**

*WITH MAP AND ILLUSTRATIONS*

ISBN : 978-93-5324-543-6 (HB)

First Published, Chicago, 1900

Published, 2020

*Published by*

Facsimile Publisher
12 Pragati Market
Ashok Vihar, Ph-2
Delhi-110052
E-mail: books@facsimilepublisher.com

*Printed at:* G. Print Process, Delhi.

**Two Thousand Years of Missions Before Carey**

Author: Lemuel Call Barnes

# Two Thousand Years of Missions Before Carey

BASED UPON AND EMBODYING MANY OF THE EARLIEST EXTANT ACCOUNTS

BY

LEMUEL CALL BARNES

MINISTER, FOURTH AVENUE CHURCH
PITTSBURG

WITH MAP AND ILLUSTRATIONS

CHICAGO
THE CHRISTIAN CULTURE PRESS
1900

To

THE TWO

Who Have Done Most

To Kindle and To Foster

My Interest in Missions,

## FORESPEECH.

It is said that Shakspere owed much of his broad mental vision to the accounts of the world's exploration made available in English by Richard Hakluyt and that Milton was still deeper in debt to the same work. A large outlook on God's world is the necessary basis of lofty inspiration. But the "Principal Navigations" of missionary enterprise have never been brought together in any one book or set of books. After preparing the copious bibliography of missions for the London Conference in 1888, Dr. Jackson, Secretary of the American Society of Church History, said in the journal of that society:

> We have some short histories which try to give an outline of the story: e. g., Mr. Smith's "Short History of Christian Missions." . . . But no one who is interested in the subject thinks of being satisfied with a few pages written at second hand on the story of the spread of Christianity during 1800 years.

The list of slight but helpful sketches has been increased since 1888. On special fields, periods or phases of mission work discussions of great value and real scholarship have been published, *e. g.*, Dennis' "Christian Missions and Social Progress" and Noble's "Redemption of Africa." There are books almost without number on missions of the nineteenth century

—"The Missionary Century." Those books which pay some attention to a longer period give but little space to the earlier times and next to none to any time between the primitive and the recent times, except for the Continent of Europe. The bibliography of the New York Conference of 1900 will show the gap of 1888 still unfilled.

All the missions originating in Europe for one thousand years—half of the period assigned us for study—were of necessity Roman Catholic missions. The neglect to consider these would be inexcusable in the present work. The largest missionary library in America has made no effort to procure books on Roman Catholic missions. Most Protestant accounts of missions ignore the Roman missions or touch them but slightly, not to say slightingly. In like manner the only Roman Catholic history of missions in general treats of Protestant missions for the avowed purpose of disparagement. The present work is an endeavor to treat all missions of all denominations before the era of Carey with critical, but perfectly friendly, fairness.

The mass of scattered details to be kept in mind at once in a continuous history of world-wide missions is so great that chronological treatment of the whole together would be unavoidably confusing. A geographical framework lends itself far more surely to unity and clear-cut outlines. A chronological conspectus is furnished in a table at the end. The events on each field are considered for the most part in the order of their occurrence.

No space has been taken to consider matters which are perfectly germane, are, in fact, a part of the whole theme of missions in a country, such as its geography, its racial types, its language and literature, its general history in the period considered, its theology, above all its morals. Even the sources, resources and machinery of the missionary work have had to be omitted or but incidentally treated. That vital half known as the home side of foreign missions would require and deserves a separate treatise.

Some of the territory surveyed here as being covered by prosperous Christian missions was afterwards lost to Christianity. Part of it has not been recovered to this day. But our line of study is not the history of Christianity in any part of the world, it is the story of the propagation of Christianity in every part of the world. Efforts to reconvert or proselyte are not within our aim.

For help rendered it is a pleasure to record gratitude to the British Museum and all the large libraries of Boston and vicinity, New York, Baltimore, Washington and Chicago. There is multiform and extended obligation to the library—composed of more than one hundred thousand volumes—which the city of Pittsburg has gathered in the buildings provided for the purpose by Mr. Carnegie. This collection has been made in five years with the highest judgment, and is administered in the true missionary temper by Mr. E. H. Anderson and his able assistants.

Inability to name each separate author who has helped in the preparation of the work is deeply regretted. The Bibliography attached can only in part cover the need. The debt of gratitude of one who attempts to write a history in even one department covering the whole earth during two thousand years is simply incalculable. The findings of fact by other students have been freely used and have been often the only dependence for information. But very few quotations have been indulged from second-hand accounts, however enticing.

On the other hand, the pages have been freely enriched with quotations from the primary sources of information, so that the reader may have the privilege of seeing for himself and building in his own way on the original foundations of knowledge concerning the subject before him. This, which is always refreshing, is peculiarly desirable in a field like the present, about many parts of which available writings are so few that it is impracticable for the general reader to correct the view of one student by that of another. Thus, so far as the plan of the work and the limitations of the author allowed, the reader has been made an original student. It is more spiritually enkindling to walk in the light than it is to walk in some reflection of it, especially some second, third, or, perhaps, thirteenth, reflection. The aim has been, however, to introduce the words of even the primary authors, never merely for the sake of the special enjoyment they give, but only when they have such clearness without need of comment and such progress of thought as to directly carry on the narrative.

The extant records of the later generations of missions are naturally more full than of the earlier. Yet the most significant record of all is that of the first thirty-four years of Christian missions given us in the Gospels and the Acts. Quotations from these earliest of all extant accounts are made in the rendering of the Twentieth Century New Testament.

It is hoped that no important missionary effort which is on record during the Two Thousand Years has failed of mention. But limitations of space have required plain and condensed statement. Too often repression of incident and of glowing appreciation has been unavoidable. Opportunity for the necessary research, in the midst of the duties of an exacting pastorate, has been possible only by the kindness of a church which is in fact as well as in theory devoted to missions—a people who endeavor to pray with deep sincerity, "Thy kingdom come." If this little study in missions is of any use to the cause, the contribution is theirs.

In addition to valuable suggestions from several personal friends, there is one nearer still, a most sympathetic and earnest coadjutor in every missionary purpose of life, who has assisted in the present work by obtaining material from Spanish sources and writing much of chapter X, besides making the Index of Names and Subjects and rendering invaluable aid in the finishing of the whole book.

# CONTENTS.

## Part I—GENESIS OF MISSIONS.



## Part II—DISTRIBUTION OF MISSIONS.

### Asia.



### Africa.

## Europe.



## Arctic Regions.



## America.



## Part III—CONTINUITY OF MISSIONS.

# LIST OF ILLUSTRATIONS.

ARRANGED IN ALPHABETICAL ORDER

*Raphael.*

PAUL ON MARS' HILL.

*"'For we are also His offspring.'"*

## CHAPTER I.

# ETHNIC MOVEMENTS MISSIONARY.

1. On Mars' Hill. 2. God in Athens. 3. God never abdicates. 4. Strategic Hellas. 5. The Greeks gifted. 6. Scattered abroad. 7. Roman rule. 8. Highways of missions. 9. Favorable laws. 10. World-wide conceptions. 11. "That rabble of gods." 12 Wanted—a conscience.

1. The Greek race furnished the finest embodiment of ethnic culture. Athens was the Queen of Gentile Cities,

"the eye of Greece, mother of arts
And eloquence."

Paul the Missionary, looking that queenly culture straight in the eye, at the moment of his highest inspiration, had the insight to see and the breadth of sympathy to say that the soul of ethnic development is God. A smaller man would have been too narrow to see it. A man less inspired would have been too conventional to say it. But the pre-eminent missionary, swayed by the supreme Spirit, divined the reality and put it in words as plain as sunbeams. He not only said what any high-souled Jew might possibly have said about God, "The God who made the world and all things in it—he I say, Lord from the first of

Heaven and Earth, does not dwell in temples made by hands, nor yet do human hands minister to his wants, as though he could need anything, since he is himself the giver to every one of life, breath and everything else," but he added, in words so luminous that to this day many Christians are dazzled by them and fail to grasp their full intensity of meaning: "He made every race of men from one stock and caused them to settle on all parts of the earth's surface, first fixing a duration for their Day and the limits of their settlement, so that they might search for God, if after all they might feel their way to him and find him."

2. The living God has never slumbered or slept in his purpose of good for all humanity. He has been alive and the life of all life in every age and in every land. His energy has been the moving force in all human progress. Intractable materials have been used, however unconsciously to themselves, for his high and holy purposes. Within all the migrations, colonizations and civilizations of men, the living God is the impelling power. Paul declares that the boundaries of Greece are determined by him as well as the boundaries of Palestine. Men of Athens are his offspring as well as men of Jerusalem.

The life of God in the life of mankind, like his life in a vine, sends it upward and outward. Every impulse onward is a mission, a divine sending. Hebrew "mal'ak" (messenger), Greek "apostle," Latin "missionary," Anglo-Saxon "sent" are all one word in different tongues. "Go" is the core of the idea and

God is the ultimate Author of all going. He is the universal Sender. "It is in Him that we move." The fountain of the "going" in the human race lies deeper than words, deeper than reasoning; it wells up out of the divine depths of ultimate Being. All men and all races of men that amount to anything move under the brief but tremendous commission, "Go." With or without the intervention of thought, even anterior to the development of highly specialized organs of intelligence, this one short and sharp command, like a bolt out of heaven, smites and charges the very nerves of life. Things which do not "go" never lived or else they are dead. Human life itself is a mission. Men are sent of God.

3. When the results of any particular sending are wide-reaching, we see plainly that it was a mission. When an *ethnos*, a whole race, is concerned, it becomes conspicuous and demands devout study. We can not get too distinctly before us the fact that every ethnic movement, from Abraham to Dewey, is a mission, a sacred sending. God has somehow said, "Go." Faith insists that even when there is a large admixture of unholy human passion, God is somewhere behind the movement. He never abdicates the office of Commander-in-chief. The sin-reared cross of Jesus Christ is a supreme example of this fact. There was the mission of missions.

The inscription on that cross "was written in Hebrew, in Latin, and in Greek." These were the families of mankind which had most directly to do with the sending of God's great purpose of love throughout the world. Each one of them had a mission of its own to perform.

4. Look, first, at the divine mission of the Greeks. "The limits of their settlement" secured them an admirable training for a special mission in the world. Separated by natural boundaries from the effacing inundations of barbarism, they had opportunity to develop a high degree of civilization. Like the young of marsupial animals, they were carried in a pocket of the continent of Europe until they had time to grow strong. Their comparative safety in that peninsular home of theirs is marked by the meaning of such great words in human history as Marathon, Salamis, and Thermopylæ. These were gateways at which they were able to stay the inflow of the hordes of barbarians. The little land itself was so divided by mountains and by estuaries of the sea as to promote independence in the various neighborhoods, and individuality of character. The center of Greek life was the municipality. The cities of Greece were practically the states of Greece. And these little cities acquired a feeling of independence and a sense of freedom never before enjoyed on the face of the earth. Among them humanity reached a pitch of vigorous individuality which it never had possessed. For its size Greece had an immense sea-coast, which called out sea-faring, commercial and colonizing habits in the people. To this day, though so long under the heel of the Turk, they are the keen tradesmen of the Levant, the "Yankees" of the Orient. This land was midway between the East and the West, so that it

was constantly in close touch with both the Orient and the Occident. Greece is a part of Europe, but the Athenians, to-day, in ordinary conversation, speak of "going to Europe" as if they were inhabitants of another continent. This little land was at the pivotal point in the history and in the development of the nations of antiquity.

5. Again, the "search for God," of which the apostle speaks, made by this wonderful people carried them in purely intellectual attainments far beyond any other people who had ever lived. The philosophy of the world at this moment is rooted in the ideas which were developed and put into words by the great Greek masters of thought. Not only did theories of life reach an advanced stage of development among them, but the putting of ideas into forms of beauty was so highly developed that their art has never since been equaled in many directions. In sculpture Phidias and Praxiteles have had no rivals in all the ages since their day. In literature we still speak of Homer, Æschylus, and Demosthenes as living masters. The missionary appealed to their own poets. "His offspring, too, are we."

The Greeks had a linguistic gift which fitted them for world-wide service. Their language had become so facile an instrument of thought and feeling that they were able to excel all other people in expressing the finer shades of the experiences of the spirit. This language of theirs, so highly and finely developed, became the vehicle for bringing the messages of God in the Scriptures to the ears of all mankind. Centuries before Christ came into the world the Old Testament writings had been translated into the Greek tongue. Christ and the apostles made most of their quotations from the Scriptures out of this Greek translation. It was through the medium of this language that the Gospel could be preached from end to end of the Roman world. Everywhere there were men and women who understood Greek. The prevalence of the Greek language has been well called a temporary suspension of the confusion of tongues. Such was the mission of this people in preparing a vehicle in which the divine thought could be carried to all mankind.

6. The people, so wonderfully fitted to be the pioneers of a higher life, were sent by the almighty purpose throughout the world. The hand by which God thrust them forth on their mighty mission was an ambitious man, Alexander the Great. Full of Greek sentiment as well as of personal ambition, he started on his tour of eastern conquest. In ancient Troy, of which Homer had sung, he poured out libations to the gods of the Greeks, and then entered upon that career which carried him from land to land as a restless conqueror until he stood on the banks of the great river of India. In a remarkably short lifetime he founded city after city, named many of them after himself, and one of the greatest of them, Alexandria in Egypt, became a center of philosophy, of art, of education, and of religious thought, for many centuries afterward. In his conquest of the world Alexander carried the Greek language everywhere so that it became the vehicle of the Gospel which was to be preached. It is impossi-

ble for us to see how the Word of God, even after Jesus had brought it in perfection, could have reached the world had not the Almighty Father first prepared this Greek nation and this marvelous Greek tongue, and then sent that man of colossal ambition, the son of Philip, in his course of conquest throughout the world.

7. Now, turn for a moment to the divine mission of the Romans. They were given a genius different from that of the Greeks, but a genius in itself as great, a genius for discipline, for organization and for government. The Roman legions were the most splendid bodies of soldiers in the world. Not only were they equipped with magnificent brute force, but they were subjected to a discipline which affected the higher phases of life. Everywhere in the New Testament when we come in contact with a Roman military officer we come in contact with a man of high soul, a noble gentleman as well as a soldier. These men were sent throughout the world gradually; not suddenly, like the versatile, mercurial Greeks, who flashed in a few months over the world like a meteor nucleated about Alexander and almost as suddenly passed out of political power. They left only the more spiritual elements of their life, their thought and their language, strewn over the world. But the Romans moved slowly from land to land. As they went they assimilated each country in some way to Rome, made it tributary to the Mistress of the World, so that in course of time the whole civilized earth was under a single government, as never before or since; and this government was efficient and practical in its administration of affairs.

8. The Romans cast up highways for the transmission of the Gospel everywhere. The Roman roads started from the golden mile-stone in the City of the Seven Hills in five directions, and ran throughout the empire. Even in the remote provinces these roads were so perfect, so much better than our best pavements of today, that a man could read a manuscript book as he rode along in his carriage. The eighth chapter of Acts tells us of such an experience. This great system of highways made it possible for the messengers of the cross to carry the message from end to end of the empire. A man could start at Jerusalem, and going over the same road along which the Ethiopian went, reach Alexandria in Egypt, then go westward to Cyrene, and on past old Carthage to the Pillars of Hercules. Crossing the straits into Spain, he could drive through that land and through all Gaul. Having crossed the British Channel, his chariot wheels need not stop short of the Scottish border. On the return trip he could pass through the Netherlands, through Germany, Switzerland and the Danubian regions to the Hellespont, then through Asia Minor and Syria until he reached Jerusalem. This would have been a circuit of seven thousand miles on splendid Roman highways cast up at the will of the Commander-in-chief of all nations, in order that the Gospel might run, have free course and be glorified. On this great circle and its radii there was a system of post stations for the convenience of those who were able to ride. It was along these thoroughfares that the messengers of Christ found the possibilities of distant travel, though they generally went on foot.

9. More important than the highways was the protection to life that was given by the laws of the Romans. They extended the realms of peace and safety. Wherever they went they carried the protection of law and order. You remember how often Paul appealed to it. In Jerusalem, the sacred city of his own nation, he appealed to the law of Rome. In Philippi, at his first point of attack on the continent of Europe, he appealed to the Roman law. The spread of the Gospel was under the ægis of this Roman law, which until the present hour is the basis of the law of civilized nations. World-wide peace had been established at the time of the coming of Jesus. The great Latin writers are never tired of singing the praises of this age of peace. The Gospel had an opportunity, as it could not possibly have had if there had been two score of nations, half of them warring with the other half through this mighty stretch of the civilized world, instead of the one majestic, calm, mighty, Roman government.

10. It was the mission of the Romans in the world not only to prepare the way but also to prepare the mind for the all-embracing message. They created wide-reaching conceptions into which the Gospel of a universal Fatherhood and a man-wide brotherhood could be received. Cicero says: "This universe forms one immeasurable commonwealth and city, common alike to Gods and mortals. And as in earthly states certain particular laws, which we shall hereafter describe, govern the particular relationships of particular tribes, so in the nature of things doth an univer-

sal law, far more magnificent and resplendent, regulate the affairs of that universal city where gods and men compose one vast association." The Romans, as well as the Greeks, prepared the mental way for the Gospel.

11. There is a further mission which Greeks and Romans had in common. They worked out a complete demonstration of the fact that men, even under the most favorable conditions for feeling their way to God, fail to find him fully without a special revelation of his love and beneficent will. Listen to this statement of the apostle himself, which is so clear on this point that there is no mistaking it: "Men of Athens, on every hand I see signs of your being very religious. Indeed as I was going about and looking at the objects that you worship, I observed an altar on which the dedication was inscribed, 'To AN UNKNOWN GOD.' What then you are worshiping without knowledge is what I am now preaching to you." Their ignorance of God had descended further even than agnosticism. Their polytheism had fallen into atheism. At first the Romans had few gods, but whenever they took a walled city they evoked the gods of that city to come out and join the Roman side, then they would establish them as Roman deities. By this and other processes it came to pass that the gods of Rome were almost innumerable, and the more gods there were the less became the real worship of any god. The system of polytheism became so vast that it tumbled to ruin. Seneca, one of the great Roman thinkers, says; "All that rabble of gods which

the superstitions of ages have heaped up we shall adore in such a way as to remember that their worship belongs rather to custom than to reality." Cicero more than once quotes Cato as saying that he did not see how the soothsayers could avoid laughing each other in the face.

12. With the decay of sincerity in religion had come, what always comes sooner or later along with that, a decay in morals. The social life of the Greek and Roman world had very little in it which we can admire. Its amusements were sights of bloodshed. Julius Cæsar put into the circus for the amusement of the people two contending armies, five hundred foot soldiers, three hundred cavalrymen and twenty elephants, to fight a sanguinary contest. Augustus, the magnificent, from whom the Augustan age is named, put pairs of gladiators to fight each other to death until ten thousand men had been slain. Political life was as corrupt as social life. That high-souled devotion to the interests of the public which once had marked the Romans and lifted them into power was changed into a greedy scramble for place. The name of Nero is almost a synonym of everything that is base in human history. The domestic life, the very center of all worthy life in any nation, was as full of corruption as the social and political life. The Romans boasted that for five hundred years, in the early and heroic days, there never had been a single divorce among them, but the era came when divorces were so common that women reckoned time by the number of their divorces and suc-

cessive husbands. Children were often unwelcome, and were thrust out to die by exposure unless some charitable hand should rescue them. This practice was not limited to the debased as it is now, but was allowed by law, and was advocated by Aristotle and other great masters of thought in the Greek-Roman world. Even Plato—the soul who stood nearest to Socrates and most completely reflected the thought of that lofty master—Plato advocated the destruction of children that were not wanted.

The running glimpse which we have now taken of prominent characteristics of the ethnic world has been enough to show that the great non-Jewish races had a vital part in preparing the way for the coming of the King and for the advancement of his kingdom throughout the world. They did it by their miserable failures as well as by their magnificent achievements.

CHAPTER II.

## THE MESSIANIC RACE MISSIONARY.

13. Patriarch and poets. 14. Prophets. 15. The dispersion in Asia. 16. In Africa. 17. In Europe. 18. Everywhere. 19. The New Testament as to the dispersion. 20. Hebrew mission-houses. 21. Pagan antagonism. 22. Distinct propagation. 23. Philo a missionary. 24. He advocates a liberal missionary policy. 25. Hebrew missions commonly unappreciated. 26. Bible translation. 27. Its uses. 28. Hebrew missions fruitful. 29. Conspicuous converts. 30. Among the masses. 31. Juvenal's testimony. 32. Converts numerous. 33. Hebrew missions the genesis of Christian missions.

13. In the germinal promise, at the very tap-root of the Hebrew nation, lay the missionary idea, to be carried up through all its growth: "In thy seed shall all the nations of the earth be blessed." In the gracious foliage of the national religion, the Hebrew Hymn-book, it appears again and again.

"Ask of me, and I will give thee the nations for thine
inheritance,
And the uttermost parts of the earth for thy possession." (Ps. 2:8.)

"I will make thy name to be remembered in all generations;
Therefore shall the peoples give thee thanks for ever and ever." (Ps. 45: 16-17.)

"He shall have dominion also from sea to sea,
And from the River unto the ends of the earth. . . .
Yea, all kings shall fall down before him:
All nations shall serve him. . . .
And men shall be blessed in him;
All nations shall call him happy." (Ps. 72: 8, 11, 17.)

"Jehovah hath made known his salvation:
His righteousness hath he openly showed in the sight of the nations. . . .
All the ends of the earth have seen the salvation of our God."
Make a joyful noise unto Jehovah, all the earth:
Break forth and sing for joy; yea sing praises."
(Ps. 98:2, 3, 4.)

14. The missionary thought of Israel came to full blossom and once, at least, to actual fruitage in the great preachers of the nation. "The word of the Lord came unto Jonah the second time, saying arise, go unto Nineveh, that great city, and preach unto it the preaching that I bid thee." The reluctance of the prophet to be sent, to be a missionary, and his utter disgust at the success of his mission in saving the heathen at the behest of God, whom he reproached with being "a gracious God and full of compassion," show that even the well known purpose of God could not yet

become permanently effective in his people. The evangelizing of Nineveh was a sort of abortive, preliminary fruitage, a foretoken of the fact that, as soon as the essential reality of religion should be sufficiently developed in the people, it would bear that kind of fruit.

This inevitable growth was stimulated and expressed, brought to the stage of abundant bloom, by the school of national preaching of which Isaiah was the head.

"For the earth shall be full of the knowledge of Jehovah,
As the waters cover the sea." (Isa. 11:9.)

"And many nations shall go and say,
Come ye, and let us go up to the mountain of Jehovah,
And to the house of the God of Jacob;
And he will teach us of his ways,
And we will walk in his paths:
For out of Zion shall go forth the law,
And the word of Jehovah from Jerusalem."
(Micah 4:2.)

"I Jehovah have called thee in righteousness,
And will hold thine hand,
And will keep thee, and give thee for a covenant of the people,
For a light of the Gentiles." (Isa. 42:6.)

"Listen, O isles, unto me;
And hearken, ye peoples, from far. . . .
It is too light a thing that thou shouldst be my servant
To raise up the tribes of Jacob,

And to restore the preserved of Israel:
I will also give thee for a light to the Gentiles,
That thou mayest be my salvation unto the end of
the earth. . . .

"Lo, these shall come from far:
And, lo, these from the north and from the west;
And these from the land of Sinim." (Isa. 49: 1, 6,
12.)

These are only a few of the many missionary messages of the prophets.

After the blossoming period of the great poet-preachers had passed and the petals of their prophecies covered the ground, it almost appears as if the fruit had begun to set as seen in the dreams of Daniel. "I saw in the night visions, and, behold, there came with the clouds of heaven one like unto a son of man, and he came even to the ancient of days, and they brought him near before him. And there was given him dominion, and glory, and a kingdom, that all the peoples, nations, and languages should serve him: his dominion is an everlasting dominion, which shall not pass away, and his kingdom that which shall not be destroyed." (Dan. 7: 13-14.)

15. The growth of the expectation that all nations should some day know the one true God advanced most rapidly just when those who were able to make Him known were being scattered most widely among the nations. The ideal and the actual developed side by side, though without much conscious relation to each other. But each development profoundly helped the

other. They both sprang out of the same purpose of God.

It is estimated that 350,000 Hebrews, first and last, had been carried captive to the Euphrates and beyond. Fewer than 50,000 returned. Hence even if there had been no increase, six were left by their own choice in the land of exile for every one who returned. By the beginning of our era these had increased to millions, according to their own historians. These Eastern Jews claimed to be less mixed in blood and to be stricter in religion than those in Palestine. Thousands of families were transplanted from Babylonia to Asia Minor at one time by Antiochus the Great.

In Antioch and other Syrian cities there were large numbers of Jews, so many in Damascus that 10,000 of them were put to death there at one time.

16. Egypt was a favorite land of immigration for the people of Palestine. It was like going from the stony uplands of New England to the fat valley of the Mississippi. Famous migrations were those made in the times of Abraham, of Joseph, and of Jeremiah. A remnant of the last named migration remained and was augmented from time to time. At the time of the foundation of Alexandria immigration was stimulated by conferring on Jews the right of citizenship the same as upon the Greeks themselves. Philo, the great Alexandrian Jew, contemporary of Jesus, tells us that two of the five quarters of the city were Jewish and that there were one million Jews in Egypt, i. e., one-eighth of the whole population.

In Africa, west of Egypt, Strabo divides the population of Cyrene into four classes—citizens, agriculturists, foreigners, and Jews. Later on, in the time of Trajan, Cyrene was a chief center of Jewish revolt.

17. From the records of Paul's work we see that Jews were numerous in Macedonia and Greece as well as in Asia Minor. To Rome itself the first considerable Jewish population was brought after the conquest of Jerusalem by Pompey, 63 B. C. Sixty years later 8,000 Jews resident in Rome joined a deputation to the Emperor, which came from Palestine. Dion Cassius, writing about A. D. 230, says of the Jews in Rome: "Often suppressed, they nevertheless mightily increased, so that they achieved even the free exercise of their customs."

18. The kinsmen of Jesus, with the same basic ideas of religion on which He built, had been carried by captivity and by commerce throughout the Roman world as the pioneer corps of missionaries of the one true and living God. Jews were scattered, not only through the Roman world and its borders but far beyond, even in India and China. There were colonies of them on oases of the African Sahara to its uttermost wastes between Morocco in the West and Timbuctu on the River Niger.

19. The first sentence of the first Christian writing which has been preserved dedicates it "to the twelve tribes which are of the Dispersion." Thus the brother of Jesus, in this earliest extant missionary tract, rests his undertaking on the same fundamental fact in which the world-wide wonders of Pentecost had been grounded. "Now there were dwelling at Jerusalem

Jews, devout men, from every nation under heaven." These Hebrews were not mere travelers abroad; they were natives in the foreign countries; "hear we, every man his own language, wherein we were born." They occupied the whole circuit of the civilized world with "Judea" as a center. The North, "Cappadocia, Pontus, Asia, Phrygia"; the East, "Parthians, Medes, Elamites, and dwellers in Mesopotamia"; the South, "Arabians and dwellers in Egypt"; the West, "dwellers in the parts of Libya about Cyrene, Cretans and sojourners from Rome." Thus, on that first day of sufficient heat for the germination of the seed, it fell into God-made Hebrew soil which had been transported through all the known continents, Asia, Africa, and Europe.

20. Philo says that "in all the towns thousands of houses of instruction were open, where discernment and moderation and justice and all virtues generally were taught." We know that Paul found them in Corinth, in Athens, in Berea, in Thessalonica, in Ephesus, in Iconium, in Antioch, in Pisidia, and sometimes more than one in a city, as for example, in Salamis in Cyprus, and in Damascus. Josephus says that in Antioch in Syria there was one which was particularly elegant and to which the Greek rulers had presented brazen vessels which had been carried away by Antiochus from the temple in Jerusalem. Early Jewish epitaphs have been found in Rome which mention by distinctive names seven different synagogues in that city. One of the synagogues in Egypt was regarded as a sort of second temple only less sacred than the one in Jerusalem. In Alexandria there were

synagogues with pleasant shade trees about them, and at least one of imposing proportions and architecture.

Besides the synagogues there were regular places of meeting for worship under the open sky. This is not surprising when we remember that Greek theaters were built without roofs. Paul found such a place of prayer at Philippi. The synagogues throughout the empire made monotheism visible, as it were, to every passer-by. They at least punctuated the cities with interrogation points as to the possibility of a religion without idolatry. When the time came they furnished a platform on which Christ could be proclaimed.

21. The Jews could not keep their light under a bushel. It was too unique to go unnoticed. Classic writers refer to them with supreme contempt and with a disgust so deep as to prove that Judaism had made a real impression on the popular mind. The religion of the Hebrews called out more than passing jibes. Positive literary attacks were made by Manetho, Apolonius Molon, Lysimachus, Chæremon, and Apion. In meeting these attacks the defenders of Israel carried the war into the enemies' country and pointed out plainly the weak places in current polytheism.

Plutarch seriously argued that the Jews' abstinence from swine's flesh showed that they paid divine honors to this animal. Juvenal sneers that they "accorded to pigs the privilege of living to a good old age," and that "swine's flesh is as much valued as that of man." He attributed their Sabbath observance to laziness. Tacitus and Pliny thought that they were practically atheists because they would not pay divine honors to idols or to the Emperor.

A Roman historian records of one of the noblest of Roman Emperors and philosophers, Marcus Aurelius, that as "he went through Palestine on his way to Egypt, again and again painfully excited with disgust at the vile and tumultous Jews, he is said to have exclaimed 'O Bohemians, O Huns, O Poles, at length I have found people more uncivilized than you.'"

The work of Josephus, "Against Apion," is preserved and is an elaborate defense and advocacy of Judaism. A large aim in the other writings of Josephus was to put Judaism in a favorable light before the Roman world.

22. Efforts still more distinctly missionary were made to commend the Hebrew religion to the Gentiles. They were made by a method which is condemned by modern standards, but which was commonly used in ancient times, the method of sheltering the truth advocated under the authority of well known names. Emil Schürer calls it "Jewish Propaganda Under a Heathen Mask," and describes the advocacy of Jewish ideas attributed to Hystaspes, Hecatæus, Phocylides and in many "smaller pieces." The most interesting to young people who are studying the ancient classics are verses attributed to Hesiod, Homer, Aeschylus, and Sophocles. Perhaps the most influential at the time, certainly the most extensive Jewish tracts for the heathen, were the Sibylline Oracles. The Roman world believed that Sibyls, inspired, half-mythical women, had from time to time uttered prophecies about morals and religious worship and about

unseen and future things. Some of these were collected and sacredly guarded in Rome. Others were floating about. Long before the time of Jesus, and later, Christians (?) composed verses advocating their views and published them as Sibylline Oracles. These are freely used by the church fathers in defense of the faith.

The testimony of Jesus is conclusive as to the missionary activity of the Jews in his day. "You scour both land and sea to make a single convert." It was not their zeal in winning converts which he lamented, but the hollowness of religion in the missionaries themselves. While such vigorous efforts at conversion were made by even the narrow and exclusive Jews of Palestine, the Hellenists or Grecian Jews, being far more open-minded themselves, were more sound-hearted and effectual in missionary endeavor.

23. Perhaps the noblest single worker in bringing the Hebrew faith to bear on the Gentile world was Philo, known as Philo the Jew. He belonged to a family of great wealth and political influence in Alexandria. He was sent, late in life, on a commission to the Emperor, in behalf of the Jews. But his own interests were chiefly religious and philosophical. He was a most loyal Israelite and at the same time a thorough-going Greek philosopher. Many of his works are commentaries on the Bible, into which he manages to interpret the leading ideas of Plato and other philosophers whom he regarded as divine men, forming a sacred society. A large group of his writings were especially intended to commend the religion of Israel

to Greek minds. One of his favorite ideas was that God communicated with his creation through the *Logos*, the Word.

24. In his work on Monarchy he describes the attitude of the ideal ruler toward converts from false religions to the true, with a breadth of sympathy seldom surpassed by Christian missionaries themselves.

"And he receives all persons of a similar character and disposition, whether they were originally born so, or whether they have become so through any change of conduct, having become better people, and, as such, entitled to be ranked in a superior class; approving of the one body because they have not defaced their nobility of birth, and of the other because they have thought fit to alter their lives so as to come over to nobleness of conduct. And these last he calls proselytes, from the fact of their having come over to a new and God-fearing constitution, learning to disregard the fabulous inventions of other nations, and clinging to unalloyed truth.

Accordingly having given equal rank and honor to those who come over, and having granted to them the same favors that were bestowed on the native Jews, he recommends those who are ennobled by truth not only to treat them with respect, but even with especial friendship and excessive benevolence. And is not this a resasonable recommendation? What he says is this:

'Those men who have left their country and their friends, and their relations, for the sake of virtue and holiness, ought not to be left destitute of some other cities, and houses, and friends, but there ought to be places of refuge always ready for those who come over to religion; for the most effectual allurement and the most indissoluble bond of affectionate good will is the mutual honoring of the one God.' Moreover, he also enjoins his people that, after they have given the proselytes an equal share in all their laws, and privileges and immunities, on their forsaking the pride of their fathers and forefathers, they must not give a license to their jealous language and unbridled tongues, blaspheming those beings whom the other body looks upon as gods, lest the proselytes should be exasperated at such treatment, and in return utter impious language against the true and holy God; for from ignorance of the difference between them, and by reason of their having from their infancy learnt to look upon what was false as if it had been true, and having been bred up with it, they would be likely to err."

25. These words of the greatest Hebrew mind contemporary with Jesus, along with other facts which form a part of missionary history, show that the popular notion about the extreme exclusiveness and unmissionary temper of the Jews should be greatly modified, if not, indeed, reversed. In another connection Prof. Harnack has said that "the Judaism of the dispersion, in distinction from the Palestinian, claims to-day our particular attention, as we know that it was in many ways both the prelude to Christianity and the bridge leading over to it." Increased comprehension of the facts in the case generally shows that in spiritual as in biological history the real break in continuity is less than surface appearance seems to indicate.

26. The supreme missionary work of the Messianic race before Christ was the translation of the Scriptures. This is always fundamental in the pioneer work of missions. It was the chief service and achievement of Carey and of Judson. The Greek-speaking Jews or Hellenists were most numerous and influential in Alexandria. They needed the Scriptures in their every-day language, and they gradually translated them, through a period of perhaps 200 years. The first portion to be completed was the first five books. Long afterward a legend arose that the Egyptian King, Ptolemy Phila-

delphus, sent to Palestine and obtained seventy-two Elders, six from each tribe, whom he entertained royally in Alexandria while they translated all the Scriptures in seventy-two days. Hence the common name of the translation is the Septuagint or the LXX. They are said to have been housed on the Island of Pharos—the famous lighthouse island—and to have compared their work one with another, all agreeing upon the result. But the translations themselves indicate that they were made at different times, by men of decidedly different tastes and habits. Some are very free translations or paraphrases, others are so extremely literal and Hebraistic in style that they do not convey their meaning clearly in Greek. Still it was a magnificent achievement to put the Sacred Writings into the language of the whole civilized world. This translation took the place of the original Hebrew even in Palestine.

27. The translators did two great missionary services. First, they put the Scriptures within reach of the heathen long before Christ. The tradition—in this particular reasonable—asserts that the translation was required by the authorities of the great Alexandrian library. That the Greek version of the Hebrew Scriptures had missionary uses is not a mere Christian fancy thrown back over their translation. It is stated in emphatic terms by Philo the Jew. After describing the making of the Septuagint he gives expression to the following truly Jewish and at the same time magnificent missionary hope:

"In this way those admirable, and incomparable, and most desirable laws were made known to all people, whether private individuals or kings, and this too at a period when the nation had not been prosperous for a long time. And it is generally the case that a cloud is thrown over the affairs of those who are not flourishing, so that but little is known of them; and then, if they make any fresh start and begin to improve, how great is the increase of their renown and glory? I think that in that case every nation, abandoning all their own individual customs, and utterly disregarding their national laws, would change and come over to the honor of such a people only; for their laws shining in connection with, and simultaneously with, the prosperity of the nation, will obscure all others, just as the rising sun obscures the stars."

In later times, Aquila, himself a Jewish convert from heathenism, made a new translation into Greek.

The other great missionary service of the LXX was its use by Christ, the Apostles, and other early Christian missionaries. The translated Scriptures were the seed-baskets for saving the world. The Old Testament quotations by Christ and the Apostles are usually made from the LXX. For several generations it was the only Bible which the Christians used. Out of this version into Greek translations were made into at least eleven other tongues.

28. Hebrew missions were not without fruit. The religion of Israel had great rational and moral superiority, which widely commended it, whenever its superficial characteristics could be overlooked and superficial prejudices against it could be overcome. The celebrated Greek geographer Strabo says of Moses that:

"He declared and taught that the Egyptians and Africans entertained erroneous sentiments, in representing the Divinity under the likeness of wild beasts and cattle of the field; that the Greeks also were in error in making images of their gods after the human form. . . . Who then of any understanding would venture to form an image of this Deity, resembling anything with which we are conversant? On the contrary, we ought not to carve any images, but to set apart some sacred ground and a shrine worthy of the Deity, and to worship Him without any similitude."

29. The man who uttered this dispassionate and scholarly view of Mosaism did not himself become a Jew.

The most conspicuous converts were the royal family of Adiabene, a small kingdom on the upper Tigris in the region of ancient Nineveh. King Izates, his mother Helen and his brother Monobaz became devout converts to Judaism. Their kindred followed. Helen made pilgrimages to Jerusalem and was a generous contributor to the people in time of famine, as well as to the furniture of the temple. She and Monobaz had a palace in Jerusalem. Members of the family fought on the side of the Jews against the Romans. Monobaz succeeded Izates on the throne of Adiabene, and brought the remains of both his mother and brother to Jerusalem for burial. They built there a splendid family tomb. It is one of the best identified spots in the vicinity of Jerusalem today.

30. Multitudes of common people in all parts of the Roman Empire turned to the worship of the one true God. Josephus tells us that "many of the Greeks have been converted to the observance of the laws; some have remained true, while others who were incapable of steadfastness have fallen away again." "Likewise among the mass of the people there has been for a

long time a great amount of zeal for our worship; nor is there a single town among Greeks or barbarians or anywhere else, not a single nation to which the observance of the Sabbath as it exists among ourselves has not penetrated; while fasting and the burning of lights and many of our laws with regard to meats are also observed." We should be inclined to count these statements among the exaggerations of Josephus, were they not abundantly confirmed by such Gentile authors as Seneca and Dion Cassius, and by the statement of James at the Jerusalem conference: "For Moses, for generations past, has had in every town those who preach him, read, as he is, in the synagogues every Sabbath."

31. An unmistakable evidence of the spread and increasing power of Judaism among the Romans is given by Juvenal in his Fourteenth Satire. The evidence is the more striking because it was written in bitter hostility to the Jews. The whole satire is a noble and trenchant appeal to parents to avoid evil courses of every kind, lest their children not only copy their bad example but even outrun them in wrong-doing. Among other perils is the religion of the Jews. If the father is an adherent, observing some of the Jewish customs, the son will become a complete convert, even to the extent of circumcision.

"Sprung from a father who the Sabbath fears,
There is who naught but clouds and skies reveres;
And shuns the taste, by old tradition led,
Of human flesh, and swine's, with equal dread:—

This first; the prepuce next he lays aside,
And, taught the Roman ritual to deride,
Clings to the Jewish, and observes with awe,
All Moses bade, in his mysterious law:
And therefore, to the circumcised alone,
Will point the road, or make the fountain known;
Aping his bigot sire, who whiled away,
Sacred to sloth, each seventh revolving day."

This warning of the poet, besides showing the progress which Judaism was making among the Romans, clearly alludes to different degrees in the process of conversion to Judaism which are sometimes indicated by the expressions "Proselytes of the Gate" and "Proselytes of Righteousness"; or, as we say in connection with modern missions, "Adherents" and "Communicants."

32. While we have no statistics for those times, there is every reason to believe that there were many thousands, perhaps hundreds of thousands, of Gentiles who had come more or less within the sphere of the worship of the one true God. Josephus says of the temple that "it was held in reverence by peoples from the ends of the earth." "The Court of the Gentiles" was an important part of the sacred enclosure because many desired to come as close to the sanctuary as possible. It was separated from the inner court by an ornate stone balustrade which had at intervals signs in Greek and Latin warning all to come no further, unless they were completely naturalized in the Jewish fraternity. One of the Greek tablets was unearthed

a few years ago. Thus there has been preserved for nineteen hundred years and now brought to light a tangible and legible monument, not only of the exclusiveness of the Jews, but also of their provision for the measured approach of the Gentiles in the house of God. This "middle wall of partition" was four feet high. It remained for Christianity to break it down completely.

33. The New Covenant began where the Old Covenant left off. The missions which have sprung from the stock of the Messiah are rooted in the missions of the Messianic Race. The relation of the two is not only close, it is vital and genetic. It is a fact not commonly considered in its full significance that Christianity made its first effectual connections with the Gentile world through the mission converts to Judaism. Nothing is plainer in the pages of the New Testament than the magnificent success of Hebrew missions and, at the same time, their fundamental relation to the world-wide propagation of Christianity. Not to mention narratives in which there is strong indirect evidence that converts from heathenism to Judaism took a decisive part in the early spread of Christianity, in the following passages it is directly stated in unmistakable language. The common way of describing them, as we saw in the language of Josephus, was to speak of them as those who take part in "our worship." In selecting The Seven the disciples at Jerusalem "chose . . . Nicholas from Antioch, a former convert to Judaism." Again, "There was then in Cæsarea a man named Cornelius, a captain in the regiment known as

the 'Italian Regiment,' a religious man and one who reverenced God, as also did all his household. He was liberal in his charities to the people, and prayed to God constantly." Again, "After the congregation had broken up, many of the Jews and converts who joined in their worship followed Paul and Barnabas," but "the Jews, on their part, roused the women of position who worshiped with them, and the leading men of the town, and stirred up a persecution against Paul and Barnabas." Again, "Among the listeners was a woman named Lydia belonging to Thyatira, a dealer in purple dyes, who joined in the worship of God." Again, "Some of the people were convinced, and threw in their lot with Paul and Silas, as well as a large body of Greeks who joined in the Jewish services, besides a considerable number of women belonging to the leading families." Again, Paul "argued in the synagogue with the Jews and with those who joined their worship there." Again, "he left and went to the house of a certain Titus Justus, a man who joined in the worship of God." Again, at a much earlier day, we read "some of us are visitors from Rome, either Jews by birth or converts, and some Cretans and Arabians." Thus we are explicitly told that converts from heathenism to Judaism took a first place and a leading part in the early spread of Christianity in many of the great centers of its propagation; in Jerusalem, in Cæsarea, in Pisidian Antioch, in Philippi, in Thessalonica, in Athens, in Corinth, in Rome. There is every reason to believe that the same was true elsewhere, at least in all the cities, certainly so in Syrian Antioch.

The primary mission work of the Messiah was done by the Messianic Race. The law was a tutor to lead, not only the Hebrews, but also the heathen, to Christ. It was significant of a world-wide fact that "among those who had come up to worship at the festival were some Greeks, who went to Philip of Bethsaida in Galilee, and said: 'We should like, sir, to see Jesus.'"

## CHAPTER III.

# THE MESSIAH MISSIONARY.

34. The missionary origin of Jesus, (a) earthly, (b) heavenly. 35. His missionary characteristics, (a) positive, (b) negative. 36. His missionary methods, (a) industrial, (b) itinerant, (c) medical. 37. His missionary fields, (a) formalists, (b) the lapsed, (c) non-Jews. 38. His missionary pupils. 39. His great commission. 40. His dominant ideal missionary.

34. **Jesus of Nazareth** was in every sense of the word a missionary. In Him the missionary tendencies of the Messianic Race culminated. In Him was a new beginning, a fresh deposit and source of missionary energy. Before Christ the missionary movement had only crept and crawled. It was in a larval state. With Him it took wings, it reached the perfect state. He was the image, the true and complete embodiment of the spirit of missions. In Him it became reproductive. He was the original and the originator of missions.

His own origin was missionary. We have seen to what extent it was so on its earthly side, but it was pre-eminently so on its heavenly side. He was repeatedly described, especially by himself, as the Sent—that is, the Missionary. If instead of the Anglo-Saxon "sent" we were to use a word of Latin origin meaning the same, we should better gather the force of this favorite thought of Christ about himself. The following are a few of His statements as rendered in the Twentieth Century New Testament: "As the living Father made me His Messenger, and as I live because the Father does, so those who take me for their food will live because I do." "For myself I do know Him, for it is from Him that I have come, and I am His Messenger." "'If God were your Father,' Jesus replied, 'you would love me, for I came out of God Himself, and am now here; nor have I come of myself, but I am His Messenger.'" "And this enduring life is to know Thee as the only true God, and Thy Messenger, Jesus, as the Christ." "Just as I am Thy Messenger to the world, so they are my messengers to it." "Oh, righteous Father, though the world did not know Thee, I knew Thee; and these men knew me to be Thy Messenger." These are but a few of the many plain statements to the same effect. The primal name of Jesus Christ is the Word—that is, the expression, the utterance, the message. In his ultimate nature he was the going forth of the infinite Life, the making known of the divine love, the proclamation of the eternal purpose of good for humanity. "For God so loved the world, that He gave His only Son, that no one who believes in Him might be lost, but that all might have enduring life."

35. Jesus was missionary in the character of his work as well as in his origin. The negative side of all missionary work is the destruction and displacement of false and imperfect conceptions of life and

duty. It is always an innovation. Jesus was the first and greatest of innovators. The world into which he came was firmly encased in customs and traditions. It was loaded down with the accumulations of ages. His own Jewish world was completely enthralled in traditionalism. People did not venture to speak or act, or even think, except along lines which were consecrated by long use. "Then some Pharisees and Rabbis came to Jesus and said: 'How is it that your disciples break the traditions of our ancestors?' His reply was: 'How is it that you on your side break God's commandments out of respect for your own traditions?' " He did not hesitate to attack wrongs which were entrenched, not only in custom, but also in the deepest selfish interests of men. They had turned the house of worship into a market and money exchange. At the very outset of his ministry he unhesitatingly overturned these practices. The Roman world as well as the Jewish, into which he came, was in bondage to custom and to the pride of precedent. The humble Nazarene promulgated principles which were bound to undermine and break down the ponderous rule of "the kingdom strong as iron."

But the chief work of a missionary is positive rather than negative. He destroys only in the process of clearing the way for constructive effort. Jesus was a missionary in making known the true relations of God to men, where, previous to his mission, they were unknown or but partly known. God had been esteemed as the almighty Creator and Ruler, the great Sustainer, the Predestinator. This was true of the best informed portions of mankind. They had caught only fragmentary glimpses of the reality. They worshiped refracted and broken rays of the Light. In too many cases these rays were distorted by human passion and sin, so as to be utterly false to the reality. Into such a world Jesus effectually brought the true and simple conception of God as "our Father." His proclamation of God was as fresh and radical, even to the monotheistic Jews, as that made by missionaries to the benighted in any age. A corresponding part of his missionary work was that of inducing men to enter into right relations with God. In his day and in all days the tendency of man is to attempt to reach God through many intermediate measures. Jesus insisted that men can come, ought to come, and are divinely urged to come into direct, immediate, and personal fellowship with the infinite Friend. "A time is coming, and indeed is already here, when the true worshipers will worship the Father spiritually, with true insight; for such is the worship that the Father desires. God is Spirit; and those who worship Him must worship spiritually, with true insight." His missionary work included also the engendering of right relations of men to one another. A new society was to be the outcome of his work. Stratifications in caste and artificial rank were to be completely broken up. All his followers were to become one, even as he and the Father were one. He instituted a hitherto unknown fellowship. Every endeavor to elevate communities in the social scale which is made by modern missionary effort is a true following of the original Missionary.

36. The methods of the work of Jesus were missionary.

In the earlier stages of his work he was an industrial missionary. It is not without significance that Jesus, during the larger part of his life, was "the carpenter." This is simply mentioned by the New Testament writers, but the instinct of the followers of Jesus in later times has fastened on the fact as being full of meaning for human life. It is regarded as a recent discovery in education that manual training is promotive in a high degree of spiritual results. In many instances young people who have failed to be aroused mentally by any other means acquire intellectual zest and tone through manual discipline. In many different ways, ranging from laboratory work to athletics, educators are giving large and ever larger place to the element of physical training. This most natural and effective education Jesus enjoyed, and through his devotion to manual pursuits for so many years he has made it impossible for any true missionary to undervalue the importance of leading people into better industrial ways, and, through industrial discipline, into higher and firmer character.

When Jesus entered upon his more public career he became an itinerant missionary. It is a characteristic of the missionary spirit that it ever seeks to enter the regions beyond. It is not satisfied, and can not be satisfied with cultivating fields already long tilled. Though Jesus tried again and again to lift the Nazarenes into a larger life, and though he made Capernaum his "own city" and the center of his operations for many months at a time, still he was always essentially an itinerant. In his brief ministry he went back and forth many times between Judea and Galilee. He went from city to city and from village to village proclaiming the good news of the kingdom. Itinerating was characteristic of all his work. "Crowds of people began to look for him; and when they came up with him they tried to detain him and prevent his leaving them. Jesus, however, said to them: 'I must take the good news of the Kingdom of God to the other towns as well, for this was the object for which I was sent.'"

Jesus was a medical missionary. Considering the amount of attention which he gave to the healing of the body, it is remarkable that his followers have been so slow in making much of this form of missionary work. With Jesus it was so conspicuous an element that multitudes followed him only as a Healer and flocked to him because of this mission of his. In addition to all the special cases which are recorded we are told more than once that he healed all those who came to him. When we remember that they flocked about him largely on this account we see that as no one else who ever lived Jesus was a medical missionary.

37. Jesus was distinctly missionary in his choice of people to be objects of special effort. First of all he came to the lost sheep of the house of Israel; that is, to believers in an imperfect form of the true religion. The resuscitation of effete religious life, giving to men higher and broader ideals than they have cherished,

is an essential part of missionary endeavor. In many portions of Europe and Asia to this day nothing radical and thoroughly renovating can be accomplished until the decadent forms of Christianity have been regenerated.

He was also distinctively missionary in devoting himself to the unprivileged classes. Slum work is decidedly missionary in its nature. Jesus devoted himself to that work to such an extent that it came to be thought of as a characteristic of his life. He was known as "the friend of publicans and sinners." "The common people heard him gladly." He expressly announced that he "came to seek and save that which was lost."

From the necessities of the case his ministry was absorbed largely in work for the imperfectly religious and for the unprivileged classes. But there are many traces of his devotion to the widest reaches of humanity. It is significant that men representing one of the most influential forms of ethnic faith brought tributes to the cradle of Jesus. In earliest infancy he was carried out of his own land, even to another continent. He gave an early portion of his public ministry to the half heathen Samaritans. To one of them he made his first recorded statement of his Messiahship and a most profound and clear announcement of true spiritual religion. Toward the end of his ministry we find him again working among the villages of the Samaritans. Hateful as the name Samaritan was to every Jew, Jesus made one of the most admirable characters which he ever delineated a Samaritan.

In another direction he passed out of the boundaries of Palestine into the neighborhood of Tyre and even of more distant Sidon; there he performed one of his most gracious and significant acts of mercy. He chose for the Mount of his transfiguration lofty Hermon, on the extreme borders of the Holy Land, from the summit of which Damascus, the most ancient representative of heathen cities, can be distinctly seen. In his brief and necessarily limited ministry there are many indications of the widest outreach in his thoughts and sympathies. One of the moments of most intense agitation in his whole career was during the last days, when "some Greeks" sent word that they wished to see him. It was then that he said: "Now I am troubled at heart and what can I say?" Then there "came a voice from the sky." "The crowd of bystanders who heard the sound exclaimed, 'That was thunder!' Others said 'it was an angel speaking to him!' Jesus said: 'This world is now on its trial. The spirit that rules it will now be driven out; and I, when I am lifted up from the earth, will draw all men to myself.'"

38. Perhaps we can gain our highest view of the Messiah as missionary from the fact that he was the originator of missions. A large feature of his ministry was his selection of a group of men in whom he could instil the missionary spirit and whom he could train for missionary work. The training of the Apostles was undoubtedly a leading aim of his life. He selected them with great care, calling them into closer and closer relations with himself, then kept them with him, imbibing his own spirit and way of working.

The pupils in his training school he called *Apostoloi*, that is, the sent out—in other words, missionaries. It is made as plain as words can make it that they were chosen for this kind of work. "The harvest is heavy," he said, "but the laborers are few, so pray to the owner of the harvest to send laborers to do the harvesting." Then calling his twelve disciples to him Jesus gave them authority over wicked spirits so that they could drive them out, as well as the power of curing every kind of disease and sickness.

Later he coupled with these many more and sent them out for a special mission, a sort of trial endeavor in missionary work. "The Master appointed seventy-two other disciples and sent them on, two and two, in advance, to every town and place that he was himself intending to visit. The harvest, he said, is heavy but the laborers are few, so pray to the owner of the harvest to send laborers to do the harvesting. Now, go." Many scholars think that the number seventy, or, according to the best documentary evidence, seventy-two, was significant in the missionary direction. This was commonly thought of as the number of the heathen nations, the opinion being based on the enumeration in the tenth chapter of Genesis.

Concerning the extent to which the Apostles carried out the meaning of their title, we have only glimpses in the New Testament writings. There are many traditions, some of which undoubtedly reflect historic facts as to the range of these primitive missionaries. In later chapters we shall have occasion to notice some of the results of their work.

The father of church history, Eusebius, writing within two hundred years after the death of the last of the Apostles, tells how they and those whom they had directly inspired carried the message far and wide.

"Alongside of him [Quadratus] there flourished at that time many other successors of the Apostles, who, admirable disciples of those great men, reared the edifice on the foundations which they laid, continuing the work of preaching the gospel, and scattering abundantly over the whole earth the wholesome seed of the heavenly kingdom. For a very large number of His disciples, carried away by fervent love of the truth which the divine word had revealed to them, fulfilled the command of the Saviour to divide their goods among the poor. Then, taking leave of their country, they filled the office of evangelists, coveting eagerly to preach Christ, and to carry the glad tidings of God to those who had not yet heard the word of faith. And after laying the foundations of the faith in some remote and barbarous countries, establishing pastors among them, and confiding to them the care of those young settlements, without stopping longer, they hastened on to other nations, attended by the grace and virtue of God."

39. That there might be no mistake about the missionary purpose of his religion and the real culmination of all his ministry, Jesus put his intention in plain words before he finally parted from his disciples. On the mountain in Galilee "Jesus came up and spoke to them thus: All authority in heaven and on earth has been given to me. Therefore go and make disciples of the nations." Finally the last thing before the ascension, lest they forget the principal word which he had to leave with them as the very essence of his intention, he reminded them as follows: "Scripture says that the Christ should suffer in this way, and that he should

rise from the dead on the third day, and that repentance for forgiveness of sins should be proclaimed on his authority to all the nations, beginning at Jerusalem. You yourselves are to be witnesses to all this."

40. More significant than any single detail in the missionary history and the institution of missions by Jesus is the ideal which he created concerning the extent and the all-inclusive purposes of the gospel. If he personally had not said or done anything which could be called specifically missionary, still the expansive conceptions which he gave to his followers must sooner or later have come to birth in missionary activity. It was clear that his work was not for Palestine alone and not for Israel alone. It was for all mankind. "The world" was a frequent and significant phrase in the original gospel. The central thought in many of his parables was the thought of growth. The Kingdom of Heaven was almost always said to be like growing things. It was like grain developing into a harvest. It was like seed growing into a tree. It was like the yeast plant propagating itself until the whole mass should be filled with its life.

By the parable of the wicked tenants he drew from their own lips the verdict of the leaders of the Jewish nation that the Owner should "let the vineyard to other tenants." That there might be no mistake in understanding the teaching as meaning the extension of religious opportunity to the non-Jewish world, he added, "for this reason the Kingdom of God, I tell you, will be taken from you, and given to a nation that does produce the fruit of the Kingdom." This teaching he at once pressed further by a parable of the marriage feast, with its unmistakable declaration of a gospel invitation for every soul in the outside, heathen world. "Then he said to his servants, 'The feast is ready, but those who were invited were not fit to come. So go to the cross-roads, and invite to the feast every one you find.'" On his final journey toward Jerusalem he had spoken the dinner parable of invitation to the unprivileged classes. Arrived at the national capital itself, in the last solemn week, he spoke this other dinner parable of the invitation to the unprivileged nations:

"When you give a lunch or a dinner, do not ask your friends, or your brothers, or your relations, or rich neighbors, for fear they should invite you in return, and so you should be repaid. Instead of that, when you give a party, invite the poor, or the crippled, or the lame, or the blind." Thus he illuminated his teaching by the parable of the dinner invitation, which he carried beyond the select social circle, to those who lived in the streets and alleys of the town and, further afield still, to the people of the country roads and lanes. No wonder that soon after, "the tax-gatherers and godless people were all drawing near to Jesus to listen to him; but the Pharisees and Rabbis found fault; 'this man actually welcomes godless people, and has meals with them!' they complained." This is what called out that matchless missionary chapter about the stray sheep, the lost coin and the prodigal son.

On a much later occasion after another parable about two sons which he addressed to "the chief priests and counsellors of the nation," he spoke words which a most ardent worker for the "submerged tenth" could not surpass in intensity if he were arraigning the privileged "four hundred" of today, "Believe me, tax-gatherers and prostitutes are going into the Kingdom of Heaven before you."

The conception of the worth of man which Jesus introduced, the worth of every man, every woman and every child, was such that those who receive it are bound to strive for the betterment of every human being. When we realize that God is the Father of us all and we are brothers, it is impossible to be contented with our own individual safety and comfort and prospect in life without care for the other children of the same infinite love. It is not only by splendid example and by formal command, but also and still more by the very essence and innermost spirit of Christ, that Christians must be missionaries.

CHAPTER IV.

# SYRIA.

41. Inspiration. 42. Inauguration. 43. Only outlines recorded. 44. City missions, (a) medical, (b) beneficent, (c) social, (d) incisive, (e) providential, (f) institutional, (g) sacrificial, (h) fruitful. 45. Home missions. 46. Samaria. 47. The African. 48. Damascus and Paul. 49. Phoenicia. 50. Antioch. (a) beginnings, (b) development, (c) base of foreign missions. 51. One missionary in the days of the crusades. 52. Permanent results of the original missionary work in Syria.

41. The missionary movement had been groping onward through the centuries. During the last quarter of a millennium it had acquired considerable distinctness. Jesus came and gave it glowing features, with a heart-beat. He put into it the breath of life. He inspired missions.

When the spirit of Jesus became the actual inspiration of his followers, they were "invested with power from above," as he had promised. The Spirit of the Master, the Breath of God among the disciples, was all at once luminous, vocal and wide-reaching. It is best not to attempt to elaborate or even to paraphrase the story of the final inspiration of missions. The story itself is inspired.

"In the course of the Harvest Thanksgiving-day the disciples had all met together, when a noise like that of a strong wind coming nearer and nearer suddenly came from the sky, and filled the whole house in which they were sitting. Then they saw tongues of what appeared to be flame, separating, so that one settled on each of them; and they were all filled with the holy Spirit, and began to speak with strange 'tongues' as the Spirit prompted their utterances.

There were then staying in Jerusalem religious Jews from every country in the world; and when this sound was heard, numbers of people collected, in the greatest excitement because each of them heard the disciples speaking in his own language. They were utterly amazed, and kept saying in their astonishment:

'Why, are not all these Galileans who are speaking! How is it that we each of us hear them in our own native language? Some of us are Parthians, some Medes, some Elamites; and some of us live in Mesopotamia, in Judea and Cappadocia, in Pontus and Roman Asia, in Phrygia and Pamphylia, in Egypt and the districts of Libya adjoining Cyrene; some of us are visitors from Rome, either Jews by birth or converts, and some Cretans and Arabians—yet we all alike hear them speaking in our tongues of the great things God has done.' Everyone was utterly amazed and bewildered."

42. "The Great Commission" is the mission of Jesus expressed in words. Missions are the mission of Jesus expressed in lives. In proportion as the Breath of the Master breathes in his people, they are missionaries at heart and missionaries in deed. Men without God, unphilanthropic men, look upon missions as the outcome of fatuous feeling. Men who recognize God as the Living Reality for all men and all times see that missions are inevitable, God must be proclaimed abroad. "Men of Judea," said **Peter,** "and all you who are staying in Jerusalem, let me tell you what this means, and mark my words. You are wrong in thinking that these men are drunk; indeed it is only nine in the morning! No! This is what was spoken of in the Prophet Joel—

"'It shall come about' in the last days, God said,
'That I will pour out my Spirit on all mankind.'"

It was a typical day, that "Harvest Thanksgiving-day." Fifteen countries heard the gospel, all the ancient classic world stretching from the Tigris to the Tiber. No wonder that they were "in the greatest excitement because each of them heard the disciples speaking in his own language." The stars had never looked on such a sight before. It was the dawn of a new day on the planet earth. A Christianizing force of three thousand was created at once. How many of them belonged abroad, and so returned with the gospel story to every country in the world, we are not told.

43. We are reminded at the outset that the bulk of the missionary history of the world has never been recorded with paper and ink. Its record was only in melting hearts and in the transformation of lives and of society. The outcome abides in an uplifted human race. But materials for reproducing the story of the process do not exist, except in scanty and scattered fragments. As we look along the ages we can catch only glimpses like bits of landscape from a car window. The educational value of the journey will depend largely on the student's power of realizing to himself the fact that a great country lies beyond the range of his vision, a country of field and forest, of mountain and stream, of lonely stretches or of teeming centers of life.

The earliest record follows the normal order of development, which had been the order of promise. "When the holy Spirit has come upon you, you shall be witnesses for me not only in Jerusalem. but in the whole of Judea and Samaria, and to the very ends of the earth." There came first five or six years of city missions, then ten or twelve years of home missions. It was about sixteen years before foreign missions were definitely undertaken.

44. All the record that is left of the five eventful years of the city mission period is contained in five chapters of Acts (2:43-8:1). It begins by telling us that "a deep impression was made upon every one" by the events of Harvest Day and the work which followed. Some of the features which accompanied their work were typical of those which have pertained to city mission work ever since.

The first thing mentioned is that they gave large attention to ministry for the suffering and diseased. Curing the sick, the lame and the blind formed a considerable portion of their work. The same thing with different facilities for accomplishing the end is undertaken now through visiting nurses, dispensaries and hospitals. A city mission work which fails to follow the apostolic lead falls short of one of its best means of grace.

The work was characterized by great generosity in giving. No vigorous work in cities can be performed without large outlay of money. They carried it to the extent of Christian socialism. Whatever the name or precise methods used, the efficient work requires liberal sharing of earthly goods. "Not one of them claimed any of his belongings as his own, but everything was held for common use." "Indeed there was no poverty among them, for all who were owners of lands or houses sold them, and brought the proceeds of the sales and laid them at the Apostles' feet; when every one received a share in proportion to his needs." One of the disciples gave a telling example for all time of Christian brotherhood. "A Levite of Cyprian birth, named Joseph (who had received from the Apostles the additional name of 'Barnabas'—which means 'The Preacher') sold a farm that belonged to him, and brought the money and laid it at the Apostles' feet." To meet the needs of life and growth religious worship and fellowship must be frequent; preaching once a month or even twice a week cannot compete with other absorbing interests of the people. "Every day, too, they met regularly in the Temple Courts and at their homes for the breaking of bread."

They had a joyous social life. Solemn formalities without sincere, hearty, good fellowship must always fail to reach the hearts and lives of people. They partake "of their food in simple-hearted gladness, continually praising God." Such a life and ministry gave the Christians great and desirable influence in the community. They are recorded as "winning respect from all the people." As a result there was a constant ingathering, "and the Lord daily added to their company those who were in the path of salvation."

Practical and pointed preaching was one of the leading features of this city mission work. There was no dwelling on pleasant platitudes. The Apostles gave their testimony to the work of Christ and to the sins of his murderers without fear or favor. Such plain and thorough-going missionary work, attacking the evils of people high in social standing, was bound to bring upon the missionaries intense dislike and officious interference. Again and again they were arrested, prohibited from preaching, flogged and imprisoned. Still the work went on and accumulated momentum.

Always in city mission work people ally themselves to the movement who are not sincere. The false professions of Ananias and Sapphira in one form or another reappear in every age. On the other hand such work is sure to be helped and guided by surprising providences. More than once the enterprise escaped destruction when no way of escape appeared to be possible. As missionary work in a city increases in breadth a multitude of details must be kept well in hand. There is no way to do this without a careful organization, hence the "institutional church." The necessity for this was early seen. One of the first steps in this direction was taken in the choice of the seven almoners of the churches' bounty.

At length the Christian movement gained such headway that its general public discussion was involved. Both natives and foreigners took part in the general debate, "but some members from the Synagogue known as that of the Freed Slaves and the Cyrenians and the Alexandrians, as well as visitors from Cilicia and Roman Asia, were aroused to action and began disputing with **Stephen.** The five years under consideration ended with the first missionary martyrdom of a long succession through the ages down to the present day. Earnest city mission work has taken the life of many a man and woman devoted to it by processes inevitable, and yet so slow that they are never thought of as being martyrs to the cause.

We have no means of knowing how many people turned to Christ in the city of Jerusalem during that five years. We only know that early in the time "the number of the men alone amounted to some five thousand." Doubtless there were as many women as men. If anything like the modern proportions prevailed, there must have been some fifteen thousand disciples in all that time. It may be that by the end of the period twenty-five thousand people or more had given some sort of allegiance to the new faith.

45. The home mission period of Syrian Missions, though more than twice as long as the city mission period and though covering an area vastly wider, is recorded in the same number of chapters of Acts (8-12). It is obvious that only typical features are given.

Home missions are true missions, divine sendings. It was not by their own motion that the disciples left Jerusalem in order to work in wider fields. God had to drive them out with a sword. "A great persecution broke out against the church which was in Jerusalem; and its members were all scattered over the districts of Judea and Samaria, with the exception of the Apostles, and those who were scattered in different directions went from place to place, with the Good News of the Message."

46. The first special work noted is work for a foreign population. Samaria had been settled by immigration many generations before this. But the population had never become fully assimilated to the religion of the

land of Israel. Eight years before the mission of Philip Jesus himself had spent two busy days in Samaria and "many from that town came to believe in Jesus—Samaritans though they were—on account of what the woman said. And many more came to believe in him on account of what he said himself." Whether any permanent results of this work were found by Philip or not we do not know, but the gospel as he proclaimed it obtained a ready entrance into many hearts. The Samaritans evidently were given to superstition. A charlatan of the first magnitude held strong sway among them. The work of the missionaries came to a sharp crisis in connection with him. The record is intense and vivid to the last degree. "When Simon saw that it was through the placing of the Apostles' hands on them that the Spirit was given, he brought them a sum of money, with the request: 'Give me, too, the power you possess, so that, if I place my hands upon any one, he may receive the holy Spirit.' 'Take your money to perdition with you!' Peter exclaimed, 'for thinking God's free gift could be bought with gold! You have no share or part in our Message, for your heart is not right with God. So repent of this wickedness of yours, and pray to the Lord, that, if possible, you may be forgiven for such a thought; for I see that you have fallen into bitter jealousy and are in bondage to iniquity.' "

47. The next work was with a foreigner, though possibly of Hebrew extraction, a man from another continent and possibly of another color. It was home mission work for an African. It belongs to the missionary history of that continent, but it is also a

typical example of the wide-reaching importance of wayside opportunities in home missions.

48. In the home mission field lay Damascus, counted the most ancient city in the world. It was evangelized to some extent, we know not how, in the earliest days of Christianity. There were so many followers of the Nazarene there that Saul the persecutor went thither to make arrests. His conversion is an eminent example of the principle that the supply of missionaries for the work abroad always depends on the cultivation of the home field. The lofty life and death of Stephen and the heroic character and bearing of hundreds of other Christians who endured hardships as seeing Him who is invisible were used by the Holy Spirit in breaking down at last the stubborn will of the man who was to become the pre-eminent missionary to the heathen.

"'Saul, Saul, why are you persecuting me? You are punishing yourself by kicking against the goad.' 'Who are you, my Lord?' I asked. 'I am Jesus, whom you are persecuting,' the Master said; 'but get up; stand upright, for I have appeared to you for the express purpose of appointing you to work for me, and to bear witness to the revelations of me which you have already seen, and to those in which I shall yet appear to you, when delivering you from your own people and from the heathen. It is to them that I am now sending you, to open their eyes, and to turn them from darkness to light, and from the power of Satan to God, so that they may receive pardon for their sins, and a place among those who have become God's people, by faith in me.'"

Under this commission **Saul** did some work immediately in Damascus.

49. The Apostles themselves did not remain all the time in Jerusalem, but took an active part in the homeland missions. "While traveling about in all directions,

Peter went down to visit the people of Christ living at Lydda." We see him going from Lydda to Joppa and from Joppa to Cæsarea. At Cæsarea he did a mission work of the highest significance. "There was then in Cæsarea a man named Cornelius, a captain in the regiment known as the 'Italian Regiment,' a religious man and one who reverenced God, as also did all his household."

Here Christianity laid hold of one who had already been converted from heathenism to Judaism. He was one of the noble examples of the results of Hebrew missions. "He was liberal in his charities to the people, and prayed to God constantly." The turning of this man to the Christian faith was widely recognized at the time as being a marked event.

"The Apostlés and the Brethren throughout Judea heard that even the heathen had welcomed God's Message. But when Peter went up to Jerusalem those converts who held to circumcision began attacking him on the ground that he had visited people who were not circumcised, and had had meals with them. So Peter began and explained the facts to them as they had occurred." Later, "the Apostles and Officers of the Church held a meeting to look into this question. After a good deal of discussion Peter rose and said: 'You, my brothers, know well how God chose long ago that, of all of us, I should be the one by whose lips the heathen should hear the Message of the Good News and believe it.'"

On the first occasion Peter's explanation ended,

"'as then, God had given them the very same gift as he gave us when we learnt to believe in the Master, Jesus Christ—who was I that I should be able to thwart God?' On hearing this statement, they ceased to object, and broke out into praise of God. 'So even to the heathen,' they said, 'God has granted the repentance which leads to Life!'"

The conversion of Cornelius had great significance from a missionary point of view because he was a Roman soldier. In the succeeding centuries the army had much to do with the spread of Christianity.

50. The culmination of this period of home mission work was the establishment of Christianity in Antioch, the capital of the country. The city was important in itself. Here we find missionary work succeeding on a large scale. The extremely brief record of Luke includes the statement that "a large number of people joined the Master's cause." His account of what took place there shows that it soon became a great center of Christian life. It was the third city in importance in the Empire. Its principal street extended five miles and was lined with splendid temples, dwellings and places of business. Two miles of the way it was paved with marble.

Christianity had obtained such headway in Antioch by the year 115 that the Emperor Trajan visiting there was advised to seek its overthrow by disposing of its leader, **Ignatius**, which he did.

Ignatius was given in charge to ten soldiers, "ten leopards," as he terms them in his Epistle to the Romans, and was ordered to be taken to Rome to be devoured by beasts for the diversion of the people.

It is a long time before we have other distinct accounts of Christianity in Antioch. According to Dr. James Orr.

"When it [The Church of Antioch] does become distinctly visible in the middle of the third century, it is as a seat of ecclesiastical influence of the first rank. The extraordinary splendor of its episcopate, and elaboration of its church service, under the notorious Paul of Samosata; its influential councils and important theological school; the magnificent Golden Church reared later by the liberality of Constantine; its prominence in the Arian controversies; the utter failure of Julian's attempt to restore Paganism in it—readers of Church History will remember his chagrin when, having gone to celebrate with all pomp the festival of Apollo at the Temple of Daphne, he found only a single old priest, sacrificing a goose at his own expense; the flourishing state of the church, numerically, at least, under Chrysostom—all this shows that, even before the change of the political relations, Christianity must have been practically in the ascendant in the city. . . . We have the express testimony of Chrysostom that in his day, before the year 400, the Christians were a majority in the city; and this is borne out by the separate figures he gives, showing the population to have been 200,000, and the number of the Christian community about 100,000."

In addition to its importance in itself, the capital of Syria was of the utmost importance as becoming the first great base of operations in foreign missions.

"There were at Antioch, among the members of the Church there, some Prophets and Teachers. Their names were Barnabas, Simeon, who went by the name of 'Black,' Lucius of Cyrene, Manaen, foster-brother of Prince Herod, and while they were worshiping the Lord and fasting, the holy Spirit said: 'Set Barnabas and Saul apart for me, for the work to which I have called them.' Accordingly, after fasting and prayer, they placed their hands on them and sent them on their way. "So Barnabas and Saul, sent on this mission by the holy Spirit, went down to Seleucia, and sailed from there to Cyprus. On reaching Salamis, they began to tell God's Message in the Jewish Synagogues; and they also had John with them to help them."

When these first foreign missionaries returned they brought reports to the home church of their three years' mission abroad. "After their arrival, they gathered the church together, and gave an account of all that God had done with and through them, especially how he had opened to the heathen a door to the Faith; and at Antioch they stayed with the disciples for a long time."

Among the most useful and distinguished Christians of the early centuries were natives of Syria. Not only Ignatius but Justin the Martyr, and Eusebius and Sozomen, the early church historians, were Syrians. Jerome, the father of biblical scholarship, did a large part of his work in Bethlehem.

51. In later centuries Christian Europe poured itself like a mighty flood through Syria in the name of the cross. The land came to be ruled under that sacred sign; but the Crusades cannot be counted as missionary enterprises in any true sense.

Syria, however, was the first foreign field of Francis of Assisi, one of the noblest missionaries that the world has known. He set on foot a movement which has sent thousands of missionaries into all parts of the world. We shall meet the Franciscans again and again in Asia and Africa and America. It is interesting to remember that in 1223 the founder of their order went on a mission to the home land of the Saviour. Lovers of missions will enjoy reading the Life of Francis, by Sabatier, a Protestant, and a thoroughly appreciative as well as critical biographer.

52. The original missionary work in Syria so established Christianity in that land of its birth that all the vicissitudes of changing empire, and even of Mohammedan conquest and re-conquest, have never effaced the Christian faith. Hundreds of thousands of Syrians still bow the knee to Christ.

CHAPTER V.

# ASIA MINOR.

53. **Cyprus.** 54. Paul and Sergius Paulus. 55. The visit to Galatia. 56. The effect of the first recorded missionary sermon. 57. Iconium, Lystra and Derbe. 58. The return of the missionaries. 59. The second and third missionary journeys in Southern Asia Minor. 60. Ephesus and Western Asia Minor. 61. Apollos and Priscilla and Aquila in Ephesus. 62. Paul's wide-reaching work in Ephesus. 63. Two other apostles. 64. Great success in Northern Asia Minor according to Pliny. 65. Gregory in New Cæsarea. 66. Justin Martyr.

53. The island of Cyprus is one of the natural stepping stones between the East and the West. England in our own day deems it worth while to hold portions of it as essential to her highway between Asia and Europe. It was one of the earliest points touched by Christianity outside of Syria. Some of "those who had been scattered in different directions in consequence of the persecution that broke out about Stephen went as far as . . . Cyprus telling the Message, but only to Jews." Copper obtained its name from the name of this island where it was early found. Possibly the estate of **Barnabas,** here, which he had sold for the common good contained mining interests.

At any rate he was at home on the island of his birth to which he came with two comrades—one of them a religious protégé of his, the other his cousin—prospecting for something more precious than metal. They went from place to place through the island seeking people who might be ready to take the pearl of great price. The results are unrecorded, except at one point, the capital.

54. There, events of the greatest significance in the history of missions were to occur. Christianity having left the provinces of its birth and started on an aggressive career in the empire, was summoned into the presence of the imperial Proconsul. He was a man of marked intelligence, and represented to some extent the best attainments of Roman or Western paganism. More significant than the presence of the Proconsul was that of an influential member of his court who was a recognized representative of oriental paganism, "Elymas the Magian." He was, very likely, the court physician and astronomer or rather astrologer. Sergius Paulus availed himself of whatever wisdom the East had to offer. Thus Christianity, on its first foreign mission field, stood face to face with what the pagan world had to offer in the way of practical light from Zoroaster to Seneca. This island court reflected the spiritual condition of the whole empire. The inquisitive, restless and hungry Occident was seeking to satisfy itself on the insights and the superstitions of the Orient. The whole energy of Saul, hitherto a figure second to Barnabas, was aroused and called into action, as they confronted the embodiment

of heathen darkness. "You incarnation of deceit and fraud!" he exclaimed. The public overthrow of this member of the order of the Magi in the presence of the Roman Proconsul proved its importance at once. The Proconsul "became a believer in Christ, being greatly struck with the teaching about the Master." The large-minded historian Luke seized on this point for record in his story of missions and marked it by thereafter placing Saul as the foremost missionary and calling him by his Gentile name, Paul.

55. From Cyprus the three missionaries, with **Paul** now in the lead, sailed to undertake a mission on the mainland. But after the intense excitement of the great crisis between Christianity and paganism at Paphos, the highly sensitive organism of Paul suffered reaction in the enervating and malarious climate of Pamphylia. It was necessary to go at once to the highlands of Southern Galatia. **John Mark** demurred at this change of plan and left the party. Barnabas, however, continued the journey with Paul across the mountains and over to Pisidian Antioch, which lay 3,600 feet above the sea. We know from Paul's own pen that it was physical malady which brought him to this region. There are many conjectures as to the nature of the malady. But, taking all the scattered hints into account, it seems probable that it was some extremely painful, occasionally disabling and even loathsome, affection of the eyes. One who has suffered from acute inflammation of the optic nerve would not think "a tent-peg in the flesh" too strong a phrase with which to characterize it. What-

ever the disease may have been, it is a significant fact in missionary history that this was the means used by providence to determine where the first mission in Asia Minor should be planted. Paul, instead of being defeated by physical disabilities, turned them to account in his mission. He was so earnest in spirit that his unsightly appearance instead of turning people away from the gospel called out their interest and sympathies.

56. After weeks of patient work, he preached a sermon in the synagogue one day which aroused the whole community of Jews and their proselytes. It was so impressive that some one made memoranda of it, so that we still possess a brief abstract. It is of great interest, not only as a sermon which set a whole town to thinking, but also as being the first report of a Christian sermon preached in the foreign mission field. It was addressed to Jews and to those whom their missions had converted to Judaism. It did not offend them. On the contrary, as they were going out they begged for the repetition of its teaching. They even followed Paul and Barnabas after they had left the house of worship. The favor of God through his own mercy, instead of through ritual merit, was a boon, a good-news indeed. The missionaries "urged" the inquirers "to continue to rely on the mercy of God." Crowds came the next Sabbath, including many of the heathen townspeople. Saved by grace was a precious note to them also. But the Jews could not bear the thought that Gentiles were being welcomed into the family of God without first coming through

*Raphael.* PAUL AND BARNABAS AT LYSTRA.

the ritual door, and so "they became exceedingly jealous." But the missionaries spoke out with utmost plainness and said: "It is necessary that God's Message should be told you first; but since you reject it and do not reckon yourselves worthy of the Enduring Life—why, we turn to the heathen! For this is the Lord's order to us—

"'I have destined thee for a light to the heathen, to be the means of salvation to the ends of the earth.'"

Many of the heathen were delighted on hearing this and became Christians. The work spread among them throughout the whole region of which Antioch was the center. At last, however, Jewish bigotry drove the missionaries out of that section of the country

57. They went about eighty miles southwest, to Iconium. Their experiences at Antioch were repeated here. Luke gives a brief narrative which be begins with the statement that "the same thing occurred in Iconium." At Lystra, 18 miles southwest of Iconium, the missionaries appear to have found no Jewish synagogue and to have come into immediate contact with raw paganism. The rude villagers, on seeing a deed of mercy, first wanted to worship the benefactors as gods, then in swift reaction wanted to kill them. The event of greatest importance at Lystra in the spread of the gospel was the coming to Christ there of a young man by the name of Timothy. Paul and Barnabas, driven from Lystra by Jews of Antioch and Iconium, went southeast to Derbe. There they "made many disciples."

58. The missionaries were now at a point where they

might naturally have returned to Antioch in Syria by the land route. Instead of doing this they went back through the places where they had met such bitter hostility. They did it for the sake of establishing the converts and organizing them into groups for permanent service. On the way home they preached in Perga, but did not revisit Cyprus. On reaching the Mother Church in Syrian Antioch "they gathered the Church together, and gave an account of all that God had done with and through them, especially how He had opened to the heathen a door to the Faith; and at Antioch they stayed with the disciples for a long time." This first truly foreign mission was carried through in the years 46 to 49.

59. After two years in Antioch and Jerusalem, spent largely in getting the home field into right relations with the work for the heathen, Paul set out on a second missionary tour, taking for a companion **Silas.** They went, overland this time, into the region formerly visited, coming first to Derbe. At Lystra Paul took **Timothy** into the missionary staff. The results of this second tour in South Galatia were admirable. "So the Churches grew stronger in the Faith and increased in numbers from day to day." But the missionaries were followed by that bane of Christianity in all ages and lands, Judaizers, men who are determined to make religion turn on ceremonies, on the symbols, instead of or the realities. Hence, three years after his second visit, Paul wrote to these Galatian churches that wonderful letter which has been the *magna charta* of Christian life and liberty ever since. Soon after he made

THE TEMPLE OF DIANA, EPHESUS.

another visit in Galatia on his third missionary tour. "After making some stay in Antioch, he set out on a tour through the Phrygian district of Galatia, strengthening the faith of all the disciples as he went." This is the last that is known of missionary work in Southern Asia Minor.

60. Ephesus was the metropolis of Western Asia Minor and the center of its heathen worship. Its temple of Diana was more than 342 feet long and 163 feet wide as shown by modern measurements of the foundations. Great fragments of its splendid marble columns and architraves fascinate the eye of the visitor to-day. Our illustration shows how it would appear if it were restored on the old lines of magnificence and beauty. In Paul's day it was venerable with more than three hundred years of history. It contained the image of Diana "which fell down from Jupiter" as the people believed. It enshrined a still greater treasure, as we should think, a painting of Alexander the Great by Apelles the famous Greek artist. That was rated at a money value equal to about $200,000. This building was not only a temple and an art museum, it was also a safe deposit bank containing immense quantities of money and jewels. No wonder that pilgrims from everywhere wished to take home with them little models of the building in terra cotta, marble or silver. Diana deftly moulded or carved within made the memento a sacred shrine.

61. The first missionary of whom we know in Ephesus was **Apollos.** He was filled with Old Testament learning and with zeal for John the Baptist and for

the Christ. But he had started on his mission without understanding the meaning of the Day of Pentecost. Converts in Ephesus knew what it was to be baptised for forgiveness of sins but not the far higher reality of being baptized into the Spirit of Jesus. An earnest business woman and her husband who had learned elsewhere that Christianity is not mainly a negative but a positive experience, a living of the divine life, did what they could to correct the serious blunder of Apollos. Meantime, Paul had been longing to reach the religious metropolis of Asia Minor. He had tried his best to do so in the year 51 on his second missionary journey westward, but had been prevented by unmistakable indications of providence. On the way back, three years later, unable as yet to stop long himself, he did the next best thing by bringing with him and leaving there **Priscilla** and **Aquila.** "They put into Ephesus, and there Paul, leaving his companions, went into the synagogue and addressed the Jews. When they asked him to prolong his stay, he declined, saying, however, as he took his leave, 'I will come back again to you, please God,' and then set sail from Ephesus."

62. Within a few months he was able to keep his conditional promise. Once here at the goal of his missionary longing, Paul stayed and worked longer than we have record of his doing at any other place, some three years. Though he was bold in his proclamation of Christ, the final break with the Jews did not come for three months. When he was excluded from the synagogue, he secured a public lecture hall in which to pro-

*Doré.* PAUL AT EPHESUS.

claim the good news. He also went from house to house, not in ordinary pastoral calls on disciples, but in specific effort for the unevangelized. He was able to reach not only the city but the whole region of which it was the commercial and religious center. "This went on for two years, so that all who lived in Roman Asia, Jews and Greeks alike, heard the Lord's Message." This wide effect was accomplished by reaching people who visited the city and doubtless also by sending out native evangelists. Philemon and Epaphras of Colossæ were Paul's converts, though he never visited that place in person. The burning of the books of the magicians and the great riot in the theater, caused by the falling off in the trade in Diana shrines, are two unmistakable indications as to the extent and success of Paul's mission at Ephesus. Perhaps the most beautiful and touching summary of mission work in all literature is Luke's record of Paul's address to the Ephesian Elders on his final separation from them. But he never gave up his influential connection with the field. When a prisoner in Rome four or five years after leaving Ephesus, he wrote the three charming, practical and inspiring letters to this region, "Philemon," "Colossians" and "Ephesians."

63. Two or three years later we gain a glimpse of the fact that Christianity had been widely planted in Asia Minor. **Peter** wrote to converted Jews who lived in five different provinces of Asia Minor, "Pontus, Galatia, Cappadocia, Asia, and Bithynia." Paul had directly labored only in Galatia and Asia, so that there must have been many earnest missionaries of whom we

have no record. The oldest form of the traditions about the fields of labor of the Apostles assigns to Asia Minor, Peter and John.

About the labors of John there we are reasonably sure. Probably only two or three years after Peter's letter to the Christians in five provinces, John wrote to seven churches in the one province of Asia.

64. There is a precious testimony to the early success of missions in Northern Asia Minor which comes to us from the pens of two distinguished Romans, a letter of Pliny, governor of the combined provinces of Bythinia and Pontus on the Black Sea, to Trajan and the emperor's reply. They were written in A. D. 112 or 113. Pliny is asking for advice as to what measures he ought to pursue in suppressing Christianity. In reporting what he has already done he declares that he has compelled many to renounce Christ and to offer libations before the statue of the emperor, adding, "none of which things it is said can such as are really and truly Christians be compelled to do." He says that "others named by the informer admitted that they were Christians, and then shortly afterwards denied it, adding that they had been Christians, but had ceased to be so, some three years, some many years, more than one of them as much as twenty years, before." According to Pliny, then, there were Christians in that region before the year 100. He was writing at Amisos, a great seaport in the extreme northeast of Asia Minor. Putting one indication with another Prof. Ramsay concludes that Christianity must have been introduced about Amisos not far from the

year 70. Let Pliny tell us what the character and extent of it were in his day:

"They affirmed, however, that this had been the sum, whether of their crime or their delusion; they had been in the habit of meeting together on a stated day, before sunrise, and of offering in turns a form of invocation to Christ, as to a god; also of binding themselves by an oath, not for any guilty purpose, but not to commit thefts, or robberies, or adulteries, not to break their word, not to repudiate deposits when called upon; these ceremonies having been gone through they had been in the habit of separating, and again meeting together for the purpose of taking food—food, that is, of an ordinary and innocent kind. They had, however, ceased from doing even this, after my edict, in which, following your orders, I had forbidden the existence of fraternities. This made me think it all the more necessary to inquire, even by torture, of two maid-servants, who were styled deaconesses, what the truth was. I could discover nothing else than a vicious and extravagant superstition; consequently, having adjourned the inquiry, I have had recourse to your counsels. Indeed, the matter seemed to me a proper one for consultation, chiefly on account of the number of persons imperiled. For many of all ages and all ranks, aye, and of both sexes, are being called, and will be called, into danger. Nor are cities only permeated by the contagion of this superstition, but villages and country parts as well; yet it seems possible to stop it and cure it. It is in truth sufficiently evident that the temples, which were almost entirely deserted, have begun to be frequented, that the customary religious rites which had long been interrupted are being resumed, and that there is a sale for the food of sacrificial beasts, for which hitherto very few buyers indeed could be found. From all this it is easy to form an opinion as to the great number of persons who may be reclaimed, if only room be granted for penitence."

65. There is an interesting glimpse of missionary activity in the northern part of Asia Minor in the middle of the third century. **Gregory,** of a distinguished

family, an enthusiastic pupil of Origen, became pastor of New Cæsarea A. D. 240. It is said that he found but seventeen Christians in that pagan town and that when he died thirty years later he left but seventeen pagans there. The precise numbers may be rhetorical. But the general fact of his missionary service and success is undoubted. He was called the Wonder-worker. He was a man of inspiring personality. Such men often heal the body as well as the soul. Gregory of Nysa, in another part of Asia Minor, writes of his friend Gregory of New Cæsarea eight years after the latter's death, and tells how crowds used to gather early in the morning, when Gregory "preached, questioned, admonished, instructed and healed. In this way, and by the tokens of divine power which shone forth upon him, he attracted multitudes to the preaching of the Gospel. The mourner was comforted, the young man was taught sobriety, to the old fitting counsel was addressed. Slaves were admonished to be dutiful to their masters; those in authority to be kind to their inferiors. The poor were taught that virtue is the only wealth, and the rich that they were but the stewards of their property and not its owners."

66. We cannot better close our study of missions in Syria and Asia Minor than with the story of the conversion of a Syrian which took place probably in Asia Minor. **Justin Martyr** was born at Nablous, in Samaria, only about eighty-five years after the ministry of Jesus to the woman and the men of that town. His parents were neither Samaritans, Jews nor Christians, but heathen and people of some means. Young Justin

was able to gratify his hunger for knowledge. He traveled far and wide studying in one after another of the schools of philosophy. But nothing fully satisfied the needs of his mind. He shared the common contempt of the philosophers for Christians until he had seen the calmness and evident sincerity with which Christians met martyrdom. He was so far impressed, after a time, that he wished that some one would stand out and cry aloud with tragic voice, "Shame, shame on the guilty, who charge upon the innocent the crimes of themselves and their gods!" About this time as he was walking one day on the seashore for philosophic contemplation "a certain old man, by no means contemptible in appearance, exhibiting meek and venerable manners," entered into conversation with Justin and plied him with philosophic questions after the manner of Socrates. Pointing finally to the insufficiencies of Plato, Pythagoras and the philosophers in general, the wise missionary led him to study the Old Testament prophets. Speaking of the effect of this conversation on himself, he says:

"A flame was kindled in my soul; and a love of the prophets, and of those men who are friends of Christ, possessed me; and whilst revolving his words in my mind, I found this philosophy alone to be safe and profitable. Thus, and for this reason, I am a philosopher. Moreover, I would wish that all, making a resolution similar to my own, do not keep themselves away from the words of the Saviour. For they possess a terrible power in themselves, and are sufficient to inspire those who turn aside from the path of rectitude with awe; while the sweetest rest is afforded those who make a diligent practice of them."

Justin continued to wear his philosopher's cloak and

it sometimes inclined inquirers to him. His philosophy was Christianity and he became its earnest missionary both by word and by pen. We shall see him, later in Italy, addressing the emperors themselves in behalf of Christianity.

CHAPTER VI.

# PERSIA.

67. "The East." 68. Story of Abgar and Jesus. 69. The correspondence. 70. Apostolic work. 71. Early work. 72. Bardaisan and Edessa. 73. The Apostle of Armenia. 74. Results. 75. Georgia. 76. Nestorians. 77. Extent of Nestorian missions. 78. Saul and Origen in Arabia. 79. A political mission. 80. Mohammed. 81. Moravians in Persia.

67. The word Persia is used here to cover the great expanse of country which has been included at one time or another in the Persian Empire, lying between Asia Minor and Syria on the one hand and India and Central Asia on the other. It included the Armenian Mountains, the Mesopotamian Valley and the Arabian Desert as well as Persia proper and other adjacent regions. It was "the East." It is probable that some knowledge of the new Messiah penetrated the East during the life of Jesus himself. What did the Wise Men tell after they had returned from Bethlehem? Later, during his public ministry, is it possible that no rumor of the amazing Galilean Healer and Prophet floated Eastward on the wings of travel and trade?

One still sees on the pathways of Palestine long trains of laden camels going back and forth to and from the East. Suffering humanity is ever alert to learn of any one who can alleviate its pains.

68. According to a very ancient account, accepted as authentic by Eusebius, one of the kings of the nearer East sent to the Nazarene Healer for help; most scholars believe that the story is largely or wholly legendary, though there have been some experts in this realm of knowledge who have thought that the account rests on a solid basis of fact. There is enough of possibility in it, not to say probability, to make it a natural preface to the history of missions in the East.

69. Eusebius, writing not later than A. D. 324, says:

"The divinity of our Lord and Saviour Jesus Christ being noised abroad among all men on account of his wonder-working power, he attracted countless numbers from foreign countries lying far away from Judea, who had the hope of being cured of their diseases and of all kinds of sufferings. For instance, the King Abgarus, who ruled with great glory the nations beyond the Euphrates, being afflicted with a terrible disease which it was beyond the power of human skill to cure, when he heard of the name of Jesus, and of his miracles, which were attested by all with one accord, sent a message to him by a courier, and begged him to heal his disease. But he did not at that time comply with his request; yet he deemed him worthy of a personal letter in which he said that he would send one of his disciples to cure his disease, and at the same time promised salvation to himself and all his house. Not long afterward his promise was fulfilled. For after his resurrection from the dead and his ascent into heaven, Thomas, one of the twelve apostles, under divine impulse, sent Thaddeus, who was also numbered among the seventy disciples of Christ, to Edessa, as a preacher and evangelist of the teaching of Christ. And all that our Saviour had promised received through him its fulfillment.

You have written evidence of these things taken from the archives of Edessa, which was at that time a royal city. For in the public registers there, which contain accounts of ancient times and the acts of Abgarus, these things have been found preserved down to the present time. But there is no better way than to hear the epistles themselves which we have taken from the archives and have literally translated from the Syriac language in the following manner:

"*Copy of an epistle written by Abgarus the ruler to Jesus, and sent to him at Jerusalem by Ananias the swift courier.* 'Abgarus, ruler of Edessa, to Jesus, the excellent Saviour who has appeared in the country of Jerusalem, greeting. I have heard the reports of thee and of thy cures as performed by thee without medicines or herbs. For it is said that thou makest the blind to see and the lame to walk, that thou cleansest lepers and castest out impure spirits and demons, and that thou healest those afflicted with lingering disease and raisest the dead. And having heard all these things concerning thee, I have concluded that one of two things must be true: either thou art God, and having come down from heaven thou doest these things, or else thou, who doest these things, art the Son of God. I have therefore written to thee to ask thee that thou wouldst take the trouble to come to me and heal the disease which I have. For I have heard that the Jews are murmuring against thee and are plotting to injure thee. But I have a very small yet noble city which is great enough for us both.'

"*The answer of Jesus to the ruler Abgarus by the courier Ananias.* 'Blessed art thou who hast believed in me without having seen me. For it is written concerning me, that they who have seen me will not believe in me, and that they who have not seen me will believe and be saved. But in regard to what thou hast written me, that I should come to thee, it is necessary for me to fulfill all things here for which I have been sent, and after I have fulfilled them thus to be taken up again to him that sent me. But after I have been taken up I will send to thee one of my disciples, that he may heal thy disease and give life to thee and thine.'

"To these epistles there was added the following account in the Syriac language: 'After the ascension of Jesus, Judas, who was also called Thomas, sent to him Thaddeus, an apostle, one of the seventy.'"

Eusebius proceeds to tell, still quoting from the archives of Edessa, how **Thaddeus** healed Abgar, refusing to take any money in return, and proclaimed Christ to him and his people. Later accounts greatly enlarged and embellished the story of the conversion of Abgar and his realm. All that we can be sure of on the testimony of Eusebius is that the Gospel was introduced in that part of Mesopotamia long before the year 300. The first missionary may have been Thaddeus, the Apostle, or one of the seventy by the same name.

70. We know that many of the people present on the Day of Pentecost belonged in what we are calling Persia. "Some of us are Parthians, some Medes, some Elamites and some of us live in Mesopotamia." If no word went into the East from the lips or the bodily ministry of Jesus, he soon spoke there in the Spirit. Waiting and expectant harps on the willows of the waters of Babylon caught up the glad tidings that the Hope of Israel had come. We have good reason to think that Peter the missionary to the circumcision carried out his mission in the Euphrates Valley, where so many more of his brethren in the flesh had their homes than lived in Palestine or in any other part of the world. Babylon was the most natural place for him to be found writing his Epistle in the seventh decade of the first century.

71. It is affirmed by tradition that before the end of

the first century **Mar Maris** planted a church at Seleucia-Ctisephon, the winter capital of the Parthian or Persian kings, and that from here he made a successful evangelizing tour through Doorkan, Cashgar, the two Iraks, El Ahwaz, Yemen and the Island of Socotra. At a very early date it is certain that Christianity in Syria spread into the adjacent regions eastward. A significant event in the progress of missions always is the putting of the Sacred Writings into the language of the people. The Scriptures were translated into the Syriac language, probably at Edessa, as early as the second century. This was the first translation of the New Testament.

72. The first missionary in the East, after the apostolic days, of whom we have definite knowledge, was **Bardaisan,** a high-born native of Edessa. He was a counsellor of Bar-Manu, the Abgar of his day, and appears to have been the instrument of his conversion. Abgar, like Cæsar, was the title of a long succession of rulers. From the time of Abgar Bar-Manu (about 200), Baalistic symbols cease to appear on the coins of Edessa and the cross takes their place. It is possible that Bar-Manu was the first Christian Abgar, and that after one hundred years the story of his conversion was attributed to the much earlier Abgar of Christ's day and was glorified by local pride into the account which Eusebius found in the Edessene archives. There was a Christian meeting-house in Edessa by the year 203, for we have record of its destruction at that time by flood. The Roman Emperor, Caracalla, spent the winter of 216 at Edessa and, hav-

ing sent Bar-Manu to Rome in chains, sought to make **Bardaisan** deny the Christian faith, but he witnessed instead a bold confession. Bardaisan then went into Armenia in the hope of making converts there also. We see him again holding serious conference with men from India, who were envoys to Elagabalus Cæsar. Though Bardaisan is the first missionary in the East after the first century whose name we know, he himself tells us that already Christianity had spread in Parthia, Media, Persia and Bactria, *i. e.*, throughout the whole region which we are studying in the present chapter.

Edessa stood near one of the great highways of the globe. It was but twenty miles from Haran, where the clan of Abraham had stopped for a time in its migration from the East to the West. Nearly four millenniums later England has projected a railway to India along this route. It was at this strategic point that Bardaisan fell in with the envoys from India to Italy and conferred with them on the highest themes.

73. The Armenians lay claim to the accounts of Christianity in connection with the Abgars and with Edessa as being their own history. There are other traces of the introduction of the faith into Armenia before the year 300. There were doubtless many believers scattered through the land. But the Christianization of the country in general took place in the early part of the fourth century. No country can more correctly name a single missionary as its apostle than Armenia. **Gregory,** called the Illuminator, carried the light of the gospel through Armenia. His father

was a Parthian invader of the country, whose whole family was exterminated by the Armenians except the infant son Gregory. He was rescued and taken to Cæsarea in Cappadocia, Asia Minor. There he was brought up in the Christian faith. When about 25 years old he went to Armenia and ingratiated himself with the king, Tiradates III, without the latter's knowledge of the terrible enmity between their fathers. But on a great occasion Gregory refused to worship Anahid, one of the idols of Tiradates, and even preached Christ to him. The king put Gregory to torture, and on learning who he was had him flung into a dark and slimy dungeon to die. But one of the Christians already in the land brought him food daily for fourteen years. The king became afflicted with a terrible disease and his sister dreamed that the release of Gregory would insure recovery. This proved true, and gave Gregory an opening for the free proclamation of the gospel. Tiradates, his wife, his sister and many of their retainers were converted.

74. A national council was summoned, which adopted Christianity and sent Gregory to Cappadocia to be ordained in his old home, Cæsarea. This was about the year 302. Immediately on his return, accompanied by a band of missionaries, it is said that in twenty days 190,000 people received baptism. **Tiradates** was the first great sovereign to become a Christian. He preached Christ with zeal himself and took Gregory with him on a royal missionary progress through the land. At one time, according to the oldest account we have, in the course of three days, 150,-

000 of the king's troops, clothed in white robes, went down into the Euphrates River and came up out of the water as baptized Christians.

It is certain that Gregory was the enlightener of Armenia. He went from place to place proclaiming Christ. But he could not have accomplished what he did without many earnest co-laborers. At first he brought these from Cappadocia. In writing back for more helpers he said, "Those whom thou hast given to me I account as precious pearls." **Zenobius** and **Epiphanius** were eminent among them. The following sentence from one of his letters asking for more helpers shows one of the secrets of Gregory's success as the Illuminator, "Especially do thou send **Timotheus,** Bishop of the Adonians, whom thou didst praise for his acquaintance with the Scriptures, a thing very necessary for this country." As fast as he could he raised up a native ministry. He is said to have ordained 400 pastors. Schools were established under the patronage of the king. Gregory died after about thirty years of service. He was one of the master missionaries of the world.

75. In the region of Georgia the faith was introduced in the fourth century, by a Christian woman, **Nouni,** who was carried there as a captive to be a slave. Her beautiful character won the interest of all who knew her. By prayer she is said to have brought about the cure of the queen from a serious ailment. This led to the conversion of both queen and king. They zealously promoted the faith in their realm, obtaining missionaries from both Tiradates,

their over-lord, and from Constantine the Great. Nouni herself made missionary journeys through the country and was its true apostle.

76. To return to Edessa, the planting of Christianity there was significant, not only for itself and for Persia, including Armenia, but also for the whole oriental world. What Antioch was to the West, Edessa was to the East, a fountain of far-reaching missionary activity. It was here and at Nisibis, not far away, that Nestorianism had its chief seat.

Early in the fifth century Nestorius, Archbishop of Constantinople, objected strenuously to the new fashion of calling Mary of Nazareth the "Mother of God" and to some allied metaphysical speculations about the nature of Christ, which seem to us more correct than his own theories, but which were then just coming into vogue. An ecclesiastical council was convened at Ephesus to settle these disputed questions. It was called to order by Cyril, Archbishop of Alexandria, the bitter foe of Nestorius, before the friends of the latter from Syria reached the town. In a single day (June 22, A. D. 431) a strong partisan conclusion was reached which has been counted orthodoxy ever since. After four years of struggle most disgraceful to all concerned, Nestorius was driven into exile. His followers were put under the ban of the emperor four years later still. Like the persecution of an earlier day in Syria, it proved to be a good thing for the cause of Christ, since the Christians were scattered abroad and went everywhere preaching the word.

The Nestorians being driven out of Edessa by imperial persecution, crossed the boundary of Parthia and made Nisibis their headquarters. Here they had a flourishing theological seminary, which was, in fact, the greatest missionary training-school that the continent of Asia has ever had.

77. One of the wide missionary movements from Persia was southeastward into India, another was eastward throughout Mongolia and China. In Persia itself Nestorianism entered into possession of a great body of Christianity, which had been planted long before. The record of the planting has been lost. As often elsewhere, we get a distinct view of the results of missions only by the record of persecutions which endeavored to counteract those results. Christianity had spread so widely that in the fourth century, during a persecution by Shapur II lasting thirty-five years, 16,000 clergy, monks and nuns, whose names were recorded, were cruelly put to death, besides uncounted thousands of Christians who were not in religious orders. There was then a period of forty years of peace, followed by thirty years more of most fiendish persecution. Thus in the Persian, as well as in the better known Roman, empire, Christianity made its way in the face of terrific opposition. The Magi as a whole were untrue to the vision which three of their number had followed at the beginning. As a class they sought to quench the star of Bethlehem in blood. But the churches survived and, gaining more liberty, multiplied and spread abroad, for some five hundred years after Shapur's persecution, till the Nes-

torian Patriarch at Seleucia-Ctesiphon (near Bagdad, and the ancient Babylon from which he took his title) had twenty-five metropolitans under his jurisdiction, with bishops under each metropolitan, and a vast army of clergy, with uncounted multitudes of believers scattered all the way from Edessa to Peking and from Lake Balkash (in modern Russia) to the southern point of India. Neale, the competent English historian of the Eastern church, doubts whether the Pope of Rome at this time had more ecclesiastical power than the Patriarch of Babylon. It is certain that the Roman Church of those days was far inferior to the Nestorian in the extent of its missionary endeavor. The Nestorians have, in fact, never been rivalled in that vital phase of Christian life, unless by the Jesuits and the Moravians.

78. Concerning Arabia as a mission field little is known. It is generally assumed that Saul's three years there were for study, contemplation and adjustment of soul to the light which had so dazzled him on the way to Damascus. We can not imagine him silent, however, as to the new faith that was in him. But if, as seems natural to suppose, he went to that part of Arabia which contained the lofty mountains of Sinai, which had meant so much to his predecessors, Moses and Elijah and to the whole people of Israel, there were few inhabitants to whom he could communicate the gospel. He was shut up for the most part to communion with the past and with his God.

In the third century an Arabian emir sent to Alexandria an earnest request that its great Christian teacher, Origen, come to give information about Christianity. We cannot doubt that he responded by going or by sending some one as a missionary. In A. D. 244 ecclesiastical life in Arabia was so far advanced that a council was called to examine the theology of one of the pastors, Beryllus, of Bostra. Origen attended the council and succeeded in straightening out the kinks of thought in Bostra.

79. One hundred years later the Emperor Constantius sent a splendid embassy to the Homeritæ who occupied the southern coast of Arabia and believed themselves to be descendants of Abraham by Keturah. They practiced circumcision and they furnished a refuge for Jews who had been persecuted elsewhere. The emperor sent the emir a missionary, **Theophilus,** accompanied by a present of two hundred horses, and requested permission to build three churches in the places frequented by Roman traders. The Arab ruler was so well disposed that he built the churches himself, one at Aden; one at the capital, Dafur; and the other on the Persian Gulf. Theophilus, however, was a politician quite as much as a religious missionary. So far as we have record the Christian work was not followed up.

80. If Saul as a young convert had possessed the peerless missionary ability which he afterward developed and had plunged into the most thickly peopled part of Arabia, and if Origen had devoted his magnificent powers to evangelization instead of to speculation, Christianity might have been so planted in Arabia

as to supplant completely its gross idolatry and to leave no need of the monotheistic reformation with which Mohammed began there and no start for the career by which he secured the blotting out of half the map of Christendom. Instead of being the False Prophet, he might then have become an Arabian Luther. Oriental Christianity needed such an one in his day as much as occidental Christianity needed him a thousand years later. There is no way of knowing how much of the reformation in religion which Mohammed did accomplish was due to **Sergius Bahare** of Bostra. This degenerate Nestorian became an intimate associate of the prophet and communicated to him his own poor apocryphal knowledge of Christ.

81. In the vast region which we are calling Persia there was much missionary activity among the Tatars in the thirteenth and fourteenth centuries. But that is best understood in connection with China and Tatary, to be considered in later chapters. There is but one other missionary episode in this region which must be noticed at present. In 1747 two of the Moravian brethren, **Fred Wm. Hocker,** a physician, and **J. Rueffer,** a surgeon, set out for a mission to the followers of Zoroaster, a few of whom remained in Persia, the Parsees. When they reached Aleppo, they learned that Persia was in a state of practical anarchy and that Nadir Shah himself was extorting money from Jews and Christians in his realm by brutal torture. One of the brethren wavered, but the other insisted on perseverance. They procured two camels and joined a caravan of 1,500 of those ungainly ships

of the desert. They reached Bagdad just in time to catch another caravan which was starting for Persia with an armed guard of half a hundred soldiers. Crossing a wild ridge the caravan was attacked by two hundred Kurdish robbers and the hired guard quickly retreated. The missionaries were robbed of everything and left with scarcely any clothing even. One of them was thrust in several places with a spear and was finally knocked insensible with a club. He recovered after a time and dragged himself fifteen miles to the nearest human habitation, where he found his brother missionary in a similar plight. Kindly Persians supplied them with garments. These were of such coarse hair-cloth that their bruised bodies suffered agony, but they plodded on afoot. They were overtaken by robbers again, but finally reached Ispahan. Here the English resident, Mr. Pierson, took them to his own house and provided for them. But he showed them that there was no use of their undertaking to go farther, since the territory of the Parsees had just been plundered, both by the Shah and by the Afghans, and the prosperous remnant of one of the noblest of the non-Christian faiths had been either destroyed or scattered. After many more thrilling experiences the brethren reached Egypt, where one of them died, but the other, after three years of absence, at last arrived in Herrnhüt to tell the story to the little church there, already accustomed to accounts of most heroic missionary endeavor.

## CHAPTER VII.

# INDIA.

82. Characteristics. 83. The first introduction of Christianity. 84. Pantænus. 85. The Nestorians. 86. Monumental evidence. 87. The introduction of Roman Catholic missions. 88. Francis Xavier. 89. Robert de Nobili. 90. Beschi and Geronimo Xavier. 91. The testimony of Sir Thomas Roe. 92. John de Brito. 93. Dutch missions in Java. 94. In Amboyna. 95. In Ceylon. 96. The first Danish mission in India. 97. Christian Friedrich Schwartz.

82. The people of India naturally have a more intimate interest for us than any other people outside of Europe and European colonists, because they are more nearly related to us in blood. Their mother language, Sanskrit, proves beyond a doubt that they are of the same branch of the human family to which we belong, the Aryan, sometimes descriptively called the Indo-European. They are also marked in having a more refined and subtle intellectual life than any other non-Christian people, except the Greeks and Romans. In some directions their spiritual development surpasses that of any other part of the human race, ancient or modern, Christian or non-Christian. Society, however, is rigidly stratified and the masses of the people

are debased and imbedded in a low conglomerate of polytheism. The human soil of India, though apparently rich and inviting beyond all others, is extremely hard to work. The great harvests of nineteenth century missions there have been chiefly from the sub-soil of the non-Aryan races in the land. But in the centuries with which we have to do in the present course of study there were many faithful toilers. We must notice five distinct plantings of Christianity in India before Carey, the Primitive, the Nestorian, the Romish, the Dutch Presbyterian, and the Danish Lutheran plantings.

83. India was known to the ancients, was conquered by Alexander, i. e., the northern borders of it, and is mentioned in the book of Esther. It has been conjectured, though without proof, that in the account of the Day of Pentecost we should read Indian instead of "Judean"—the words are more alike in Greek than in English. It is clear from their names that many of the articles of commerce in Solomon's day came from India. It is certain also that there was a colony of Jews in India from whom representatives might have come at Pentecost. Tradition asserts that the Apostle Thomas went as a missionary to India. A Christian community which has existed there from early times bears his name and even shows his grave.

84. There is no reason to doubt that Christianity was taken to India in the first century. But the first positive name and date on record belongs to the second century, **Pantaenus,** between 180 and 190 A. D. Pantænus was a stoic philospher who had become a

Christian and the head of a famous Christian college in Alexandria, Egypt. His pupils, Clement and Origen, were among the greatest of early Christian teachers and writers. Clement says that Pantænus was "a man of learning who had penetrated most profoundly into the spirit of Scripture." Eusebius says that he "was distinguished as an expositor of the Word of God." Jerome, in one of his letters, says "Pantænus was sent to India that he might preach Christ among the Brahmins." He found Christians already there and using an early edition of the Gospel of Matthew, from which he brought back a copy to Alexandria. There is no means of knowing the extent of the work of the primitive missionaries in India. At the council of Nice (A. D. 325) there was present a "Bishop of India." He was really Bishop in Persia. As India had been included in the Persian Empire, the Christians there were counted within his jurisdiction.

85. In the last chapter we saw how the Nestorians were scattered throughout Asia. If now we turn to a native Hindoo history of the Malabar coast, India, we find that one **Thomas Cannaneo,** a Syrian, was allowed by one of the Rajas to settle there. He became very wealthy and was the progenitor of a numerous family. Again two Syrian Bishops, **Mar Sapor** and **Mar Peroses,** were extremely well received by a Raja and were permitted to build a church.

The tradition of the Malabar Christians, often called the St. Thomas Christians, is that the Thomas who led their forefathers to Christ was the Apostle of that name. But it was, doubtless, some later Thomas, probably one of the Nestorians leading a band of that sect after it was driven from the Greek Roman Empire by the Emperor Theodosius. The current names and customs of the people, their use of a form of the Syrian language, their well-known later ecclesiastical relations and other data, leave no question that the main evangelizing agency was Nestorian. In the sixth century an Egyptian merchant, Cosmas, surnamed Indicopleustes (Indian Voyager), turned monk and wrote vivid accounts of what he had learned. His work, entitled "Topographia Christiania," is an invaluable record of the early spread of Christianity. He says:

"So that I can speak with confidence of the truth of what I say, relating what I myself have seen and heard in many places that I have visited. . . . Even in the Island of Taprobane [Ceylon], in Farther India, where the Indian Sea is, there is a church of Christians with clergy and a congregation of believers, though I know not if there be any Christians farther on in that direction, and such is also the case in the land called Male, where the pepper grows. And in the place called Kalliana [Malabar], there is a bishop appointed from Persia as well as in the isle called the Isle of Dioscoris [Socotra], in the same Indian Sea. The inhabitants of that island speak Greek, having been originally settled there by the Ptolemies who ruled after Alexander of Macedon. There are clergy there also ordained and sent from Persia to minister among the people of the island and a multitude of Christians. We sailed past the island, but did not land. I met, however, with people from it who were on their way to Ethiopia, and they spoke Greek."

These words were written not later than 547 A. D.

Many of the early Nestorian converts were from

NESTORIAN TABLET OF INDIA.
(SEVENTH CENTURY)

the Brahmin and another of the highest of the Hindoo castes. For centuries the Christian community enjoyed great liberty and prosperity.

86. A precious monument of the work of the Nestorian missionaries was unearthed near Madras about the year 1547. It is an altar slab with a dove hovering over a cross cut in relief. On the margin are inscriptions belonging to the seventh or eighth centuries, one in Syriac, "Let me not glory except in the cross of our Lord Jesus Christ," and one in Pahlavi, "Who is the true Messiah and God alone and Holy Ghost." A more impressive monument of Nestorian missions is the continued existence of Malabar Christians. One thousand years after the first Nestorian planting in India the Portuguese found there one hundred villages composed entirely of Nestorian Christians, and in all the country 1,400 churches, with 200,000 souls. These people paid a slight tribute to the Rajas, but were governed in matters both temporal and spiritual by their own archbishop, who received ordination from the Nestorian patriarch in Persia. They used Syriac in all their church services, permitted their priests to marry and admitted no images in their simple meeting-houses. Through native political oppression and through still more shameful Romish persecution they had been reduced by the time of Carey to 116 churches all told, eighty-four united to Rome and thirty-two still independent. They recovered somewhat in the nineteenth century, so that they are as numerous now as they were four hundred years ago, when the Portuguese unhappily discovered them. It is a pleasure to

know that the census of British India in 1891 found 200,467 souls as a living monument of the early Nestorian missions.

87. During the Middle Ages a number of Franciscan and Dominican monks visited India with more or less vagrant missionary aims. But one need be mentioned here. **Jordanus,** a Dominican, was sent out in 1430 as a real missionary bishop. He wrote a book on the "Wonders of the East." The following passages indicate the temper of his work:

"In this India there is a scattered people, one here, another there, who call themselves Christians, but are not so, nor have they baptism, nor do they know anything else about the faith; nay, they believe St. Thomas the Great to be Christ! There, in the India I speak of, I baptized and brought into the faith about three hundred souls, of whom many were idolaters and Saracens. And let me tell you that among the idolaters a man may with safety expound the Word of the Lord; nor is any one among the idolaters hindered from being baptized throughout all the East, whether they be Tatars, or Indians or what not!

"As God is my witness, ten times better [Christians] and more charitable withal be those who be converted by the Preaching Minor friars to our faith than our folk here, as experience hath taught me. And of the conversion of those nations of India I say this, that if there be two hundred or three hundred good friars who would faithfully and fervently preach the Catholic faith, there is not a year which would not see more than X. thousand persons converted to the Christian faith. For whilst I was among these schismatics and unbelievers, I believe that more than X. thousand, or thereabouts, were converted to our faith; and because we, being few in number, could not occupy or even visit many parts of the land, many souls (woe is me!) have perished, and exceeding many do perish for lack of preachers of the Word of the Lord.

. . . How many times have I had my hair plucked out and been scourged and been stoned God Himself knoweth and I, who had to bear all this for my sins, yet have not attained to end my life as a martyr for the faith as did four of my brethren. Nay, five Preaching friars and four Minors were there in my time cruelly slain for the Catholic faith. Woe is me that I was not with them there!"

88. Portuguese Christianity, as we shall see later, did splendid work during the sixteenth century in Africa and in South America. But in India it was marred by its more than wasted, its wicked and destructive, efforts to bring over the Syrian Christians to the Roman rite. It annihilated more than it proselyted. The story is full of thrilling and sickening episodes. But we draw the veil over such so-called mission work. It was not planting. It was, at the best, only transplanting. It was mainly uprooting.

The record of Portuguese Romanism in India, however, is partly redeemed by the brilliant career, under its auspices, of the first and most famous Jesuit missionary to the heathen, **Francis Xavier.** It is true that it was he who suggested the introduction of the Inquisition in India. It is true that he never learned the language of the natives. It is true that he was too restless to stay long enough in one place to do permanently effectual work. It is true that he was loaded down with the superstitions of his time. But it is also true that he burned with genuine zeal for souls and that he took through India, Malacca, Japan and to the gates of China the first flaming torch of modern times to announce the Light of the World. He had a consuming love for his benighted fellows and so was a man after God's own heart. He was so high in heroic purpose that he flamed as a heavenly meteor not only across the continent of Asia, but also above the horizon of sleepy Christendom. It was he, more than any one man before Carey, who started the beacon fires of missions, which, after four hundred years, are to be seen ablaze on every mountain range of the earth and glowing in almost every valley.

Five young Spaniards, including Xavier, together with one Frenchman and one Portuguese, all students in the University of Paris, had pledged one another to undertake a mission to the Mohammedans in Palestine, or if not practicable there, then wherever the Pope might send them. This was the beginning of the "Company of Jesus," as it was soon after named. Ignatius Loyola, the first "General" of the order, had been a soldier, and he formed his missionary band on lines of the strictest military and more severe than military discipline. According to the ultimate constitution, thirty-one years were to be spent by every candidate in a course of training of which the central principle was the obliteration of self-will and the substitution of the will of the General, which was assumed to be the will of God. In this way the lofty motto of the company was to be made effective, "For the Greater Glory of God."

One day in 1540 Francis Xavier received orders to start the next day for a mission to India, under the auspices of the king of Portugal. He arrived at Goa, the Portuguese settlement, two years later, after a distressing voyage in which, though sick himself much of the time, he had been a ministering angel to the rough and wicked soldiers with whom he sailed. He immediately began work by ringing a large bell through the streets of Goa ànd urging that children be sent to him for instruction in the Christian religion. After five months he went to the pearl fisheries, on the Gulf of Manor, and for fifteen months lived in close brotherhood with the low caste, degraded people, ringing his bell, ministering to all and preparing a catechism for their instruction. His next mission was in the kingdom of Travancore, on the other side of the southern point of India. Here he established over forty missionary stations and in a single month baptized ten thousand natives. So the story runs. Then he labored for a time in the Malay Peninsula and Archipelago. Large successes are attributed to him there.

89. One of the most famous, some think infamous, successors of Xavier in India was Robert de Nobili. He was a man of aristocratic birth, a nephew of Cardinal Bellarmine and a grandnephew of Pope Marcellus II. He carried the principle of becoming all things to all men that he might save some, to such an extent as to lay himself open to the accusation of surrendering both Christianity and truth itself. He made himself master of the language and the religious literature of the natives and then conformed strictly to the social requirements of caste, living the life of a rigid, ascetic Brahmin devotee, but inculcating Christianity. He came to have numerous converts. A Capuchin missionary, who was afterward expelled from his own order, published in Europe a book in which he accused

Nobili and the Jesuits of unblushing fraud upon the natives. Most Protestant writers, though not all, have fully credited the charges of the Capuchin and have diligently repeated them. The Pope and others of Rome for a time accepted them as containing much truth, but finally ecclesiastical censure was removed. Nobili certainly conformed to Hindoo social and theological requirements in a way which no conscientious and democratic Christian could possibly allow. But he is entitled to state his own case:

"Besides my manner of life, my food and costume, and my using exclusively the services of Brahmins, there is another circumstance which aids me powerfully in making conversions; it is the knowledge which I have acquired of their most secret books. I find it stated in them that their country originally possessed four laws, or vedas; that three of these laws are those which the Brahmins still teach at the present day, and that the fourth was a purely spiritual law by virtue of which it was possible to attain the salvation of the soul. . . .

"I take occasion to point out to them, that they are living in fatal error, that neither of the three vedas which they recognize has power to save them; that in consequence all their efforts are vain, and this I prove to them by citing the very words of their sacred books. These people have an ardent desire of eternal happiness, and in order to merit it devote themselves to penance, alms deeds, and the worship of idols. I profit by this disposition to tell them that if they wish to obtain salvation, they must listen to my instructions; that I have come from a remote country with the sole object of bringing salvation to them, by teaching them that spiritual law which, by the confessions of their Brahmins, they have wholly lost. I thus adapt myself to their opinions, after the example of the Apostle, who preached to the Athenians the Unknown God."

In the Madura mission, of which Nobili was the head, 100,000 converts were gathered. At our distance in time and standards it is impossible to say to what extent they were really converted. In one respect only can we be sure that Nobili and his fellow-workers were right; that was in making themselves masters of the point of view of the people whom they sought to save.

90. **Constantius Beschi,** like Nobili, adopted the mode of life of a Brahmin penitent. He was one of the greatest Tamil scholars in India and was so regarded by the literati. The Nabob Tricheropalle made him his prime minister.

**Geronimo Xavier,** a nephew of Francis, was employed at the court of Akbar, the great Mogul emperor of India—who, though a Mohammedan, was somewhat of an eclectic in religion—to write for him "Persian Histories of Christ and of Peter." The account given by Akbar's minister, Abulfazl, is interesting:

"Learned monks also came from Europe, who go by the name of Padre. They have an infallible head called Papa. He can change any religious ordinances as he may think advisable, and kings have to submit to his authority. These monks brought the gospel and mentioned to the Emperor their proofs for the Trinity. His Majesty firmly believed in the truth of the Christian religion, and wishing to spread the doctrines of Jesus, ordered Prince Murad to take a few lessons in Christianity by way of auspiciousness, and charged Abulfazl to translate the gospel. Instead of the usual Bismillah-irrahmanirrahim, the following lines were used—

*Ai nam i tu Jesus o Kiristo,*

(O Thou whose names are Jesus and Christ),

which means, 'O thou, whose name is gracious and blessed';

and Shaikh Faizi added another half in order to complete the verse—

*Subhanaka la siwaka Ya Hu*

(We praise Thee, there is no one besides Thee, O God!)"

One of the wives of Akbar was a Christian and some of the Princes were baptized.

91. Early in the eighteenth century Sir Thomas Roe visited the court of the Great Mogul as an ambassador of England. Thus we have a contemporary Protestant view of the Jesuit missions. The quaint and simple statements of the recorder of the embassy do credit to his own fairness as well as to the work of the Jesuits:

"In this Confusion they Continued vntil the tyme of Ecbarsha, father of this king, without any Noice of Christian profession; who, beeing a Prince by Nature just and good, inquisitiue after Noueltyes. Curious of New opinions, and that excelled in many virtues, especially in Pietye and reuerence toward his Parentes, called in three Iesuites from Goa, whose cheefe was Ieronimo Xauier a Naurroies. After their arriuall hee heard them reason and dispute with much Content on his and hope on their partes, and caused Xauier to write a booke in defence of his owne profession against both moores and Gentilles; which finished, hee read ouer Nightly, causing some part to be discussed, and finally granted them his lettre Pattentes to build, to preach, teach, conuert, and to vse all their rites and Ceremonyes, as freely and amply as in Roome, bestoweing on them meanes to erect their Churches and places of deuotion. So that in some fewe cittyes they haue gotten rather *Templum* then *Ecclesiam.* In this Grant he gaue grant to all sortes of men to become Christians that would, eauen to his Court or owne blood, professing it should bee noe cause of disfauaour from him. Here was a faire beginninge, a forward spring of a leane and barren haruest.

"Ecbar-shae himselfe continued a Mahometan, yet hee began to make a breach into the law; Considering that Mahomett was but a man, a King as he was, and therefore reuerenced, he thought hee might proue as good a Prophett himselfe. This defection of the King spread not farre; a Certayn outward reuerence deteyned him, and so hee dyed in the formall profession of his Sect."

92. **John de Brito,** a Portuguese nobleman, who had great difficulty in securing the king's permission to leave his personal service, came to be one of the most devoted and successful of the missionaries in India, where he toiled for twenty years, suffering terrible tortures and finally death for Christ. He had baptized many thousands, four thousand the last year of his life. This was more than one hundred years after Xavier, whose work had inspired the youthful imagination of De Brito and had led him into the foreign field. Xavier had a long line of brilliant successors in India. There were nearly a million of Roman Catholics there when Carey arrived.

93. In 1610 the Dutch came into possession of a portion of the populous island of Java. The capital of all their possessions in the Indian Ocean was established there at Batavia.

**Justus Heurnius** was one of the most distinguished of the early Dutch missionaries. Son of a medical professor in the newly founded University of Leyden, he took the medical course of study. After five years of travel in France and England he returned and took a theological course. He was eager to go to India as a missionary, but both the Dutch and the English East India Companies were opposed to missions until long after this time. He wrote a vigorous book to arouse his countrymen to their missionary duty. This was in 1618. Six years later the East India Company sent him to Batavia. He began at once to work for the natives, both Malays and Chinese. He translated the Creed, the Lord's Prayer and the Ten Commandments into Chinese, making also a Dutch-Latin-Chinese dictionary.

His earnest evangelistic spirit led him to advocate the independence of the church from the East India Company. On this account he was arrested and imprisoned. On release he went to the Island of Amboyna. Here and in neighboring islands he gave himself to work among the natives. He won many of the people for whom he toiled. Missionaries of Islam were active there at the same time and poisoned his food. Though it did not take his life immediately, he never entirely recovered from the effects of the poison and was obliged to return to Holland. There, before his death in 1652, he revised a version of the Gospels and translated the Acts, the Psalms and a liturgy into Malayan. He also prepared a dictionary and put some of the Psalms into Malayan rhymes. He was a devoted missionary and an efficient advocate of missions one hundred years earlier than the Moravians.

The best thing that the Dutch did in Java was to translate the Scriptures into the Malay language and to publish them there in the Arabic character in 1758. But the missions do not appear to have made a deep impression on either the heathen or the followers of Mohammed, though there came to be 100,000 nominal converts in Java. Islam has made more converts from heathenism than Christianity has made in Dutch India.

94. In the Island of Amboyna, in 1686, it is said that the inhabitants, both pagans and Mohammedans, submitted to baptism, so that one missionary had 30,000 converts.

The Dutch admiral, Stavorinus, however, who visited Dutch India near the end of the eighteenth century, sums up the religious history of those regions during some hundreds of years, in a most discouraging way:

"The Amboynese," he says, "were in former times, as the Alforese are at present, idolators; but the Javanese, who began to trade hither in the latter end of the fifteenth, and in the beginning of the sixteenth century, endeavored to disseminate the doctrines of Mahomet here, and they succeeded so well that in the year 1515, that religion was generally received.

"The Portuguese arriving here in the meantime endeavored likewise to make the Roman Catholic religion agreeable to the inhabitants, and to propagate it amongst them; which, in particular, took place, according to Rumphius, in the year 1532, on the peninsula of Leytimor, but those of Hitoe have, to the present day, remained firmly attached to the Mahomedan faith, whence, in contradistinction to the Leytimorese, they are called Moors.

"When our people came to Amboyna, and the Portuguese were expelled from the island, the Protestant religion was gradually introduced; yet the unpleasing result of these frequent changes of religion has been, as might naturally be expected, that, from blind idolators, they have first become bad Roman Catholics and afterwards worse Protestants. The practice of idolatry can not yet be wholly eradicated; this, added to the prevalence of the superstitions which disgrace Christianity among the followers of the Roman Catholic persuasion, and the almost universal negligence and want of zeal of our ecclesiastics in these regions, almost entirely takes away the hope that the salutary doctrines of the gospel will ever be deeply rooted here, and that the Amboynese will ever be cured of their deplorable blindness."

Stavorinus says that when the number of Reformed Church ministers in Java was counted complete there were twelve of them, "six of whom preach in the Dutch, four in the Portuguese and two in the Malay languages." Thus but two were in the strictest sense missionaries.

95. After 1658 the Dutch held sway in Ceylon for one hundred and forty years, having largely displaced the Portuguese. They displaced them in ecclesiastical as well as in political relations to the natives. The Dutch were as intense and as determined in their religious convictions as were the Portuguese. One wishes that it could be said that these Calvinists were more Christlike in spirit than the Jesuits had been. In both cases the colonial government was brutal to the last degree. At the same time it required the natives to profess the Christian faith. In Ceylon Buddhists were informed by proclamation that 'baptism, communion in the State Church, and subscription to the Helvetic Confession, were essential preliminaries not only to appointment to office, but even to farming land.' Natives of Ceylon who had been brought into the Church of Rome by force and by worldly inducements, were now made Presbyterians by similar means. They were required to repeat the Lord's Prayer, the ten commandments, a morning and evening prayer and a grace before and after meals. When the school teachers certified that they had memorized these, they were baptized. The missionaries did not

know their language. In this way 40,000 were "converted" in four years. There were generally only from twelve to fifteen ministers in the island for the work among natives, colonists and all.

In the line of education, however, the Dutch were truer to the qualities which made them in Holland the world's foremost champions of light and liberty. They divided Ceylon into two hundred and forty parishes, with a school for boys in each parish, and established an academy for the education of teachers and evangelists. Some native ministers were educated in Europe. Each school had three or four teachers if needed. Over every ten schools a catechist was placed to visit and examine monthly the schools in his charge. One of the Dutch ministers was assigned a larger district for superintendence and annual inspection. They also provided the foundations of a Christian literature, even publishing the whole New Testament and the Book of Genesis in Cingalese in 1783. **Baldaeus,** one of the best known ministers, wrote a description of the country in which he gives a detailed account of thirty-four churches for the natives, with cuts of several meeting-houses, which were at the same time school-houses. The "hearers" in these thirty-four parishes number 30,950 and the "scholars" 16,460.

In 1722 there were counted in the Dutch churches in the East Indias 424,392 natives. Besides the chief centers already named, mission work was done by the Dutch in Sumatra, Timor, Celebes, Bonda, Terante and the Moluccas. On Formosa see §§ 177-184.

96. The first Danish missions to India were sent early in the eighteenth century. The chaplain of the King of Denmark, Lütken, had been imbued with the spirit of the earnest religious life known as Pietism, in the University of Halle, Germany. He stirred the king with a feeling of moral obligation to his non-Christian subjects in the Danish colonies. The chaplain was authorized to find suitable men for a mission to the heathen and to undertake the work with them. He **obtained at Halle, Bartholomew Ziegenbalg and Henry Plütschau.** After a trying seven months' voyage they arrived at the Danish port of Tranquebar, in 1706. This was 150 miles south of Madras on the opposite side of the peninsula of India from the principal fields cultivated by Xavier more than sixty years before. The missionaries put themselves to school with children, learning to write the Tamil alphabet in the sand. Ziegenbalg made such rapid progress that in two years he began the translation of the Scriptures and a year later could speak the language with fluency.

As has generally been true in the history of early modern foreign missions, the European colonists were far more obstructive to the work than the pagan natives themselves. The Danish governor of Tranquebar at the outset treated the missionaries with harshness and finally cast Ziegenbalg into prison, where he lay suffering intensely from the tropical heat for four months. It was only the absolute mandate of the Danish king which secured any chance whatever for the work. Beginning with outcast slaves, converts were gathered and a church was formed. Ziegenbalg died after thirteen years of service for India. But he had translated and scattered abroad the New Testament, prepared a dictionary and many religious tracts, thirty-three in all. He left 355 converts. The mission continued under the patronage of the kings of Denmark for 120 years. It is still maintained by the Leipsic Mission Society with a fair degree of success.

87. **Christian Friedrich Schwartz,** consecrated in childhood by his dying mother to the service of Christ and educated at the University of Halle, arrived at Tranquebar in 1750. He had partly learned the Tamil language from a returned missionary at Halle, so that in only four months after his arrival in India he was able to preach his first sermon to the natives in the church which had been dedicated just before the death of Ziegenbalg, thirty years earlier. After fifteen very useful years he was transferred to Trichinopoli, in the interior. Here, too, he lived and toiled in apostolic simplicity, "his daily fare a dish of boiled rice with a few other vegetables." He was "clad in a piece of dark cotton cloth woven and cut after the fashion of the country." At the end of twelve years he had baptized 1,238 converts, built an orphan asylum with his salary of $500 a year received as chaplain of the British garrison, and, by the aid of the commandant and others, built a church-house accommodating 2,000 people.

The last twenty years of his apostolate he spent in Tanjore, a center of Hindu worship, containing one of the most stately pagodas of India. Within four years two churches were established. The moral character of Schwartz was so commanding that all classes, both native and foreign, held him in the highest esteem and even reverence. On the occasion of a formidable native uprising under the haughty Mohammedan Hyder Ali, that potentate refused to treat with an English embassy, but said, "Send me the Christian. He will not deceive me." He meant Schwartz, and no nobler tribute was ever paid to Christian character. The humble missionary went and saved thousands of lives by his intercession. The Rajah of Tanjore made Schwartz the guardian of his adopted son and heir, Serfogee. The slab in the chapel over his grave says, in part, "His natural vivacity won the affection, as his unspotted probity and purity of life alike commanded the reverence, of the Christian, Mohammedan and Hindu. The very marble that here records his virtues was raised by the liberal affection and esteem of the Rajah of Tanjore, Maha Raja Serfogee."

Before Carey baptized his first convert in 1800 there had been 40,000 converts in the Tranquebar mission.

CHAPTER VIII.

# CHINA AND TATARY.

98. Three periods. 99. The Nestorian monument of Si-gnan-fu. 100. Royal reception of Olopun. 101. Progress and reverse. 102. More imperial favor. 103. Conclusions from the monument. 104. Close of the first period. 105. The Kerait Tatars and Prester John. 106. Jenghiz Khan. 107. Carpini's phenomenal journey to Karakorum. 108. Report of Sempad. 109. A great debate in Karakorum. 110. Characteristics of Tatar rule. 111. Kublai Khan's request for missionaries. 112. John of Monte Corvino. 113. His journey, reception and helpers. 114. Converts and education. 115. Appeal for more workers and supplies. 116. Church building. 117. Work in Southern China. 118. Progress there. 119. Odoric of Pordenone. 120. State of the missions about 1330.

98. There were three distinctly marked and apparently successful periods of missions in China before 1800, with complete gaps between them. In the eighth century Christianity had gained a numerous and influential following. It seemed in a fair way to pervade the land. Then it was almost entirely effaced. The same was true again in the fourteenth century. The leaders in the first period of missionary work were Nestorians, in the second period Franciscans, in the third period Jesuits.

99. One of the precious missionary records of the

world was preserved by being buried in China for seven or eight hundred years. Near the great city of Ch'ang-an, in the fu or department Hsi-an, province of Shenshi, northwestern China, some workmen digging a trench in the year 1625 came upon a stone tablet seven feet long and three feet wide, covered with characters, mostly Chinese, but a few of them Syriac. The Chinese are fond of ancient monuments, having a considerable collection in this very city of Ch'ang-an. The governor of the city took this one in charge. There were no foreigners in the place at that time, but a native Christian sent a copy of it to some Jesuit missionaries. It has been reproduced by copies and "squeezes" many times since 1625, and has been frequently translated. Its authenticity was questioned by Voltaire and others. But even so critical a historian as Gibbon said of them that they became "the dupes of their own cunning, whilst they are afraid of a Jesuitical fraud." It has been decided by competent scholarship that this is a genuine monument inscribed by Nestorian missionaries A. D. 781. It is commonly called the Nestorian monument of Si-gnan-fu, a current spelling of the place where it was found.

The interest of this document in stone is so great from every point of view that we must regret that our space does not permit the reproduction of it all. The first part is a statement concerning the being of God, the sin of man, the coming and teachings of Christ and the beneficent work of Christian missionaries. The second part is a sketch of the Nestorian missions in China from A. D. 635 to 781. The third

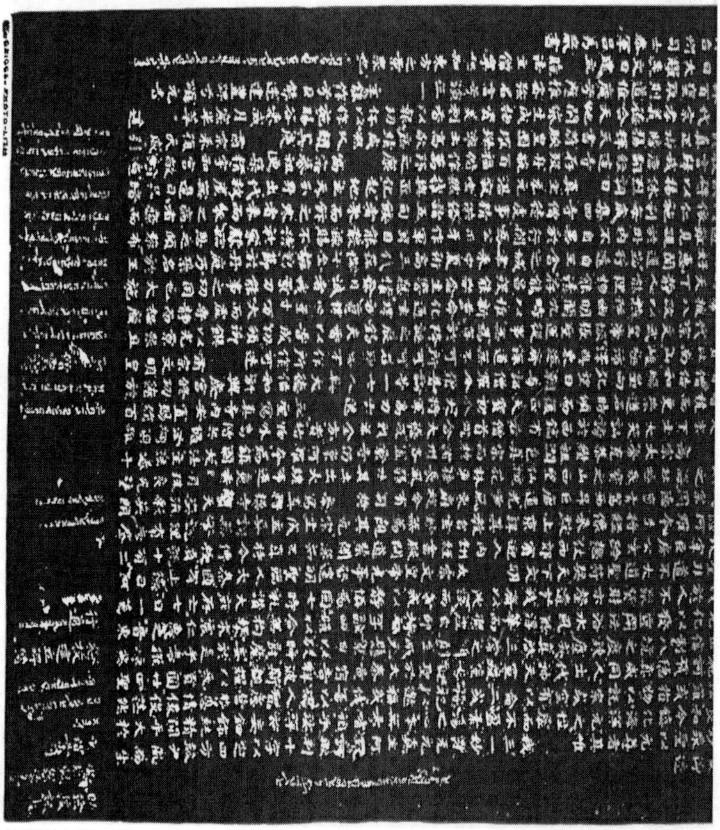

NESTORIAN TABLET

( EIGHT

SI·GNAN·FU, CHINA.

NTURY)

part is a poem in praise of the "Illustrious Religion," as Christianity is always named on the monument, and eulogistic of the Chinese emperors who favored this religion. Several notes are added, partly in Syriac, giving the names of ecclesiastics, including the one who erected the stone, Yezd-buzid. The whole inscription as translated by Prof. Legge of Oxford has some 3,500 English words. We must confine our selection to some paragraphs from the second or historical portion of the record, using Prof. Legge's translation.

100. "When the Accomplished Emperor T'âi Tsung (A. D. 627-649) commenced his glorious reign over the (recently) established dynasty (of T'ang), presiding over men with intelligence and sagehood, in the kingdom of Tâ Ts'in (Roman Empire), there was a man of the highest virtue called *Olopun*. Guiding himself by the azure clouds, he carried with him the True Scriptures. Watching the laws of the winds, he made his way through difficulties and perils. In the ninth year of the period Chang-kwan (A. D. 635), he arrived at Ch'ang-ân. The emperor sent his minister, Duke Fang Hsüan-ling, bearing the staff of office, to the western suburb, there to receive the visitor, and conduct him to the palace. The Scriptures were translated in the Library. (His Majesty) questioned him about his system in his own forbidden apartments, became deeply convinced of its correctness and truth, and gave special orders for its propagation. In the twelfth Chang-kwan year (638), in autumn, in the seventh month, the following proclamation was issued:—'Systems have not always the same name; sages have not always the same personality. Every region has its appropriate doctrines, which by their imperceptible influence benefit the inhabitants. The greatly virtuous Olopun of the kingdom of Tâ Ts'in, bringing his scriptures and images from afar, has come and presented them at our High Capital. Having carefully examined the scope of his doctrines, we find them

to be mysterious, admirable, and requiring nothing (special) to be done; having looked at the principal and most honoured points in them, they are intended for the establishment of what is most important. Their language is free from troublesome verbosity; their principles remain when the immediate occasion for their delivery is forgotten; (the system) is helpful to (all) creatures, and profitable for men:—let it have free course throughout the empire.'

"The proper officers forthwith, in the capital in the Ward of Righteousness and Repose, built a Tâ Ts'in monastery, sufficient to accommodate twenty-one priests. The virtue of the honored House of Châu had died away; the rider in the green car had ascended to the west; the course of the great T'ang was (now) brilliant; and the breath of the Illustrious (Religion) came eastward to fan it. The proper officers were further ordered to take a faithful likeness of the emperor, and have it copied on the walls of the monastery. The celestial beauty appeared in its many brilliant colors, the commanding form irradiated the Illustrious portals; the sacred traces communicated a felicitous influence, forever illuminating the precincts of the (true) law. . . . .

101. "The great emperor Kâo Tsung (650-683) reverently continued (the line of) his ancestors. A beneficent and elegant patron of the Truth, he caused monasteries of the Illustrious (Religion) to be erected in every one of the Prefectures, and continued the favour (of his father) to Olopun, raising him to be Lord of the Great Law, for the preservation of the state. The Religion spread through the Ten Circuits. The kingdoms became rich and enjoyed great repose. Monasteries filled a hundred cities; the (great) families multiplied in the possession of brilliant happiness.

"In the period Shăng-li (698-699), the Buddhists, taking advantage of their strength, made their voices heard (against the Religion) in the eastern capital of Châu, and in the end of the year Hsien-t'ien (712) some inferior officers greatly derided it; slandering and speaking against it in the Western Hâo. But there were the chief priest Lo-han, the greatly virtuous Chi-lieh and others, noble men from the golden regions, all eminent priests, keeping themselves aloof from worldly influences, who joined together in restoring the mysterious net, and in rebinding its meshes which had been broken.

"Hsüan Tsung (713-755), the emperor of the Perfect Way, ordered the king of Ning and the four other kings with him to go in person to the blessed buildings, and rebuild their altars. The consecrated beams which had for a time been torn from their places were (thus) again raised up, and the sacred stones which had for a time been thrown down were again replaced. . . .

"In the third year of the same period (744), in the kingdom of Tâ Ts'in there was the monk of *Chî-ho*. Observing the stars he directed his steps to (the region of) transformation; looking to the sun, he came to pay court to the most Honorable (emperor). An imperial proclamation was issued for the priests Lo-han, P'û-lun and others, seventeen in all, along with the greatly virtuous Chî-ho, to perform a service of merit in the Hsing-ch'ing palace.

102. "The emperor Sû Tsung (756-762), Accomplished and Intelligent, rebuilt the monasteries of the Illustrious (religion) in Ling-Wû and four other parts. His great goodness (continued to) assist it, and all happy influences were opened up; great felicity descended, and the imperial inheritance was strengthened.

"The emperor Tâi Tsung (763-779), Accomplished and Martial, grandly signalized his succession to the throne, and conducted his affairs without (apparent) effort. Always when the day of his birth recurred he contributed celestial incense wherewith to announce the meritorious deeds accomplished by him, and sent provisions from his own table to brighten our Illustrious assembly. As Heaven by its beautiful ministration of what is profitable can widen (the term and enjoyment of) life, so the sage (sovereign) by his embodiment of the way of Heaven, completes and nourishes (the objects of his favour).

"In this period of Chien-chung (780-783), our present emperor, Sage and Spirit-like, Accomplished alike for peace and war, develops the eight objects of government, so as to degrade the undeserving, and promote the deserving; and exhibits the nine divisions of the scheme (of Royal government), to impart a new vigour to the throne to which he has illustriously succeeded. His transforming influence shows a comprehension of the most mysterious principles; (his) prayers give no occasion for shame in the heart. In his grand position he yet is humble; maintaining an entire stillness, he yet is observant of the altruistic rule. That with unrestricted gentleness he seeks to relieve the sufferings of all, and that blessings reach from him to all that have life is due to the plans of our (Illustrious Religion) for the cultivation of the conduct, and the gradual steps by which it leads men on. That the winds and rains come at their proper seasons; quiet prevail through the empire; men be amenable to reason; all things be pure; those who are being preserved flourish, and those who are ready to die have joy; every thought have its echo of response; and the feelings go forth in entire sincerity:—all this is the meritorious effect of its Illustrious power and operation."

103. During most of the time then, for about one hundred and fifty years, by approval of the emperors, Christianity was allowed to have free course in China with the three other systems of religion in the country —Confucianism, Taoism, and Buddhism. One period without the royal favor is mentioned. From Chinese histories we know that at that time an empress violently assumed the reins of government and that she was a conservative in thought, even reactionary. It is striking to find that China had such similar experiences at the end of the seventh and of the nineteenth centuries.

The distance of the missionaries in China from their home land in Persia in those days is impressively shown by the fact that the inscription says that it was made when Hanan-Yeshu' was the Nestorian patriarch, and that it was in the year 781. But we know from the ecclesiastical history of western Asia that Patriarch Hanan-Yeshu' died before the end of 778. After more than three years, then, the most conspicuous item of their home-church news had not yet reached them. Think, then, what a daring venture it was one hundred and fifty years earlier for Olopun and his comrades to start on their long journey to the land of Sinim! Must we not add him to our list of missionary heroes?

104. There is no unmistakable information as to Christianity in China before the time of Olopun. There are traditions like that imbedded over and over again in the liturgy of the Nestorian Christians of India. "By St. Thomas hath the Kingdom of Heaven taken unto itself wings and passed even unto China." This tradition is a late one and of no value. But the fact that there was a Christian bishop of Maru and Tus A. D. 334 shows that missions had early reached as far east as Khorasan. There is also record of a bishop at Samarkand in 503.

Not long after the flourishing times of the Si-gnan-fu monument, we know from Chinese history that one of the emperors suppressed a large number of Buddhist monasteries, requiring 260,000 monks and nuns to return to secular life. At the same time he made the same requirement of three thousand who were all or in part Christian missionaries. These are the words of the edict concerning the latter: "As to the religions of foreign nations, let the men who teach them, as well those of Tâ Ts'in as of Mu-hu-pi, amounting to more than three thousand persons, be required to resume the ways of ordinary life, and their unsubstantial talkings no more be heard." This was in 845, only 64 years after the erection of the Nestorian monument. It gives a hint as to the number of Christian teachers in China then. Nestorian Christianity there probably did not recover from this blow, at least not for centuries, although Buddhism—which had more than eighty times as many representatives—did recover. We shall see evidence appearing 450 years later that Christianity may not have become quite as extinct as a Mohammedan author, Abulfaraj, would have us believe. His account shows, at any rate, that missionaries were still sent to China. He says:

"In the year 377 (A. D. 987), behind the church in the Christian quarter (of Baghdad), I fell in with a certain monk of Najran, who seven years before had been sent to China by the Catholics, with five other ecclesiastics, to bring the affairs of Christianity in that country into order. He was a man still young, and of a pleasant countenance, but of few words, opening his mouth only to answer questions. I asked him about his travels, and he told me that Christianity had become quite extinct in China. The Christians had perished in various ways; their Church had been destroyed; and but one Christian remained in the land. The monk, finding nobody whom he could aid with his ministry, had come back faster than he went."

Layard found in an old Nestorian church in the Kurdistan Mountains some China bowls suspended from the ceiling and grimy with age, which he was assured had been brought from China by missionaries in the days of the great Nestorian missions to that empire.

105. The second period of missions in China was during the sway of the great Mongol rulers of Asia, commonly known at the time as Tatars. It must include work thousands of miles from China, but only in territory ruled, for a part of the time, at least, by the sovereigns of China. Among Europeans China was know as Cathay, and the rest of the empire as Tatary.

The first mission to the Tatars of which we have much knowledge was at the beginning of the eleventh century, though some of the Turks in the region east of the Caspian Sea were converted two hundred years earlier. A Nestorian metropolitan see existed there. The pioneers of the missionary enterprise farther east are said to have been Christian merchants. It must have been a thrilling day for the Christians at Bagdad when the Nestorian Patriarch there received word from the Archbishop among the Tatars at Merv, east of the Caspian, that the ruler of the Kerait Tatars, more than 2,500 miles still farther east, had requested that missionaries be sent to him and his people and had declared that two hundred thousand of his subjects were ready to follow him in baptism. The requested missionary force was sent. This was between the years 1001 and 1012. The Keraits became a Christian tribe. This fact is confirmed by Rashid-eddin, the Mohammedan historian of the Mongols. Some of these Keraits occupied the region around the great northern bend of the Hoang Ho River of China, and some of them were in regions still farther north. Exaggerated accounts of the ruler of this tribe started all Europe into wild ideas which were cherished for centuries about a certain Prester John, a wonderful priest-king, who ruled in fabulous splendor and power over most of Asia.

106. Christianity continued among the Keraits for more than four hundred years. But after only two hundred years Jenghiz, Khan of a neighboring Tatar people, completely overcame the Keraits. Sweeping southward into China and westward across all central Asia, Jenghiz and his successors subdued the whole continent and much beyond, even to the heart of Europe. They overran Poland and Hungary. All Europe shuddered at the name of Tatar. Still there was a feeling that these dreadful barbarians might be Christianized. They were not at first Mohammedans, but the subduers of Mohammedans, to the delight of Christendom. The myths about Prester John were attached more or less to all the Tatar sovereigns. The Pope sent missionary ambassadors to them.

107. He intrusted the first mission to **John of Plano Carpini**, one of the immediate followers of Francis of Assisi. Carpini started from Lyons in the spring of 1245 and, accompanied by **Benedict of Poland**, reached the camp of the Great Khan the following summer. Karakorum, the seat of Tatar empire for the first two or three generations, is in the heart of northern Mongolia, 900 miles northwest from Peking, 350 miles south of the southern tip of Lake Baikal, Siberia. Carpini was sixty-five years of age and very corpulent. He made the unprecedented journey into the wilds of

central Asia and brought back a report to the Pope in two years and a half. It was a journey of 10,000 miles. He must have been a man of matchless tact and determination, as well as devotion. He arrived at Karakorum when Tourakina, the widow of the last khan, was acting as regent, and endeavoring to secure the election of her son. Princes and chieftains gathered from literally all parts of Asia, and the Queen Dowager's favorite, Kuyuk, was elected. The rude gorgeousness of the canvas capital of the world and its ceremonies are outside of our present field of interest. The new khan gave audience repeatedly to the missionary ambassadors. When they asked him if the reports which had reached the West were true, that the Khan of the Tatars was a Christian, he answered: "God knows it, and if the Pope wishes to know it, too, he has but to come and see." The answer was more discreet than satisfactory. He was found to have many Oriental Christians in his service. Tourakina was thought to favor Christianity more than other religions, but really all religions were favored alike. The Great Khan sent the Pope a letter in which he replied to the papal remonstrance against the slaughter of Christian nations, saying: "God has commanded me to annihilate them and has delivered them entirely into my hands." This answer would seem to be plain enough to have dispelled forever the rosy myth of Prester John, a Christian priest-king ruling the Orient. Carpini brought to Europe the first modern knowledge concerning Cathay (China). It was clear and correct as far as it went.

108. In 1246 the King of Armenia sent his brother Sempad to secure the favor of the khan. Here is an extract from Sempad's report. It confirms Carpini's account as to the vastness of the territory represented in the assemblage for the election of Kuyuk, and gives intensely interesting information as to the extent of Nestorian Christianity and its treatment by the Great Khans. It shows, too, how the religious tolerance of the Tatar khans, so far in advance of the practice of Christendom in those days, fostered the impression that the khan himself must be a Christian. The letter naïvely reveals the fact that the notions of the khans in that respect were far superior to those of Sempad, the writer.

"We understand it to be the fact that it is five years past since the death of the present Chan's father [Okkodai]; but the Tartar barons and soldiers had been so scattered over the face of the earth that it was scarcely possible in the five years to get them together in one place to enthrone the Chan aforesaid. For some of them were in India, and others in the land of Chata, and others in the land of Caschar and of Tanchat. This last is the land from which came the Three Kings to Bethlem to worship the Lord Jesus which was born. And know that the power of Christ has been, and is, so great, that the people of that land are Christians; and the whole land of Chata believes in those Three Kings. I have myself been in their churches and have seen pictures of Jesus Christ and the Three Kings, one offering gold, the second frankincense, and the third myrrh. And it is through those Three Kings that they believe in Christ, and that the Chan and his people have now become Christians [!]. And they have their churches before his gates where they ring their bells and beat upon pieces of timber. . . . And I tell you that we have found many Christians scattered all over the East, and many fine churches, lofty, ancient, and of good architecture, which have been spoiled by the Turks. Hence the Christians of the land came before the present Khan's grandfather; and he received them most honorably, and granted them liberty of worship, and issued orders to forbid their having any just cause of complaint by word or deed. And so the Saracens who used to treat them with contumely have now like treatment in double measure . . . and let me tell you that those who set up for preachers [among these Christians], in my opinion, deserve to be well chastised."

109. When Louis IX. of France heard a description of the barbarities of the Tatar invaders of eastern Europe, he exclaimed: "Well may they be called Tartars, for their deeds are those of fiends from Tartarus." The extra letter "r" which he thrust into their name for the sake of his serious pun has stayed there ever since in the popular usage.

Louis sent **William Rubruk,** a Fleming, and two other Franciscans, as missionaries to the Great Khan. When they reached Karakorum, Mangou, the successor of Kuyuk, was on the ivory throne. He appointed a great public discussion by representatives of Buddhism, Mohammedanism and Christianity, forbidding on pain of death any quarreling. Rubruck had a preliminary conference with the Nestorians, in order that the two sects of Christians might co-operate. How often missions have brought sectarians together! A Buddhist priest from China called on Rubruk to open the discussion, and is said to have admitted after the debate was over that the Christian had the best of the argument.

"The Nestorians then entered the lists against the Mussulmans, but the latter declared that there was no ground for dispute; that they regarded the Christian law as a true one, and believed all that the Gospel contained; that they acknowledged one God alone, and prayed to him every day. 'This conference being then ended,' says Rubruk, 'the Nestorians and Saracens chanted together with a loud voice, but the pagans said nothing at all; and after that the whole assembly drank together pretty freely.' The day after the public controversy, Mangou sent for Rubruk, and began to make a kind of confession of faith. 'We Mongols,' said he, 'believe that there is one God, by whom we live and die, and towards whom our hearts are wholly turned.' 'May God give you his grace that it may be so,' said Rubruk, 'for otherwise it is impossible.' The emperor went on: 'As God has given the hand several fingers, so has he prepared for men various ways, by which they may go to heaven. He has given the Gospel to the Christians, but they do not obey it; he has given soothsayers to the Mongols, and the Mongols do what their soothsayers command, and, therefore, they live in peace.'"

Having finished his statement of the case, the ruler of Asia dismissed the missionaries. They reached home in 1255.

110. During the Tatar sway more than at any time before or since, the long land route was open between the Mediterranean and the China Seas. This was preeminently true from the middle of the thirteenth to near the middle of the fourteenth centuries—that is, in the days of the early successors of Jenghiz Khan, Okkodai, Kuyuk, Mangou and Kublai. Kublai Khan, grandson of Jenghiz, removed the Mongol capital to northern China (Peking), and later carried the Tatar sway through all China to its southern coasts and even over the confines of Burma into the Malayan Peninsula. Reigning at Peking from 1259 to 1294, he was the sovereign of a larger part of the planet than has

ever been under the scepter of any other one man. His dominion stretched from the Strait of Malacca to the Arctic Ocean, and from the Yellow Sea to the Black Sea. He was a man of unusually broad and enlightened views. He won the hearts of the conquered Chinese, and at the same time gathered about his court not only merchants, but also learned men from all parts of the world. It was in his days that the Polos of Venice made their journeys to China and resided there. Modern critical scholarship proves that Marco Polo's account, long thought to be largely fabulous, is to be relied upon with confidence as to important facts. Kublai had many Nestorian Christian subjects, as well as Buddhists, Mohammedans and Jews. He allowed them all complete liberty. He was himself something of an eclectic in religion. On Christian festival days he had the Gospels brought to him and reverently kissed them. He said that there were four great prophets—Mohammed, Jesus, Buddha and Moses. One of his nephews, Nayan, raised a revolt and carried it on under a Christian banner. When the insurrection had been overcome Kublai forbade any railing at the religion of the defeated, saying that the reason that the God of the Christians refused to hear their prayers and prosper their course was because he was too just and good to favor their rebellion against rightful authority.

111. Kublai commissioned Nicolo and Maffeo Polo, Marco's father and uncle, to go as envoys to the Pope, asking for one hundred learned men to come to China to instruct the people in western knowledge and in the Christian religion. They reached Venice in 1270, but

the Papal chair was vacant until 1271, because the French and Italian cardinals could not unite in electing a candidate for the office. Finally Gregory X. sent two Dominicans in answer to this appeal, which ought to have stirred every heart in Christendom to strenuous effort. It was a clear call for the conversion of the largest empire on which the sun ever shone. The two sent turned back before they had gone far on the long journey. If only the hundred missionaries asked for in Kublai's noble Macedonian appeal had been sent, to say nothing of thousands whose lives were withering in monasteries for want of philanthropic activity, who can tell what the effect might have been at that favorable moment on the destiny of China? The question is made more insistent by the effective work which we find a handful of missionaries doing in China, almost a generation later. But, alas! the poor Pope was kept too busy with factions of the cardinals and with European politics, connected with the hope of another crusade in behalf of the sepulcher in Palestine, to guide much of the church's energy toward the redemption of the millions of living souls in China and on the whole continent of Asia. There are thousands of parish popes in every sect of Christendom still, who see the relative importance of things much as Gregory saw them.

112. After Gregory X. and six other popes had run their brief careers, a mission to China was undertaken by a most worthy member of the order of Francis of Assisi, **John of Monte Corvino.** He was sent out when fifty years of age, and toiled more than

thirty-five years with deserved success. He found the Nestorian Christians there in great numbers, results of the early missions or of some later planting by that missionary people. His proselyting trials and struggles with them are to be regretted and are outside the range of our present studies. But he did true missionary work as well. The following extracts from his letters home are the best description of his work. They are pathetic as to his isolation. After some twelve years' absence, he writes: "I am surprised that until this year I never received a letter from any friend or any brother of the order, nor even so much as a message of remembrance, so that it seemed as if I were utterly forgotten by everybody." In his first letter he asks for books and for helpers. How much it sounds like the appeals of modern missionaries for more workers! In a later letter he says: "But none should be sent except men of the most solid character."

"CAMBALEC [PEKING], CATHAY, Jan. 8, 1305.

113. "I, Brother John of Monte Corvino, of the order of Minor Friars [Franciscans], departed from Tauris, a city of the Persians, in the year of the Lord 1291, and proceeded to India. And I remained in the country of India, wherein stands the church of St. Thomas the Apostle, for thirteen months, and in that region baptized in different places about one hundred persons. The companion of my journey was brother *Nicholas of Pistoia*, of the order of Preachers [Dominicans], who died there, and was buried in the church aforesaid.

"I proceeded on my further journey and made my way to Cathay, the realm of the Emperor of the Tatars, who is called the Grand Cham [Khan]. To him I presented the letter of our lord the Pope, and invited him to adopt the Catholic Faith of our Lord Jesus Christ, but he had grown too old in idolatry. However, he bestows many kindnesses upon the Christians, and these two years past I am abiding with him.

"The Nestorians, a certain body who profess to bear the Christian name, but who deviate sadly from the Christian religion, have grown so powerful in those parts that they will not allow a Christian of another ritual to have ever so small a chapel, or to publish any doctrine different from their own. . . .

"In this mission I abode alone and without any associate for eleven years; but it is now going on for two years since I was joined by Brother *Arnold*, a German of the province of Cologne.

114. "I have built a church in the city of Cambaliech [Peking], in which the king has his chief residence. This I completed six years ago; and I have built a bell-tower to it, and put three bells in it. I have baptized there, as well as I can estimate, up to this time some 6,000 persons; and if those charges against me of which I have spoken had not been made, I should have baptized more than 30,000. And I am often still engaged in baptizing.

"Also I have gradually bought one hundred and fifty boys, the children of pagan parents, and of ages varying from seven to eleven, who had never learned any religion. These boys I have baptized, and I have taught them Greek and Latin after our manner. Also I have written out Psalters for them, with thirty Hymnaries and two Breviaries. By help of these, eleven of the boys already know our service, and form a choir and take their weekly turn of duty as they do in convents, whether I am there or not. Many of the boys are also employed in writing out Psalters and other things suitable. His Majesty the Emperor moreover delights much to hear them chaunting. I have the bells rung at all the canonical hours, and with my congregation of babes and sucklings I perform divine service, and the chaunting we do by ear because I have no service book with the notes. . . .

115. "Indeed, if I had had but two or three comrades to aid me 'tis possible that the Emperor Cham would have been bap-

tized by this time! I ask then for such brethren to come, if any are willing to come, such I mean as will make it their great business to lead exemplary lives and not to make broad their own phylacteries.

"As for the road hither, I may tell you that the way through the land of the Goths, subject to the Emperor of the Northern Tartars, is the shortest and safest; and by it the friars might come, along with the letter-carriers, in five or six months. . . .

"It is twelve years since I had any news of the Papal court, or of our order, or of the state of affairs generally in the west. Two years ago indeed there came hither a certain Lombard leech and chirurgeon, who spread abroad in these parts the most incredible blasphemies about the court of Rome and our Order and the state of things in the west, and on this account I exceedingly desire to obtain true intelligence. I pray the brethren whom this letter may reach to do their possible to bring its contents to the knowledge of our lord the Pope, and the Cardinals, and the agents of the Order at the court of Rome.

"I beg the Minister General of our Order to supply me with an Antiphonarium, with the Legends of the Saints, a Gradual, and a Psalter with the musical notes, as a copy; for I have nothing but a pocket Breviary with the short Lessons, and a little missal; if I had one for a copy, the boys of whom I have spoken could transcribe others from it. Just now I am engaged in building a second church, with the view of distributing the boys in more places than one.

"I have myself grown old and gray, more with toil and trouble than with years; for I am not more than fifty-eight. I have got a competent knowledge of the language and character which is most generally used by the Tartars. And I have already translated into that language and character the New Testament and the Psalter, and have caused them to be written out in the fairest penmanship they have; and so by writing, reading and preaching I bear open and public testimony to the Law of Christ."

116. In his second letter, dated April, 1306, he describes his church building operations:

"I began another new place before the gate of the Lord Cham so that there is but the width of the street between his palace and our place, and we are but a stone's throw from his Majesty's gate. Master Peter of Lucolongo, a faithful Christian man and great merchant, who was the companion of my travels from Tauris, himself bought the ground for the establishment of which I have been speaking, and gave it to me for the love of God. And by the divine favor I think that a more suitable position for a Catholic church could not be found in the whole empire of his Majesty the Cham. In the beginning of August I got the ground, and by the aid of sundry benefactors and well-wishers it was completed by the Feast of St. Francis with an enclosure wall, houses, offices, courts and chapel, the latter capable of holding two hundred persons. On account of the winter coming on I have not been able to finish the church, but I have the timber collected at the house, and please God I hope to finish it in summer. And I tell you it is thought a perfect marvel by all the people who come from the city and elsewhere, and who had previously never heard a word about it. And when they see our new building, and the red cross planted aloft, and us in our chapel with all decorum chaunting the service, they wonder more than ever. When we are singing, his Majesty the Cham can hear our voices in his chamber; and this wonderful fact is spread far and wide among the heathen, and will have the greatest effect, if the divine mercy so disposes matters and fulfils our hopes.

"From the first church and house to the second church which I built afterwards, is a distance of two miles and a half within the city, which is passing great."

117. In 1317 the Pope sent out seven more Franciscans as missionary bishops, with the appointment of archbishop for Monte Corvino. Three of them died on the way in India. Another returned from that country

to Europe. The following extracts from a letter of one who reached the field, **Andrew of Perugia,** show the progress of the mission, especially its development in Southern China. Zayton, the center of operations there, lay more than a thousand miles straight south of Peking. It has been identified with the modern city of Tsiuan-chau, which is only 170 miles up the coast from Swatow:

ZAYTON, January, 1326.

"On account of the immense distance by land and sea interposed between us, I can scarcely hope that a letter from me to you can come to hand. . . . You have heard then how along with Brother *Peregrine,* my brother bishop of blessed memory, and the sole companion of my pilgrimage, through much fatigue and sickness and want, through sundry grievous sufferings and perils by land and sea, plundered even of our habits and tunics, we got at last by God's grace to the city of Cambaluc, which is the seat of the Emperor the Great Chan, in the year of our Lord's incarnation 1308, as well as I can reckon. There, after the Archbishop [Corvino] was consecrated, according to the orders given us by the Apostolic See, we continued to abide for nearly five years; during which time we obtained an *Alafa* [allowance] from the Emperor for our food and clothing. . . .

"There is a great city on the shores of the Ocean Sea, which is called in the Persian tongue Zayton [Tsiuan-chau] and in this city a rich Armenian lady did build a large and fine enough church, which was erected into a cathedral by the Archbishop himself of his own free will. The lady assigned it, with a competent endowment which she provided during her life and secured by will at her death, to Brother *Gerard,* the Bishop, and the brethren who were with him, and he became accordingly the first occupant of the cathedral.

118. "I caused a (another) convenient and handsome church to be built in a certain grove, quarter of a mile outside the city, with all the offices sufficient for twenty-two friars, and

with four apartments such that any one of them is good enough for a church dignitary of any rank. In this place I continue to dwell, living upon the imperial dole before-mentioned, the value of which, according to the estimate of the Genoese merchants, amounts in the year to 100 golden florins or thereabouts. Of this allowance I have spent the greatest part in the construction of the church; and I know none among all the convents of our province to be compared to it in elegance and all other amenities.

"And so not long after the death of Brother Peregrine I received a decree from the Archbishop appointing me to the aforesaid cathedral church, and to this appointment I now assented for good reasons. So I abide now sometimes in the house or church in the city, and sometimes in my convent outside, as it suits me. And my health is good, and as far as one can look forward at my time of life, I may yet labor in this field for some years to come; but my hair is gray, which is owing to constitutional infirmities as well as age.

"'Tis a fact that in this vast empire there are people of every nation under heaven, and of every sect, and all and sundry are allowed to live freely according to their creed. For they hold this opinion, or rather this erroneous view, that every one can find salvation in his own religion. Howbeit we are at liberty to preach without let or hindrance. Of the Jews and Saracens there are indeed no converts, but many of the idolaters are baptized; though in sooth many of the baptized walk not rightly in the path of Christianity."

119. The wandering Franciscan, **Odoric of Pordenone,** after his adventures in India, carried the bones of martyrs in that land to China, the original destination of the martyred missionaries, going through Burma and the southwest provinces of China. He deposited the venerated burden which he had brought with incredible toil at the mission in Zayton. He journeyed next northward clear across China, visiting

several cities where there were Franciscan missionaries. At last he reached Cambalec [Peking].

"I, Friar Odoric, was full three years in that city of his [the Great Khan's], and often present at those festivals of theirs; for we Minor Friars have a place assigned to us at the emperor's court, and we be always in duty bound to go and give him our benison." He speaks of "our own converts to the faith, of whom there be some who are great barons at that court, and have to do with the king's person only."

Having in his own way aided the missions in China, this roving missionary advanced into what we now call the closed land of Tibet. He found at the capital Christian missionaries. After sixteen years of itinerating over all southern Asia, including a number of the islands, he arrived home in 1330. In a short time he was about starting again for farther Asia, with a company of young missionaries, when he fell ill. Odoric was disinclined to tell of the great things which he had seen and done. But he received a formal command from the superior of his order to give an account. He was too feeble to write himself, and was obliged to dictate to another. The zeal of the amanuensis or of some admiring copyist may have misunderstood or exaggerated the number originally given; but the record which has reached us is of more than 20,000 converts baptized by Odoric.

120. **William Adam**, one of the missionaries of the Persian Khanate, was on a visit to the capital of the Grand Khan when John of Monte Corvino died (1328). He wrote by order of the Pope an account of "The State and Government of the Great Khan of Cathay." He says that all the people of Peking mourned for the good

man. Pagans as well as Christians paid the strongest tokens of respect. In the thirty-six years of Corvino's ministry in Peking he had earned the highest esteem. He is said to have been instrumental in the conversion of 30,000 unbelievers. The Pope appointed **Nicolas,** another Franciscan, to succeed Corvino at the head of the work in China. He set out with thirty-two other missionaries for his distant field. The party can be traced only into the heart of the vast Tatar realms, which were at this time beginning to revert to chaos. The whole company was probably murdered. Nothing was heard of them after 1338.

The papal Archbishop of Sultania, in Persia **John de Cora,** made a brief record of the state of the missions in China (A. D. 1330) soon after the death of Monte Corvino. He says of the Grand Khan that "most willingly doth he suffer and encourage the friars to preach the faith of God in the churches of the pagans, which are called *vritanes* [monasteries]. And as willingly doth he permit the pagans to go to hear the preachment of the friars; so that the pagans go very willingly, and often behave with great devoutness, and bestow upon the friars great alms."

The following paragraph from John de Cora shows that the Nestorians, who had done so much in China from the seventh to the ninth centuries, and had been instrumental in the conversion of the Kerait Tatars in the eleventh century, had been actively at work since, perhaps ever since, so that now, in the fourteenth century, they were numerous and influential:

"These Nestorians are more than thirty thousand, dwelling

in the said empire of Cathay, and are passing rich people, but stand in great fear and awe of the Christians. They have very handsome and devoutly ordered churches, with crosses and images in honor of God and the saints. They hold sundry offices under the said emperor, and have great privileges from him; so that it is believed that if they would agree and be at one with the Minor Friars, and with the other good Christians who dwell in that country, they would convert the whole country and the emperor likewise to the true faith."

CHAPTER IX.

# CHINA AND TATARY, CONTINUED.

121. The divisions of the Tatar sovereignty. 122. Missions in the Khanate of Kiptchak. 123. In the Persian Khanate. 124. In the Khanate of Chagatai. 125. The close of the second period. 126. Missions to China from the Philippines. 127. First permanent modern mission. 128. Adam Schall. 129. Martini. 130. Schall and the Emperor. 131. Ferdinand Verbiest. 132. Numerical results. 133. Jesuit compromises. 134. Emphasis placed on the baptism of infants. 135. Genuine conversions. 136. A noble ideal. 137. Medical work. 138. Church building. 139. Conclusion.

121. Kublai was the last of the Khans to be monarch of all the Mongols. His actual government was confined mainly to the eastern portion of the country. The continental sovereignty fell into five great divisions, the Grand Khan being counted suzerain and receiving tribute from the others. In the northwest was the Khanate of Kiptchak, from Western Russia to the Merv oasis; in the west, the Khanate of Persia, from Asia Minor to Khorasan; in the south the Empire of the Great Moguls of India; in the center the Khanate of Chagatai, known as the Middle Empire, from Khorasan to the Desert of Gobi; in the east the empire of the Grand Khan, from the Desert

of Gobi to the southern coast of China. Into every one of these huge Mongol realms Christianity was carried between the eleventh and the fifteenth centuries.

122. The influence of Christianity on the Great Mogul of India has been noticed in the chapter on that land. We may take space for only a glimpse of the work in the remaining Khanates. Kiptchak, with its capital, Serai, in Russia north of the Caspian, was in the hands of the Golden Horde of Tatars. Usbeck, a grandson of Jenghiz, ruled. He fell under Mohammedan influence and persecuted the Christians in his realm. Pope John XXII. sent him in 1318 an earnest letter of remonstrance and of exhortation to become a Christian. Near Serai there was a Franciscan missionary monastery. In 1334 one of its inmates, **Stephen,** a Hungarian, apostatized to Islam. The Mohammedans of the capital made a great celebration over the event. But when the poor man was placed on a platform in the Mosque to declare his new faith before thousands, his conscience overcame him and he spoke out clearly for Christ. As a result, he suffered a prolonged and terrible martyrdom.

123. In the Persian Khanate we have the name of one of the Oigour Tatars, **Jaballaha,** who had been appointed Nestorian Archbishop of Peking. Just then the Patriarch died and Jaballaha, at the request of a Tatar Khan was raised to the Patriarchate. At the head of the whole Nestorian Church he vigorously prosecuted missions among his fellow Mongols. Later, however, he joined the Church of Rome (1304). There were repeated negotiations between Argoun, the

Tatar Khan of Persia at the end of the thirteenth century, the Pope and European kings, including Edward I. of England (1272-1307), for a combination of forces against the Mohammedans in Syria. Many of the chief people about Argoun were baptized, including one of his sons, whose mother was a zealous Christian. This Queen was a great-granddaughter of Ung-Kalm, one of the early Christian Khans of the Keraits in their far eastern homes. The first lieutenant and the physician of Argoun became Christians. The Persian Khans fluctuated between Christianity and Mohammedanism, most of them remaining pagans at heart.

Karbende Khan, son of Argoun, founded a new capital in 1305, calling it Sultania, which grew rapidly into greatness and splendor. Here **Franco of Perugia** and a number of other Dominicans did effective work. Before many years there were twenty-five Christian churches in Sultania. In 1318 it was made the seat of an Archbishopric. Six missionary bishops were put under the direction of Franco.

In Northwest Persia the Franciscans labored and are said to have had 10,000 converts by the end of the century.

124. In the Khanate of Chagatai ("Middle Empire"), south of Lake Balkash, the followers of Francis of Assisi had an active mission and a church building in the capital, Almalic. **Francis of Alexandria,** a medical missionary, gained great influence over the Khan by healing a fistula. The Khan allowed one of his sons, a lad of eight, to be baptized and taught by the Franciscans. One of the missionaries was **Pascal of**

Vittoria, Spain. He wrote a letter home in 1338, telling how he had reached his field after a tedious journey by boats on the Black Sea, River Volga and Caspian Sea, then in carts drawn by camels—"for to ride those animals is something terrible." He gives us a thrilling glimpse of missionary work in the very heart of Asia in the fourteenth century:

"I was long tarrying among the Saracens, and I preached to them for several days openly and publicly the name of Jesus Christ and his gospel. I opened out and laid bare the cheats, falsehoods and blunders of their false prophet; with a loud voice, and in public, I did confound their barkings; and trusting in our Lord Jesus Christ I was not much afraid of them, but received from the Holy Spirit comfort and light. They treated me civilly and set me in front of their mosque during their Easter; at which mosque, on account of its being their Easter, there were assembled from divers quarters a number of their *Cadini, i. e.*, of their bishops, and of their *Talisimani, i. e.*, of their priests. And guided by the teaching of the Holy Ghost I disputed with them in that same place before the mosque, on theology, and regarding their false Alchoran and its doctrine, for five-and-twenty days; and in fact I was barely able once a day to snatch a meal of bread and water.

"But by the grace of God the doctrine of the Holy Trinity was disclosed and preached to them, and at last even they, in spite of their reluctance, had to admit its truth; and, thanks be unto the Almighty God, I carried off the victory on all points, to the praise and honor of Jesus Christ and of Holy Mother Church. And then these children of the devil tried to tempt and pervert me with bribes, promising me wives and hand-maidens, gold and silver, and lands, horses and cattle, and other delights of this world. But when in every way I rejected all their promises with scorn, then for two days together they pelted me with stones, besides putting fire to my face and my feet, plucking out my beard, and heaping upon me for a length of time all kinds of insult and abuse. The blessed God, through whom poor I am able to rejoice and exult in the Lord Jesus Christ, knoweth that 'tis by his marvelous compassion alone I have been judged worthy to bear such things for his name.

"And now I have been graciously brought to Armalec, a city in the midst of the land of the Medes ["Middle Empire"], in the vicariat of Cathay. . . . Fare ye well in the Lord Jesus Christ, and pray for me, and for those who are engaged, or intend to be engaged on missionary pilgrimages; for by God's help such pilgrimages are very profitable, and bring in a harvest of many souls. Care not then to see me again, unless it be in these regions, or in that Paradise wherein is our Rest and Comfort and Refreshment and Heritage, even the Lord Jesus Christ."

Two years after the writing of this letter the new emperor, Alisolda, commanded all Christians in his domain to became Saracens or forfeit their lives. Pascal and six other missionaries yielded their lives rather than to deny Christ.

125. The daring and brilliant missionary work of the Franciscans in far Cathay and in all the realms of the Tatars drew rapidly to a close. Ten years after the death of Monte Corvino, the Great Khan at Peking sent an embassy to the Pope (A. D. 1338), who sent in return a number of Franciscans with **John de Marignolli** at their head. On the way he visited the mission in Chagatai and reached Peking in 1342. He remained four years in China, he and his company of thirty-two people being royally entertained by the Great Khan, who bade them take back to the Pope a request for a cardinal to be appointed for China. But none could be sent. In 1368 the Tatar dynasty in

China was overthrown. Foreigners were driven from the country. Christianity was so nearly extinguished that it was difficult for the missionaries of the next period to find even its traces. The descendants of Jenghiz, ruling over the rest of Asia, fell into such violent and incessant strife among themselves that anarchy began a long reign and the interior of the continent was closed to the outside world.

126. Before the departure of the last of the mediæval missionaries of whom we have certain record, and the arrival of the pioneer missionary of the modern period, two hundred years elapsed. Francis Xavier died (1552) on an island (San-Chan, near Canton) on the coast of the land which he was seeking to enter. Meantime the old Cathay of the Mongols had been forgotten. It was a long time before anyone thought to identify it with China. A new road had been discovered to the Orient by sea around the Cape of Good Hope and another new road around the globe across Mexico. It was by the latter that the first modern missionary actually entered China.

Only ten years after the beginning of permanent missions in the Philippines, they became a base of operations for the regions beyond. As the quaint record runs, which was made by Juan G. de Mendoza and translated into English within thirteen years after the event, it was determined by the Augustinians at Manila that "The religious men shoulde bee frier **Martin de Herrada** of Pamplona, who left off the dignitie of prouinciall, and was a man of great learning and of a holy life; and for the same effect had learned the

China tongue, and manie times for to put his desire in execution did offer himselfe to bee slaue vnto the merchants of China, onely for to carry him thither; and in companie with him should go frier Hieronimo Martin, who also was verie well learned, and of the cittie of Mexico." This was in 1575.

July 2, 1578, the first Franciscans reached the Philippines, fourteen in number, with **Pedro de Alfaro** at their head. He was eager to go on to China, especially after the conversion of a Chinaman at Manila, and, not being able to gain the governor's consent, he took three of his companions, none of them seamen, and slipped away without permission in a small boat. They finally reached Canton. This mission, with all its bold venturesomeness, came to no permanent results. But Mendoza's charming account of these events, in which he had some part, ought to be read by every one who can get access to Park's translation, made in 1588.

127. It was only four years after the heroic attempt of Alfaro that a permanent missionary lodgment in China was effected (1583). This was achieved by **Matteo Ricci** and two other members of the Company of Jesus. Ricci toiled for nearly eighteen years in southern China, then made his way in a long evangelistic tour through great obstacles across the country to Peking (1601). Without knowing it, he was following the track of Odoric two hundred and fifty years before. His knowledge of science, especially mathematics, procured him admission to government circles and employment. He

JOHANN ADAM VON SCHALL.

(As a Mandarin.)

made a better map for the emperor than he had possessed. His Majesty ordered ten copies painted on silk and hung in his palace. The Jesuits decorated the margins with Christian texts and symbols.

In 1610 the Chinese astronomers had predicted an eclipse of the moon, far from the true time. The missionaries' prediction proving to be correct, won them additional influence. Ricci religiously refused any remuneration for his public services, but was rewarded with the privilege of promulgating Christianity. One of the high officers of the empire, Seu by name, was converted and christened Paul. Some of the descendants of Paul Seu are to this day in the Roman fold. Three princes of the imperial family joined the church and afterward suffered the severest penalties for their faith. Paul Seu and his daughter Candida were instrumental in building thirty-nine churches in various provinces and in printing one hundred and thirty Christian works in Chinese. He also had much to do in the reversal of an edict of expulsion in 1622, after it had been in more or less efficient operation for seven years.

128. The next great missionary in China was a man of Teutonic race, **Adam Schall** of Cologne. He most worthily wore the mantle of Ricci. From the work of Schall in one of the provinces, Paul discovered his talents and introduced him to the Emperor. He became the Astronomer Royal and in conjunction with another missionary, **Giacomo Rho**, revised the imperial calendar. He was so useful to the government that his work continued through three reigns, the second of

the three being the beginning of a new dynasty (1644), that of the Manchu Tatars, who are still on the throne. Again, as in the time of Jenghiz, four hundred years before, the southern provinces held out against the Tatar usurpers longer than the northern. There Yunlie, one of the old imperial family, was proclaimed emperor. His mother, wife and son were baptized as Helena, Maria and Constantine. Two Christian generals made good headway for a little time against the Tatar army. But the Manchus soon completed the conquest of the country. Yunlie and Constantine lost their lives and Helena was taken captive to Peking.

129. At the time of the Tatar invasion the Jesuits were scattered throughout China. Many of them perished with their flocks at the hands of the fierce invaders. But many escaped. The following story by Verbiest concerning **Martini** throws vivid light on the ways of both missionaries and Tatars:

"As soon as he learnt that the Tartars were about to enter the town, he put upon the door of his house an inscription in these words: 'Here resides a doctor of the divine law, come from the Great West.' In the vestibule he placed a number of tables covered with books, telescopes, burning-glasses, and similar articles, which excite great admiration and respect in those countries. In the middle of it all he erected an altar, and placed upon it an image of the Saviour. This spectacle was attended with all the effect which he anticipated. The Tartars were much impressed, and far from injuring any one, their chief sent for the father, received him very favorably, and, unwilling to compel him to forsake the national dress, he asked him frankly if he had any objection to having his hair cut off. As the father made no opposition the captain had it cut off in his presence; and when the father observed to him laughingly that the Chinese dress which he still wore did not suit with his shorn head, the Tatar took off his own boots and cap and made him put them on; and after entertaining him at his own table, he sent him back to his church with letters and passports, which effectually protected him and his fellow-Christians from the insults of the soldiery."

130. Under the Emperor Chunchi, many converts were made and churches were built. The missionary force from Europe was greatly increased. Verbiest tells us that the Emperor

"Chunchi placed the most boundless confidence in his [Adam Schall's] honesty and was so well assured of his affection that he always listened patiently to the frequent and severe rebukes which this faithful servant administered to him, though they might condemn many of his pleasures; and even if he did not invariably reform his conduct, he had the candor to confess that he would have done better to have followed his advice. The grandees, who saw what a powerful influence Father Adam exerted over the mind of the prince, often employed him to communicate what they had not the courage to say themselves."

Then follow a number of specific instances. Hopes were entertained of the Emperor's conversion. But he fell into sin and idolatry much as Solomon had done centuries before him.

After the death of Chunchi, a regency was in charge of the government for a time. It was memorialized by the bonzes, leaders of paganism, and induced to institute a vigorous persecution. Even Schall, after all his invaluable services, was loaded with irons and condemned to be strangled and cut in pieces. The sentence was recalled later, but the venerable scholar, broken down, suffered a stroke of paralysis and died at the age of seventy-eight years.

131. Another Teutonic missionary, a Fleming, **Ferdinand Verbiest,** succeeded Schall as the scientific advisor of the Emperor. Verbiest learned the Tatar language so as to be able to instruct the young sovereign without the intervention of an interpreter. At the Emperor's behest he also superintended the casting of cannon, and turned out three hundred and twenty pieces of artillery. These wise sons of Loyola did not forget their direct missionary work and their standing secured opportunity for a host of the Company of Jesus to invade various parts of China. Verbiest was followed to the grave not only by a large gathering of his fellow missionaries, but also by Mandarins especially appointed by the Emperor to pay that tribute. Verbiest's place as Superintendent of the Board of Mathematics was filled by another missionary, **Pereira** Verbiest and Pereira stood so close to Kang-hi that he took them with him on his annual hunting expeditions into the wilds beyond the great wall.

132. The standing of the learned missionaries at court kept the way open for missionary work throughout the country. A great many obscure but devoted men of the Company of Jesus worked in the ways thus opened. They were followed by not a few Franciscans and Dominicans. At the death of Ricci, the first modern missionary in China, in 1610, after twenty-seven years of labor, there were more than three hundred churches there. The work was so carried on by the coadjutors and successors of Ricci that by the year 1664 1,616 churches had been established in five provinces. In that year there were said to be 257,000 converts

under the care of the Jesuits and 10,000 more in churches organized by the Dominican and Franciscan missionaries. In 1672, according to Pereira, "a maternal uncle of the Emperor and one of the eight perpetual generals who command the Tatar militia received baptism and from that time the gospel has spread so widely over China that the number of Christians is estimated at 300,000."

133. In China, as in India, the Jesuits made compromises with heathenism which will not bear the light of the highest standards of Christian morality. It was well that they were closely watched by rival religious orders of their own church. As early as 1645 the question was referred to the authorities in Rome "Whether in regard to the frailty of the people, it could be tolerated for the present that Christian magistrates may carry a cross hidden under the flowers which were presented at the heathen altars and secretly worship that, while they are in outward form and appearance worshiping the idol." This duplicity was forbidden from Rome. Many similar questions arose. Two violent parties were formed. The method of the Jesuits in China became a prominent part of the world-wide indictment against them. They are not to be justified; but it is only fair to moderate the bitterness of condemnation by looking through their own eyes at their perplexities and their way of meeting them. **John de Fontenay,** writing in 1704, describes without disapproval the way in which a native helper dealt with an inquirer.

"The young man owned frankly to his countryman, that his

relations often performed the ceremony of honoring their Ancestors. Now should I refuse to join with them on these occasions they would turn me out of doors; and perhaps inform against me to the Mandarins, as one who is wanting in the respect and gratitude due to parents. This is the reason why I cannot possibly become a Christian.

"But who told you, replied the Catechist, that you may not assist at these ceremonies after your conversion? I myself, by God's grace, am a Christian, and I assist at those ceremonies when necessarily obliged to it. The Christian religion forbids us only to ask or expect favors or blessings from our deceased parents; to believe that it is in their power to do us any, or that they are present in the picture; to suppose that they come to hear our prayers, or to receive our gifts. It also will not permit our burning paper money, or pouring on the ground the wine which we offer to them. But it does not forbid our owning the obligations which we have to them, for our birth and education; nor thanking them for it, by falling prostrate before the picture on which their names are writ, and by offering them our possessions. If I may be allowed, says the young man, to go with my parents, and fall prostrate before the images of my ancestors, I have no further difficulties to struggle with, and will turn Christian this instant. The Catechist brought him to me two days after, telling me the frame of mind he was in. The young man begged my pardon for having so long resisted the celestial grace, and besought me to baptize him, declaring that neither himself nor his relations expected any blessing from their ancestors in paying them the accustomed honors. I did not think it proper to exclude a man who had so lively a faith from the kingdom of heaven."

134. With the missionaries of Rome in every land the great hope of saving souls rested on infant baptism. The following is an account of that feature of their work in China, as given approvingly by Verolles:

"The agents in this work are usually elderly women, who have experience in infantile diseases. Furnished with innocent pills and a bottle of holy water, whose virtues they extol, they introduce themselves into the houses where there are sick infants and discover whether they are in danger of death, and in this case they inform the parents and tell them that before administering other remedies they must wash their hands with the purifying waters of their bottle. The parents, not suspecting this pious ruse, readily consent, and by these innocent frauds we procure in our mission the baptism of 7,000 or 8,000 infants every year."

135. It is to be profoundly regretted, for the sake of the world, that the widespread, often sincere and truly heroic work of the Company of Jesus must be seriously discounted. Every honest mind will cherish with satisfaction the knowledge that their work was not all bad nor always bad. The following, related by **De Chavagnac** in 1701, is a sparkling rill out of the great stream of real religion introduced into China by the Jesuits:

"We are now laboring at the conversion of a Tartarian officer, who was prevailed upon by an accident which reflects great honor on the Christian religion to get himself instructed of the law of Christ. He was going on horseback to Peking, when happening to let fall his purse, a poor Christian artificer who saw it fall took it up and ran after him in order to restore it. The officer surveyed the poor man with an air of contempt, and not knowing his business, spurred his horse; notwithstanding which the Christian would not go away, but followed him quite home. There the exasperated Tartar first gave him foul language and asked him what he wanted; to which the Christian replied: 'My only business is to return you your purse.' This surprised the Tartar, who then changing his note, inquired how he came to return him his money, contrary to the customs of the Empire, which permit every man to keep whatever he finds. To this the artificer replied: 'I am a Christian and am enjoined to do as I have now done by the precepts of the religion I profess.' This answer raised the officer's curiosity, who thereupon was desirous of knowing what this religion was. Accordingly he visited our fathers, listened to them, and seemed to entertain the highest esteem for the several particulars they told him, concerning the mysteries and maxims of the Christian law. We hope grace will compleat what has been so happily begun in him."

136. De Chavagnac, in response to request from his superior officer in Europe, sent home an account of what he thought a missionary in China ought to be. This ideal, expressed with French clearness and charm at the beginning of the eighteenth century, is worth keeping in mind at the beginning of the twentieth century. Chinese characteristics remaining the same, the qualifications for work among them do not greatly change.

"First, Persons are required, who have formed the strongest Resolution to suffer all Things for Christ's sake; and to become new Men, as it were, not only as they must change their Climate, their Dress, and their Food; but still more, as they must practice Manners, the very reverse of those of our Countrymen the French. That Man who has not this Talent, or will not endeavor to acquire it, should lay aside all Thoughts of coming to China. Those also are unfit who are not Masters of their Temper; for a Man of a hasty Turn would sometimes make dreadful Havock here. The Genius of the Chineze requires Men to be Masters of their Passions; and especially of a certain turbulent Activity, which is for bearing down every Thing. A Chineze has not Abilities to comprehend, in a Month, what a Frenchman can inform him of in an Hour. He must bear patiently with that Indolence and Slowness of Apprehension which is natural to them; must boldly inculcate the Truths of Religion to a Nation, who stand in fear of no one but the Emperor; whose only Thirst is that of Money, and who consequently are wholly indifferent with regard to all Things relating to Eternity. Every Missionary who is not inspired with the strongest Spirit of Patience and Moderation is put to the most severe Trial.

"The Difficulty of the Chineze Language, and its Character, requires also a Person who delights in Study; though he finds nothing pleasing in it, except the Hopes that he may one Day employ it successfully to the Glory of God. As he always has an Opportunity of learning something on these Occasions, he consequently may spend a great Part of his Time this way; and he must accustom himself perpetually to shift from Action to Study, and from Study to his Ministerial Functions. Farther, 'tis well known that the Chineze boast their being the most civilized and most accomplished People on Earth, but an European can scarce conceive how difficult it is for a Foreigner to acquire the Chineze Politeness. The Ceremonial of this Country is surprisingly fatiguing to a Frenchman, it being one Business to acquire the Theory of it and another to put it in Practice. In proportion as a Person excels in the European Sciences, the more likely it is for him to ingratiate himself with the Nation in Question (particularly with their great Men), who have Foreigners in the utmost Contempt. Thus you perceive, reverend Father, how absolutely necessary it is for a Person to have the strongest Command over his Passions, in these Missions more than in any other. I omit to mention the Christian and Religious Virtues he ought to possess; without these it is impossible for any Man, either here or in any other Country, to save his own Soul, or to make any considerable Progress in the Conversion of others."

137. The influence of the Jesuit missionaries at the Chinese court continued into the eighteenth century. Not only their science, but also their practical arts, especially that best of missionary arts, the art of medicine, gave them deserved standing. Let the account stand in the original words of De Fontanay:

"But the circumstance which procures us the greatest access to, and credit with, the chief officers of the Empire is the favor with which the Monarch is still so gracious as to indulge us, and which we endeavor to render ourselves worthy of by the service we do him. For although he does not seem to pursue, with so much assiduity as formerly, the study of mathematics, and the rest of the European sciences, in which he is very skillful, we nevertheless are obliged to go frequently to the palace, that Prince having always some question or other to propose. He employs day and night in works of Charity, Brothers *Frapperie, Baudin* and *de Rodes,* who are expert at healing wounds and preparing medicines, he sending them to visit the officers of his household, and persons of the highest distinction in Peking, whenever they are indisposed, and is so well satisfied with their services that he never makes a progress into Tartary, or the Provinces of the Empire, without taking one of them with him. This great monarch is also exceedingly well pleased with Father *Jartoux,* and Brother *Brocard,* they going every day to the Palace, by his Majesty's express order. The former is exceedingly well skilled in algebra, mechanics, and the theory of clocks; and the latter has a very delicate hand in making various curious works which please the Emperor. But though they are so much employed by the Prince, they yet find time to preach Christ, and to instill his doctrine into such officers of the Palace as are ordered to treat with them. . . .

138. "On the front of the fine church lately built by us in the first inclosure of the Palace, in sight of the whole empire, the following words are engraved, in gold, in large Chinese characters: *Tien-chu tung-chi Kien; Coeli Domini Templum mandato Imperatoris erectum: i. e.* 'The Temple of the Lord of Heaven, built by the Emperor's order.' This is one of the most beautiful edifices in Peking; we not having spared any of those ornaments, etc., which might raise the curiosity of the Chinese; and invite to it the Mandarins, and the most considerable personages of the Empire, thereby to get an opportunity of speaking to them concerning God, and instructing them in our mysteries. Though this church was not quite finished when I left Peking, nevertheless the Heir-apparent,

the Emperor's two brothers, the Princes their children, and the greatest Lords of the Court, had been several times to view it. Such Mandarins as are sent into the Provinces, excited by the like curiosity, come thither also; and there form to themselves a favorable idea of our religion, which is of great service to us when they return to their several governments."

139. Early then in the eighteenth century the Roman Church was well established in China. As our present pursuit is not church history, but the first planting of Christianity, we are not to follow further the story of Rome in China. By the year 1724 she had sent five hundred missionaries to that land in the modern period. Ricci had the start of the first Protestant missionary in China by just two hundred and twenty-five years.

All honor to the Nestorians, Franciscans and Jesuits who gave their lives according to their light for the redemption of China.

CHAPTER X

# THE PHILIPPINE ISLANDS.

140. The missionary motive in the Spanish conquest. 141. "Conquests for the benefit of the conquered." 142. Magellan as a missionary. 143. The responsiveness of the Filipinos. 144. The baptism of King Humabon and his family. 145. The cross substituted for idols. 146. The expedition under General Legaspi. 147. Urdinæta's return to Spain. 148. Supplies for the mission. 149. The success of Herrera's mission to Spain. 150. The development of the mission work in the islands. 151. The attack of the Chinese corsair. 152. Captain Ammon's pursuit. 153. Attempts to send missionaries to China. 154. Captain Ammon's return to China with two "ambassadors from Manila." 155. The return to Manila. 156. The resentment of the Chinese captains. 157. Herrera's second visit to Spain to secure missionaries. 158. The devotion of the early friars. 159. Some results of the early mission work. 160. The support of the missions. 161. A voyage of one of the galleons. 162. The religious orders in the Philippines. 163. Missions to foreign residents in Manila. 164. The Ladrone Islands.

140. Antonio de Morga, for eight years Lieutenant Governor of the Philippines in the first generation of Spanish occupation, tells in the preface to his work on the Philippines, published in Mexico, 1609, how large a place the missionary motive held in the world-wide conquests of Spain. We shall see this more fully in connection with Spanish missions in America. But,

listen a moment to old Antonio de Morga. He says of the Spaniards:

"By the valor of their indomitable hearts, and at the expense of their revenues and pròperty, with Spanish fleets and men, they have furrowed the seas and discovered and conquered vast kingdoms in the most remote and unknown parts of the world, leading their inhabitants to a knowledge of the true God, and to the fold of the Christian church, in which they now live, governed in civil and political matters with peace and justice, under the shelter and protection of the royal arm and power which was wanting to them; weighed down as they were by blind tyrannies and barbarous cruelties, with which the enemy of the human race had for so long afflicted them and brought them up for himself.

"From this cause the crown and scepter of Spain has come to extend itself over all that the sun looks on, from its rising to its setting, with the glory and splendor of its power and majesty; but surpassing any of the other princes of the earth by having gained innumerable souls for heaven, which has been Spain's principal intention and wealth."

141. These glowing words as to the conquests of Spain for the benefit of the conquered, which we are hearing echoed by the United States three hundred years later, are more just and truthful concerning the work of the Spaniards in the Philippines than almost anywhere else. There the lust for gold found less stimulus to brutalize their dominion than it had found in Mexico and Peru.

One of the particulars in which the Filipinos were much better treated than the natives of New Spain or Mexico was in the entire abolition of slavery in the archipelago by papal brief, dated April 18, 1591. It emancipated all slaves and prohibited any enslavement of the natives for the future.

Even Foreman, who describes at length the quarrels of the Church with the State in these islands, and of the religious orders with each other, and goes into detail about the black sheep among the friars, says that it was the missionaries rather than the soldiers who established Spanish rule and civilization in the islands. He also says that "for many years after the conquest, deep religious sentiment pervaded the State policy, and not a few of the Governors-General acquired fame for their demonstration of piety."

142. The Spanish conquest of the Philippines began with the landing of **Magellan** on the island of Cebu in 1521. He was received by the Filipinos with friendliness, and he made blood brotherhood with the king of the island of Cebu. Pigafetta, who accompanied Magellan and was the historian of the voyage, tells the story of the first attempt to evangelize the Filipinos. Magellan

"Told them that we were all alike subject to the same divine laws, as we were all alike descended from Adam and Eve. He added other observations from holy writ, which afforded much pleasure to these islanders, and inspired them with desire of being instructed in our religion; so much so, indeed, that they besought the captain to leave with them, at our departure one or two men capable of teaching them, who would not fail of being held in great honor. But the captain informed them that if they wished to be Christians his priest would baptize them, but that he could not on this occasion leave any of his people behind him; but that he would return on a future day, and bring with him priests and monks to instruct them in all things belonging to our holy religion.

143. "At this they expressed their satisfaction, and added that they themselves would be glad to receive baptism; but that they must first consult their monarch on this subject.

Each of us wept for the joy which we felt at the good will of these people. The captain then admonished them by no means to be baptized through any dread with which we might have inspired them, nor through any expectation of temporal advantage; for it was not his intention to molest any one on account of his preferring the religion of his fathers; he did not, however, disguise that those who should become Christians would be more beloved and better dealt with. Every one upon this exclaimed that it was neither out of dread of nor complaisance towards us, that they sought to embrace our religion, but from a spontaneous emotion, and of their own will."

144. The King, after some deliberation, promised the captain to embrace the Christian faith, and Sunday, the 14th of April, was fixed upon for the ceremony.

"With this intent a scaffold was raised on Saturday in the place we had already consecrated, which was covered with tapestry and branches of palm. . . . About forty of us landed, exclusive of two men armed *cap-a-pie*, who followed the royal standard. At the instant of our landing the vessels fired a general salute, which did not fail of alarming the islanders. The captain and the King embraced. We ascended the scaffold, on which were placed two chairs for them, one covered with red and the other with blue velvet. The chiefs of the island were seated on cushions, and the rest of the assemblage on mats. . . . The captain then taking the King by the hand conducted him to the platform, where he was drest entirely in white, and was baptized, together with the King of Meffana, the Prince, his nephew, the Moorish merchant, and others, in number five hundred. The King, who was called Rajah Humabon, received the name of Charles, after the Emperor; the others received other names. Mass was afterwards celebrated, after which the captain invited the King to dinner; but his Majesty excused himself, accompanying us, however, to the boats which took us back to the squadron, on which another general salute was fired.

"Soon as we had dined we went on shore in great numbers, with our almoner, to baptize the Queen and other women. We ascended the platform with them. I showed the Queen a small image of the Virgin with the infant Jesus, with which she was much affected and delighted. She begged it of me to replace her idols, and with great willingness I acceded to her request. The Queen receivd the name of Jane, from the mother of the Emperor; the Prince's spouse that of Catherine, and the Queen of Meffana that of Isabella. On that day we baptized altogether more than eight hundred persons—men, women, and children. . . .

145. "After erecting a large cross in the middle of the place, a proclamation was issued ordering that all who were inclined to become Christians should destroy their idols and substitute the cross in their stead. . . .

"At this time all the inhabitants of Cebu and the neighboring islands were baptized, those of one village in one of the islands alone excepted, who refused obedience to the injunctions of the King or our captain-general; after burning the village, a cross was erected on the spot, because it was a village of idolaters; if the inhabitants had been Moors, i. e., Mahometans, a pillar of stone would have been raised to mark the hardness of their hearts. . . . The captain-general landed every day to hear mass, on which occasion many new Christians also attended, for whom he made a kind of catechism in which many points of our religion were explained."

Poor Magellan lost his life in a foolish expedition against some of the enemies of the new "Christian King." Then the latter conspired with Magellan's slave and interpreter to destroy all the Spaniards. So ended the first mission to the Philippines. Many years after, when actual missionaries came to Cebu, they found a crucifix there, still held in great veneration by the natives.

146. It was not until forty-three years later than

the visit of Magellan that Philip II., whose name had been given to the islands, organized an expedition to take possession of them for Spain and the church. It was on the Mexican coast of North America that he had four ships and a frigate fitted out for this work. The expedition, including six Augustinian missionaries and four hundred soldiers under command of the intrepid but prudent Legaspi sailed from The Port of the Nativity, Mexico, in November, 1564, and reached Cebu in April, 1565. The natives were shy and fearful at first, but finally opened their port for the conquest of the archipelago. The missionaries, with **Urdinaeta** as their leader immediately began active work among the people.

147. When terms of peace had been made with Tupas, King of Cebu, and the natives had sworn allegiance to the King of Spain, promising to pay him tribute with a part of their harvests, General Legaspi sent Urdinæta to report the success of the enterprise to the court of Mexico and to the King. Urdinæta was also commissioned to make a chart of the route from the Philippines to Mexico. The voyage was a rough one. Two pilots, a mate and sixteen sailors died on the way. The survivors were received with great joy in Mexico. Some time later Urdinæta went on to Spain, carrying to the King the reports of General Legaspi and submitting his own chart of the route, in which he had indicated the course of the disastrous wind, which the sailors had named *hurracan.*

At the Spanish Court Urdinæta was eulogized as the true discoverer of a path through the unknown sea.

On his return to Mexico on account of his age he was relieved of active service. He died there in June, 1568, at the age of seventy.

148. Acapulco, on the western coast of Mexico, was for many years the only port of departure for missionaries and missionary supplies to the Philippines. There was one expedition each year, employing generally but one ship, occasionally two. The hardships endured in the early voyages were unspeakable, costing many lives.

On the death of Urdinæta **Herrera** succeeded him in office. He baptized a niece of the native King, Tupas, who was in the retinue of General Legaspi. Later King Tupas himself, his son and many of the principal inhabitants of the islands, asked and received baptism. In June, 1569, General Legaspi sent Herrera to consult with the court in regard to points of discussion with the Portuguese, to inform the King of the progress of the work and to enlist more missionaries, either of the Augustinian or of other orders, to assist in carrying on the missions. Meantime **Martin de Herrada** was left as the only worker except for the companionship and help of two worthy laymen who had come to his aid from Salcedo (see § 126).

As Herrera was leaving the island he met **Juan Alba** and **Alonzo Jimenez**, who were arriving. Taking them with him he returned to Cebu to discuss plans for work in his absence. It was decided that Herrada should remain in Cebu, Jimenez should go to Mastate and later to Camarines, and Alba to Panay. General Legaspi had decided to place his headquarters at Panay because he could more easily collect provisions there than in Cebu. His soldiers were marauding through the islands in which the three missionaries were trying to instil the principles of Christian character.

149. In 1570 Herrera returned, accompanied by six Augustinian helpers with orders from the king to establish communities in the islands. King Philip bestowed on General Legaspi the title of Governor. Herrera was also made the bearer of titles of property from King Philip II. for the captains and soldiers who had distinguished themselves in the conquest of the islands. The Spanish chronicler of this fact adds significantly that the bringing of these titles "assured to the religious workers the reward of their arduous labors." In the following year Governor Legaspi moved the seat of government for the colony from Panay to Manila, the metropolis, even then, of the archipelago.

150. The members of the little band of missionaries were scattered through the islands separated from each other by hundreds of miles.

In spite of the distances and of the perils of traveling in unknown seas, Herrera, as Provincial, made many visits to different parts of the archipelago in performing the duties of his office. In returning to Manila from one of these expeditions his boat struck a rock. Herrera's greatest misfortune in connection with the wreck was the loss of his books, which, to quote the language of a chronicler of the time, "were many and well chosen." But the expedition which had cost him the loss of his books had given him a new knowledge of the people and the territory under his jurisdiction.

In the following year, when the Provincial of Mexico sent to him six new workers, Herrera called all the missionaries together to revise their earlier plans. With a desire to systematize the work and give it greater efficiency, he assigned to each his territory and his work. Convents or churches were to be built in the most important places. In the plan of the Provincial, the erection of a convent was to signify the establishment of a ministry and the formal creation of a civilized village.

151. In 1574 "The New Christendom" was attacked by an army under the command of the Chinese corsair, Li Ma Hong. The natives of Mindoro, Tondo and Manila rebelled and joined the corsair. Two missionaries of Mindoro were seized by the revolting natives and tied in the woods, where they were kept for four days awaiting the result of Li Ma Hong's attack. The marauders burned the church and convent of Manila with all their furnishings, including valuable gifts from King Philip II.

The Spaniards resisted, then attacked their well-equipped enemies and finally succeeded in blockading Limahon's entire fleet within their harbor. It was found necessary to pacify and win back the revolting natives to allegiance to Spanish rule. This task was accomplished by two missionaries, **Marin and Orta.** The Provincial accompanied the Governor in the column of attack against the corsair. So Church and State combined to resist attacks from without.

152. At the time of Li Ma Hong's attack on Manila he had been closely followed by Captain Ammon, who

was under orders from the Chinese government to find him and reduce him to submission. Finding him blockaded in the harbor of Manila with his forces apparently in the power of the Spaniards, Captain Ammon asked for a conference with the Governor and was most cordially received, not only by the Governor and his retinue, but by the Provincial and his coworkers.

153. Neither the zeal of the missionaries nor the ambition of the Governor had been satisfied with the conquest of the Philippines. The missionaries had a strong desire to evangelize China. Legaspi had tried again and again to send embassies of peace to the Emperor. Conferences had been held with the captains of the commercial barges, which came frequently from China. They had discouraged the project of sending missionaries and declared that entrance to China had been forbidden to all foreigners. This refusal to admit people of other lands was said to be based on a superstitious belief common among the people that if foreigners should be allowed to enter they would eventually dominate China.

In 1572 **Albuquerque,** one of the most zealous and successful of the Augustinian missionaries, learning that China would receive as slaves men of any nationality, offered himself to a Chinese captain to be sold in order that he might carry the gospel of freedom into that land. Governor Legaspi forbade him to go in the capacity of a slave, but promised to try to secure for him a more propitious way of accomplishing his desire.

Now the coming of Captain Ammon with a request

for help in securing the subjection of Li Ma Hong to Chinese authority seemed to open the way for the introduction of missions from the Philippines to China.

154. The Governor gave the Chinese slaves that he had taken from Limahon to Captain Ammon to be returned to China and promised to deliver Li Ma Hong "alive or dead" with all his forces into the hands of the Chinese.

Captain Ammon returning to China to report to the government and to bring an escort for Li Ma Hong and his fleet, took with him, at the request of the Governor, two missionaries, as special ambassadors from Manila. The only result of the embassy was a courteous exchange of letters, compliments and presents, after which the viceroys very politely invited the ambassadors to return to their own port. They sent them back with new captains and boats, and exhorted them to secure for China the friendship of their Spanish King and to deliver Limahon, dead or alive, to the Chinese authorities. Permission was granted them to return to China when this should be accomplished.

155. Arriving at Manila they found that Li Ma Hong had succeeded in raising the blockade and escaping. Don Francisco Sande had been installed as Governor. He accepted the presents which had been intended for his predecessor, and after expressing his appreciation of them, he asked the captains to take with them, on their return to China, two missionaries, Albuquerque and Herrada. The captains consented to this, but quite unwillingly. They had hoped to secure Limahon and to be handsomely rewarded by China for his capture,

but he had escaped before their arrival. They had expected to receive presents and titles from the Philippine Governor, but, contrary to the counsel of his advisers, he bestowed nothing upon them.

156. Offended by what they considered lack of consideration on the part of the Spaniards, they avenged themselves on the missionaries and their three Indian servants. Disembarking at Zimbales they beheaded the servants, disrobed the missionaries, tied them to strong trees and tore open their flesh with flogging, then left them there unconscious and half dead. After two days they were found by Sergeant Moronis, who nursed them until they were so far recovered as to be able to be taken back to Manila. Later, hoping to undo the harm which he had done, Governor Sande sent Marin to the Court of Spain to represent to the King the advantages of friendly relations with China and to describe the mistake which he had made and its unfortunate effect on the relations existing between China and the Philippines.

Philip II. appointed an imposing embassy to go to Peking carrying messages of affection and valuable presents. After many delays the embassy was finally abandoned.

157. On the departure of Li Ma Hong and his forces the missionaries began anew their task of building churches and founding communities.

Herrera went again to Spain to enlist more missionaries. He secured forty Augustinians and several Franciscans, and started with them for the Philippines by way of Mexico. The hardships of the voyage were so great that they were exhausted and ill. Only six of those who had left Spain found themselves able to proceed farther than Mexico. These six, with three others who joined the company in Mexico, had nearly reached Manila when they were wrecked by a typhoon. With great difficulty they reached a neighboring island, where they all, including Herrera, died at the hands of the savage natives, in 1576. In the following year seven Augustinians and seventeen Franciscans came to Manila to engage in missionary work.

158. Whatever may be true of their successors, the inheritors of wealth, position and power, there is no reason to doubt that the friars who went to the Philippines in the early days of the Spanish occupation were unselfish in their zeal to carry the gospel where it had not been known. The period of which we are treating ended more than one hundred years ago. Many writers have commended the devotion and faithfulness of those early missionary friars who, "with no other arms than their virtues," made the Spanish name loved, and "gave to the King as by miracle 2,000,000 more of Christian subjects." The Spanish flag floated beside the cross, upheld by a mere handful of soldiers and with the expenditure of "scarcely a drop of blood."

Dampier, the English navigator, reporting his visit to the Philippines in 1796, says:

"In every village is a stone church, as well as a parsonage house for the rector, who is constantly one of the monks. These last, who all of them are Europeans, are very much respected by the Indians, while the secular clergy, who most commonly are Creoles, are held in contempt; hence the Government shows great deference to the rectors;

for, generally speaking, the Indian always consults them on entering upon any enterprise and even as to paying taxes."

159. Mendoza's account, written about 1584, and translated soon after into the English of that day, gives a picturesque view of the conditions existing in the islands twenty years after the beginning of serious missionary work:

"According vnto the common opinion, at this day there is conuerted and baptized more then foure hundred thousand soules, which is a great number; yet in respect of the quantitie that are not as yet conuerted, there but a few. It is left undone (as aforesaid) for want of ministers, for that, although his maiesty doth ordinarily send thither without any respect of the great charge in doing the same, yet by reason that there are so many ilands, and euerie day they doo discouer more and more, and being so far off, they cannot come vnto them all, as necessitie requireth. Such as are baptized doo receiue the fayth with great firmenesse, and are good Christians, and would be better, if that they were holpen with good ensamples; as those which haue beene there so long time are bounde to doe; that the lacke thereof doth cause some of the inhabitants so much to abhorre them, that they would not see them once paynted vpon a wall. . . . That some of them forthwith receiued the baptisme, and that others did delay it, saying that because there were Spaniard souldiers in glory, they would not go thither, because they would not be in their company."

Mohammedanism had three hundred years the start of Christianity in the southern group of the Philippines. Terrible persecutions were suffered by the Christian converts at the hands of both pagans and Mohammedans. It is said that there were more than six thousand martyrs before the end of the sixteenth century. By the end of the next century Christianity was firmly established.

160. A Spanish writer of the time says: "Without the help of the friars it is of little use for us to try to conquer the Indians by force of arms. Hidden in the woods they would refuse to pay tribute or to do service for the Spaniards."

The astute King, realizing the material advantages secured for his realm by the missionaries, was glad for political reasons to promote their enterprises. The missions in the Philippines were largely supported by the monopoly which the King of Spain had of the trade of the islands. The annual galleon between Manila and Acapulco, Mexico, carried rich cargoes of spices and silks from China, not fewer than fifty thousand pairs of silk stockings a year, and from India various fabrics, especially calicoes (named from Calcutta) and chintz. The King assigned a certain number of bales to each of the missionary orders. They either filled their allotted bulk of cargo themselves or sold the privilege to others. The trade was worth about three millions of dollars a year. It was this enormous trade between Peru and Mexico on one side and the Orient on the other, through the Philippines, which introduced the Mexican dollar as a standard of value in China, so that our missionaries there to this day say of their expenses, so much, "Mexican." The Italian traveler, Careri, went in the galleon from Manila to Acapulco in 1697 and describes at length the miseries of the voyage, and tells also of the prodigious profits made by those in charge.

161. On the last day of June, 1743, the galleon Nostra Signora de Cabadonga, which had sailed from

Manila eleven months before, heavily laden with a rich cargo, landed it safely on the shores of America. She made the return voyage with a light cargo of cochineal and other products, but with a fresh relay of missionaries and with 1,313,843 Mexican dollars for the support of the missions, besides 35,682 ounces of virgin silver. After four months of continuous sailing almost straight westward, as the map of her track from her own log book shows, she was almost in sight of the Cape of the Holy Spirit, her gateway into the Philippines, when Commodore Anson, of England, who had been lying in wait for her a whole month at that point with his ship, The Centurion, opened fire upon her. Though he has not half as many men as are standing to the thirty-six guns of our Lady of Cabadonga, most of those that he has being mere boys, his Anglo-Saxon skill in maneuvering and in handling the guns, after a sharp fight causes the Spaniards to strike their colors with loss to them of 67 killed and 84 wounded, while the British loss is but 2 killed and 17 wounded. When the prisoners were brought aboard they were disgusted as well as astonished to see that they had been beaten by a mere handful of British lads.

Hundreds of years the galleons went and came, generally in safety, carrying means and men for missions from America to the Philippines.

162. Before the close of the eighteenth century the Augustinians had founded seventy distinct missions in the Philippines. They were preaching in eight different dialects. Their missions were scattered through twenty provinces. About three-quarters of a million of

inhabitants were gathered under their immediate care in Christian villages. In the years 1565-1800 twelve hundred and sixty Augustinian monks were engaged in these missions, and nearly two hundred and forty served as teachers and college professors.

The Augustinians have been assumed to be the first missionaries to the Philippines. They were the first, doubtless, to begin a work there which has continued uninterruptedly to the present day. But the first teachers of Christianity in the islands were not members of any of the religious orders, but "private clergy," chaplains of ships, whose teachings remained and prepared the soil for later workers, though their names perished.

Franciscan missionaries reached the islands twelve years after the Augustinians. In 1581 the first bishop arrived. He was a Dominican and brought with him from Mexico others of his own order. Not long after the Jesuits and the Recollets followed. All these missionary orders were very successful, according to their standards, in winning the natives to Christianity.

It was not till the year 1700 that natives were admitted to full membership in the brotherhoods. On account of the native uprisings this privilege was taken away in 1872.

163. Even before the way was open for modern missionaries to go from the Philippine Islands to China and Japan some of the people of those lands received the gospel through what might be called the home mission work of the Philippine missionaries.

Chinese swarmed in Manila before 1600, and the government enacted stringent laws for their exclusion, allowing only certain needed classes of tradesmen and workmen to remain on certificate.

They were compelled to live in specified districts and never to be found within the walls after the gates were closed, on pain of death. The Dominicans carried on a vigorous mission among them, having two missionary settlements and a hospital for their especial benefit. There was a quarter occupied by the christianized Chinese to the number of 500. But their conversion proved not to be very genuine or stable, being largely feigned with the hope of business and social advantage to be gained.

Among the Japanese, on the other hand, who were far less numerous and of a much higher grade, the Franciscans carried on a mission which resulted in many genuine conversions.

164. Magellan discovered the Ladrone Islands and landed at Guam in the same year in which he visited the Philippines, 1521. In 1668 a Jesuit mission from Mexico was established under the direction of **Diego.** By 1695 the natives were nominally christianized. The mission met with many reverses, and at times with determined hostility on the part of the people. The Jesuit **Faure**, with twenty-two others of the same order, visited the Ladrones in 1709. He speaks of the islands as having been "consecrated by the blood of so many of our martyrs." He says: "We continued no longer than was necessary for taking in some refreshments, but six of our Jesuits staid behind, their assistance being very much wanted for the ease of the first mis-

sionaries, most of whom were bowed with age and incapable of discharging their ministerial duties."

According to Anson, who visited Guam in 1741, there were then "near four thousand native inhabitants." But he says that there were said to have been above fifty thousand people only sixty years before his visit.

In 1771 Crozet found only about 1,000 native inhabitants in the Ladrones. But he speaks in the highest terms of the treatment which they were at that time receiving from the Spanish governor, M. Tobias, and the missionaries. There were five of the latter belonging to the order of Augustine, though the Company of Jesus had formerly had charge of the work.

## CHAPTER XI.

# JAPAN AND FORMOSA.

165. The pioneer missionaries. 166. Xavier in Kioto and Oita. 167. Xavier and Carey—a contrast. 168. Work in Bungo and Hirado. 169. Nagasaki becomes the headquarters of Christianity. 170. The Goto Islands. 171. Summary of exclusively Jesuit work. 172. Franciscans from the Philippines. 173. Dominicans and others from the Philippines. 174. Native helpers. 175. Numerical results. 176. Attempted obliteration not quite successful. 177. Dutch missions in Formosa. 178. Report of George Candidus. 179. Great work of Robert Junius. 180. School work. 181. Methods. 182. A printing press and Dutch humor. 183. Compulsion and religious liberty. 184. The last stand.

165. The first missionary to Japan was that great forerunner of all modern missionaries in Asia, **Francis Xavier.** In India he wrote:

"I have been informed by many of an island, Japan, situated near China, inhabited by heathens alone, not by Mahometans, nor by Jews; and that it contains men endowed with good morals, most inquisitive men, intelligent, eager for novelties respecting God, both natural and divine novelties concerning God. I have resolved not without great pleasure of mind, to see that island also."

At Malacca Xavier had met a Japanese by the name of Hanjiro (Anger), who had committed a murder and been driven into exile. Hanjiro had an active conscience and the missionary found him hungering for peace of mind. As a result the Japanese and his servant were converted and were baptized and taught by Xavier.

Hanjiro guided the apostle to Japan, was his interpreter there and his active coadjutor. The other members of this first mission were **Jean Ferdinand** and **Cosmé de Torres**. They landed at Kagoshima, Hanjiro's home, in southwestern Japan, August 15, 1549. Some of the relations of Hanjiro soon received Christian baptism. The ruler of the district and his wife are said to have been greatly impressed with a picture of Mary and the infant Jesus depicted on a tablet which was one of Hanjiro's treasures. On the departure of a Portuguese trading vessel, however, the ruler's interest departed and he prohibited further preaching. The ship sailed to the port frequented by foreigners in the island of Hirado (Firando), 130 miles northwest of Kagoshima. Xavier went thither, overland most of the way. He planted a mission there, leaving Cosmé de Torres in charge.

166. The restless apostle and his three remaining comrades set out for Kioto, the western capital of Japan on the main island, nearly 400 miles eastward from Hirado. Xavier carried a box containing vestments and vessels for celebrating mass. With his burden and barefooted in mid-winter he tramped the long distance over hill and dale, some of the way in the snow. He preached on the streets, but political commotions, as well as his own unpropitious estate, prevented his obtaining the interview which he desired with either the Mikado or the Shogun. After all his

FRANCIS XAVIER.

pains in reaching the capital, he stayed but two weeks. Either on this trip or on a separate journey from Hirado, Yamaguchi was visited. But the forlorn mission band found no welcome there.

In Oita (Fucheo), on the Bungo Channel, 130 miles northwest of Kagoshima, the missionaries found their most receptive field. The Portuguese traders co-operated with Xavier and he obtained a cordial welcome on the part of the ruler of the province of Bungo, who appointed a public discussion of religion and declared the result of it to be in favor of the new faith. Xavier always believed in the use of political power for the propagation of Christianity. He not only practiced extreme poverty, but when it appeared to him that pomp and ceremony would do more good he used that. He received $15,000 from Europe during his brief mission in Japan.

167. After only two and a half years in the Sunrise Kingdom this flying scout of missions set sail November 20, 1551, hoping to enter next the great land of China. Xavier was a man of extremely sensitive emotional nature. Some of his letters show him in the depths of discouragement, almost hopeless as to the conversion of the Asiatics; and others show him on the mountain crest of millennial vision. With him, as with some other great pioneers of missions, the love of travel had much to do with shaping his career. What we might call the geographical sense was strong in William Carey and had much to do with his appreciation of the needs of the world; but it did not master him as it mastered Xavier. Carey settled to the steady, pro-

longed work in one place, which is far less exhilarating and makes larger drafts on spiritual resources. Carey conscientiously accepted that kind of work as his mission. When he had come to be recognized as one of the great scholars of the world, he expressed the wish that if people must say anything about him they should merely say that he could "plod." The restless Xavier never learned to use any Asiatic language. Carey learned enough of thirty-six languages and dialects to translate completely or partially the Scriptures into them. Thus he put the sacred literature which had originated in Western Asia into the native tongues of more than half the population of the whole continent. But the Kingdom of Heaven uses explorers as well as settlers. Japan seems to have given Xavier more satisfaction than India. This is not surprising considering the mental mobility of the Japanese. Xavier said of them: "This nation is the delight of my soul."

168. Cosmé de Torres, who had been appointed by the Jesuit college in Goa, India, to accompany Xavier, was in charge of the mission work after Xavier left Japan. The mission prospered in the province of Bungo. Two of the bonzes (Buddhist priests) had been inquirers for some time. One day when Torres had been giving to an assembly some account of Paul's conversion one of the bonzes exclaimed to the whole gathering: "Behold, O Japanese! I, also, am a Christian! and as I have hitherto imitated a Paul by my opposition to Jesus, so will I follow him henceforth by preaching to the heathens. And you, my friend," he added, turning to his companion, "come with me; and

since together we have disseminated error, now together let us teach the truth." These men were baptized under the names **Paul** and **Barnabas.**

In 1557 Paul and a Jesuit, **Balthazar**, undertook a fresh work at Hirado. Many were converted, including a governor of two small islands in the vicinity. Before long, however, persecution arose at Hirado, and the first recorded martyrdom for the faith in Japan was there. A master had forbidden his slave to attend the Christian assembly on pain of death. She replied that she would do all her duty to him, but also her duty to God. When she returned the next time from religious service he met her with a drawn sword. She knelt quietly before him and he cut off her head at one blow.

169. Several of the daimios, the feudal barons or territorial nobles of Japan, commonly called kings in the Jesuit accounts, adopted Christianity. **Sumitando,** the Daimio of Omura, was one of the most zealous of these. He had been convinced of the truth of Christianity, it is said, by reading a book written in Japanese by one of the missionaries, **Villela**, to answer objections of the bonzes. The fact must be recognized that at the same time Sumitando saw that it would be a great advantage to him to have the Portuguese trade center in his barony. He laid out on a large scale the city of Nagasaki at that prosperous seaport, a few miles south of his seat, Omura, and gave the Jesuits and merchants large jurisdiction there. In 1562 a Christian church was built. The town grew rapidly and became one of the great ports of Japan, and the headquarters of Chris-

tianity. In 1567 "there was hardly a person who was not a Christian." Sumitando came with forty of his chief retainers and they were baptized by Torres. The daimio adopted the methods which were in vogue in European Christendom at the time and sought to compel uniformity of creed. He destroyed idolatry with a strong hand. His course resulted in an insurrection of the heathen party, but he was able to put it down.

170. The daimio of the Goto Islands, the western group of Japan, asked for missionaries. Torres sent **Almeida and Lewis** in 1566. Later **John Baptist de Monti** baptized the baron's son, who succeeded to the estate. **Alexander Valignan** was a sturdy missionary in Goto for some years. Arima, another baron, was early brought under the influence of Christianity.

171. Cosmé de Torres guided the missions in Japan until his death in 1570, more than twenty years after his landing on the shores of Japan with Xavier. The record runs that he had baptized 30,000 pagans with his own hands. Fifty churches had been founded. A number of mission schools had been established. He was succeeded in the charge of the work by **Cabral.** The Company of Jesus prosecuted their work in Japan with continued vigor.. For forty-four years they occupied the field alone. At the end of that time (1593), they had 130 missionaries on the ground.

172. Then other orders joined in the work. For nearly fifty years (1593-1640) active and heroic missionary enterprises in Japan were conducted from the Philippine Islands. In spite of the protests of the Jesuits, who claimed Japan as their peculiar territory, Francis-

cans were sent from Manila. They went first as government ambassadors and negotiated treaties for trade between the Philippine and Japanese islands. But they had missions most at heart. **Pedro Bautista** was the leader. He had three other barefooted friars and four laymen with him. Permission was granted them to build a church at Meaco, near Osaka, which was opened in 1594. But, instigated by Portuguese merchants and perhaps by the Jesuits, the governor of the provincial capital, Nagasaki, prohibited the Franciscan propaganda. These missionaries were less politic than those of the Company of Jesus. The Emperor himself became alarmed at the spread of the new religion in his realm and issued an edict against it. Bautista went to Manila, however, and secured a fresh authorization from the Governor and a new relay of missionaries. In 1603 **Diego Guevara** founded the convent of Bungo and **Estasio Ortiz** that of Usuki. Two years later **Ferdinand de San Jose** created a church in Sayki, the residence of the King of Bungo. Later still he built the convents of Angota and Nagasaki.

The Emperor of Japan, finding that the work was being carried on with more vigor than ever, had the Philippine missionaries arrested and condemned to death by crucifixion. Others were only banished, thus losing, as a Philippine author says, "the greatest hope of their lives, the hope of being able to seal the preaching of the Gospel with their blood." But twenty-six missionaries and native converts were mutilated and exhibited from town to town and finally crucified on a hill near

Nagasaki. Foreman justly asks: "Would Buddhist missionaries in Spain have met with milder treatment at the hands of the Inquisitors?" The Emperor justified his course in a letter to the Governor of Manila on the ground that the missionaries had entered his realm under the false guise of ambassadors. The Jesuits declared that the Franciscans had died under the ban of the church, having violated a bull of the Pope, which had assigned Japan to Francis Xavier. But neither Emperor nor Jesuit, nor the cross could deter the ardent missionaries. More went, Dominicans as well as Franciscans. In 1622 four of the latter and two of the former, along with many natives, were burned to death. The authorities at Manila, both civil and ecclesiastical, forbade the throwing away of any more lives in Japan. Still missionaries longed to go and employed Chinese junks to carry them. A bull of Pope Urban VIII. declared those who had laid down their lives for Japan to be martyrs and saints.

173. The first Dominicans to go as missionaries from Manila to Japan were a band of five with **Francis de Morales** at the head. They dedicated their first church in Japan at Quiodomari in 1606. A little later they built three churches in the province of Figen. In 1610 they built one in the imperial capital, Tokio, and soon after another in Osaka.

The Augustinians of the Philippines also had workers in Japan under the leadership of **Ferdinand of St. Joseph.** In 1612 there were on the field four of this order, nine Dominicans, fourteen Franciscans and one hundred and twenty-three Jesuits. In spite of much jealousy the various orders co-operated to a considerable extent in the common work. For instance, they combined in building hospitals. The plain facts of history in many lands show that sectarianism in the Roman church has been as intense as that outside of it, and neither better nor worse.

174. As in every land the most vital work of evangelism was performed by the people of the land. **Hanjiro** was the spokesman of Xavier. He translated the Gospel of Matthew and some ritual documents into Japanese. The members of the nobility who were converted had a great deal to do with the spread of Christianity, but not they alone. A poor, blind peddler of combs and needles, christened **Matthew,** went everywhere in his business earnestly proclaiming Christ from house to house. One of the noblemen attributed his conversion to the convincing words of this Matthew.

175. There are various estimates of the number of converts, ranging from 600,000 to 2,000,000. A most exact statement is made as to the number converted in one period of only nineteen years (1603-1622). It is 239,339. Many of the converts had little Christian instruction. It is no wonder that multitudes apostatized in the hour of trial. The wonder is that so many stood the test. There are said to have been 37,000 martyrs. It is certain that Christianity was thickly planted in all southwestern Japan, with Nagasaki as a center.

176. As we are studying the planting, not the uprooting of Christianity, we must leave the subject here,

only remarking that one of the most terrific persecutions that the world has ever seen apparently succeeded in eradicating the new faith from Japan. The museum in Tokio contains specimens of the little metal crucifixes which all Japanese subjects suspected of Christianity were required to trample under foot. Here is the final imperial decree:

"So long as the sun shall warm the earth, let no Christian be so bold as to come to Japan, and let all know that the king of Spain himself, or the Christian's God, or the great God of all, if he violate this command, shall pay the forfeit with his head."

In spite of such decrees posted about Japan till after the middle of the nineteenth century, when Roman Catholic missionaries were permitted to resume work in the country, they found in the vicinity of Nagasaki 10,000 people who had been keeping up some Christian prayers and practices which had been handed down through the 200 years of desolation. It was a thrilling moment, the 17th of March, 1865, when the first group of these came to the new Roman Catholic church in Nagasaki and said to the French missionary, **M. Petitjean.** "In our hearts, all we who are present are the same as you," and, speaking of the village from which they had come: "At home nearly every one thinks as we do." Later, copies of prayerbooks used in the Christian communities were brought, which proved, "with the exception of some faults of pronunciation and mistakes in copying," to contain correct translations of the Lord's Prayer, the Apostle's Creed and five or six other formulas which had been taught by the missionaries six generations before.

177. Early in the seventeenth century the Japanese had won from the Chinese and held possession of a portion of the island of Formosa. They were expelled by the Dutch, who built in 1624 two forts on the west coast, Zealandia and Providentia. They held possession for nearly forty years. During that time they carried on extensive missionary operations among the natives. Twenty-nine different ordained ministers labored there, but most of them for only a few months each. Their work was as brilliant as that of the Jesuits in other places, and of much the same character as far as depth and permanence are concerned.

Mr. William Campbell's "Account of the Missionary Success in the Island of Formosa" renders an invaluable service to all serious students of missions by putting the primary documents within reach. The following extracts will not only enable the original actors in Formosa to tell their own story, but will also give us a reliable glimpse into the missionary methods of the Dutch in their wide oriental possessions.

178. **George Candidus,** the first missionary to Formosa, when he had been there sixteen months was able to write:

> "I have used great diligence to learn the language of the people and to instruct them in the Christian faith, and have succeeded so far that, a fortnight before Christmas of the present year, there were one hundred and twenty-eight persons who knew the Prayers and were able to explain in the most satisfactory manner the principal Articles of the Christian faith, but who, for certain reasons, have not yet been baptized."

Candidus argued for the Dutch retention of that island in words which sound the same as those used two hundred and seventy years later by people of the United States in respect to islands very near Formosa: "The island should not be abandoned or given up by us; for, in that case, it would either be annexed by the Spaniards or fall into the hands of the Japanese, who would not afford any shelter or protection to the Christian religion."

179. The second missionary, **Robertus Junius,** rendered distinguished service. At the end of thirteen years he could report that one thousand and seventy people had been baptized at a single station, Soulang, "and a proportionate number in the other villages," of which he names five. The most satisfactory station was Sinkang. The following from the same letter shows clearly the sort of mission work done by the Hollanders and its success:

"More and more their former manners and customs are disappearing, and they are conforming to our ways; which shows that it requires time and proper instruction to convert the heathen. It would be very desirable if the good example of Sinkang as regards Christianity could be imitated by the other villages, the inhabitants of which, however, are all baptized, and most of them married according to Christian rites. They also regulate their outward conduct in every respect according to the Christian Church in Holland, and are very punctual in their attendance at God's House on the Sabbath, coming to church in the morning and evening to be instructed in the Christian religion, or rather to repeat what they have already learnt, in order that they should thus remember it better. . . . The priestesses, who were so serious an obstacle to our work, have now lost all power, and are treated with contempt on account of the many falsehoods they formerly promulgated; nor are they allowed to enter any houses except their own, being thus prevented from practicing their former idolatry. The schools continue to flourish, and many of the people can read fluently and write fairly well."

After Mr. Junius returned to Holland a friend of his there sent on some account of his work to a Mr. Jessie, who published an English translation in 1650. Speaking of the large number of baptisms he says,

"of which number of persons, so Dipt in Water, the Infants of persons in covenant are not reckoned."

Of the adults he says,

"Moreover, many of them are so able, in such fervencie of spirit to poure out their prayers before God, Morning and Evening, and before and after taking of Meat, and in other Necessities; and that with such comlinesse and fitnesse of speech, and with such moderation and decencie of gesture; that may provoke tears to such as heare and behold them. And there are some of them, that being called to pray about any matter or businesse, are able to perform it in conceived prayer, *ex tempore,* so readily, in such fit expressions, and with such arguments and pithinesse, as if they had been spending some houres for the contriving and so framing of them."

180. In 1643 there were six hundred children in the schools, "including some who can write fairly well in Latin characters." The following from a letter of the Consistory of Formosa to the Classis of Amsterdam reveals a mission work of such genuine as well as phenomenal character that one is led to hope that there was more of real value in the mission work of the Dutch in Ceylon, Java and elsewhere than is commonly thought. Still, the small number of communicants in the model village where so many hundreds had been baptized shows that the work was not of the deepest kind:

"The daily instruction is regularly continued, and much progress is made, the brunt of the work falling upon our native teachers, who perform their work most admirably; for which reason we have induced the Governor to grant them a real per month each, in the hope that Mr. Junius, on arriving in Batavia, will be able to get their salaries increased. There are fifty of them in these six villages who are all thoroughly instructed in the principles of the Christian faith, and able to communicate to their countrymen the saving knowledge in such a way that even many of the Scripture Readers (lit. Sick-Visitants) could not be compared with them.

"Little confidence can be placed in the Dutch schoolmasters, some of them giving very great offence to those weak Christians; and although one of them was recently decapitated on account of his misdeeds, others still refuse to take warning from this punishment, and persevere in their wickedness; so that, not long ago, we were obliged to deliver another who behaved scandalously into the hands of the civil authorities.

181. "Our brother the Rev. Robert Junius has baptized in these six villages upwards of five thousand and four hundred persons; of whom all that are living—with the exception of the young children—repeat fluently the 'Law of God,' the 'Articles of Belief,' the 'Lord's Prayer,' the 'Morning and Evening Prayers,' the 'Prayers before and after meals,' and the 'Questions concerning the Christian Religion,' which is a catechism Mr. Junius will show to you. More than a thousand couples have also been united in marriage by him, and so far as we know, they all live in conformity with their marriage vows.

"Some months ago our beloved colleague administered the Holy Communion to the chiefs of Soulang and more than sixty people of Sinkang; who all, with proper reverence, partook of the Lord's bread and drank from His cup, by this conduct giving the assurance that they really partook of the blessing which the Holy Communion holds out to us."

**Daniel Gravius,** one of the most learned and also highly esteemed ministers at Batavia, Java, then capital of the Dutch East Indies, nobly insisted, in spite of the protests of his congregation, on going as a missionary to Formosa.

The missions suffered seriously from the short term of service in vogue, generally but two or three years, seldom more than four or five. Junius, who had such great ingatherings, remained twelve years. Only one other man was so long on the field. The Formosa Classis made pleading appeals to Holland for greater permanency of service.

182. They also begged for a printing-press, so that lessons in the hands of the people might help to stability. Their appeal on this point reveals a great weakness in their methods:

"Perhaps it is sufficient to give you a slight idea of the method followed in the education of these new converts (a method which leads us to urge our request with much earnestness) when we state that the instruction given in our numerous and populous villages is *viva voce*, the people having to repeat what has first been recited to them by one or two of the schoolmasters. Now, as a great many persons have to be instructed, and as we must avoid straining their powers too much, they receive lessons in companies, and each company only once every two or three weeks. We have thus very little hope that the instruction given in one week will be remembred by them during the interval; our frequent experience being that, when the time for instruction comes round again, they have forgotten everything and have gone backward—all this arising from the want of books, and from their own weakness of memory and unwillingness to remember what has been told them."

These staid and honest Dutchmen were not without gleams of humor. Witness the following paragraph in their plea for a printing press:

"There is no need to fear that the multitude of writers or

authors which may unexpectedly arise will entail greater expenses on the Company or become a burden to the churches; since it is our intention—if the present request be granted—to keep this current so effectively in check that there will be no danger of the water at any time rising so high as to cause an inundation or the breaking of the dykes."

183. The civil and ecclesiastical government of Formosa, growing impatient with the native slowness to adopt Christian religion and morals, enacted that "idolatry in the first degree shall be punished with public whipping and banishment." But the law was annulled by the Supreme Council of the Dutch East India Company at home. Their communication on this subject, dated Amsterdam, April 16, 1660, is worthy of the thrilling history of Holland in regard to religious liberty:

"Our conviction is that if we cannot influence the inhabitants by precept and instruction, they are much less likely to be influenced by severe punishments of this kind; and as we are of opinion that Christians ought in no case to resort to such measures, it has greatly surprised us that the Consistory should have given consent to their adoption in the present case. Thus, although the object be to Christianize the natives, we cannot refrain from declaring that these measures sorely displease us, because they may be considered harsh and cruel, and because they are contrary to the spirit and character of the Dutch nation."

184. The Dutch were driven out of Formosa by the Chinese under a general named Koxinga, and their work was swiftly obliterated. In the midst of their heroic and desperate struggle to hold their ground they adopted the following resolution:

"To open negotiations with Koxinga; but, first of all, to consider: That in all negotiations the principal object to be kept in view is that, henceforth, our clergymen shall have full and perfect liberty to instruct the Formosan Christians who, by the grace of God, have already been taught the principles of his Gospel. The most strenuous efforts are to be made to have this condition granted, inasmuch as we take nothing else so much to heart as the honor of God's most holy name, and the establishment and progress of the Reformed religion."

CHAPTER XII.

# EGYPT AND ABYSSINIA.

185. African influence in early Christianity. 186. Hadrian's criticism. 187. Christian education in the second century. 188. Missionary literature written in the second century. 189. Clement's "Exhortation to the Heathen." 190. The work of Origen. 191. Early successes and reverses of Christianity in Egypt. 192. Francis of Assisi. 193. Extract from the letter of a crusader. 194. Moravian missions. 195. Cyrene. 196. Ethiopia. 197. Candace's treasurer. 198. Frumentius and Edessius. 199. Athanasius organizes a missionary expedition. 200. Nubia.

185. Of twenty greatest names in the history of Christianity in the first four centuries after the apostles more than one-half belong to Africa. Remembering Origen, Athanasius and Augustine, one cannot hesitate to say that Africa exerted the chief moulding influence on the first half-millennium of Christianity, and to a large extent on all the ages since. Even before Augustine, in the early formative centuries, more than half of the Ante-Nicene Library is of African origin.

We may never know who was the first to carry a knowledge of the Messiah into the land which had sheltered him in his infancy. It was the land which had cradled the Messianic race and its emancipator, Moses, and, later on, it became the nursery of missionary Judaism with its noble Philo. It seems natural to think that some true Israelite must have told there of the Prophet of Nazareth even before his ascension. It is certain that but ten days after that event "dwellers in Egypt" heard about Christ in the tongue wherein they were born.

The traditions about the fields of labor of the apostles are too confused and many of them too late to be reliable. But at least five writers as early as the third century state that **Mark** labored in Egypt. There seems no reason to doubt that he planted Christianity there in the first century.

186. The first contemporary notice of Christians in Egypt, however, is from the pen of an enemy, occurring in a letter from the Emperor Hadrian (A. D. 117-138) to the Consul Servanus. Hadrian, fond of travel and of architecture, was also a curious observer of society. He did not see the sober and sincere Christianity which could have been found in Alexandria, but rather the superficial forms of philosophy and eclectic religion which existed in that cosmopolitan city. He says:

"I have become perfectly familiar with Egypt, which you praised to me. It is fickle, uncertain, blown about by every gust of rumor. Those who worship Serapis are Christians, and those who are devoted to Serapis call themselves bishops of Christ. There is no ruler of a synagogue there, no Samaritan, no Christian presbyter, who is not an astrologer, a sooth-sayer, a quack. The patriarch himself (*i. e.*, the Jewish patriarch, for there were no Christian patriarchs at this time), whenever he comes to Egypt, is compelled by some to worship Serapis, by others to worship Christ."

187. From better informed sources it is known that

within a hundred years after the last of the apostles there was a large well-to-do Christian community in Alexandria, having church buildings of their own. There were twelve city parishes with pastors. A Christian school had been established beside the great heathen university for which the city was famous. The new Christian school was one of the first of missionary training schools. It admitted both men and women. The first principal of this school was **Pantaenus**. He was well versed in Greek philosophy. Only half a dozen lines from his scholarly pen have been preserved to our day. They are concerning the relations of the Greek to the Hebrew verb. We know that he went on a missionary tour to India, leaving his school work for the time in the hands of his brilliant pupil, **Clement**, who was a good example of the effect of the missionary work of Pantænus among "the heathen at home," who existed, not as an excuse but as a reality in those days. Clement had been reared in the proud pagan schools of Athens. But not satisfied with what philosophy could teach him, he wandered far abroad in search of knowledge. At last in the teacher of the little Christian academy held in the house of Pantænus, he found that for which his soul hungered.

188. On the death of Pantænus Clement became head of the school and the author of many learned works. All but the names of most of them have been lost. Three of his works remain, however, filling two good-sized volumes. Of the three two are as distinctly missionary in their composition and purpose as any which have been written by Carey or Ashmore. One

of these he entitled "An Exhortation to the Heathen," the other "The Instructor," this last being intended to teach the converts from heathenism how to follow Christ in all things. Clement's "Exhortation to the Heathen" is one of the first of missionary writings, not only in point of time, but also in breadth of sympathy, in charming scholarship and in fervor of evangelistic appeal. A history of missions would be seriously defective without a glimpse of the contents of this great missionary document which was written fewer than one hundred years after the Apostle John had laid down his pen. The translation occupies one hundred pages in the Ante-Nicene Library. We can take only a paragraph here and there from the pages which expose with a keen and merciless pen the combination of immorality and folly in the mythology and in the idolatry of heathenism, then recognize the gleams of truth and the inspiration of some of the loftiest reaches of pagan philosophers and poets, passing on to the true dignity of man in fellowship with the Word of God, the Light of the World.

189. "Let the secret shrines of the Egyptians and the necromancies of the Etruscans be consigned to darkness. Insane devices truly are they all of unbelieving men. Goats, too, have been confederates in this art of soothsaying, trained to divination; and crows taught by men to give oracular responses to men. . . . We must not either keep the Pythagoreans in the background, who say: 'God is one; and He is not, as some suppose, outside of this frame of things, but within it; but, in all the entireness of His being, is in the whole circle of existence, surveying all nature, and blending in harmonious union the whole—the author of all His own forces and works, the giver of light in heaven, and

Father of all—the mind and vital power of the whole world—the mover of all things.' For the knowledge of God, these utterances, written by those we have mentioned, through the inspiration of God, and selected by us, may suffice even for the man that has but small power to examine the truth. . . .

"Let your Phidias, and Polycletus, and your Praxiteles and Appelles, too, come, and all that are engaged in mechanical arts, who, being themselves of the earth, are workers of the earth. 'For then,' says a certain prophecy, 'the affairs here turned out unfortunately, when men put their trust in images.' Let the meaner artists, too—for I will not stop calling—come. None of these ever made a breathing image, or out of earth moulded soft flesh. Who liquefied marrow? or who solidified the bones? Who stretched the nerves? Who distended the veins? Who poured the blood into them? Or who spread the skin? Whoever could have made eyes capable of seeing? Who breathed spirit into the lifeless form? Who bestowed righteousness? Who promised immortality? The Maker of the universe alone; the Great Artist and Father has formed us, such a living image as man is. But your Olympian Jove, the image of an image, greatly out of harmony with truth, is the senseless work of Attic hands. For the image of God is His Word, the genuine Son of Mind, the Divine Word, the archetypal light of light; and the image of the Word is the true man, the mind which is in man, who is therefore said to have been made 'in the image and likeness of God,' assimilated to the Divine Word in the affections of the soul, and therefore rational; but effigies sculptured in human form, the earthly image of that part of man which is visible and earth-born, are but a perishable impress of humanity, manifestly wide of the truth. That life, then, which is occupied with so much earnestness about matter, seems to me to be nothing else than full of insanity. . . .

"As, then, we do not compel the horse to plough, or the bull to hunt, but set each animal to that for which it is by nature fitted; so, placing our finger on what is man's peculiar and distinguishing characteristic above other creatures, we invite him—born, as he is, for the contemplation of heaven, and being, as he is, a truly heavenly plant—to the knowledge of God, counselling him to furnish himself with what is his sufficient provision for eternity, namely, piety. Practice husbandry, we say, if you are a husbandman; but while you till your fields, know God. Sail the sea, you who are devoted to navigation, yet call the whilst on the heavenly Pilot. Has knowledge taken hold of you while engaged in military service? Listen to the commander, who orders what is right. As those, then, who have been overpowered with sleep and drunkenness, do ye awake; and, using your eyes a little, consider what mean those stones which you worship, and the expenditure you frivolously lavish on the matter. . . .

"For just as, had the sun not been in existence, night would have brooded over the universe notwithstanding the other luminaries of heaven; so, had we not known the Word, and been illuminated by Him, we should have been nowise different from fowls that are being fed, fattened in darkness, and nourished for death. Let us then admit the light, that we may admit God; let us admit the light, and become disciples to the Lord."

190. We get a vivid idea of the extent of early missionary activity in Africa when we remember that Clement was preceded by Pantænus and that Clement completed his own prodigious labors, of which we have spoken, by the year 202.

In that year he was driven from Alexandria by imperial persecution. But the work did not cease. A young man by the name of **Origen**, but eighteen years of age, was appointed his successor at the head of the training school. Origen became one of the greatest scholars and most voluminous writers the Christian world has ever had. One of his latest writings and the one commonly counted of the greatest interest in modern times was a missionary document, though much less directly so than the writings of Clement. A work had been written by one Celsus attacking Christianity all along the line so elaborately that unbelievers to this day have invented little that is new to say against it. Origen took up the extensive attack and met it point by point in a great work of 620 chapters entitled "Against Celsus." As many a self-supposed genius would have been saved needless repetition of labor already performed by consulting the records of the Patent Office, so many an upstart critic of Christianity might well have saved himself useless repetition of paganistic invention by first carefully reading Origen against Celsus.

191. By such colossal championship Christianity was firmly seated in Egypt. On that throne a little later "Athanasius against the world" wielded a scepter which to the present hour influences the thought of Christendom.

Christianity not only attained great depth and height in Egypt at an early date, but also wide extent. As early as the year 235 a council was attended by twenty bishops. This, however, was scarcely past the middle of the early missionary period in the land of the Pharaohs. The evangelization of the country seems to have reached a sort of culmination about the year 400, when the Emperor Arcadius granted one of the heathen temples in Alexandria to the Christians for a church. They opened up the secret sanctuary and made a public procession to display the obscene and ridiculous objects which they had found in the temple. The pagans were

FRANCIS OF ASSISI.

so incensed that they fortified themselves in the splendid temple called the Serapeum and dragged in many Christians, torturing them and putting them to a cruel death. This was one of the final outbursts of paganism. The Emperor transformed the Serapeum itself into a church.

In the seventh century the shock of Mohammedanism shattered, but failed to destroy, Egyptian Christianity. The Koptic Church still exists as an immovable, but also, alas! an immobile remnant.

192. Early in the thirteenth century **Francis of Assisi,** the Father of modern missions, made a brave effort to infuse a new tide of Christian life into Egypt. In 1213 he endeavored to go to Syria, and a little later to Morocco, but without success. In 1219 he sent to Morocco a devoted band of missionaries, who found martyrdom there. He, with eleven others, went to the Levant. Leaving a part of his comrades in Syria, he followed a crusading army to Egypt. In the very height of the hostilities there he made his way to the headquarters of the Sultan of Egypt. The perfectly transparent simplicity and sincerity of Francis were appreciated by the Saracen and he was allowed opportunity to present the claims of Christ in the midst of the camp of the followers of Mohammed. Here is an extract from a letter written at the time to friends in Europe by one of the crusaders:

193. "The master of these Brothers is Brother Francis; he is so lovable that he is venerated by every one. Having come into our army, he has not been afraid, in his zeal for the faith, to go to that of our enemies. For days together he announced the word of God to the Saracens, but with little success; then

the sultan, King of Egypt, asked him in secret to entreat God to reveal to him, by some miracle, which is the best religion."

194. Near the end of the period we are studying a more persistent missionary effort was made in Egypt. This time it was by the Moravians, who, the world over, share with Franciscans and Jesuits the honors of missionary zeal.

In 1752 Hocker, the same Moravian missionary who had been through such terrible experiences in attempting a work in Persia, undertook a mission to Abyssinia. For more than thirty years the Brethren endeavored to effect their object through Egypt as a base. Some of their experiences were highly heroic. But at last the attempt to enter Abyssinia was abandoned and likewise the base of operations in Egypt.

195. Since it was Simon of Cyrene who had the unique distinction of helping Jesus in carrying the cross to Calvary, we can but wish that we had some details of the early preaching of the cross in Simon's country. We only know that it became one of the earliest of missionary fields, and, it would seem, a radiating center of the missionary spirit. Without doubt some of the "dwellers in the parts of Libya about Cyrene" carried the pentecostal fire home. It is to the everlasting glory of this part of Africa that only eight years after Pentecost it was men of Cyrene, along with those of Cyprus, who were the first of the followers of Jesus persistently to preach the gospel to the heathen, which they did so effectually at Antioch that "a great number that believed turned unto the Lord." One of these early missionaries was Lucius of Cyrene. It

seems natural to think that his comrade in the work, "**Simeon that was called the Black**" was a man with much real African blood in his veins. The name, however, may have been no more significant of that than "Simon Black" would be now. But we know from Herodotus that the Greek settlers of Cyrene coalesced with the natives more than colonists elsewhere have done. We have seen that it was also a favorite Jewish colony. Whether of Greek, Negro or Jewish stock, the first missionaries outside the immediate apostolic circle were men of Africa.

196. Ethiopia, from the days of the Homeric mythology till now, has been a region of fascination and mystery. One catching glimpses of its ancient splendors appreciates the words of Purchas, the old English compiler of the "Relations of the World." After giving the titles of the King of Ethiopia running through several lines, he says: "Heere are names enough to skarre a weake braine."

The ancient capital of Ethiopia, a vast and indefinite region, was Meroe, the famous island in the upper Nile.

The later center of the country, so far as the history of Christianity is concerned, was on the lofty tablelands of Abyssinia which lie two perpendicular miles above sea level. As the kingdom of Meroe declined, the seat of the empire ascended to the highland province, where it has been enthroned ever since. Axum, the capital, was a great city in the early Christian centuries. But, independently of tradition and custom, the evidence of language is too strong to be questioned, showing that the Abyssinians are of Semitic stock, probably from Arabia, the land of the Queen of Sheba.

Whether the friendliness to Jeremiah of Ebed-Melech, an Ethiopian, is significant or not as to the relations of his country to Judea, is doubtful. But the prophecy of Isaiah is full of promise:

"Thus saith the Lord, The labor of Egypt and the merchandise of Ethiopia, and the Sabeans, men of stature, shall come over unto thee and they shall be thine; they shall go after thee; in chains they shall come over; and they shall fall down unto thee, they shall make supplication unto thee, saying, surely God is in thee; and there is none else, there is no (other) God."

197. It is known that for hundreds of years both before and after Christ, Ethiopia was ruled by a line of queens whose title was Candace. About the year 35 a high financial officer of the Candace of that day, who was either of Hebrew extraction or a convert of Jewish missionary effort, was riding in his carriage on a Roman road in southern Syria reading a manuscript of Isaiah as he rode. The prophet who made such glowing predictions about Ethiopia may well have been a favorite with the Israelites of that region. There came running to him a Christian missionary, whose name meant Lover of Horses, but who, like many another missionary, was on foot. The courteous courtier took the missionary to a seat beside himself in the carriage and learned a deeper meaning in Isaiah than he had ever been able to divine for himself. After some miles of this traveling together the royal officer begged the privilege of using for himself the emblem of burial with Christ and resurrection with him to a new life.

The record takes us no further, but that must have been a great day for Ethiopia. Let the imagination follow Candace's treasurer home to the lovely island capital on the upper Nile and see him there making known and spreading abroad the wonderful new life which he had found.

198. But it is nearly three hundred years to the next record of missionary history. Two young men from the city of Tyre were on a voyage with their uncle through the Red Sea. The ship touched on the African coast for water. The barbarians there, who had lately thrown off the Roman yoke, put to death the passengers and crew, but were touched with mercy at sight of the two boys whom they found studying their lessons, and took them alive to the king of Abyssinia, who soon discovered their gifts and made one of them, **Frumentius,** his secretary and the other, Edessius, a cup-bearer. The king bequeathed liberty to his two Tyrian attendants, but the widowed queen persuaded them to stay and educate the heir to the throne. Frumentius, finding himself in a position of great influence, encouraged Roman merchants to cultivate Christianity in Abyssinia.

199. When their royal pupil became of age they resisted all entreaties to remain longer and returned, Edessius to Tyre to visit his relatives, but Frumentius to Alexandria, to tell its famous pastor, Athanasius, of the opening for missions in Abyssinia. The mighty champion of orthodoxy had interests higher than the forming of creeds and was quick to seize the opportunity to extend the kingdom of heaven. He cut eccle-

siastical red tape and exalted this stranger at once to the bishopric, (338) sending him, accompanied by helpers, as missionary to Abyssinia. Athanasius wisely said, "What other man shall we find such as thou art, in whom is the Spirit of God, as he is in thee, who will be able to discharge these duties?" Frumentius became known as the Father of Peace, and through his agency Christianity was firmly established in Abyssinia. There it has stood for more than a millennium and a half, a veritable Gibraltar in the midst of great seas of paganism and Mohammedanism.

200. There are confused accounts of the planting of Christianity in Nubia not far from the same time, but we lack accurate history for the details of the work. We know, however, that Christianity flourished there from the fourth to the twelfth century. The King of Dongola did not become a Moslem till the fourteenth century. The work of Islamising Nubia was not fully completed till the sixteenth century.

CHAPTER XIII.

# NORTH AND WEST AFRICA.

201. Characteristics of early Christianity. 202. Tertullian. 203. Literary activity. 204. The Donatists. 205. Western version of the Scriptures. 206. Christianity's opportunity. 207. Islam's success. 208. Franciscans and Dominicans in Africa. 209. The conversion of Raymond Lull. 210. Lull's intellectual crusade. 211. His mission to North Africa. 212. His return from banishment. 213. His martyrdom. 214. The evangelizing of the Canary Islands. 215. Growth of Christianity there. 216. Maritime enterprise and missions. 217. Henry the Navigator. 218. His missionary motive. 219. The dark side of his enterprises. 220. Diego Gomez in West Africa. 221. John II. of Portugal sends a missionary expedition. 222. Work in Congo land. 223. Livingstone's characterization of Jesuit work. 224. Roman Catholic characterization of the same work. 225. French and Spanish missions. 226. Moravian efforts. 227. English and Scotch missions. 228. Jesuit missions in East Africa. 229. Madagascar.

201. Christianity was carried very early and very widely into North Africa, i. e., the part of Africa of which Carthage was the center. We know this from the fact that when definite accounts begin, only one hundred years after the death of John the Evangelist, there are already many churches with multitudes of

members and well organized ecclesiastical life in every important city and town. Tertullian says as early as A. D. 202 that in the cities of Africa the Christians were about equal in number to the pagans.

The propagation of Christianity there was opposed with extreme violence and attended for a long time by bloody persecutions. Twelve Christians at Scellium (Cosreen) are said to have been the first to lay down their lives as Christian martyrs in North Africa.

Two of the best authenticated martyrs in early Christian history are Perpetua, a young mother of high birth whose father repeatedly endeavored to persuade her to recant, and Felicitas, a young slave mother. With equal devotion high and low together preferred to be thrown to the furious beasts of the arena rather than to deny Christ.

202. The missions in North Africa were distinguished not only by rapid success and by great heroism but also by intellectual leadership. The first great name in Western Christendom is **Tertullian.** He was born in North Africa about A. D. 150. He was educated for the law. At forty years of age he was converted and became a Christian minister. He became, too, an advocate of the more spiritual type of Christianity, insisting on the presence of the Spirit of God in the hearts and in the minds of his people. Such an earnest Christian in the midst of heathenism was sure to be engaged in missionary service. Even before he was ordained he wrote an advocacy of Christianity, showing its great superiority to paganism. In it he expressed a thought which is constantly

repeated to this day as, "The blood of the martyrs is the seed of the church." So stated it is a misquotation in form, though not in fact. His actual words, appealing to the Roman rulers, were: "Go zealously on, good presidents, you will stand higher with the people if you sacrifice the Christians at their wish, kill us, torture us, condemn us, grind us to dust. . . . Nor does your cruelty, however exquisite, avail you; . . . the oftener we are mown down by you, the more in number we grow; the blood of Christians is seed."

These words are near the end of the "Apology," almost one hundred pages of vigorous, earnest, fearless, sometimes racy, always luminous and stirring, words. Of the forty works of Tertullian which have come down to us, three others are arguments with the heathen, "On Idolatry," "To Scapula," and "To the Nations." The last is as extensive as the "Apology."

203. For two hundred and fifty years the churches in North Africa led the van of Latin Christianity. After the most formidable opposition in her history old Rome had conquered Carthage. But now the countrymen of Hannibal were giving law to Rome. Tertullian **was followed by Cyprian,** Cyprian by **Arnobius**, and Arnobius by **Augustine.** The missionary writings of Cyprian were "On the Vanity of Idols" and "A Testimony against the Jews." On the border of Numidia southwest of Carthage was the town of Sicca Veneria. It was distinctively given over to the most debasing forms of paganism. There Arnobius was a popular teacher of rhetoric. He was converted to Christianity

and wrote "Against the Heathen," a work which makes a volume of 364 pages in the Anti-Nicene Library. We need not be surprised to find this teacher of rhetoric quoting or referring to 69 different writers of classic antiquity. His knowledge of Christianity was somewhat defective, but he was able to make an elaborate assault on paganism. These men of Africa were the chief teachers of the Roman Church. Augustine is, in fact, still counted the master mind of all occidental Christianity. Over the portals of Trinity Church, in Boston, are carved, after the four evangelists, Paul and Augustine. A third stone in the series remains uncut. There is no man yet who has wielded so wide a sceptre, both intellectual and ecclesiastical, as Augustine, bishop of the provincial town of Hippo in North Africa.

204. It has been said that one of the greatest achievements of Augustine was breaking the supremacy of the Donatists. They were the Protestants of the fourth and succeeding centuries in North Africa. They were more than Protestants, they were Puritans. They were more than Puritans, they were Baptists. None of these titles apply to them, perfectly, of course. They fell into many serious blunders, but they tenaciously held, in theory, at least, to a converted church membership. At their best they were not only more numerous and influential, but also more Christian than the Romanists there. These Donatists became the chief missionary force of North Africa working in the barbarian borderlands of the Roman territory,

often with great success, and even extending their missions to more remote regions.

205. One of the marked features of the evangelization of North Africa was the making here of the first translation of the Scriptures into a Western tongue. This old Latin version was the foundation of Jerome's rendering which became the Vulgate, *i. e.*, common version of Western Christendom, to which all later translations, till very recent times, were religiously conformed. The ancient and passing King James version in English, which is still so dear to many, savors of North African Latin as truly as it does of the original Hebrew and Greek.

206. In the height of Christianity's glory in Northern Africa there were 900 churches of Christ in that region. Oh, that they had understood their calling! If, instead of spending their chief strength in the theological and ecclesiastical arena, they had turned their magnificent powers to the evangelization of all Africa, instead of being still "The Dark Continent," it might have become the most luminous portion of the whole planet a thousand years ago. A favorite text with Augustine was "Go out and compel them to come in." His application of it was that the civil and ecclesiastical authorities should compel heretical Christians to profess orthodoxy. If he had only used this watchword of his in the missionary sense in which the Master gave it and instead of looking northward to the Bishop of Rome had yearned southward to Africa's millions, the history of Christendom might have become spiritual instead of ecclesiastical, and the Mo-

hammedans would not have found all the northern half of Africa so ripe and easy a prey before their overwhelming onset.

207. Even as it was it took Islam a long time fully to dispossess Christianity in North Africa. Islam conquered the Barbary States politically in the seventh century, dogmatically in the course of about 200 years after that. By the end of the eleventh century Islamism had begun to spread and take root in the Soudan. By the middle of the thirteenth century all the Soudan was under Mohammedan influence. In the next century it became well established in Darfur, the last of the great Soudan States to receive it. In Nubia Islam superseded Christianity during the twelfth to the fourteenth centuries. The king of Dongola became a Moslem just before 1350. The work was not completed till the sixteenth century. It took Islam nearly eight hundred years completely to displace Christianity in North Africa. The lost ground has never been recovered.

208. Early in the thirteenth century Francis of Assisi sent five missionaries to Morocco. Before the end of the century two hundred of these missionaries were martyred at the hands of Moslems. The Dominicans, Brothers Preachers, as they call themselves, arose at about the same time as the Franciscans. Dominic was exalted in later days. But during his real life he was not a great personality. Francis in his actual life embodied the apostolic ideal in a high degree and was the example that led Dominic to adopt the missionary

model for his order. Though Francis was the "Father of the Poor" and Dominic the "Hammer of Heretics," the early followers of the latter did not a little mission work for non-Christians, too, as their successors have done in the centuries since. They founded missionary training-schools at Murcia, Spain, and Tunis, Africa. They gave nearly as many missionary martyrs to middle-age Africa as did the Franciscans, all, however, to little avail.

209. One of the most striking of the futile attempts to reach the Moslems with the gospel was that of **Raymond Lull.** In an age of crusades and armed knights his was the knight-errantry of true evangelizing love. His father had helped the king of Spain to drive the Moors from the Balearic Isles off the Spanish coast and had been rewarded with lands on the island of Majorca. To that estate Raymond was born in 1234. He became seneschal of the island, but lived a dissolute life, embroidered with a dilettante interest in poetry. At the age of thirty-two, as he was writing a silly love song, the thought of the crucified Christ forced itself upon his mind. His passionate self-love was changed into holy devotion which controlled the remaining forty-five years of his life. The memory of Francis of Assisi was still warm in the world and exerted a shaping influence on the aims of Lull. If he never became a Franciscan, he worked as a layman in hearty accord with the purposes of Francis.

210. At last he secured from the king the endowment of a Franciscan monastery in Majorca as a

missionary training school. He had tried to secure from popes and other potentates the turning of all monasteries into that work. Meantime he bought a Mohammedan slave and spent nine years in learning Arabic and making himself familiar with Moslem literature. He also developed a new system of scholastic learning by which he hoped irresistibly to convince Mohammedans and other unbelievers. He went about again and again through Europe awakening an interest in this intellectual crusade. His writings are said to have numbered more than one thousand articles. Scores of them have come down to us in print and many still unprinted are preserved in various libraries. His system of learning seems artificial and fanciful now, but he secured a large following in the University of Paris and in other places where he gave courses of lectures. The Lullists made substantial head against the skeptical Arabic philosophy which had crept through Christendom. He finally secured at a council held in Vienne, France, a decree that chairs of Arabic and other oriental languages should be established at Oxford, Paris, Salamanca and Rome to fit men for direct missionary work among Mohammedans and other non-Christians.

211. But this great scholar and leader of thought was not contented without personally undertaking missions to the Moslems in North Africa. He had a terrible shrinking from the perils involved. He embarked at Genoa and then drew back. He seems to have done so a second time, returning in a fever of fear and shame. But at last he got away with a calm and

brave heart which dared everything. In Tunis he secured a conference with the Moslem scholars and teachers whom he hoped to convert by his irrefragible logic and who likewise hoped to convert him. The inevitable result was that he was thrown into prison and ordered to be beheaded. But one of the Moslem teachers, out of respect for Lull's learning and sincerity, secured the commutation of the sentence to banishment (1292).

212. After returning to Majorca he sought to convert Mohammedans and Jews there and later went on a mission to Cyprus and even to distant Armenia. But his heart was still in North Africa, though he was forbidden to return there on pain of being stoned to death. But go he would. At Bugia he openly preached Christ in the market place. He was cast into a dungeon, where he remained six months, using every opportunity to persuade the Mohammedan doctors of divinity to exchange arguments with him. He challenged them to write a defence of their faith. They esteemed him as a sincere fanatic and returned him to Europe. He suffered shipwreck on the way and narrowly escaped drowning. In Genoa he secured large contributions, 30,000 guilders, to equip another mission to North Africa.

213. In 1314 he landed for the third time and succeeded in restraining his zeal sufficiently to do a quiet work for a whole year, when he broke forth in open denunciation of Mohammed, and was stoned to death at nearly eighty years of age. This Majorcan Spaniard may have been somewhat Quixotic, but he was a

man of vast learning who believed in rational religion and in the conversion of the world, not by force, but by persuasion. Raymond Lull was a William Carey five hundred years before the Christian world was ready to understand and co-operate with him.

214. The Canary Islands were permanently colonized at the beginning of the fifteenth century, under the leadership of a baron of Normandy, **Jean de Bethencourt.** The conversion of the natives was one of the leading purposes of the conquest and colonization, nominally at least. Bethencourt took with him his chaplain **Pierre Bontier** and a Franciscan, **Jean le Verrier**. In due time, these missionaries were able to write "The Canarian, a book of the Conquest and Conversion of the Canarians." The following is the first sentence in their preface:

"Inasmuch as, through hearing the great adventures, bold deeds, and fair exploits of those who in former times undertook voyages to conquer the heathen in the hope of converting them to the Christian faith, many knights have taken heart and sought to imitate them in their good deeds, to the end that by eschewing all vice, and following virtue, they might gain everlasting life; in like manner did Jean de Bethencourt, knight, born in the kingdom of France, undertake this voyage, for the honour of God and the maintenance and advancement of our faith, to certain islands in the south called the Canary Islands, which are inhabited by unbelievers of various habits and languages."

215. In 1404 a native chief and his family were baptized.

"After this all in the island (Lancerote) came one by one to be baptized, both small and great; and therefore an instruction was drawn up as simple as possible for the guidance of those who were already baptized and for the preparation of those who by the grace of God should afterward receive baptism."

The "Instruction" which they drew up is admirable for the time.

The next year two other chiefs came for baptism, one bringing twenty-two candidates with him, the other forty-seven.

"From that time forward all the people came to be baptized; some now, some then, according as their dwellings might happen to be scattered about the country. . . They are baptized in a chapel that M. de Bethencourt has had built; and they mingle with his people and share all their comforts. The said Lord de Bethencourt has commanded that they should be treated with the utmost gentleness."

The founder of the colony further showed his interest in the religious welfare of the islands by visiting the Pope and securing the appointment of a "Bishop of all the Canary Islands." The man chosen was **Albert de las Casas.** The bishop

"demeaned himself so well, so graciously, and in such a pleasant manner, that he found favor with all the people, and was the cause of many great blessings to the whole country. He preached very often, now in one island and now in another."

216. The history of missions in West Africa introduces us to the most creditable feature in the great enterprises of the age of maritime discovery. Along with the love of money and of power there was not only a praiseworthy spirit of investigation, but a motive deeper still, the desire to extend the knowledge and blessings of Christianity to the pagan world. To Portugal belongs the glory of leading in the movement for finding the lost world.

217. **Henry the Navigator** might well be called the Apostle of Discovery, not only because his was the great pioneer spirit which initiated the opening of

maritime highways to four continents—Africa, Asia and the two Americas—but also because in doing it he had a genuine missionary intention. Though an Infante, *i. e.*, royal prince of Portugal, he withdrew from political life, except when needed as a crusader or a peacemaker, and devoted his princely resources of both mind and fortune to scientific study, map-making and exploration. He took up his abode on that southwestern point of Portugal which thrusts itself well out into the Atlantic Ocean, built there an astronomical observatory and dispatched thence his caravels, the best craft afloat, singly and in whole fleets during a period of forty years. He opened pathways and made them permanently frequented on the Atlantic westward and southward. Men commissioned by him rediscovered the Azores and colonized them, discovered the Madeira, the Canary and the Cape Verde islands, colonizing the two former groups, and, most important of all, crept down the African coast more than 1,300 miles beyond the point which had been believed to be the last which human beings could possibly reach. It was the impulse of Prince Henry which sent his countrymen around the Cape of Good Hope to India. The son of Columbus tells us that "it was in Portugal" that his father began to think that, if men could sail so far south, one might also sail west and find lands in that quarter."

218. The old chronicler Azurara, who wrote by command of Henry himself, gives five reasons for the Prince's earnestness in making discoveries, dwelling most on the last,

HENRY THE NAVIGATOR.
(In Mourning Dress.)

"The fifth reason was his great desire to make increase in the faith of our Lord Jesus Christ and to bring to him all the souls that should be saved,—understanding that all the mystery of the Incarnation, Death and Passion of our Lord Jesus Christ was for this sole end—namely the salvation of lost souls—whom the said Lord Infant by his travail and spending would fain bring into the true path."

219. It is true that Henry's men kidnapped the natives of West Africa, inaugurating the long and terrible ages of slave-raiding on that coast. We see the crime as no man perceived it in those days or for many a day after. But, however greed ruled the conduct of the sea-rovers who did the work, there is no doubt that Henry himself and many others were sincere in their belief that they were doing God and man a service in bringing the heathen to Christendom. It is said that they were generally well treated, frequently as if members of the families in which they lived. Most of them were brought into the church. Azurara's chronicle says near the end:

"At the commencement of this book I assigned five reasons by which our high-souled Prince was moved to send his ships so often in the toil of this Conquest, and because me seemeth I have given you a plentiful understanding of the first four, . . . it remaineth for me to tell you of the fifth reason, and to fix the certain number of the souls of infidels who have come from those lands to this, through the virtue and talents of our glorious Prince. And I counted these souls and found they were nine hundred twenty and seven, of whom, as I have said before, the greater part were turned into the true path of salvation."

220. The first glimpse of actual mission work in West Africa itself shows that Islam had reached the Cape Verde region more than four hundred years

ago. It is the account of **Diego Gomez,** one of Prince Henry's explorers.

"There was a Bishop there of his [the local chief's] own faith who asked me about the God of the Christians, and I answered him as God had given me to know; and then I questioned him about Mahomet, whom they believe. At last the King was so pleased with what I said that he sprang to his feet and ordered the Bishop to leave his country within three days, and swore that he would kill any one who should speak the name of Mahomet from that day forward. For he said he trusted in the one only God and there was no other but He, whom his brother Prince Henry worshiped.

"Then calling the Infante, his brother, he asked me to baptize him and all his lords and women. He himself would have no other name than Henry, but his nobles took our names, like James and Nuno. So I remained on shore that night with the King, but did not baptize him, as I was a layman.

"Then again on shore the King asked me to baptize him but I said I had not leave from the Pope; but I would tell the Prince, who would send a priest. So Nomimansa at once wrote to Prince Henry to send him a priest and some one to teach him the faith, and begged him to send him a falcon with the priest, for he was amazed when I told him how we carried a bird on the hand to catch other birds."

221. In 1482 an expedition sent by John II of Portugal landed at Mina on the Gold coast. The squadron of ten vessels carried materials, even stones and tiles, for building a fort and a church. Besides soldiers it brought a good complement of missionaries and two hundred workmen for building the fort and church. The young king had many discouragements presented to his attention by those opposed to his project. But he said: "If one African be thus converted to the faith, the threatening obstacles will easily be surmounted."

**222.** In 1484 Diego Cam entered the mouth of the Congo. He sent some of his men into the interior to find the king of the country and took four of the natives to Portugal. King John received the Africans with joy and sent them back, as Diego had promised, at the end of fifteen months, loaded with presents to their king and taking him an earnest request that he and his people would become Christians. On this trip Diego himself visited the Congo king and had the pleasure of taking to Portugal Cazuta, one of the chief men, as an ambassador, with the request that Cazuta and his attendants be instructed in Christianity and baptized and that missionaries be sent for the conversion of all the Congoese. After two years of instruction Cazuta and his suite were baptized, the King and Queen of Portugal standing as sponsors. In 1490 a large company of missionaries from Portugal accompanied Cazuta home. The King of Congo and his head men were soon all baptized along with multitudes of the people. But the missionaries insisted that a Christian man could be the husband of one wife only. The old African king thoroughly repudiated such newfangled notions curtailing his most cherished rights, and the people were mostly with the king. But he died soon after, and the Portuguese succeeded after hard fighting in establishing the heir Alfonso, who was disposed to adhere to the Christian teaching, as the ruler of the country.

From Congo Christianity was carried into many neighboring countries, such as Sundia, Pango, Concobella and Maopongo. The Negroes were charmed with the gorgeous pageantry which was a part of Christanity as presented by the Capuchins, but they rebelled constantly against the moral requirements.

223. Different religious orders worked in West Africa first and last. The Company of Jesus was perhaps the most efficient. David Livingstone, with characteristic breadth of view, gives them credit for greater permanency of results than is commonly conceded. He says, in substance:

"In Africa the Jesuits were wiser in their generation than Protestants. Theirs were large, influential communities, proceeding on the system of turning the abilities of every brother into the channel in which he was most likely to excel. One fond of natural history was allowed to follow his bent. Another fond of literature found leisure to pursue his studies. He who was great in barter was sent in search of gold-dust and ivory. While performing the religious acts of his mission to distant tribes, he found the means of aiding effectually the brethren whom he had left in the central settlement."

In another place, Livingstone uses the following language:

"It is now [1854] quite astonishing to observe the great numbers who can read and write in this district. This is the fruit of the labors of Jesuit and Capuchin missionaries, for they taught the people of Ambaca; and ever since the expulsion of the teachers by the Marquis of Pombal (1759) the natives have continued to teach each other. These devoted men are still held in high estimation throughout the country to this day. All speak well of them (as padres Jesuitas); and, now that they are gone from this lower sphere, I could not help wishing that these our Roman Catholic fellow Christians had felt it to be their duty to give the people the Bible, to be a light to their feet when the good men themselves were gone."

224. Roman Catholic missionaries themselves have pointed out the weaknesses and failures of the work

in unequivocal terms. Two of them are quoted by F. P. Noble as follows. Bæsten, a Jesuit of Belgium, says:

"The first conversions (1491-1549) were too precipitate. Insufficient account was taken of the difficulties against the lasting and sincere practice of Christianity."

One hundred years ago a Capuchin by the name of Zuccelli wrote:

"Assuredly the misery is great! Here is neither honor nor reputation, knowledge or conscience, faith nor word of God, state nor family, government nor civilization, discipline nor shame, polity nor righteousness, fear of God nor zeal for souls. Great as are the sins, scandals and vices this people commit every moment, you can never bring them to shame. You can say nothing of them except that they are but baptized heathen, who have nothing of Christianity save the bare name without works. Utter ruin impends over the land, the people, the mission. There is no wisdom, reason, policy, counsel; none troubles himself about the common weal. Civil wars, enmity, murder, robbery, superstition, devilish arts, incest and adultery are the people's and the prince's virtues. Deceit is in full vogue. As there is no fortified place of refuge, men hide themselves in the wilderness."

225. The French as well as the Portuguese sent missionaries to the West Coast. In 1635 five Franciscans were sent to the mouth of the Ossinece. Other bands of missionaries followed them. In 1701 Father **Loyer** was sent by the Pope as an Apostolic Prefect. He took with him a native who had been educated in France and baptized with great hopes, the King of France standing as godfather. But the convert proved faithless and the mission nearly fruitless.

The Spanish followed the Portuguese and French in missionary endeavor on the West Coast. In 1652 fifteen Capuchins were sent to Sierra Leone. They were reinforced from time to time and made converts and built churches.

226. In 1737 Moravians sought to establish a mission in Guinea. Five times they sent reinforcements, eleven missionaries in all, but all perished on the malarious field before they could get a foothold.

227. The missionary efforts of the English in West Africa before 1800 were not great. In 1751 a missionary of the Society for the Propagation of the Faith, **Thomas Thompson,** having labored five years in New Jersey, went to Cape Coast Castle on the Gold coast "for the sole purpose of converting the Negroes to Christianity." He remained only three years and baptized nine adult Negroes. But he failed to learn the language, and his quaint account does not leave a very happy impression as to his real missionary zeal. But he sent three natives to England to be educated. One of them, **Philip Quaque,** was ordained in 1765 and served as chaplain of the fort at Cape Coast Castle for more than fifty years.

In 1797 the Scotch Missionary Societies sent men thither. Guinea was a fatal field to all alike—Portuguese, French, Spanish, Moravians, English, Scotch.

228. The Portuguese entered Africa from the East Coast also and the Jesuits prosecuted missions from that side far into the interior. The most appreciative account of their work in the East as well as in the West is that of David Livingstone:

"Indeed, missionaries of that body of Christians [Roman Catholic] established themselves in a vast number of places in

Eastern Africa, as the ruins of mission stations still testify; but not having succeeded in meeting with any reliable history of the labors of these good men, it is painful for me to be unable to contradict the calumnies which Portuguese writers still heap on their memory. So far as the impression left on the native mind goes, it is decidedly favorable to their zeal and piety, while the writers referred to roundly assert that the missionaries engaged in the slave trade, which is probably as false as the more modern scandals occasionally retailed against their Protestant brethren. Philanthropists sometimes err in accepting the mere gossip of coast villages as facts, when asserting the atrocities of our countrymen abroad while others, pretending to regard all philanthropy as weakness, yet practicing that silliest of hypocrisies—the endeavor to appear worse than they are—accept and publish the mere brandy-and-water twaddle of immoral traders against a body of men who, as a whole, are an honor to human kind. . . . We cannot believe that these good men would risk their lives for the unholy gains which, even were they lawful, by the rules of their order they could not enjoy; but it would be extremely interesting to all their successors to know exactly what were the real causes of their failure in perpetuating the faith."

229. The Portuguese made some attempt to introduce Christianity in Madagascar early in the seventeenth century, but with no permanent result. Near the middle of that century French missionaries worked for some twenty years about Fort Dauphine. But they undertook to compel adhesion to Christianity by force. They were driven out of the country by the natives and their work disappeared.

CHAPTER XIV.

# SOUTH AFRICA.

230. Dutch rule in southern Africa. 231. The first governor's attitude toward the natives. 232. The destruction of Bosjesmen. 233. "Hottentots not admitted." 234. Formalities of religion. 235. Baptismal emancipation. 236. School regulations. 237. Appeal to the Moravians. 238. George Schmidt. 239. His reception in Cape Town. 240. Baboon Glen. 241. Boer resentment. 242. Late success. 243. Value of study of anti-missions.

230. Nineteenth century missions in Africa have had some brilliant successes. But the story of missions on that continent before 1800 is a sad one. In northern Africa it is a story of great achievements and great reversions. In western Africa it is a story of splendid but foiled intentions and endeavors. In southern Africa the story of missions is chiefly a story of anti-missions.

In their 150 years of undisputed opportunity the Portuguese attained no permanent colonies or missions in southern Africa. The English took possession of that part of the world just at the close of our period. A century and a half previous to the English occupation the Dutch held sway there, beginning in 1652.

By every right of humanity and of creed it ought to have been a century and a half of earnest evangelization of the natives. Instead of that, it was a century and a half of nearly unmitigated barbarism toward them. The early Roman Catholic misrepresentatives of Henry the Navigator in West Africa, and the modern Mohammedan slave raiders in East Africa, have neither of them surpassed the Dutch Calvinists of South Africa in brutal inhumanity. They hunted the natives down like wild beasts, organizing annual raids upon them called "commandoes." In 1774 the Colonial Government gave orders that the whole race of Bushmen not yet destroyed or enslaved be at once reduced to slavery or exterminated.

231. This was near the end of Dutch rule, as well it might be. But listen to the cold-blooded statements of the first governor, Jan van Riebeck, which show not only the hardness of his heart but also the great prosperity of the unsuspecting natives when the long process of extermination began, unprovoked except by greed. This part of his journal is dated December, 1652, according to Dr. A. C. Thompson's extract:

"The Hottentots came, with thousands of cattle and sheep, close to our fort, but we could not succeed in traffic with them. We feel vexed to see so many fine herds of cattle, and not to be able to buy to any considerable extent. If it had been indeed allowed, we had opportunity enough to deprive them today of ten thousand head; which, however, if we obtain orders to that effect, can be done at any time, and even more conveniently, because they will by that time have greater confidence in us. With one hundred and fifty men, eleven thousand head of black cattle might be obtained without danger of losing one man; and many savages might be taken without resistance, in order to be sent as slaves to India, as they will always come to us unarmed. If no further trade is to be expected with them, what should it matter much to take at once six or eight thousand beasts from them? There is opportunity enough for it, as they are not strong in number, and very timid, and since not more than two or three men often graze a thousand cattle close to our cannons, who might be easily cut off."

232. The raids proposed at the outset with such cold heartlessness were of frequent occurrence in later years. Almost one hundred and fifty years later Thomas Pringle, an eyewitness, describes one of them as follows:

"I still shudder when I think of one of the first scenes of the kind which I was obliged to witness in my youth, when I commenced my burgher service. It was upon a commando under Carl Kortz. We had surprised and destroyed a considerable kraal of Bosjesmen. When the firing ceased, five women were still found living. The lives of these, after a long discussion, it was ordered to spare, because one farmer wanted a servant for this purpose, and another for that. The unfortunate wretches were ordered to march in front of the commando; but it was soon found that they impeded our progress, not being able to proceed fast enough. They were therefore ordered to be shot. The scene which ensued often haunts me up to the present hour. The helpless victims, seeing what was intended, sprang to us, and clung so firmly to some of the party that it was for some time impossible to shoot them without hazarding the lives of those they held fast. Four of them were at length despatched, but the fifth could by no means be torn from one of our comrades, whom she had grasped in her agony; and his entreaties to be allowed to take the woman home were at last complied with. She went with her preserver, served him long and faithfully, and, I believe, died in the family. May God forgive the land!"

233. With such an attitude toward the natives prevailing from first to last, it is not surprising that over

the door of at least one of the Dutch churches should have been the notice, "Dogs and Hottentots not admitted." This is anti-missions consistently carried out.

But we must not be unfair to the Dutch in South Africa. They are not the only people known to history who have been keen in theology and punctual in ritual, while at the same time blind in sociology and wicked in political and industrial relations. We must credit them with being honest men and sincere Christians according to their stage of development. The most enlightened communities even yet are not far enough in advance of them to be unable to understand their attitude toward peoples counted inferior. There are said to be church doors over which is the notice—in hieroglyphics distinctly read by the people—"Social Hottentots not wanted here." There are many unmissionary Boers in various places.

234. When the Dutch took possession of the Cape they expressed the pious hope that "their rule might tend to uphold righteousness and plant teaching among the wild and savage natives of the country."

They took the pains from the start to have a careful observance of formal religion in their colony. Before the colony was counted large enough to have an ordained chaplain, it had a minister of lower ecclesiastical rank called "Comforter of the Sick." He was to read sermons on Sunday. One of the first ventured to offer some remarks of his own. He was severely called to order by the authorities through ecclesiastical headquarters in the East Indies, then in the Netherlands. The first white child born at the Cape of Good

Hope was a son of the "Comforter." But there appears to have been no thought of providing any comfort for the natives. They were counted merely as the heathen in the land to be dispossessed. These Dutchmen were as sound in their Calvinism and as pious in their everyday phraseology as were the Puritans of the same period in America. But they had no Roger Williams to seek the conversion and welfare of the natives.

235. This much, however, is true of them; if one of the blacks professed Christianity he was immediately freed and was treated in many respects as if white. The line of mere color was not deeply drawn in those days. For instance, a Bengalese slave girl of Admiral Bogært, having been baptized and liberated, was spoken of in the same terms as the admiral's own niece, "de eerbare jonge dochter." In the first sixty-six years of the colony 46 adult slaves and 1,121 slave children were baptized. But the law of baptismal emancipation was bitterly opposed and finally repealed. Ten leading South African Dutch clergymen in a document published for the English-speaking world in 1900 say that the law was repealed "on account of the abuses to which it led." But they refrain from telling what they mean by "abuses."

236. In another direction, however, these gentlemen by acquainting themselves with all the missionary facts in the early history of their church might have made a better showing than they did. It is to the missionary credit of the early Dutch at the Cape that their very first school was opened for the teaching of slave chil-

dren, imported from the West Coast, to say prayers and to repeat the Heidelberg catechism. **Peter Van der Stall** was the teacher. It was soon closed in connection with the great dispute about the baptism of the children of slaves. But not long after a school was opened for the children of the colonists, with a tuition of two shillings a month, but to slave and Hottentot children the schooling was free, "for God," as the regulations stated. The school began with seventeen pupils, four of them being slave children and one a Hottentot. Eva, a slave girl, brought up in the governor's house, was baptized. After a time she married a surgeon and explorer of the company. But later she proved to be very immoral. Experiences with this first convert may have had something to do with forming the missionary views and policy of the Dutch in South Africa.

237. The slight missionary tendency of the early days seems to have ceased by the end of the seventeenth century, for when the Danish pioneer missionaries in India, Ziegenbalg and Plütschau, stopped at the Cape on their way out in 1706, they found that the Boers did not permit their slaves to be baptized. The account sent to Europe by these men and other information as to the condition of the natives in South Africa at last stirred the conscience of devout men in Holland sufficiently to lead to their writing a letter about it to the young church of Moravian refugees in Saxony, who had four years before sent to the West Indies their first missionaries.

238. But seven days after the arrival of this appeal

at Herrnhüt, **George Schmidt** started for Holland on his way to South Africa. It took the Dutch more than one hundred years to ask some one else to go. It took the Moravians less than a week actually to start. The Dutch East India Company in Amsterdam appointed clergymen to examine Schmidt. They tried to convince him that it was dangerous and foolish to go. They said to him: "The language of the Hottentots is extremely difficult. They have nothing but wild roots to feed upon. What do you think of that?" His answer was: "With God all things are possible; and as I have assurance that it is the will of God I should preach the gospel to the Hottentots, so I hope firmly in him that he will carry me through the greatest difficulties." It was a whole year before Schmidt could get passage from Holland to the Cape. While he waited he supported himself as a common laborer. His book education was very limited, but he had already at twenty-seven years of age had six years of spiritual discipline by imprisonment for the sake of the gospel in Bohemia. On the voyage to South Africa he was able to lead three ungodly passengers to Christ.

239. On reaching Cape Town in 1737 the Moravian was received with contempt and derision by the colonists. But he found two natives who lived some fifty miles away, one of them speaking Dutch, who conducted him to their kraal. There he built himself a hut and laid out a garden. Schmidt, like Xavier, never learned the language of the people of his mission. The Hottentot language in addition to the ordinary sounds of human speech has many different

"clicks," some of them like the sound which we frequently make in driving a horse. But he taught them through an interpreter. His earnestness soon won to Christ a Dutch corporal stationed near. Some other colonists were converted.

240. His Boer neighbors in general were so hostile to him that they procured his removal to a wild spot ten miles beyond their frontier farms. In this place, called Bavianskloof, *i. e.,* Baboon Glen, he so quickly built a new hut and planted a garden that the natives were impressed by the lesson of industry. Eighteen Hottentots had followed him and others soon gathered about, so that he had a school of fifty to whom he taught the Dutch language and the Christian religion. After three years his first convert from the heathen was baptized.

241. When the news reached Cape Town that Hottentots were being treated as men and even as Christians the authorities were fully aroused. This was more than the Boers would endure. Some of the converts were sent for and were examined by the clergyman of the town. He found them able to read and to give an intelligent account of their faith. To his great credit, in view of the prevailing public sentiment, he expressed his satisfaction and his approval of the work. But the authorities were determined, and Schmidt was sent back to Europe. But he never gave up the hope of returning. He lived for forty-one years, praying daily for Africa. He was an evangelist, but most of the time a day-laborer. After attending church one Sunday when he was seventy-six years

old he went home, rose Monday morning, worked in his garden, then went in and knelt down to pray for Africa. In that attitude the Lord took him home as he took Livingstone long after.

242. George Schmidt, the first missionary to South Africa, in his six years there had the privilege of baptizing only seven natives. But fifty years later, when the Moravians were permitted to resume the mission, people were found who turned eagerly to the missionaries because their fathers had told them to follow the good men who would come to teach them the narrow way. One woman whom Schmidt had baptized by the name of Magdalena, now eighty years of age and nearly blind, came bringing a Dutch New Testament which he had given her and which she was carefully preserving wrapped in two sheepskins. Seven converts were now baptized the first year. For five years their place of worship was under a great pear tree which had been planted by George Schmidt. The name of Baboon Glen was now changed to Vale of Grace, Gnadenthal. But this renewed mission, at the end of the eighteenth century, was still meeting with intense opposition on the part of the Boers.

243. The story of anti-missions in Dutch South Africa is a part of the history of missions and not the least instructive part. The missionary spirit is simply unselfishness, generous regard for others, the disposition to share with them in our highest privileges. Its reward is richness of life, enduring life. Its opposite is selfishness, which is the very essence of sin, ending inevitably in self-destruction. For one

GNADEN THAL, SOUTH AFRICA.

hundred and fifty years the Boers refused to share not only Christian hopes and helps but even the name of manhood with the natives. If they had been liberal they might have built up a power of which they could not have been easily dispossessed.

The same selfish spirit working later in another direction refused to share manhood suffrage with the men who brought capital and enterprise to develop the country.

A generous fraternal policy might have unfolded the Boer republics into commonwealths of vast power and independence. As a result of the contrary disposition, at the end of another hundred years the land which was still in the hands of the Boers has been taken from them.

Thus, in the last quarter of a millennium, on virgin and propitious soil planted with seed from Holland, the best stock in Europe, the experiment has been wrought out to a finish, the experiment of living unto one's self, even the larger self of one's own kin and social circle. And sin or selfishness when it is finished bringeth forth death. Not only for individuals, but for whole groups of people, however well born and religiously gifted, the anti-missionary spirit holds within itself the germs of inevitable perdition.

CHAPTER XV.

# GREECE AND ITALY.

244. Alexander and Paul. 245. Distinction of the first church in Europe on record. 246. Hunting work. 247. One of the great plantings. 248. The nobility near Olympus. 249. In "The Eye." 250. At Corinth. 251. The Sacred Literature of the New Testament began in the land of letters. 252. Post-apostolic epistles to and from Corinth. 253. Recent romantic discovery. 254. Athenian philosopher's argument for Christ. 255. Paganism in Greece slowly expires. 256. Crete. 257. Record of missions in Italy meager. 258. First quarter of a century. 259. Paul in Italy. 260. Christians numerous according to Tacitus. 261. Days of Domitilla and Clemens. 262. Revelation of the catacombs as to the success of missions. 263. Missionary writings of Justin Martyr. 264. A conspicuous conversion by the power of the Old Testament. 265. Other missionaries.

244. To the new Troy which had arisen over the ashes of the old Homeric city came Alexander, the son, of Philip of Macedon. It was a moment when the ideality which was in him rose to high tide. He poured out prayers and libations to the Homeric gods. He had turned aside to make this his first act on the Asiatic continent. Then he swept on from victory to victory till Macedonian energy ruled the continent from the Hellespont to the Indus.

Nearly four centuries later an Asiatic of greater

MARS' HILL, TO-DAY.

ideality stood on a higher stratum of the same Ilium. Paul too was a man of prayer and libation. He too heard a voice calling him to continental conquest. He had no phalanx with him, but he plunged into Europe and organized a force of world-conquering quality out of the tested Macedonian material. In less than six months he could inspirit his little army with the fact of its already wide conquests. "From you has sounded forth the word of the Lord, not only in Macedonia and Achaia, but in every place your faith toward God has gone forth."

The Macedonian stream of energy eastward was physical and intellectual, observed of all men. The Macedonian stream of energy westward was vital and spiritual and went "without observation."

245. It was twenty-one years after the resurrection of Jesus that **Paul, Silas, Timothy** and **Luke** landed on the shores of Europe with the Good News. It had been brought to parts of the continent earlier, but this is the first recorded mission. It was Paul's second missionary journey. Luke, perhaps himself a Macedonian, had joined the party at Troas. Possibly it was after an earnest twilight talk with Luke that Paul had his dream there. It was a man whom he saw. But women were the first to receive the Message in Europe. Lydia, Euodia and Syntyche were the nucleus of Paul's first church in Macedonia, and they made it at once more than a mission church, even a missionary church. Lydia was so well-to-do that she could entertain the three missionaries in her home. We know not whether the jailor and the rest of the

young church had much means or not. What we do know is that within a month after their own organization they sent two distinct contributions to support missionaries in the regions beyond.

246. Paul and Silas are soon on their way westward. At the end of a three days' march they enter the metropolis of Macedonia, named after Alexander's sister Thessalonica. See them, footsore and dust-laden, tramping along the imperial Via Egnatia, the highway between Orient and Occident. It was the axis of the city when Cicero dwelt here in exile as it continues to be to this day.

As they walk wearily along the street, they stop at certain places of business. They are looking for work. At last in one of the alcove, cupboard-like shops the proprietor sitting on his folded feet engages them to work for a pittance in the haircloth goods of his trade and theirs. It is a season of scarcity. Bread is six times the ordinary price. Even with all the contributions from Philippi, they are obliged to make excessively long days, toiling over the coarse fabric far into the night. If some realistic artist would paint us the picture, our attention would be fixed on the central figure, his furrowed face and possibly troublesome eyes bending over the work of his roughened fingers in the light of a dim wick. It is well for the world that there was a Jewish traditionalism mightier even than Jewish greed. Every seventh day meant rest. Thessalonica is to-day one of the largest Jewish cities in the world and its Sabbath cessation is more than Puritanic. To Paul it meant not the opportunity for much-needed sleep, but the opportunity for pouring divine life into the moral stagnation of the Macedonian capital.

247. He had but one message to bring on the three Sabbaths of his opportunity, viz., the God-sent Life given unto men to the last extremity and yet victoriously alive in its self-giving. This is the Messiah for whom the world had been waiting, "Jesus, whom I proclaim to you." That message was fresh and radical then; in its reality it is hardly less fresh and no whit less radical still. The Macedonian mob of Greeks and Jews blindly felt the revolutionary truth and hit it off in aptest phrase. They divined that it was not simply one more myth, like the swarm of myths gathered about the snowy heights of Olympus yonder across the bay in front of their city—that it was not simply another doctrinal quibble of Jewish cabalism. Here was teaching which turned the whole selfish scheme of life "upside down." They cried aloud at the peril to Cæsarism, but they shook within at the blow to selfism. Nevertheless, a church of the disciples was formed. A few months after two short letters were sent them. Later one or two flying visits were given them. Such was the planting of the new life in Thessalonica.

From that day to this it has never utterly died out in that place. Convulsions of all kinds, seismic, racial, political and religious, have shaken the town. But Christianity has not only survived; it has from time to time made great contributions to the intellectual and religious life of the world, not least of which was rearing the men who became the missionaries for the conversion of the whole Slavonic race. The Mohammedans have ruled the city for 750 years; it still has several of the oldest and finest examples of early church architecture in existence. Many of them have been turned into mosques, but, for a wonder, the cross has not been effaced from their walls. Paul inaugurated a movement which made Thessalonica one of the mother-cities of Christendom. There in plain sight of Mount Olympus, the fabled seat of the Greek and Roman gods, he established the forces which were to drive those gods out of Europe and out of the world.

248. Everywhere Paul, though he was the special missionary to the heathen, began his work among the Jews and those whom they had converted from heathenism. In Berea, forty-seven miles southwest of Thessalonica, he found unusually open-minded Jews as well as Greeks. "These Jews of Berea were better disposed than those in Thessalonica, for they welcomed the Message with great readiness, and daily examined the Scriptures to see if what was said was true. As a consequence many of them believed it, besides a considerable number of Greek ladies of position, as well as men."

249. We find our missionary next at the most interesting point in all his wide contact with classical heathenism. His charming courtesy toward the ideas of the Athenians and his sincere appreciation of their religion are a matchless model for missionaries of all ages. "So Paul took his stand in the middle of the

CHURCH OF ST. PANTELIMON, THESSALONICA.

court, and this is what he said: 'Men of Athens, on every hand I see signs of your being very religious. Indeed as I was going about and looking at the objects that you worship, I observed an altar on which the dedication was inscribed, 'To an Unknown God.' What then you are worshiping without knowledge, is what I am now preaching to you.' " How gracious as well as wise he was a little later in quoting from some of their "own poets." Further notice of Paul at Athens has been made in our first chapter.

250. There were two great routes between Rome and the Orient, one through Thessalonica, the other through Corinth. Paul had planted Christianity in the Macedonian metropolis on the northern route. Now he settled at the Grecian metropolis on the southern route. He worked in Corinth longer than in most places, a year and a half. In addition to establishing a metropolitan church, his work here had missionary significance for other places. Here that able woman **Priscilla** and her husband **Aquila** were led into the work of Christian missions. They do not appear to have become in the strictest sense missionaries, but what is equally important, they were intimate friends and supporters of missions. We find them in that capacity later in Ephesus and also in Rome.

Professor Ramsay believes that in Corinth Paul's own missionary policy took on larger proportions and more definite plans. This development may have been connected with the deepening of his theology which seems to have taken place here. It may have been promoted also by the fact that the Proconsul, Gallio, a brother of the most influential Roman philosopher and statesman, Seneca, granted in Corinth a good measure of religious liberty and protection from Jewish persecution.

251. It was in Corinth that Paul penned his first letters, which were the first documents of the New Testament to be written. All his letters were called out by the exigencies of his missionary work. The needs of the recent converts in Thessalonica elicited the first two letters. Later, after a second visit to Corinth, the desperate needs of the Corinthians caused him to write four letters to them, two of which have been preserved.

Apollos, having been set right himself at Ephesus, did some good work in Corinth. "When he wanted to cross to Greece, the brethren furthered his plans, and wrote to the disciples there to welcome him. On his arrival he proved of great assistance to those who had, by the help of God, become believers in Christ, for he vigorously confuted the Jews, publicly proving by the Scriptures that Jesus was the Christ." But the Corinthian mission fell into bad ways, and Paul sent Timothy to help them out. Timothy failed. Then the apostle sent Titus, who had better success. Paul himself made a third visit to Corinth, remaining there three months. Then he wrote his great letter to the Christians in the capital of the empire. This letter speaks of a church at Cenchrea, the eastern port of Corinth. But for this incidental mention we should not know of this church. How many there were in Achaia unknown to us we can not say. Here as well as in Macedonia women were active. One of the officers of the church was **Phoebe.** She had been a most efficient fellow-worker of the missionaries. She was trusted with Paul's letter and was herself most cordially commended to the Romans. The events in Macedonia and in Greece proper which have now been narrated comprise about all that we know concerning missions in the land of Alexander and of Socrates They occurred between the years 51 and 58 A. D

252. Near the end of the first century Clement of Rome wrote a letter in behalf of that church to the one in Corinth. He compliments the Corinthians very highly on their Christian character. The second generation of Christians in Corinth must have been a great improvement over the first. But, alas! jealousy and discussion arose once more. Clement sums up the situation this way: "Every kind of honor and enlargement was bestowed upon you and then was fulfilled that which is written, 'My beloved did eat and drink and was enlarged and became fat and—kicked.'" Then follows a long letter of wholesome advice. It was so good that it was often read in the churches of old in the same way as the Sacred Scriptures.

In the second century Dionysius, a pastor in Corinth, wrote letters to churches in various parts of the empire, one to the church in Lacedæmon. This shows, what we can be sure of on general principles, that Christianity had spread into other parts of Greece.

253. In that century, when Hadrian visited Athens, (125) Quadratus and Aristides, Athenian Christians, presented to him memorials in defense of Christianity,

which are said to have modified his treatment of Christians. These precious missionary documents were both lost from the knowledge of the scholars for more than fourteen hundred years. But in 1889 Professor J. Rendel Harris found in the Convent of St. Catharine on Mount Sinai a veritable copy of the "Apology of Aristides" in Syriac. This led Professor J. A. Robinson to another thrilling discovery. There is a well known early Christian romance entitled "The Life of Baarlam and Josaphat," which is nothing less than the legend of Buddha worked over into a story of Christian missions. The Indian Prince is represented as inclining to Christianity when his father gathered a great assembly for public debate and appointed one of his sages to present the arguments for Christianity and to do it in such a weak way as to insure its overthrow. The sage began, and, as the romance runs, "like Balaam's ass he spoke that which he had not purposed to speak," making such a powerful argument for Christianity that he converted himself, the King, the Prince (Buddha) and all his people. Now it turns out that the wonderful argument which the sage recited is nothing else than the "Apology of Aristides," not all of it, but a very large portion. Hence we have—and have had all the time, if we had only known its identity—in the original Greek in which Aristides wrote it, his memorial to the Roman Emperor in behalf of Christianity, written at Athens only seventy-five years after Paul's address on Mars' Hill.

254. The first paragraph sounds almost like an elaborate echo of the profound thought of Paul:

"Here follows the defence which Aristides the philosopher made before Hadrian the King on behalf of reverence for God. . . . All-powerful Caesar Titus Hadrianus Antoninus, venerable and merciful, from Marcianus Aristides, an Athenian philosopher.

"I, O King, by the grace of God came into this world; and when I had considered the heaven and the earth and the seas, and had surveyed the sun and the rest of creation, I marveled at the beauty of the world. And I perceived that the world and all that is therein are moved by the power of another; and I understood that he who moves them is God, who is hidden in them, and veiled by them. And it is manifest that that which causes motion is more powerful than that which is moved. But that I should make search concerning this same mover of all, as to what is his nature (for it seems to me, he is indeed unsearchable in his nature), and that I should argue as to the constancy of his government, so as to grasp it fully,—that is a vain effort for me; for it is not possible that a man should fully comprehend it. I say, however, concerning this mover of the world, that he is God of all, who made all things for the sake of mankind. And it seems to me that this is reasonable, that one should fear God and should not oppress man."

Aristides proceeds to a searching analysis of pagan mythology showing up its deep moral degradation. He then advances as the main argument for Christianity its practical outcome in pure, noble, unselfish lives. For dignity, learning and practical sense the argument of Aristides was worthy of a successor of the great Missionary, even in Athens. As the old romancer fancied, the realities of this argument will yet supplant Buddhism and every other defective "search for God, if after all they might feel their way to him and find him."

255. But the overthrow of paganism is always a

slow process. As late as the time of Valentinian and Valens (375), heathen temples and festivals were still common in Greece. These emperors enacted stringent laws against them. A pagan Proconsul, more than three hundred years after Gallio's toleration of Christianity, had to solicit tolerance for heathenism. To the credit of the Emperor Valens it was granted. But not long after that the temples and customs of paganism fell into final disuse.

The University of Athens, however, remained in opposition to Christianity until it was suppressed on that account by Justinian I, A. D. 529, when its teachers fled to Persia. Evidently the word "pagan" did not always mean what its derivation signified, peasant. The conservatism of learning was sometimes equal to that of ignorance. But as a rule heathmen remained longest heathen. The Mainottes in the mountains of Peloponnesus did not yield to Christianity until near the end of the ninth century.

256. Christianity was planted in the island of Crete sixty miles south of Greece in apostolic times. "Some Cretans" were present on the Day of Pentecost. There are unmistakable hints of Paul's visiting six or eight different places during his fourth missionary journey, or series of journeys, of which no details are given. (A. D. 63-65.) One of these was Crete, or he could not have said in writing to Titus, "I left thee in Crete." Missions had been successful in planting the faith in a number of places—"appoint elders in every city." One of the letters of Dionysius of Corinth in the next century was written "to the church of Gor-

tyna and to the other churches in Crete." Eusebius says that in this epistle "he commends their bishop, Philip, for the numerous instances of fortitude that the church evinced under him according to the testimony of all, while he cautions them against the perversions of the heretics."

257. As we enter upon the history of missions in Italy, we are forcibly impressed with the fact that in the primitive days of human institutions men are completely absorbed in the work of founding them. It is only when they are well established that elaborate records are likely to be kept. The records of the life of Christ on earth were unwritten until from thirty to sixty years after his crucifixion. The four Gospels altogether record events occurring on not more than thirty-five days of his ministry. We wish that we could know some of the things which he said and did on the other thousand days and more of his public life, to say nothing of the ten thousand days of essential preparation.

This which is true of the beginning of Christianity itself is true of its introduction into every land. The history of missions was not written by those who alone could fully write it and we are the losers. Of no country is this want of records more impressive than of Italy. The land which was the very center of the Roman world and which was to be one of the chief seats of Christianity for many centuries was evangelized we know not how or by whom. The great historian of "Latin Christianity," Dean Milman, well says that "Christianity has ever more faithfully recorded her dissensions than her conquests."

258. A knowledge of Christ was carried to Rome not later than the year 30. On the 29th of May that year there were inhabitants of Rome who heard in Jerusalem "of the great things God has done." "Some of us are visitors from Rome, either Jews by birth or converts." Some of these "converts" from heathenism to Judaism doubtless received the message of Peter and were baptized that day. If they and others took not only a knowledge of Christ but earnest faith in him to Rome, then Christianity had been growing there for more than a quarter of a century when Paul wrote his letter to the Romans. During the latter part of that time many of his own converts and fellow-workers had gone to Rome. There were twenty-seven whom he saluted by name, giving some detail of personal acquaintance with most of them. The details show that they were his missionary coadjutors, beginning with "Priscilla and Aquila, my fellow-workers in Christ Jesus, who for my life laid down their own necks; unto whom not only I give thanks, but also all the churches of the Heathen; and salute the church that is in their house." There were probably more Christians in Rome at that time than could conveniently assemble in any one place. When Priscilla and Aquila came from Ephesus back to Rome they made their house one of the regular meeting-places of the disciples. One wonders if they were not Christian Jews when they left Rome in the time of the Emperor Claudius and whether they were sufficiently well-to-do to have owned a home there.

The well-assured strength of Christianity in Rome

is indicated by Paul's way of writing about his intended visit as being not only for work among the Romans but largely for the sake of making them a base of operations for his mission to Spain. It is also suggested by the massive character of the letter and is plainly stated in the words "your faith is proclaimed throughout the world."

259. Three years after his letter Paul reached Rome as a prisoner. On landing at Puteoli, more than one hundred miles from Rome, he was met by a group of Christians, showing that the gospel had been planted in Italy far from the capital. They persuaded Paul, **Luke and Aristarchus** to stay a week with them. During that eventful winter the party of missionaries had gained a great ascendency over Captain Julius of the Imperial Regiment, or he would not have allowed his prisoner to determine the length of the stay at Puteoli.

Once in Rome, Paul lost no time in beginning missionary work. "Three days after our arrival Paul invited the leading Jews to meet him." Having come to this first conference, "they then fixed a day with him, and came to the place where he was staying, in even larger numbers, when Paul proceeded to lay the subject before them. He bore his testimony to the Kingdom of God, and tried to convince them about Jesus, by arguments drawn from the Law of Moses and from the Prophets—from morning till evening." To those who rejected he quoted from Isaiah as to self-blinding and added: "Understand, then, that this Salvation of God was sent to the heathen; and they will listen."

Paul made such a defense before the court of Nero

that he was cleared. But it was a long process and the great Missionary used the intervals of time to the best advantage for his work. "Paul stayed two whole years in a house which he rented for himself, welcoming all who came to see him, proclaiming the Kingdom of God, and teaching all about Jesus Christ, the Master, with perfect fearlessness, and unmolested."

260. The next year after Paul's acquittal occurred an event which has given us a notice of Christianity from the pen of the great Roman historian Tacitus, including the statement that there was "a vast multitude" of Christians in Rome. On the 18th of June, A. D. 64, a conflagration started which ran unchecked for six days and left only four of the fourteen sections of the city untouched. It was believed to be one of the brutal freaks of Nero that he might rebuild the city on a scale of greater splendor and have space to open vast pleasure gardens for himself. Tacitus concludes the terrible story as follows:

"But not all the relief that could come from man, not all the bounties that the prince could bestow, nor all the atonements which could be presented to the gods, availed to relieve Nero from the infamy of being believed to have ordered the conflagration. Hence to suppress the rumor, he falsely charged with the guilt, and punished with the most exquisite tortures, the persons commonly called Christians, who were hated for their enormities. Christus, the founder of that name, was put to death as a criminal by Pontius Pilate, procurator of Judea, in the reign of Tiberius; but the pernicious superstition, repressed for a time, broke out again, not only through Judea, where the mischief originated, but through the city of Rome also, whither all things horrible and disgraceful flow, from all quarters, as to a common receptacle, and where they are encouraged. Accordingly, first those were seized who confessed they were Christians; next, on their information, a vast multitude were convicted, not so much on the charge of burning the city, as of hating the human race. And in their deaths they were also made the subjects of sport, for they were covered with the hides of wild beasts, and worried to death by dogs, or nailed to crosses, or set fire to, and when day declined, burned to serve for nocturnal lights. Nero offered his own gardens for that spectacle and exhibited a Circensian game, indiscriminately mingling with the common people in the habit of a charioteer, or else standing in his chariot. Whence a feeling of compassion arose toward the sufferers, though guilty and deserving to be made examples of by capital punishment, because they seemed not to be cut off for the public good, but victims to the ferocity of one man."

261. Before the year 100, the Emperor Domitian had his own cousin, Flavius Clemens, executed on a charge of atheism, the common charge against Jews and Christians who refused to worship idols, and the wife of Clemens, Flavia Domitilla, banished. Ancient inscriptions which have been found in modern times prove that Domitilla was a Christian. This was the period too when a pastor of the Roman church by the name of Clement wrote a letter to Corinth of which we have an undoubted copy.

262. About this time, the end of the first century, the Christians of Rome began to make the underground cemeteries called catacombs, a network of galleries dug through the soft rock with shelf-like alcoves for the bodies and occasional enlargements of the galleries where funeral services and other meetings could be held in times of persecution. They extended these catacombs as need required during nearly three hun-

dred years. After having been lost to view for many centuries these corridors of graves with their many hundreds of epitaphs, inscriptions, symbols, and even paintings, have been unsealed to give us the surest knowledge as to the wide extent of Christianity in Rome. Measurements show that there are now known 587 miles of these subterranean passages and that at the lowest estimate 1,752,000 Christians were buried in them before the year 400. Some archeologists put the numbers very much higher. But, judging from the lowest estimate, there must have been as many as 175,000 Christians living in Rome by the middle of the period of the catacombs, say 240 A. D.

The catacombs show not only that there were great numbers of Christians but also that many of them belonged to families of wealth and distinction. In Paul's day dependents in Cæsar's household were of the faith. Later, some of higher station became Christians. The first empress strongly to favor Christianity was Severina, the second wife of the infamous Elagabalus (218-222 A. D.). The Emperor Alexander Severus (222-235) put a statue of Jesus in his collection of revered men and had the Golden Rule inscribed over the gateway of the palace. There were, however, still to be, as there had been already, terrible persecutions before Christianity became strong enough to win full imperial sanction under Constantine (312). But then the capital of the empire was no longer in Italy.

263. While there is little record of the methods employed, the results which were surely attained show that there was an immense amount of earnest mission-

ary activity in Italy in the early days. One element in the process was the same as that which we have seen in Egypt, North Africa and Greece, the work of literary champions of the new faith. The best known of these in the early days in Rome was Justin, who gave up his life for Christ there (A. D. 163) in such a noble way that he has always been known as **Justin Martyr.** Having had his physical birth in Palestine, his intellectual birth in Greece or in Greek philosophy, and his spiritual birth in Asia Minor, he wore his baptized philosopher's robe to Rome and established himself there as an advocate of Christianity. He wrote two addresses to the imperial court. The first begins:

"To the Emperor Titus Ælius Adrianus Antoninus Pius Augustus Cæsar, and to his son Verissimus the philosopher, and to Lucius the philosopher, the natural son of Cæsar, and the adopted son of Pius, a lover of learning, and to the sacred senate, with the whole people of the Romans, I, Justin, the son of Priscus and grandson of Bacchius, natives of Flavia Neapolis in Palestine, present this address and petition in behalf of those of all nations who are unjustly hated and wantonly abused, myself being one of them."

Continuing, he points out the injustice, the folly and the vice of heathenism contrasted with the simple, pure life and the reasonable faith of Christianity. The two "apologies," as printed in English, cover seventy-seven pages. Justin's other great missionary writing was an argumentative "Dialogue with Trypho, a Jew." This occupies nearly two hundred pages. Justin was remarkable for his breadth of view and his generous appreciation of the religions which he was endeavoring to supplant.

264. A contemporary of Justin in Rome was **Tatian.** He had been through a similar course to that of Justin in respect of Greek philosophy and had dipped even more deeply into the heathen religions. Let him tell us how he was converted by the power of the Hebrew Scriptures:

"Wherefore, having seen these things, and moreover also having been admitted to the mysteries, and having everywhere examined the religious rites performed by the effeminate and the pathic, and having found among the Romans their Latiarian Jupiter delighting in human gore and the blood of slaughtered men, and Artemis not far from the great city sanctioning acts of the same kind, and one demon here and another there instigating to the perpetration of evil,—retiring by myself, I sought how I might be able to discover the truth. And, while I was giving my most earnest attention to the matter, I happened to meet with certain barbaric writings, too old to be compared with the opinions of the Greeks, and too divine to be compared with their errors; and I was led to put faith in these by the unpretending cast of the language, the inartificial character of the writers, the foreknowledge displayed of future events, the excellent quality of the precepts, and the declaration of the government of the universe as centered in one being. And, my soul being taught of God, I discerned that the former class of writings lead to condemnation, but that these put an end to the slavery that is in the world, and rescue us from a multiplicity of rulers and ten thousand tyrants, while they give us, not indeed what we had not before received, but what we had received but were prevented by error from retaining."

Tatian attended lectures of Justin and was accused before the authorities by the same enemy of Christianity, one Crescens. Though Justin and Tatian had so much in common, they are very different in style and tone. In his "Discourse Against the Greeks" Tatian is able to find no good in heathenism—with the possible exception of Socrates. He relentlessly holds it up to scorn.

265. Another literary advocate of Christianity in Rome was **Hippolytus** in the third century. He wrote many works. The titles of forty are preserved, eleven being commentaries on the Scriptures. Only fragments of his arguments "Against the Jews" and "Against the Greeks" are preserved.

In addition to the preaching missionaries and the literary missionaries there were—most important of all—the business men missionaries. Christianity was carried through Italy and the empire largely by the unordained Christians who commended their faith by their daily lives and their words.

CHAPTER XVI.

# SPAIN AND FRANCE.

266. Apostolic missions. 267. Early glimpses of Christianity. 268. The Council of Elvira. 269. Irenæus. 270. Martyrs for the truth. 271. Missions from monastic centers. 272. The Burgundian reception of Christianity. 273. Salvian's comparison of Romanists with Goths. 274. The conversion of Clovis. 275. The baptism of Clovis. 276. Conclusion.

266. "Having these many years a longing to come unto you, whensoever I go into Spain (for I hope to see you in my journey, and to be brought on my way thitherward by you, if first in some measure I shall have been satisfied with your company)—but now, I say, I go unto Jerusalem, ministering unto the Saints. . . . When therefore I have accomplished this and have sealed to them this fruit, I will go on by you unto Spain." Did the man pre-eminently known as the Missionary to the Heathen accomplish this purpose? Clement of Rome, who wrote before the year 100, says that Paul "taught righteousness to the whole world and reached the boundary of the West." The boundary of the West generally meant Spain, and Clement is a trustworthy witness. About the year 185 Irenæus speaks of "churches which have

been planted in Spain," and early in the next century Tertullian, in one of his sweeping phrases, speaks of "all the limits of the Spains" as believing on Christ.

The foregoing paragraph tells what is known concerning the evangelization of Spain. Each imagination must fill out the picture to suit itself. Spain was intimately related to Rome. Such Spaniards as Lucan, Seneca, Quintilian and Martial were counted Romans. Other missionaries than Paul, some of them perhaps before him, many of them certainly after him, made Christ known and loved to the "Boundary of the West." There are many and conflicting traditions of late origin and of no value as to the relations of the apostle James with Spain. Iago is the patron saint of the country. But for nearly two hundred years after Paul's day we do not find a scrap of history concerning missions in Spain or concerning Christianity there.

267. But it is certain that Christianity was spreading there during that time, for in the year 254 we get a glimpse of it in a letter of Cyprian of North Africa sent to Christians in Spain in answer to an inquiry of theirs as to a matter of discipline. He speaks explicitly of Christians in Leon, Astorga, Merida and Saragossa, places in the northwestern, southwestern and eastern parts of the peninsula. He mentions two ministers by the name of Felix and a deacon, Lælius, besides the two ministers under discipline, Basilides and Martial. His words imply that there were more than these, probably many more. The letter was called out, not by a question as to the propagation of the gospel, but by a question as to the treat-

ment of those who had relapsed into heathenism. But the record shows that the faith had been widely disseminated.

From that time on there are records of martyrs to the faith in Spain. It is impossible to separate fact from fiction in the accounts of them which have reached us. But there is no reason to doubt that there were of true-hearted Christians not a few who gladly gave up their lives rather than to deny Christ. The earliest and best accounts are in the poems of Prudentius, a highly educated man who became a devout Christian about the year 400 and sang the praises of the martyrs, thirty of them by name, some at great length. Eighteen of them belonged to the town of Saragossa.

268. About the year 305 a church council was held at Elvira, near Granada, attended by nineteen bishops and twenty-four other ministers, from various parts of Spain. The council passed eighty-one resolutions, all of which have come down to us. They show that heathenism was still rampant in the land, that persecuted Christians were strongly tempted to conform to some of the idolatrous customs, and that the churches were having a hand-to-hand struggle with the practical immoralities of paganism. But they show also that churches had been established a long time, were equipped with splendid buildings, and numbered among their members men of large wealth and of prominence in public life.

One of the bishops, the second to sign the decisions of the council, was Hosius. He became one of the most distinguished churchmen in the Roman Empire, the special counselor of Constantine, and probably the president of the Council of Nicea. Much has been recorded of him, but it is not a part of missionary history, except in one particular. It is a striking fact that the most eminent Christian minister that Spain has ever produced lived before the year 300 A. D.

269. We turn now to France. Among the earliest triumphs of the gospel of which we have record after the first century were those along the banks of the Rhone in southeastern France. Lyons and Vienne were the chief centers. Here **Irenaeus** became a great Christian leader and author before the year 200. He was a disciple of Polycarp of Smyrna in Asia Minor, who was himself a disciple of John the beloved. Lyons had been settled originally by merchants from Asia Minor. **Pothinus** a friend of Polycarp, was the first missionary whose name has reached us. He used the Greek language. But Irenæus with much pains made himself complete master of the Celtic tongue so that the gospel might take deep hold of the people at large.

270. By the year 177 Christians about Lyons were sufficiently numerous and active to bring down on themselves bitter persecution. The story of their heroism has been preserved by Eusebius in extended quotations from a letter written at Lyons soon after and sent to friends in Asia Minor. This is not like the apocryphal martyrologies of later time, but is acknowledged by all scholars to be an original and authentic record. We ought to cherish sacredly the names of these earliest known confessors of the faith with

their lives before European pagans after the days of the apostles. Those preserved are Vettius, Epogathus, Sanctus, Attalus, Blandina, Biblias, Pothinus, Maturus, Alexander and Ponticus.

Christianity had penetrated the land far beyond Lyons. At Autun, one hundred miles northward, the wave of persecution which swept Vienne and Lyons found victims. **Benignus,** a disciple of Polycarp, had carried the gospel there. One of the converts, Symphorian, a young native nobleman, refused to make obeisance to the image in a pagan procession. He was arrested, and on his way to execution his mother, a Christian, cried out to him from the walls: "My son, Symphorian, remember the loving God. Lift up thine heart and look to him. He reigns in the heavens. Be not afraid; it is not thy life they will take away this day. They will only change it for the better."

**Denys** of Paris was not Dionysius the Areopagite, as late legends aver, but a missionary pastor who suffered martyrdom in Paris about 270 A. D. Because it was in Paris he has been counted the patron saint of France. He was one of many missionaries of whose work we have no detailed knowledge who brought the gospel into Europe. There will be a great army at the final roll-call.

271. The most distinguished figure in western Gaul **was Martin,** Bishop of Tours. He was the first great promoter of monasticism in France. It was not only a contemplative but also an aggressive monasticism which he led. Like Loyola later, he had been a soldier before he became a Christian, and he went with his

company of stern ascetics throughout western Gaul overthrowing the monuments and temples of both Druidical and Roman paganism. In the last quarter of the fourth century he was instrumental in firmly establishing Christianity over a wide area. He was active to eighty years of age, when he prayed: "Lord, if I am still needed for thy people, I would not draw back from the work." His tomb became a shrine, and his words, "*Non recuso laborem,*" a watchword for missionaries in all western Europe.

On Lerins Island, off the southern coast of France, near Cannes, **Honoratus** founded and fostered a school which sent out many missionary workers. **Victricus** of Rouen, in the north of France, evangelized from that center far and wide, reaching by the year 390 as far east as Belgium.

272. By the year 400 A. D. Celtic-Roman Gaul had been extensively evangelized. Then the work of evangelization had to be done over with the foreign population formed over the country by the great Teutonic immigration. With the new race there came a new method of conversion, the wholesale or tribal method. The Burgundian was one of the early tribes to accept the Christian name. The quaint account of the ancient historian Socrates best tells the story:

> "I will now relate a thing worthy to be recorded which happened about this very time. There is a barbarous nation which have their abode beyond the river Rhine; they are called the Burgundions. These people lead a quiet life; for they are, for the most part, wood-cutters,by which business they earn wages and get a livelihood. The nation of the Hunni, by making con-

tinual inroads upon this people, depopulated their country, and frequently destroyed many of them. The Burgundions, therefore, reduced to great straits, flew for refuge to no man, but resolved to entrust themselves to some god to protect them, and having seriously considered with themselves that the God of the Romans did vigorously assist and defend those that feared him, they all, by a general consent, came over to the faith of Christ. Repairing accordingly to one of the cities of Gallia, they made request to the bishop that they might receive Christian baptism. The bishop ordered them to fast for seven days, in which interval he instructed them in the grounds of the faith, and on the eighth day baptized and so dismissed them. Being encouraged thereby, they marched out against the Hunni, and were not deceived in their expectation; for the king of the Hunni, whose name was Optar, having burst himself in the night by over-eating,the Burgundions fell upon his people, then destitute of a commander, and, few, though they were, engaged and conquered very many. For the Burgundions being in number only three thousand, destroyed about ten thousand of the Huns. And from that time the nation of the Burgundions became zealous professors of Christianity."

273. The Goths and some of the other Teutonic tribes were Arian Christians before they entered Gaul. In fact, though not in theory, they were as good Christians as the Romanists, according to the testimony of Salvian. Addressing his fellow Romanists, he said: "You think that you are better than the barbarians; they are heretics, you say, and we are true believers. I reply that in faith you no doubt excel them; but in your lives—I say it with tears—you are even worse than they."

274. The Teutonic tribe which gave name and nationality to the French had for a ruler Hlodwig, whose name was softened into Clovis and later into

Louis. On the death of his father, Clovis, though only a youth, was held aloft on a buckler by the rude Frank warriors in acknowledgment of his chieftainship. He remained a pagan till he was thirty years of age. Meantime he saw much of Roman-Celtic Christianity and allowed it liberty and protection. He married **Clotilda**, a princess of the Burgundians, who had already accepted Christianity, as we have seen. Clotilda was earnest in her Christian convictions. She insisted that their first-born son should be christened. The babe soon died and the superstition of Clovis attributed the death to the withdrawal of the protection of the heathen gods. He consented, however, though with extreme reluctance, to the christening of a second son. But he himself held firmly to paganism until one day he found himself confronted by an overwhelming force of enemies on a battlefield near Zulpich, Germany. Then he prayed to Clotilda's God to give him the victory, promising to be baptized into the name of Jesus. The leader of his foes died that night, leaving him a complete and easy victory. Clovis did not forget his pledge. He appears to have sent at once for **Vedastus**, a Christian minister, to come and give him religious instruction. On reaching Rheims, the capital of his dominions, he put himself under the tuition of **Remigius**, the Christian pastor there.

275. At an early day (December 25, 496) he acknowledged Christ in baptism. As the conversion of Clovis is counted the supreme crisis in the Christianization of Western Europe, let us have the account

in the words of Hincmar, an early successor to the Bishopric of Rheims.

"The way leading to the baptistry was put in order; on both sides it was hung with painted canvas and curtains; overhead there was a protecting shade; the streets were leveled, the baptistry of the church was prepared for the occasion, and sprinkled with balsam and other perfumes. Moreover, the Lord bestowed favor on the people that they might think that they were refreshed with the sweet odors of Paradise.

"The holy pontiff Remigius, holding the hand of the king, went forth from the royal residence to the baptistry, followed by the queen and the people; the holy gospels preceded them, with all hymns and spiritual songs and litanies, and the names of the saints were loudly invoked. . . . The blessed Remigius officiated on the solemn occasion. . . . Clovis having entered the life-giving fountain, . . . after confessing the orthodox faith in answer to questions put by the holy pontiff, was baptized by trine immersion according to ecclesiastical usage (*secundum ecclesiasticam morem, baptizatus est trina mersione*), in the name of the holy and undivided Trinity, Father, Son, and Holy Spirit. * * * Moreover, from his army three thousand men were baptized."

276. Clovis was ever a rough and ruthless warrior. Moved by the story of Christ's crucifixion, he exclaimed: "Had I been there with my brave Franks I would have avenged his wrongs." This is the noblest word that has reached us from his lips. But from his time on France was Christian in name, though not completely evangelized until many years later. There had been a long line of zealous missionary workers from Irenæus to Clotilda, whose names have faded from authentic history, but whose work has endured.

*J. Rigo.* THE BAPTISM OF CLOVIS.

## CHAPTER XVII.

# BRITAIN, IRELAND AND SCOTLAND.

277. Celtic and Roman rule in the British Islands. 278. Early spread of Christianity in Britain. 279. The legendary and the real Patrick. 280. A slave. 281. While escaping, doing missionary work. 282. Dreams and education. 283. Missionary conviction. 284. Opening work on Strangford Lough. 285. Tara, Killala Bay, Cavan and Armagh. 286. Of what church was Patrick? 287. Character of his writings. 288. Palladius, Brigida and other missionaries in Ireland. 289. The Scots and Scotland. 290. The White House mission on.. Solway Firth. 291. Strathclyde evangelized. 292. Columba and Northwestern Scotland. 293. Dunstan's tears and Northeastern Scotland. 294. The Dove-Wolf's great apostleship.

277. Every record of the early history of Christianity in the British Islands is of interest to all the English-speaking world. To that world, too, it is comparatively accessible in a great number of books on church history and to some extent in works on general history. Our concern at present, however, is only with the distinctively missionary aspect of the subject. Christianity came to England long before the English came, and it occupied a territory far wider than that settled by the Anglo-Saxons. The Celtic race, which

is still in possession of Wales, Ireland and Scotland, occupied all of British Europe at the beginning of the Christian era. The Britons of what is now England, came completely under the sway of the Roman Empire by the middle of the first century. It is possible that there were believers in Christ among the conquering legions of Claudius. Legendary history ascribes the first introduction of Christianity to at least ten different agencies, of which the Apostle Paul is one. There is no absolute proof of any of these legends.

278. As late as the time of Irenæus at Lyons, A. D. 185, there is no knowledge that Christianity had been planted in Britain. But by the year 208 Tertullian said that "places in Britain not yet visited by Romans were subject to Christ." Toward the end of the second century, then, missionaries, to us unknown, had carried the name, and, to some extent, the sway of Christ far afield among the Britons.

In the year 314 five British delegates attended the Council of Arles. A larger number appear to have been present at the Council of Ariminium forty-five years later. This is all that is known positively concerning the progress of the gospel among the Britons. Gildas, the first writer of British church affairs, draws a very pessimistic picture of the state of religion in his day, the sixth century.

It is commonly thought that the propagation of Christianity was confined largely to the Romanized portion of the people who lived about the centers of population and civilization. When the English invaded and settled the land, they destroyed or banished the Romano-Celtic people, civilization and religion, occupying all England anew with raw paganism. The remnants of Christianity were driven with surviving Britons into Wales. There, doubtless, missionaries had introduced the faith long before. There is a mass of legend about the conversion of Celtic England and Wales, but no trustworthy history.

Early British Christianity furnished Christendom one gifted man who made a profound and permanent impression on Christian thought, Pelagius. His relation to the general missionary history of the world belongs to a later chapter. But we have no details of his British life.

279. It is when we cross the Irish Channel that we come to the first brilliant chapter in the history of missions among the Celtic peoples of the British Islands. The conversion of Ireland was probably a fruit of the preceding obscure period, for the trend of competent judgment is that the apostle of Ireland was a Briton. The name of the birthplace of **Patrick** is given us in his own writings. But where it was scholars cannot be sure. It was probably near the present Kilpatrick, between Glasgow and Dumbarton. His parents and grandparents were Christians of the old British stock. Christianity had gained some foothold probably in Ireland long before Patrick's day. But he is the first of whom we have record to do a large and permanent work. It was such a phenomenal work that legends without number have gathered about it. But we have two writings which critics of

all schools are agreed in recognizing as from the hand of Patrick himself, his "Confession" or autobiographical sketch and his "Epistle to Coroticus," an expostulation with that British prince, who was possibly a nominal Christian, for allowing his soldiers to capture and sell into slavery many of the Irish converts. There are one or two other documents treating of Patrick's life which are of sufficiently ancient origin to be of real use in understanding the facts. Whether born in Gaul or in Britain, he had early Christian influences. The first sentence of his "Confession" is as follows:

"I, Patrick, a sinner, the rudest and least of all the faithful, and most contemptible to very many, had for my father Calpornius, a deacon, the son of Potitus, a priest, who lived in Bannaven Taberniæ, for he had a small country-house close by, where I was taken captive when I was nearly sixteen years of age."

280. He was sold into slavery and served Milcho, a chieftain in what is now County Antrim. His work was that of a shepherd and a cow-boy. In this life of solitary toil and exposure his religious nature developed into great intensity. He says:

"But after I had come to Ireland, I was daily tending sheep, and I prayed frequently during the day, and the love of God, and His faith and fear, increased in me more and more, and the spirit was stirred; so that in a single day I have said as many as a hundred prayers, and in the night nearly the same; so that I remained in the woods, and on the mountain, even before the dawn, I was roused to prayer, in snow, and ice, and rain, and I felt no injury from it, nor was there any slothfulness in me, as I see now, because the spirit was then fervent in me."

281. He dreamed of liberty and followed his vision

to the coast where, at first refused, he finally obtained a chance to work his passage. It appears to have been in a trading-boat which had for a part of its cargo Irish hunting dogs which were at that time highly esteemed in the Orient. After landing on the coast of Gaul the caravan had to pass through a desolate wilderness region, where it was almost impossible to obtain provisions. Some of the dogs perished by the way for want of food. This journey with pagan comrades proved to be the very missionary opportunity for which he had been longing. Let him tell the story himself:

"I hoped of them that they would come into the faith of Jesus Christ, for they were Gentiles; and this I obtained from them; and after three days, we reached land, and for twenty-eight days we journeyed through a desert, and their provisions failed, and they suffered greatly from hunger; and one day the master began to say to me: 'What sayest thou, O Christian? Your God is great and all-powerful; why canst thou not, then, pray for us, since we are perishing with hunger, and may never see the face of man again?' And I said to them plainly: 'Turn sincerely to the Lord my God, to whom nothing is impossible, that He may send us food on your way until ye are satisfied, for it abounds everywhere for Him.' And with God's help it was so done; for, lo! a flock of swine appeared in the way before our eyes, and they killed many of them, and remained there two nights, much refreshed and filled with their flesh; for many of the dogs had been left exhausted by the wayside. After this, they gave the greatest thanks to God, and I was honored in their eyes. . . . They also found wild honey, and offered me some of it, and one of them said: 'This is offered in sacrifice, thanks be to God'; after this I tasted no more."

282. Patrick was always given to dreaming, but any

vigorous young man of twenty-four, after days of scanty food followed by a bountiful feast of pork and honey, might have had the nightmare as he did. But it could have taken the Biblical form that it did take only in the mind of a man whose waking thoughts were filled with ideas from the Scriptures.

"But the same night, while I was sleeping, I was strongly tempted by Satan (of which I shall be mindful as long as I shall be in this body), and there fell, as it were, a great stone upon me, and there was no strength in my limbs. And then it came into my mind, I know not how, to call upon Elias, and at the same moment I saw the sun rising in the heavens; and while I cried out Elias with all my might, behold! the splendor of the sun was shed upon me, and immediately shook from me all heaviness. And I believe that Christ my Lord cried out for me; and I hope that it will be so in the day of my adversity, as the Lord testifies in the Gospel: 'It is not you that speak,' etc."

He hints at a number of thrilling adventures which he had in regions which we know had been and continued to be overrun by barbarians. He remained some years on the continent and probably there learned much of the crude Latin in which he afterward wrote. There are indications which point strongly to the monastic school of Martin of Tours as the source of his training, such as he had. As confirmatory of the reasons which scholars commonly adduce pointing to a relationship between Patrick and the school of Martin, we may note for ourselves the fact observed in the chapter on France, that the school of Martin was a hot-bed of missionary activity. Martin himself was noted for unflagging zeal to the end of his life. It must have been just before he passed away, if at all, that Patrick came in contact with him. Directly or indirectly, Patrick caught up the missionary torch which had turned the country people of Western and Northern Gaul from darkness to light.

283. From what we have learned of his nature and his experience, we can not be surprised at his vivid call to missionary work, at the method of the call, or at the field to which he felt himself appointed.

> "And again, after a few years, I was with my relations in Britain, who received me as a son, and earnestly besought me that then, at least, after I had gone through so many tribulations, I would go nowhere from them. And there I saw, in the midst of the night, a man who appeared to come from Ireland, whose name was Victoricus, and he had innumerable letters with him, one of which he gave to me; and I read the commencement of the epistle containing 'The Voice of the Irish'; and as I read aloud the beginning of the letter I thought I heard in my mind the voice of those who were near the wood of Focluti, which is near the western sea; and they cried out: 'We entreat thee, holy youth, to come and walk still amongst us.' And my heart was greatly touched, so that I could not read any more, and so I awoke. Thanks be to God that, after very many years, the Lord hath granted them their desire!
>
> "And on another night, whether in me or near me God knows, I heard eloquent words which I could not understand until the end of the speech, when it was said: 'He who gave His life for thee is He who speaks in thee'; and so I awoke full of joy."

284. Sailing to Ireland in obedience to the heavenly vision, Patrick landed first at Wicklow, but was driven off by the pagans. He sailed northward and entered Strangford Lough, in County Down, landing near the end of its southern arm. The local chief, Dichu, was won to Christ and gave the use of his barn to be

the first meeting-place of the disciples. The Celtic word for barn, Sabhall, has been contracted into Saul, which designates to this day the place, between Downpatrick and the shore of the lough, where stood the first Christian meeting-house in Ireland.

The missionary's heart yearned for the conversion of his old master and he went northward with that end in view. But Milcho utterly rejected the gospel brought by his former slave.

285. Patrick moved next on Tara, a stronghold of paganism on the plain of Meath. Læghaire was one of the most influential chieftains in Ireland. He had assembled at his capital, Tara, a solemn council of under-chiefs. On such a state occasion no fire was to be kindled anywhere before that on the king's own altars on Tara hill. Twelve miles northeast across the plain rose Slane hill. There Patrick on Easter eve kindled a fire. It was plainly seen at Tara. The sacred customs of the people were outraged and angry summons was sent to Patrick. But he bore himself so well in the presence of the ruler, that permission was given him to preach and Læghaire himself was converted, along with many others. Ten miles northeast of Tara lived a brother of Læghaire, who was converted. Like the wise missionary that he was, Patrick seized the occasion of a great gathering there for public games and sports to preach Christ. Numbers were converted.

It is certain from his own writings that he presented his mission work all the way across the island to the "Western Sea" near Killala Bay. After a time he was back again destroying the most sacred idols of the country in Cavan and founding a church at Armagh. There is no authentic account of his working in the southern quarter of Ireland. But, beginning about the year 400, he did for half a century the work of a pioneer missionary and founder of Christian churches and schools.

He was as truly the apostle of Ireland as any one man has ever been of a whole country. Without putting confidence in the statements of the precise number of thousands of converts assigned by biographers to one place and another, we have from his own pen a reference to spiritual sons "many thousands of whom I have baptized in the Lord."

286. It is a mistake for any modern sect to claim Patrick as belonging to itself—the Presbyterians because he ordained presbyters, the Baptists because he immersed, the Romanists because he established monasteries. All Christians had presbyters, all immersed, all believed in monasticism in those days.

The authentic records do not indicate that Patrick had any connection with the Pope or with popery, though doubtless he shared the common respect of the old Roman world. The modern Romish sect did not then exist. Patrick's grandfather was a married priest. There is no auricular confession, no adoration of Mary, no extreme unction in the reliable records of his life.

287. The most striking feature in his own writings is the frequent quotation of Scripture. The quota-

tions are from a translation earlier than the Vulgate. In the "Book of Armagh," which contains his writings and the other early accounts of him, there are besides only a life of Martin of Tours and a New Testament. This is the Latin Vulgate with the preface of Jerome, the translator, and is the earliest copy of the Scriptures in the British world. It is forever significant that the life of a preceding missionary and a copy of the New Testament should be bound up with the primitive accounts of the first distinguished missionary in the British Islands.

Among the documents about Patrick in the Book of Armagh is a hymn attributed to him, composed for a kind of Christian incantation against the sorceries of the heathen. It is possible that he wrote it. It is the oldest literary composition that we have in the Irish Celtic tongue and it reflects the simple Christian faith which Patrick planted. The following is a stanza out of the heart of it:

"5. I bind to myself to-day,—
The Power of God to guide me,
The Might of God to uphold me,
The Wisdom of God to teach me,
The Eye of God to watch over me,
The Ear of God to hear me,
The Word of God to give me speech,
The Hand of God to protect me,
The Way of God to go before me,
The Shield of God to shelter me,
The Host of God to defend me,
Against the snares of demons,

Against the temptations of vices,
Against the lusts of nature,
Against every man who meditates injury to me,
  Whether far or near,
  With few or with many."

288. Concerning other evangelizers of Ireland nothing definite is known. **Palladius,** was one of them. According to some traditions he preceded Patrick. He is often confused with Patrick. He probably came afterwards. It is quite likely that he had a commission from the Pope.

**Brigida** (Bridget, Bride) was born a few years before the death of Patrick and became the founder of many monasteries. In those days co-education was the rule. Monks and nuns studied, taught and lived in the same institution. A monastery was not one great building, but a collection of humble cottages around a central church and a dining-room-lecture-hall. It was more like John Eliot's Christian Indian villages. It was a center from which devoted men and women evangelized and educated the surrounding pagan territory. It was a university settlement. Brigida was the foremost woman in this work. But nothing authentic as to details of her work has come down to us, only a worthless mass of superstition-laden traditions. If we could have as much unmistakable record as we have of Patrick, we should doubtless find her worthy of the place which she has held in the Irish heart for fourteen hundred years.

Patrick and Brigida raised up hundreds, indirectly

thousands, of missionary workers who not only turned Ireland to Christ, but made it for one hundred and fifty years after Patrick's death the greenest spot in Christendom. It was freest from outside ecclesiastical domination and was also the brightest center of Christian learning. Best of all it became the great homeland of missionary activity for the conversion of pagan and of re-paganized Europe. In these particulars the England and Ireland of our day have exchanged places as compared with the early days.

289. Ireland was the original home of the Scots. Our Scotland was Caledonia. The Scots of Ireland gradually settled and dominated Caledonia, giving their name to the country. It was not till the tenth century that Scotia became the name of all North Britain. Scotland received not only her dominant race and name but also her religion chiefly from Ireland.

290. The first missionaries, however, were of the Roman Britons. The name of one of them, **Ninian**, has survived with great honor in Scotland. He appears to have been of a noble Welsh Christian family. His desire to visit Rome was granted. There he studied for years and was ordained. Returning through Gaul he visited Tours and caught the missionary fire from the aged Martin, who even supplied him with mechanics to build a church. This he did at Whithorn on one of the northern heads of Solway Firth. It is reputed to have been the first stone meeting-house in Scotland. It came to be known as the White House. Around it gathered the monastic village, which was a center of evangelization from about the year 400. The

results, however, seem to have been largely obliterated in the troublous times which followed the withdrawal of the Roman troops from Britain.

291. More than one hundred years after the death of Ninian another Welsh Briton, **Kentigern,** was ordained by a bishop called over from Ireland for the purpose. With Glasgow as a center Kentigern made missionary tours on foot through a wide stretch of country. He reclaimed the lapsed and preached the gospel to the unchristianized. Pagan hostility drove him out of the country for a time, but he obtained permission to found a missionary colony in North Wales. When political changes enabled him to return to the Kingdom of Strathclyde, he resumed his work there and became the leading personality in the permanent planting of Christianity in Southern Scotland. He left in charge of the work in North Wales one of his pupils, from whom the institution received **its name, St. Asaph.** Hoddam in Dumfries and Glasgow were the chief centers of Kentigern's later apostolic labors.

The event in the life of Kentigern which warms the imagination most is his meeting, about the year 584, with another aged and most revered missionary who was the apostle of Northern Scotland, Columba. These veterans of the cross are said to have met, each with a retinue of fellow-workers singing psalms of faith and victory. They embraced and kissed each other and held sweet communion together. Before separating they exchanged the staves with which they had made their missionary journeys.

292. **Columba** is the best-known missionary to Scotland. He was born in Ireland of princely stock on both sides. His great-great-grandfather was Niall, monarch of Ireland. On his mother's side he was descended from Cathæir Mor, King of Leinster. His high connections had not a little to do with his career. He was educated by the best teachers of Ireland. One of his schoolmates was Comgall, afterward the head of the famous institution at Bangor. Columba founded several monastic communities in Ireland, including Derry and Durrow. It was not until he was forty-two years of age that he engaged in foreign missions. Then he embarked with twelve companions in a currach, a boat of wicker framework covered with hides, and sailed northward to the coast of Argylshire, Scotland. Here, on the island of Hy, or Iona, three miles long and a mile wide, he founded one of the most celebrated missionary settlements of history, A. D. 563. It was near the borders between the Scots and the Picts. The former were nominal Christians. The latter, as their name signified, were painted savages. Among them Columba and his comrades went near and far carrying the gospel. They planted Christian institutions on the islands and the mainland up and down the northwestern coast, including the Isle of Skye.

293. They crossed the mountains and confronted King Bruide near Inverness. At first he closed his gates against the missionaries, but later he gave them a hearing and was himself converted. There was a decade of earnest work in northeastern Scotland, re-

sulting in the firm planting of Christianity there. One of the most efficient missionaries in the region of Aberdeenshire was **Drostan**, or Dunstan, a nephew of Columba. On the departure of his superior, who left him to prosecute the work in that wild region, Drostan wept so grievously that his tears gave name to the missionary settlement there, Dears or Deer. The name is a monument, not to the weakness, but to the heroism required to establish Christianity in the land of the painted barbarians. Drostan braved it out and planted churches all over Northern Scotland.

294. One of the rules of the missionary establishment at Iona was obedience "even unto death." So Scotland was conquered for Christ, to become a stronghold of the faith in ages yet unborn. Columba means dove, but the bearer of the name is said to have been given another name also at his baptism, Crimthann, which means wolf. His fond biographers say little of that. But he was a fighter as well as a bringer of good tidings of peace. He promoted more than one battle among the Irish clans. According to some accounts he was banished from Ireland as a result of one of them and enjoined by ecclesiastical authority to make as many converts from paganism as he had caused Christians to be slain in battle. As a matter of fact he was not banished, for he returned from time to time, and kept control, to the end, of the institutions which he had founded there in the first half of his life. He is said to have been of noble appearance. He certainly had the gifts of imperious leadership. He had also marked literary tastes. Late

in life he visited Ireland to attend a council at which the suppression of the bards who traveled in troops about the country was discussed. One of his favorite teachers in youth had been a bard, and Columba defended the order so well that it was not suppressed, but only restricted. At Iona he spent much time in writing, and made the copying of manuscripts a prominent feature of the work of the institution. The production of copies of the Scriptures and of other books for the numerous mission stations was an important part of the whole undertaking. The last work of Columba, after thirty-four years of magnificent missionary service, according to the methods of the time, was the transcription of Scripture. It was the thirty-fourth Psalm. He wrote as far as the words, "They who seek the Lord shall want no manner of thing that is good." At that point he said, "I think that I shall write no more." Between midnight and dawn of Sunday morning, June 9th, 597, he was found dead on the pavement before the altar in the church.

So profound was the impression of Columba and his mission establishment on the British Islands that for many generations all the kings of Scotland and many of other parts were brought to Iona for burial beside their great apostle.

CHAPTER XVIII.

# ENGLAND.

295. Sources of English Christianity. 296. The famous missionary puns. 297. England's apostle who never saw England. 298. The Roman missionaries landing on Thanet. 299. King Ethelbert's hospitable visit there. 300. Established at Canterbury. 301. The king's conversion and Gregory's joy. 302. Agency of women in the conversion of Teutonic peoples. 303. Edwin of Northumbria is well disposed. 304. Witenagemot to discuss Christianity. 305. Destruction of the idols. 306. The Northumbrian apostle. 307. East Angles, East Saxons, Middle Angles and Mercians. 308. West Saxons. 309. Celtic missionaries brought to Northumbria. 310. King Oswald Missionary Aiden's interpreter. 311. Earnestness of the Celtic missionaries. 312. Their wide work in England. 313. The great English apostle of the last of the tribes to be converted. 314. The South Saxons won. 315. Importance of the work.

295. Englishmen did not to any large extent receive the gospel directly from the Britons whom they had conquered. They either slew or enslaved them or drove them into Wales. The hatred and contempt were too great on both sides for any attempt to impart or to receive spiritual influences. After Celtic Christianity had made the circuit of the British Islands, it came down upon England from the North-

west and was at last the chief factor in the conversion of the Anglo-Saxons. It was from the seed-bed of Columba that most of England was planted with the gospel.

But before the germs from the North were sufficiently mature for transplanting, in the very year of the death of Columba himself, there was a noble missionary implantation from the south, from Rome through France. It was one of the notable providences in history. The English barbarians had slowly conquered the land and had settled upon it to begin a national development. It was time for this raw material of the world's best manhood to be leavened with spiritual ideals; for this coarse, rough energy to be charged, suffused, controlled by finer forces. The current of British Christianity was too much insulated to have produced the full effect needed. Then it was that fresh connection was made with the continent of Europe and directly with Rome, the central battery of light and of wide-sweeping power. Here was the accumulated storage of human civilization. The turning of its current into the formative years of the English nation has made the history of the world what it could not otherwise have been during the last thousand years.

296. The history of the mission of **Augustine** and the conversion of England has been retold so many times that it will be more useful and refreshing to most students to go back to the original accounts by the Venerable Bede than merely to add one more to the re-writings of it. We use the translations by

Mason and by Giles. The beautiful opening scene is related by the Venerable Bede himself with less assurance as to its historicity than is assumed in most of the repetitions of the story. He speaks with scholarly caution:

"I must not fail to mention a traditional belief concerning the blessed *Gregory,* with regard to the incident which first prompted him to take such pains for the salvation of the English. It is said that one day, when some merchants were newly arrived, and many articles for sale were collected in the forum, and many purchasers assembled, Gregory came amongst the rest, and saw, amongst other objects, some boys exposed for sale, with fair white bodies and attractive countenances, and with remarkable heads of hair. When he saw them, he enquired (so we are told) from what district or country they were brought. He was informed that it was from the Island of Britain, and that that was what the inhabitants were like. Again he enquired whether the people of the island were Christians, or were still wrapped in the errors of heathenism. He was told that they were heathens. He heaved a long sigh or two from his inmost heart, and said: 'Alas, the pity! that human beings with such bright countenances should be possessed by the author of darkness, and that such a graceful exterior should enclose a mind destitute of grace within!' So he enquired once more what that nation was called. The answer was, 'The Angles.' 'Good,' said he; 'they have the faces of Angels; and such should be made joint heirs with the Angels in heaven. What is the name of the particular province these boys were brought from?' The answer was, 'Ælli.' Playing upon the name, he said, 'Alleluia, the praise of God our Maker must be sung in those parts.'

"So he went to the Bishop of the Apostolic See of Rome (he was not yet Bishop himself), and asked him to send some ministers of the word to the English nation in Britain, to convert them to Christ, and said that he was himself prepared to accomplish the task, with the Lord's help, if the Apostolic

Pope should be pleased to have it so. As he was unable to accomplish this plan—for, though the Bishop was willing to grant his request, the citizens of Rome could not bring themselves to permit him to withdraw to such a distance from the city—as soon as he came to discharge the office of Bishop himself, he accomplished the long wished-for work; sending others indeed to preach, but helping the preaching to bear fruit, by his exhortations and by his prayers. This belief, received from ancient sources, I have deemed it suitable to incorporate in this Church History."

297. The forty Benedictine monks whom Gregory as Pope sent to be missionaries in England became so frightened by the accounts which they heard on the way as to the barbarism of the English, that they had their leader Augustine return to Rome "to obtain by humble entreaty from the blessed Gregory that they might not be obliged to engage upon a journey so perilous, so barbarous, so uncertain." But the determined and vigorous Pope enjoined them to lay aside their fears and do the work appointed. In order to pave the way and further their mission he wrote letters to bishops, abbots, a noble, two kings and a queen in Gaul. These and many other letters copied from the papal registry of letters put us on firm ground of history as to the mission of Augustine. Whether he had said in the market-place the bright, prophetic words attributed to him and later offered himself as a missionary to Britain or not, it is certain that, when Pope, Gregory the Great was the moving spirit in the mission of Rome to pagan England. The apostolic enthusiasm was his; the unretreating energy and the guiding brain were his.

298. In the pellucid narrative of Bede we see the self-respectful and at the same time liberal bearing of the first English king in meeting Christianity. The success of the mission was assured with such a reception.

"Fortified therefore by the encouragement of the blessed Father Gregory, Augustine, with the servants of Christ who accompanied him, returned to the work of the Word; and he reached Britain. There was at that time a very powerful king in Kent, named Ethelbert, who had extended the bounds of his empire as far as to the great river Humber, which divides the Southern English from the Northern. Upon the eastern coast of Kent there is an island, called Thanet, of considerable size—that is to say, according to the usual English reckoning, of six hundred families—separated from the mainland by the river Wantsome, which is about three furlongs broad and only to be crossed in two places: it pushes both heads into the sea. Upon this island Augustine, the servant of the Lord, came ashore, and his companions, said to have numbered about forty men. They had taken, as they were bidden by the blessed Pope Gregory, interpreters of Frank nationality; and Augustine sent to Ethelbert, informing him that he was come from Rome, and that he brought the best of messages, which promised with absolute certainty to those who obeyed it eternal joys in heaven, and that they should reign without end with the living and true God. When Ethelbert heard it, he ordered them to remain in the island to which they had gone, and necessaries to be supplied to them until he saw what to do with them. For it was not the first time that he had heard of the Christian religion; because, in fact, he had a Christian wife, of the royal family of the Franks, by name Bertha; who had been given to him by her parents on the understanding that she should be allowed to maintain without interference the system of her faith and religion, as well as a bishop named *Liudhard,* whom they had given her as a helper of her faith.

299. Accordingly, after some days, the King came to the island, and taking his seat in the open air he ordered Augustine with his companions to come and confer with him there. He had been careful not to let them approach him in any house, in obedience to an old saw, for fear that if they had any witchcraft they might, on their entrance, get the better of him and cheat him. But they, endowed with Divine power, not with that of devils, came carrying as a standard a silver cross, and a picture of our Lord and Savior painted on a panel; and as they came they sang litanies entreating the Lord for their own eternal salvation and that of those for whom and to whom they were come. And when at the King's bidding they sat and preached the word of life to him and to all his courtiers present the King replied, saying: 'They are certainly beautiful words and promises that you bring; but because they are new and unproved, I cannot give my adhesion to them and abandon what I have so long held in common with the whole English race. But as you are strangers and have come a long way to this country, and unless my observation deceives me, your desire was to impart to us also what you yourselves believed to be true and good, we do not wish to be unkind to you; on the contrary, we make a point of welcoming you with friendly hospitality, and of supplying you with what you need for your maintenance; and we put no hindrance in the way of your attaching all the adherents you can to your religious faith by means of your preaching.'

300. Accordingly he gave them lodging in the city of Canterbury, which was the capital of his whole empire; and, as he had promised, he supplied their bodily wants, and did not withhold from them leave to preach. The story goes, that as they approached the city, according to their custom, with the holy Cross and the picture of the great King, our Lord Jesus Christ, they intoned in unison this litany: 'We beseech Thee, O Lord, in all Thy mercy, that Thy fury and Thine anger may be taken away from this city, and from Thy holy house; because we have sinned. Alleluia.'

As soon as they had entered upon the lodging assigned to

CHURCH OF ST. MARTIN, CANTERBURY.
"The Mother Church of England."

them, they began to imitate the apostolic life of the early Church; serving God with continual prayers, watchings, and fastings; preaching the word of life to those whom they could reach; putting away all the things of this world as no concern of theirs; receiving from those whom they were teaching nothing but what was thought necessary for their life; themselves in all points living in accordance with what they taught, and having a mind ready to suffer any adversities, and even to die for the truth which they preached. To make a long story short, a good number believed and were baptized, wondering at their simple and innocent lives, and at the charm of their heavenly doctrine. There was near the city, on the eastern side, a church erected in old days, while the Romans were still in Britain, in honor of St. Martin, where the Queen, who was (as we have said) a Christian, was accustomed to pray. In this church the missionaries also at the outset assembled to sing, to pray, to celebrate their masses, to preach, and to baptize; until, upon the King's conversion to the faith, they received a wider permission to preach at large, and to build and restore churches.

301. Among the rest the King himself was charmed by the pure life of the holy men, and by their attractive promises, the truth of which they had confirmed by showing many miracles. He believed and was baptized. Thereupon larger numbers began to congregate day by day to hear the word, and forsook the heathen system to attach themselves as believers to the unity of Christ's holy Church. Thankful as the King was at their faith and conversion, it is said that he would compel no man to embrace Christianity; only he met believers with a specially close affection, as being fellow-citizens with him in the kingdom of heaven; for he had learned from the teachers to whom he owed his own salvation, that the service of Christ must be free, and not of constraint. He was not long before he presented those teachers with a place of settlement suitable to their condition in his capital of Canterbury, and conferred upon them possessions of various kinds which they required."

We are not left to imagination as to the joy of

Gregory in the success of his mission. He sent the news afar, writing to Eulogius, Bishop of Alexandria in Egypt, and to others. To Augustine himself he writes:

"Glory to God in the highest, and in earth peace to men of goodwill; because the grain of corn has died, falling into the earth, and has borne much fruit, that it might not reign alone in heaven. . . . Who here could express the gladness which has arisen in the hearts of all the faithful, that the English nation, by the operation of the grace of Almighty God and by your labors, brother, has had the darkness of error driven away, and has had the light of the holy faith shed upon it; that now with right devotion it tramples on the idols under which it formerly crouched in foolish fear; that it submits to Almighty God with a pure heart."

This letter continues at length and is occupied chiefly with insistent advice to the successful missionary that he is not to be elated overmuch at the wonders which God has enabled him to perform, but to keep very lowly in spirit. Gregory's letters to Queen Bertha and to King Ethelbert were as appropriate and as interesting as those to his missionary agent Augustine.

302. In the conversion of Teutonic peoples a marked place is occupied by women. It was Clotilda who led Clovis, "the oldest son of the Church" among the Franks, to accept Christ. It was Bertha who prepared the way in Ethelbert's heart and court for the reception of Christianity. Now as we cross the Humber to witness the conversion of another section of the English race, the Northumbrians, we find Ethelberga, the daughter of Bertha, an important actor. Her father had become the first Christian ruler of Kent,

the little portion of England settled by the Jutes. Her husband was to become the first Christian ruler of a much larger section of England, that settled by the English proper, the Angles. It had been agreed in the marriage contract of her mother that she was to bring from her Frankish home a Christian minister. Now it was stipulated that Ethelberga was to take from her Kentish home a Christian minister into Northumbria. **Paulinus** was the one chosen. He had been sent by Gregory in the second company of missionaries to Kent twenty-four years before this. He was well seasoned for the arduous work before him.

303. In the vicissitudes of the constant English tribal wars, Edwin, son of the chieftain of Northumbria, at three years of age had been carried for safety to Wales. There he grew up under the tuition of Christian teachers of the old British stock; but he refused to accept Christianity. After various wanderings and perils he won a decisive victory in the vicinity of Retford, A. D. 617, which put him on his rightful throne and made him a ruler over a wider realm than any Englishman had ever before governed. It reached north to the Firth of Forth, where he built an outpost, Edwin's burg (Edinburgh). Southward his suzerainty reached to the kingdom of Kent. It was into this great wild region, the first actual England, that Bertha and Paulinus came with the faith of Christ.

On Easter eve of the year 626 an envoy of the West-Saxons tried to assassinate Edwin. An attendant, Lilla by name, threw himself between the king and the poisoned dagger. The strong Saxon arm drove the two-edged knife through the body of Lilla so far as to wound the king. But Edwin's life was saved by the giving of Lilla's life. The same night Edwin's first child was born and he gave thanks to the old gods of the English. Paulinus wisely took advantage of this day of intense sensibility to urge the claims of the living God, telling the king how he had been praying for the safety of mother and child in the name of Christ. Edwin's heart was touched and he allowed the baby Eanfled to be christened, promising to consider carefully the claims of Christianity upon himself as soon as he should be victorious over the wicked West-Saxons. Eanfled and eleven more of the royal household were baptized at the season of Pentecost, the first in Northumbria. The fifty days had been sufficient time for Edwin's wound to heal and he at once set out against the West-Saxons, whom he thoroughly punished for their perfidy. On returning, Edwin kept his word and gave prolonged, careful study to the Christian teaching. We must have the rest of the story in the words of Bede, who belonged to this part of England, and took every opportunity to verify his facts.

304. "Still he said that he would confer upon the point with the princes his friends, and with his counselors, in order that if their sentiments agreed with his they might all be dedicated to Christ together in the font of life. With the approval of Paulinus, he did as he had said. Holding a Witenagemot, he asked them all, one by one, what they thought of this teaching, never before known to them, and of the new Divine worship which was preached to them.

"His head priest, Coifi, immediately answered: 'See to it yourself, O king, what manner of thing this is which is now preached to us; I acknowledge to you frankly, what I have learned beyond a doubt that there is no power and no profit whatever in the religion which we have hitherto held. None of your people has given himself with greater pains to the service of our gods than I; yet there are many who receive larger benefits and greater dignities from you, and have better luck in all their plans of doing and getting. Now, if the gods had any power, they would rather help me, their more devoted worshiper. The result is this: if on examination you find that the new things now preached to us are better and stronger, let us hasten to adopt them without any delay.'

"This advice and these prudent words were approved by another of the king's thegns, who spoke next, and added: 'Man's present life upon earth, O king, seems to me, when compared with that time beyond, of which we know nothing, to be like as if, when you are sitting at supper with your aldermen and thegns in the winter time, and a fire is lighted in the middle and the hall is warmed, but all outside storms of wintry rain and snow raging, some sparrow were to come and fly very quickly through the house, in at one door, and out at another. During the time that he is inside, he is untouched by the wintry storm, but when that little moment of calm has run out, he passes again from the winter into the winter, and you lose sight of him. So this life of men appears for a little while; but what follows it, and what went before it, we do not know at all. So if this new teaching has brought us anything sure, we should do well, I think, to follow it.' The rest of the aldermen and of the king's counselors by God's instigation followed in a similar strain.

"Coifi added that he would like to hear Paulinus speak more explicitly of the God whom he preached. When at the king's commandment he did so, Coifi hearing his words cried aloud: 'I saw long ago that what we worshiped was nothing at all; because the more carefully I sought for the truth in that worship the less I found it. But now I openly acknowledge that in this preaching shines the truth which is able to give us the gifts of life, and health, and everlasting happiness. Therefore, I propose, O king, that we should at once give over to ban and fire the temples and altars which we have consecrated to no profit.'

305. "To make a long story short, the king gave his adhesion openly to the preaching of the blessed Paulinus, and renouncing idolatry acknowledged that he adopted the faith of Christ. And when he asked the aforesaid high priest of his sacrifices who should be the first to desecrate the idol altars and temples, with the inclosures in which they stood, he answered: 'I. In my folly I worshiped them, and who rather than I should set an example to all by destroying them in the wisdom given me by the true God?' Immediately casting away vain superstition, he begged the king to give him armor and a stallion horse, to ride to the destruction of the idols; for the high priest had not been allowed to carry arms, or to ride anything but a mare. So he was girded with a sword and took lance in hand, and mounting the king's stallion, proceeded to the idols. When the multitudes saw it, they thought him mad. As soon as he drew near the temple, he flung at it the lance which he held, and desecrated it forthwith; and much delighted with the acknowledgment of the worship of the true God, he bade his companions destroy and set on fire the temple and all its inclosures. The place—the former place of idols—is shown not far from York, toward the east, the other side of the river Derwent, and is now called Goodmanham, where the high priest, by inspiration of the true God, defiled and destroyed 'the altars which he had himself consecrated.'

"So King Edwin received the faith and the laver of holy regeneration, together with all the nobles of his nation and a very great number of the people, in the eleventh year of his reign, which is the year of the Lord's Incarnation, 627, about the one hundred and eightieth year from the arrival of the English in Britain. He was christened at York, on the holy day of Easter, April 12, in the church of the Apostle Peter, which he built there hastily of wood, while he was a catechumen under instruction for his baptism."

306. Paulinus and his assistants evangelized Northumbria in both its northern and southern provinces.

"The fervor of faith and the desire for the saving laver is said to have been so great at that time in the Northumbrian people that on one occasion when Paulinus came with the king and queen to the king's abode, called At Veverin, he was detained there with them for six and thirty days, engaged in the work of catechising and baptizing; and on these days he did nothing else all day from morning till evening, but to instruct the people, who flocked to him from all the villages and places round, in Christ's word of salvation, and after the instruction to wash them with the laver of remission in the river Glen hard by. . . . .

"This was what happened in the province of Bernicia; in that of Deira, where he often stayed with the king, he used to baptize in the river Swale, which flows by the village of Catterick. For the Church in those parts was only beginning to come into existence, and they had not been able to build chapels or baptisteries. However, at Donfield, where the king's abode then was, he made a basilica."

The mission was pressed even south of the Humber.

"In regard to the conversion of this province I was told by a presbyter and abbot of the monastery of Partney, a man of great accuracy of statement, named Deda, that he had been informed by an elderly man that he had been baptized in the middle of the day by Bishop Paulinus, in the presence of King Edwin, and with him a multitude of people, in the river Trent, near a city which is called in English Tiowulfingcaster. This old man used also to describe the appearance of Paulinus, that he was a man of tall stature, somewhat bent, with black hair, and spare face, and a very thin, hooked nose, looking at the same time venerable and formidable. He had with him as his assistant James the deacon, a truly indefatigable man, and renowned in Christ and in the Church, who survived to our own times."

307. The mission in Northumbria met with a severe backset when Edwin was slain and his kingdom overrun by inland pagan tribes of English. The mission in Kent had had reverses on the death of Ethelbert. The christianization of the other Anglo-Saxon tribes was marked by many ups and downs. The chief early missionaries among the East Angles were **Felix** of Burgundy and **Fursey** of Ireland. **Cedd** was an apostle among the East Saxons. The Middle Angles were evangelized largely by Celtic workers, of whom **Diuma** and **Ceolloch** were leaders. The Angles who had settled farthest in the interior of central England were called, not West Angles, as we might expect from the other names current, but instead Mercians, *i. e.*, Bordermen. They had for king a long time a vigorous warrior and ruler, Penda. He was a bulwark against Christianity. But in his old age even Penda allowed missionaries to work among his people, declaring that his only real hatred was against those who did not live up to the new religion, "who put their faith in this new God and then did not trouble themselves to obey his commands." The Middle Angles were under his sway and it was their missionaries who worked among the Mercians proper.

308. In southern England the West Saxons were first evangelized by **Birinus**, who had been sent by Pope Honorius to carry the gospel into sections where it had not yet spread. King Cynegils accepted the faith, but his son and successor, Coinwalch, rejected it. He was married to Penda's sister. When he put her away, Penda was enraged and expelled him from his king-

dom. While in exile among the East Saxons he was converted. Later he regained his kingdom and forwarded there the missionary work of **Agilbert,** a Frenchman who "had lived a long time in Ireland for the purpose of reading the Scriptures" and "came of his own accord to serve this king and preach to him the word of life."

309. Agilbert's connection with Ireland brings before us again the Celtic influence in the conversion of England. After the overthrow of Edwin by pagans, Paulinus fled southward with Queen Ethelberga, and Christianity suffered a great decline among the half-converted Northumbrians. But after two short pagan reigns, Oswald came to the throne. He had been many years an exile and had been much in contact with the Scot-Irish mission at Iona, where he was baptized. Listen once more to Bede, whose testimony is the more impressive because he was himself in favor of the Roman as contrasted with the Celtic form of Christianity.

"Oswald, as soon as he ascended the throne, being desirous that all his nation should receive the Christian faith, whereof he had found happy experience in vanquishing the barbarians, sent to the elders of the Scots, among whom himself and his followers, when in banishment, had received the sacrament of baptism, desiring they would send him a bishop, by whose instruction and ministry the English nation, which he governed, might be taught the advantages, and receive the sacraments of the Christian faith.

It is reported that when King Oswald had asked a bishop of the Scots to administer the word of faith to him and his nation, there was first sent to him another man of more austere disposition, who, meeting with no success, and being unregarded by the English people, returned home, and in an assembly of the elders reported that he had not been able to do any good to the nation he had been sent to preach to, because they were uncivilized men, and of a stubborn and barbarous disposition. They, as is testified, in a great council, seriously debated what was to be done, being desirous that the nation should receive the salvation it demanded, and grieving that they had not received the preacher sent to them. Then said *Aiden*, who was also present in the council, to the priest then spoken of, 'I am of opinion, brother, that you were more severe to your unlearned hearers than you ought to have been, and did not at first, conformably to the apostolic rule, give them the milk of more easy doctrine, till being by degrees nourished with the word of God, they should be capable of greater perfection and be able to practice God's sublimer precepts.' Having heard these words, all present began diligently to weigh what he had said, and presently concluded that he deserved to be made a bishop, and ought to be sent to instruct the incredulous and unlearned; since he was found to be endued with singular discretion, which is the mother of the other virtues, and accordingly being ordained, they sent him to their friend, King Oswald, to preach.

310. "On the arrival of the bishop, the king appointed him his episcopal see in the isle of Lindisfarne, as he desired. Which place, as the tide flows and ebbs twice a day is enclosed by the waves of the sea like an island; and again, twice in the day, when the shore is left dry, becomes contiguous to the land. The king also humbly and willingly in all cases giving ear to his admonitions, industriously applied himself to build and extend the Church of Christ in his kingdom; wherein, when the bishop, who was not skilful in the English tongue, preached the gospel, it was most delightful to see the king himself interpreting the word of God to his commanders and ministers, for he had perfectly learned the language of the Scots during his long banishment. From that time many of the Scots came daily into Britain, and with great devotion preached the word to those provinces of the English over which King Oswald reigned, and those among them that had received priest's

orders administered to them the grace of baptism. Churches were built in several places; the people joyfully flocked together to hear the word; money and lands were given of the king's bounty to build monasteries; the English, great and small, were, by their Scottish masters, instructed in the rules and observance of regular discipline; for most of them that came to preach were monks. Bishop Aiden was himself a monk of the island called Hii, whose monastery was for a long time the chief of almost all those of the northern Scots, and all those of the Picts, and had the direction of their people."

311. The unmistakable earnestness of the Celtic missionaries and their close attachment to the Scriptures gave them great moral power as missionaries. They went everywhere preaching, not Christ and Rome, or Canterbury, but Christ and the Scriptures. The final subjugation of Northumbria to Christ was largely due to them. As in Ireland and Scotland, so-called monasteries, social settlements, were the dynamos of enlightening, christianizing power. Sometimes the head worker of a settlement was a woman. One of the most efficient of these was **Hilda**. Some of the leading ministers were educated in the establishment at Whitby, over which she presided.

312. The work of the Celtic missionaries was not confined to Northumbria, but extended through all the petty kingdoms of the Angles and the Saxons. Hodden and Stubbs, the learned editors of the original documents of early English history, say that "the whole of England, except Kent, East Anglia, Wessex and Sussex, was, at the beginning of A. D. 664, attached to the Scottish communion, and Wessex was under a Bishop, Wine, ordained in Gaul and in communion

with British bishops. Sussex was still heathen. So that Kent and East Anglia alone remained completely in communion with both Rome and Canterbury." In the year just named, however, a council was convened at Whitby in which it was concluded that the Roman ritual should be the standard. It ought to be an impressive lesson to those who are denied the privilege of being foreign missionaries themselves, that the two men who were most efficient in bringing about the conversion of England were men who never saw that country themselves, Columba and Gregory. It is a suggestive fact that only one of these two exercised his ministry in a metropolis; the other lived in a most out-of-the-way corner of the world.

313. The last of the Anglo-Saxon kingdoms to accept Christianity was that of the South Saxons. They were largely cut off from their fellows by the vast region of Andredesweald, "wood of the uninhabited district." A great section of it is known still as the Weald. It marked the progress of missions in England that their apostle was an Englishman. The king and queen had been converted some time before by the influence of royal acquaintances in the regions north. At their invitation some Irish missionaries, with **Dicul** at the head, had established a small missionary settlement. But they were not able to win many converts.

There is no more stirring story in early English Church history than that of **Wilfrid** of Northumbria. Of high birth and captivating manners he had an early ambition to be educated in Rome. An unkind step-mother had driven him from home. But the first child to be christened in Northumbria was now queen of that country. Queen Eanfled befriended young Wilfrid and sent him first to Lindisfarne, where he proved a very apt scholar, learning the whole Psalter in the translation made by Jerome in Bethlehem. She then provided for his journey to Rome. On the way he learned at Canterbury another version of the Psalter made by Jerome five years earlier in Rome. At Lyons in France Wilfrid was so popular with the Bishop, Annemund, that the latter endeavored to persuade him to give up monastic life and marry his niece, the daughter of the count of the city. But the young man continued after a time his journey to Rome. On his return to Northumbria Wilfrid became the chief champion of Rome in the Council of Whitby and was made the Archbishop of York. British missionaries had been defeated and had many of them withdrawn to Iona. But other ecclesiastical and political complications arose hostile to Wilfrid. He appealed to Rome and went there again and again, always to be indorsed. But the independent Northumbrian kings and churchmen often refused to obey Rome. Wilfrid was imprisoned under severe jailors and was repeatedly in forced or voluntary exile. But he was full of unresting energy. At one time in Frisia (Holland) he was instrumental in the conversion of hundreds from heathenism to Christianity.

314. In 681, finding no comfort among the Christian tribes of England, he made his way to the South Saxon pagans. They had been suffering from terrible famine. Many had drowned themselves to es-

cape their misery. Forty or fifty at one time, holding each other's hands, had flung themselves over the cliffs into the sea. So low was their state of civilization that they had not even learned to fish. Wilfrid, the refined and charming companion of princes and prelates, taught the poor savages of Sussex how to fish with nets and gather abundant food. There came rains and ample harvests. By his own energy, under a favoring providence Wilfrid stood forth as the redeemer of the South Saxons from destruction. It was the more striking because, fifteen years before, returning from Rome, his boat had been stranded on their shore in a storm. They were wreckers of the worst type, and had been kept at bay only by vigorous fighting till a rising tide floated the craft. Now the one they had tried to murder was the saviour of their lives. They flocked to him in crowds for baptism. So an Englishman won to Christ the last pagan tribe of the Anglo-Saxons and did it in a most humane, that is, a most Christ-like, way.

315. The seventh century saw England—which had once been Christian and then had been entirely overwhelmed with barbarous heathenism—once more transformed into a Christian land. It was now five hundred years since Tertullian had told the first certain word as to Christians in Britain. Who shall be discouraged with slowness in modern missions when we remember that it took half a millennium to bring the little British Islands to even a nominal Christianity? It took centuries more for its full sweetness and light to pervade the country. But what work ever done has been more important for the whole world?

CHAPTER XIX.

# GERMANIC REGIONS.

316. Location of Germanic tribes. 317. Ulfilas. 318. Origin of German literature. 319. Theory and life. 320. Hun invasion. 321. Noricum. 322. Severinus. 323. His civic work. 324. Columbanus. 325. Irish and English missionaries. 326. Amandus. 327. Eligius. 328. On superstition. 329. Practical Christianity. 330. Willibrord. 331. His associates in work. 332. Anglo-Saxon success. 333. Winfrid or Boniface. 334. Chaotic conditions. 335. Boniface as an organizer. 336. His helpers. 337. Women's work. 338. Walpurgis. 339. Other missionaries. 340. The oak of Geislar. 341. The end of strife. 342. The Saxons. 343. Their spiritual conquest. 344. Charlemagne's teacher. 345. East Prussia. 346. The Knights. 347. Lithuania. 348. A millennium of missions.

316. In the region of Lake Constance the sources of the Rhine and the Danube are less than five miles apart, one flowing to the North Sea and the other eastward to the Black Sea. East of the Rhine and north of the Danube lay Germanic Europe, inhabited by migratory and warring races and tribes. The absence of complete records of the time makes it impossible to write a detailed history of the conversion of these barbarous peoples to Christianity. The evangelizing forces were

almost as divers and shifting as the tribes of people with whom they worked. Our space will allow only a brief sketch of the facts which have been recorded. Stripped of legendary accumulations and omitting all minor details, the account is best remembered as grouped around a few great names.

317. **Ulfilas** was the first of the Germanic missionaries. The name of this Apostle of the Goths is often spelled Wulfila. It means little wolf and savors of a savage race and age. In the second half of the third century Goths swept downward, not only beyond the Danube, but even across the Hellespont into Asia Minor and carried thence many Christian captives into slavery. So Christianity was introduced among the wild people north of the Danube. Ulfilas came of this Christian stock. He was born A. D. 311. At twenty-one years of age he went with an embassy of Alaric, king of the Goths, to Constantinople. There he remained for ten years imbibing Christianity and something of Greek culture. He was made a church reader and labored faithfully among the Goths north of the Danube and later in territory occupied by them just south of that river.

318. Ulfilas was one of the first missionaries to give not only Christianity, but letters to a whole people. The Goths were without books, without writing. In order that they might have the Scriptures, their missionary pastor invented for them an alphabet, using modifications of the Greek letters with the addition of some characters to represent Gothic sounds for which the Greeks had no signs. He is said to have

given his people considerable literature in the way of sermons and other religious treatises; but scarcely anything has come down to us except his New Testament. He translated the whole Bible except the Books of Kings, omitting these because he feared that they would tend to feed the warlike passions of which the Goths had a superabundance already. The best copy extant of the Testament of Ulfilas is in the University of Upsala, Sweden. It is known as the silver copy, because the letters are silver on a purple background. It is extremely precious to the world because it is the earliest existing form of the Teutonic speech, the mother-language of all northern Europe and America.

319. At the time when Ulfilas learned Christianity in the Eastern Roman Empire it was dominantly Arian in theology; so he taught it to the Goths. But, like the true missionary that he was, he seems to have cared far more for life than for theories about life. Whatever the speculative notion, Christ was to him in reality the embodiment of God and Ulfilas persistently preached Christ and called him God.

320. The region of the Goths was invaded by the still more barbaric Huns, a people belonging to an utterly different section of the human race. The Goths, thus pushed from behind, under their great leader Alaric, swept in huge migrations westward. They made themselves masters away in the southward peninsulas of Europe, in Italy and in Spain. With all their barbarism, they had assimilated some elements of Christianity and in moral conduct they were little inferior to the inhabitants of the regions

which they invaded. They sacked Rome, according to the universal custom of the times, but they spared much on account of Christianity.

321. Noricum, the region about the upper waters of the Danube, being a part of the Roman Empire, was early reached by the gospel. In the second century Christianity is said to have penetrated northward from the region around the head of the Adriatic Sea. The first name of a missionary there to be handed down to us is that of **Maximilian** in the third century. In the year 304 **Flarian** was martyred by drowning in the river.

322. The Latinized portions of the country had quite generally accepted Roman Christianity when the tide of barbarian invasion swept over it, wave on wave. Then it was largely re-paganized. Amid the terrorized remnants of Christianity there suddenly appeared a man who refused to give any account of himself, but who was clearly one of the zealous hermits of Roman Africa. There was doubtless a twinkle in his eye when he said, in reply to questions: "If you take me to be a runaway slave, get ready money to redeem me when my master comes to ask me back." His name was **Severinus.** He built himself a hermitage before the gates of Vienna. He ate nothing till sunset. He had no bed but his mantle on the ground. He went barefooted, even in the deepest snow. His was the type of religious manifestation to impress the people of that time and he acquired a great ascendency, not only over the Romanized portion of the population, but even over the barbarians. He gave no

quarter to the Arian type of Christianity. But he was often able by his daring presence and appeals to rescue Christian captives from the barbarians, whether they were Arian or pagan. He raised large funds for ransoming captives and for other charitable work.

323. He stimulated the towns to defend themselves to the last against the invaders, and had the fighting men form themselves into organized companies for regular drill and discipline. He also devised improved means of commerce and promoted better municipal organization. Along the current of this broad ministry he carried his ideas of the true religion into the very hearts and lives of men, so that the Roman form of Christianity not only stood and stemmed the tide of barbarian invasion, but actually overcame the conquerors. It was not Severinus alone, but he and other unnamed missionaries who saved that part of Europe to civilization and secured the establishment of Christianity there long before a similar work was done for the regions further north. Severinus finished his career A. D. 482.

324. The next conspicuous apostles of Central Europe entered the land a hundred years after the death of Severinus and came from the opposite direction. They were Irishmen. Their leader, **Columbanus,** was a scholar as well as a missionary. He was educated in the great monastic school of Bangor, on the coast of Down, where thousands of others received efficient training under the direction of Comgall, the head of the institution. His writings show what excellent use he had made of his advantages. When past forty

years of age Columbanus, with twelve comrades, crossed over to France and after some wanderings founded a monastery amid the spurs and defiles of the Vosges Mountains at Luxeuil. The establishment attracted great numbers of men. But his unflinching protest against the gross immorality of the Court of Burgundy as well as the high standard of ascetic life at Luxeuil, which put to shame the lax and worldly lives of the Burgundian clergy, resulted in the banishment of Columbanus. With some companions he made his way to the headwaters of the Rhine and at the south end of Lake Constance founded a monastery in Bregenz. Here, though well advanced in years, he assailed the surrounding paganism with the fiery zeal of an Irish youth. He burned the temples of the Teutonic gods. He broke the cauldrons in which beer was brewed to offer to Woden. He threw gilded idols into the lake. After three years the hostility of people and rulers, along with his own restless spirit, drove him over the Alps into Lombardy, where at Bobbio, in the Apennine Mountains, he was permitted to found another monastery. There he finished his career. He is always counted one of the pioneer foreign missionaries, although the chief part of his life was not given to direct work for the heathen. But the missionary spirit dominated his course. He was the pre-eminent man among a great number of Irishmen who went on missions to continental Europe and he established centers of long continued missionary activity.

325. **Gallus** and others of his Irish comrades remained near Lake Constance and founded a monas-

tery from which the town and province of St. Gall were named. This became the great evangelizing center from which Switzerland was converted to Christ. **Eustasius,** a successor of Columbanus in the abbacy of Luxeuil, and **Agilus,** from Bobbio, both pupils of Columbanus, were the first missionaries from the West to work in Bavaria. Other Irish missionaries, **Kilian** and **Colman and Totnan,** pushed their way to Würtzburg on the River Main. These are but a few of the Irish missionaries who are said to have swarmed like bees over the continent.

Ireland was not the only part of Britain to send out foreign missionaries. England soon followed and exceeded in the great enterprise of converting Central Europe. More than a thousand years, a full, round millennium, before Carey became the apostle of India, Englishmen went as foreign missionaries to the continent of Europe.

326. The Celtic portion of the Netherlands had been much Latinized under the Romans and was well penetrated with Christianity. When the Teutonic flood came in it was met and began at once to be tinged with Christianity. Amid the many currents and counter-currents of the time the Irish missionaries introduced practices in some respects freer than the Roman, in some respects sterner and in other respects simply different, neither better nor worse. One of the strongly Romanizing missionaries was **Amandus,** a native of Aquitania. He also did vigorous work among the heathen in Flanders. He procured and used a mandate of Dagobert, the Frankish

king, that the pagans should be baptized. But he also redeemed and taught captives. He cut down from the gallows a man who was counted dead and resuscitated him, so that the people thought that a miracle had been wrought. At last multitudes overthrew their pagan altars and asked for baptism.

327. A missionary of much higher type was **Eligius.** He was a prosperous goldsmith who worked at his trade with his Bible open before him and was able to give religious instruction better than many of the clergy of the time. It was not strange that such a man should be impressed with the needs of the heathen. He gave himself up to missionary work in the wilds of Friesland (Holland). Many turned to Christ and were faithfully taught to lay aside superstitions and live kind and useful Christian lives. He was made Bishop of Noyon in 640 A. D. A pupil of Eligius put on record the following as the substance of one of his discourses:

328. "Worship not the heavens, nor the stars, nor the earth, nor anything else but God; for He, by His power alone, has created and disposed all things. Doubtless the sky is lofty, the stars are beautiful, the earth is vast, the ocean boundless, but He who made all these is greater and fairer than they. I declare, then, that you must not follow the impious customs of the unbelieving pagans. Let no man take note of what day he leaves his house, or what day he returns there, for God has made every day. Nor must any one scruple to begin a work at the new moon; for God has made the moon, to the end that it should mark the time and enlighten the darkness, and not that it should interrupt men's business and disturb their minds. Let none believe himself subject to an appointed destiny, to a lot or to a horoscope, according to the common saying, 'Every man shall be that which his birth has made him';

for God wills that all men should attain salvation and arrive at a knowledge of the truth.

329. "But on every Sunday present yourselves at the church, and when there take no thought of business or of quarrels, or of trifling conversation, and hearken in silence to the divine teaching. It sufficeth not, my friends, to have received the name of Christians if you do not the works of Christians. That man bears the name of Christian with profit to himself who keeps the precepts of Christ, who steals not, who bears not false witness, who lies not, who doth not commit adultery, who hateth no man, who returns not evil for evil. That man is a Christian indeed who puts no faith in phylacteries nor other devilish superstitions, but hopes in Christ only; who receives the wayfarer with gladness, as though he were entertaining Christ Himself, for it is said, 'I was a stranger, and ye took Me in.' That man, I tell you, is a Christian who washes the feet of his guests, and loves them as dear kinsmen, who bestows alms to the poor according to his own means, who touches not the produce of his own farm till he has given a portion to the Lord, who knows not the deceitful scale or the false measure, who lives chastely and in the fear of God, who finally, bearing in mind the Creed and the Lord's Prayer, takes care to teach them to his children and his household."

330. But the man who is accounted the apostle of Holland was **Willibrord.** A native of Northumbria and educated at Ripon, he went, for a post-graduate course, as we might say, to Ireland, at that time preeminently the land of learning and of religion. There he came under the influence of Egbert, an Englishman who had made Ireland his home and who was one of the great forces in stimulating missionary zeal. With eleven companions Willibrord set sail for Friesland and landed at the mouth of the Rhine in the year 690.

331. The names of the other members of this first band of Anglo-Saxon foreign missionaries were **Swi-**

**bert, Wigbert, Acca, Willibald, Winnibald, Ew—d, Ewald, Werenfrid, Marcellinus, Lebvinus** and **Adelbert. Acca was a skillful musician, who made music a** great help in the mission. After a time he was recalled for special work in England. Others came from England from time to time, replenishing the missionary force in Friesland. Of the original band Willibald worked at Aichstadt, Lebvinus at Deventer, Marcellinus at Overyssel. The Ewald brothers pushed on into the wilds of Saxony and were martyred there.

332. Willibrord himself came to be held in the highest esteem for his work by the Pope and by the civil rulers. The English missionaries entered into the labors of Eligius, and the other Gallic missionaries, greatly extending and consolidating the work, so that they became the real evangelizers of Holland. The Anglo-Saxons had great advantage in being of the same stock and of almost the same speech as the Frisians. Just here, however, we cannot better sum up the character of the first great English foreign missionary than in the Latin words with which Alcuin, the distinguished English tutor of Charlemagne, described Willibrord: *Omni dignitate præclarus, statura decens, vultu honorabilis, facie venustus, corde lætus consilio sapiens, ore jucundus, moribus compositus et in omni opere Dei strenuus.*"

333. Without question the most distinguished and efficient English foreign missionary before Carey was Winfrid, more frequently known by the name given him later, **Boniface.** When the company of Willibrord sailed for the mouth of the Rhine, Winfrid was a lad

but ten years of age in his native kingdom of Wessex. He was of ancient and noble family and received his education at Exeter, where he gave promise of being one of the best scholars of England. At thirty years of age he was chosen by the assembled abbots of Wessex to represent them in a council at Canterbury and he had every prospect of ecclesiastical preferment. But for a score of years ecclesiastical circles in England had rung with reports of the stirring missionary deeds of Willibrord and his comrades. Winfrid or Boniface, with only two or three companions, embarked for Friesland. There he began to work and his heart never relinquished that field of his early ideals, but brought him back there to die a martyr's death forty-five years later. But meantime it was ordered that he should spend most of his long missionary career in Germany instead of Holland.

334. The utterly chaotic social and religious condition of the people which we have noted elsewhere was at this time at its height along the central reaches of the Rhine. Old Roman-Gallic, Celt and many Teutonic tribes were seething together. In the midst of many phases of paganism Christianity had more or less foothold, but Christianity of divers aspects.

Five hundred years before the religion of the cross had followed the Roman eagles along the Roman roads to the Roman camps and towns. This early planting had been fostered by the somewhat independent Gallic type of church life. The rough and ready Frankish rulers, still half pagan in their ideals, had given it a cast of their own. Swarms of zealous Irish missionaries had woven their ideas widely through the fabric. They insisted on a different time for celebrating Easter from that observed in the south, on a different way of shaving the heads of priests. In more important aspects of church life, they were less absolutely subordinated to Rome. In some respects their protests against existing regulations command our modern sympathies.

335. But those dark, deeply involved, chaotic, times needed a great, organizing, master mind. Boniface proved to be the man for the hour. Successive Popes had the sagacity to see this and they equipped him with all needful ecclesiastical sanction, kept him away from his favorite, but less critical Netherland field and sent him here and there throughout the vast tangle of Germanic forest and Germanic society. He converted, organized and reorganized churches into the one Church of Rome. Our interest is especially in his work for the heathen. Allemani, Hessians, Bavarians, Saxons and Franks of various tribes heard the gospel from him and turned to Christ in great numbers.

It is said that one hundred thousand were baptized under his immediate direction. Doubtless many of them, like the earlier wholesale baptisms of Clovis and his three thousand followers, were merely formal, signifying no change of life and character. But there were many cases, too, of genuine conversion, proved by altered lives.

336. Boniface called to his aid a multitude of helpers, sending home to England for many of them. The monastic colleges of those days responded with a host

of student volunteers. Lull, Willibald and Denehard were among the number. **Willibald** was at that time just home from a trip to Jerusalem. **Denehard was** intimately associated with Boniface and was sent by him on delicate and important errands to Rome. The **work of Lull** so commended itself that Boniface afterward made him his own successor.

337. However it may be with Mohammedan missions, no Christian mission can succeed without the work of Christian women.

This was no less true in Germanic Europe 1300 years ago than it is on the mission fields of the world today. Many women went from England to be co-workers with men in publishing the gospel. **Lioba,** abbess of Bishofsheim, was a kinswoman of Boniface. She was said to be "beautiful as the angels, fascinating in her speech, learned in the Holy Scriptures, and canons." **Thecla,** a nun of Wimborne, was sent by Boniface from England to preside over the convent of Bischofsheim under the direction of Lioba, and, later, to be abbess of Ketzeingen on the Main.

388. **Walpurgis,** daughter of a West Saxon king, was educated at Wimborne under the direction of the abbess Tetta. In 748, A. D., she went with the abbess and several other women to take part in the missionary work which Boniface was pushing so vigorously in Germany. At first she was established near her brothers Willibald and **Winnibald** at Eichstadt. A little later the convent of Heidenham was established by Winnibald, who directed its affairs until his death, when Walpurgis succeeded him in office and was ab-

bess to the end of her life, fifteen years later. After her death a convent was erected in her honor. Many churches and chapels were dedicated to her in Germany, France, the Netherlands and England.

339. **Chinnihild** and her daughter, **Berathgith,** labored in Thuringia; **Chunidrat** was stationed in Bavaria. Other women whose names and stations have not been preserved for us left their impress on the work.

Boniface commissioned **Sturm,** a noble Bavarian pupil, to found a monastery in the midst of a vast forest in the valley of the Weser. It was called Fulda from the name of the branch of the river on which it stood. It became a center of evangelization in Germany similar to St. Gall in Switzerland.

340. The most dramatic scene recorded of the life of Boniface was that of his felling the sacred oak of Geislar. When in the midst of a multitude of pagan worshipers, he dared to lay tne glittering blade of a woodman's axe to the root of the tree dedicated to their great god Thor, they awaited the result in profound silence. To them it seemed a trial of strength between Thor and the god of this stranger. When a timely blast of wind suddenly completed his work, the awe-struck tribe turned *en masse* to Christ. The story is nowhere more charmingly and stirringly retold than in Dr. Henry Van Dyke's "First Christmas Tree."

341. At last, when seventy-five years of age, instead of going to Fulda to die in peace, as he had hoped to do, the old hero, with the fire of youth still burning in

him, led a company of missionaries into a part of Frisia which Willibrord and his successors had not yet been able to subdue to Christ. At first success attended the mission. But later, as several candidates were awaiting baptism, a horde of pagans rushed upon them. His comrades started to the defense, but he said, "Cease, my children, from strife." So the unresisting English apostle of Germany finished his warfare.

342. The sturdiest of the German tribes were the Saxons. Originally sea rovers, a portion of them had settled on the southeast shores of Britain and another portion on the northwest shores of Germany. They occupied the territory from the Yssel to the Elbe. Though Willibrord's comrades, the Ewald brothers, had given their lives in a mission to the Saxons, and Boniface had endeavored to establish missions among them, they were still intense pagans. Combining religious zeal with imperial ambition Charlemagne set out for the complete conquest of Saxony. As fast and as far as his arms reached the people were baptized by his command. Repeatedly he thought that the work was practically accomplished. But again and again the brave Saxons threw off his yoke, slaying and banishing his naturally hated religious emissaries. It was only at the end of thirty years, in 804, that the conquest was finally completed.

343. But whatever the worldly ambitions of Charlemagne, there were many earnest and sincere missionaries of the cross who followed his conquests with

gentleness and light. He was wise enough to call into the service many evangelists from the English branch of the Saxons. One of these, **Willehad,** of Northumbria, was sent into Saxony in 779. Six years later, though he had been driven out of the country once in the meantime by the stubborn Saxons, he had the privilege of baptizing Wittekind, their most able and vigorous chief.

344. One of Charlemagne's chief spiritual advisers at home was the scholarly Englishman Alcuin. Alcuin told the Emperor with perfect plainness that Christians could be made only by the gospel and not by the sword.

"Faith," he said, "must be accepted voluntarily, and cannot be enforced. A man must be drawn to it, he cannot be compelled to accept it; you may drive men to baptism, but you cannot make them take a single step toward religion. Therefore it is that those who would evangelize the heathen should address them prudently and temperately; for the Lord knows the hearts of his chosen ones and opens them to understand His word. . . . Let the preachers of the faith, then, learn by the example of the apostles; let them be preachers and not spoilers; and let them trust in him of whom the prophet bears witness, that he will never abandon those who hope in him."

Sooner or later, the spirit of these noble words had its way among the Saxons and they became among the most genuinely devoted of all the people converted to Christianity. In this connection it can never be forgotten that seven hundred years later it was a Saxon monk, Martin Luther, who led the world into more spiritual forms of Christianity.

345. The German peoples further north and east were converted very largely by military and political

means. The people in what is now East Prussia have since expanded into the chief German state and have given rule to the whole German Empire, but they were very late in accepting Christianity. The first missionaries to approach them were **Adelbert,** of **Bohemia** and **Bruno,** of Saxony just before and after the year 1000. They were both quickly martyred. The next two missionaries, two hundred years later, met the same fate. It was not until 1209 that Christianity gained a foothold among them. Then it was through the ministry of **Christian,** a Cistercian of Pomerania. He led many to Christ.

346. Most of the early missionaries were Dominicans, of whom **Hyacinth,** a Polander, was the most eminent. But the actual subduing of the country to the Christian name was accomplished by the military ardor of the Teutonic Knights. It was often a bloody work. But their commander, **Herman Balk,** was a sincere crusader and endeavored to replace force by Christian kindness as much as possible. By 1283 the cross had nominally triumphed. But the method of conversion and the fact that the Knights remained in permanent possession of vast estates, kept an undercurrent of hostility. Old pagan customs were cherished generation after generation. The people were never completely weaned away from heathenism, till they eagerly joined the Lutheran revolt against the church which had outwardly subjugated them.

347. The last Germanic land to yield to Christianity was Lithuania. Down almost to the middle of the fourteenth century Christianity was only tolerated

there by the still heathen ruler, Gedimin. His successor, Olgerd, favored Christianity. **Jagello,** the son of Olgerd, succeeded in putting a nominal end to heathenism in Lithuania, A. D. 1386. He gave a woolen coat to every one who received baptism and they came in great numbers.

348. From the Goths and Franks on through to the Prussians and Lithuanians it took a thousand years to bring the Germanic tribes under the sway, even the outward sway, of the religion of Christ.

That millennium is a complete answer to flippant critics who decry modern missionary efforts because in a few scores of years the vast populations of Asia have not accepted Christianity. Germany was a thinly peopled forest of uncivilized, unsophisticated people. Ten millenniums would be no longer, in proportion to the numbers and the profoundly entrenched religions of India and China, then one millennium was for Germanic lands.

## CHAPTER XX

# SCANDINAVIAN AND SLAVONIC REGIONS.

349. The Scandinavians. 350. Willibrord. 351. Harold Klak. 352. Ansgar. 353. Reverses. 354 The third mission to Denmark. 355. Ansgar's success. 356. Canute the Great. 357. Denmark the promoter of modern missions. 358. Ansgar's work in Sweden. 359. Destruction of the mission. 360. Re-establishment. 361. Sweden evangelized. 362. The subjugation of Norway. 363. King Olaf Tryggvison. 364. King Olaf Haroldson. 365. English missions to Norway. 366. The apostles of the Slavs. 367. Mission to the Crimea. 368. The Bulgarians. 369. An artist's mission. 370. Bohemia. 371. Origin of Slavonic literature. 372. Religion in the current speech. 373. Second summons to Rome. 374. A missionary educator. 375. Olga. 376. Vladimir. 377. The Greek "philosopher's" appeal. 378. The visit to Constantinople. 379. The baptism of Vladimir. 380. Christianizing by force. 381. Political conversions. 382. Pomerania. 383. Otho. 384. Hard-won victories.

349. It is not strange that the best ancient copy of Ulfilas' Bible is preserved at the University of Upsila. The Goths were the first of the Germanic stock to be evangelized and the Scandinavians the last large body of them to receive the gospel. The peninsula of Denmark had been the mother country of mighty men, the

conquerers and settlers of both Saxon England and Saxon Germany. The Northmen colonized also parts of France and even established kingdoms in Russia and in Sicily. The Scandinavian peoples were the hardiest, roughest, fiercest, of the whole titanic stock of Teutons. They were characterized by purity of family life and by utterly unmeasured devotion to friends and to enterprises of daring. But they were as nearly inhuman as men could be in eating and drinking and in the savage treatment of their enemies. They had no taste for the gospel of the Prince of Peace. The gentle teachings of Christianity seemed to them effeminate and totally demoralizing.

350. The English apostle of Holland, **Willibrord.** was the first missionary to the Danes. He entered the country near the close of the seventh century. Finding that he would not be permitted to remain he redeemed from slavery thirty boys by purchase, in order that he might educate them to evangelize their own country. On his retreat he and his party were wrecked on an island. While there he baptized three of his young Danes in a sacred pool of the island. This pollution of the sacred water, as they considered it, greatly infuriated the natives. When confronted by them, Willibrord bore himself in such an undaunted manner as to win the admiration of the natives. His fearlessness was a trait of character which they could appreciate. His Northumbrian forefathers had come from Denmark. He had the same indomitable blood as the islanders. He denounced their superstition without stint and proclaimed the gospel so ear-

nestly that Radbod, the chief of the island, was favorably impressed. But there appears to have been no permanent result. This was about the year 700.

351. It was not until 822 that continuous missionary work for Denmark began. Harold Klak appealed to the Emperor of the Franks, Charlemagne's son Louis, to favor his claim to the throne of Denmark. Louis, called the Pious, responded favorably and took advantage of the opportunity to send missionaries. Their leader was no less a personage than **Ebo, Bishop** of Rheims, the Primate of France. His missionary zeal took him to Denmark again and again. He baptized converts and established a station at Welnau. But after a time, King Harold was compelled to flee to Louis for protection. Near Mayence the king, queen and retinue were baptized, with Louis and Empress Judith as sponsors.

352. It was desired now to send some one with the returning royal family to be a permanent missionary. Who would go? The terrible reputation of the Danes for barbarity made most men unwilling. But there was a young man in the monastery of Corwey who longed for difficult and dangerous service. His name was **Ansgar.** He had often dreamed of high and perilous undertakings. His comrades sought in vain to deter him by portraying the savage ways of the Danes. But there was one fellow-monk, **Autbert** who decided to go with him. Emperor Louis fitted them out with an ample equipment. Once in Denmark Ansgar began to preach with burning zeal, reinforcing his words by Christ-like ministries to the people in their com-

mon trials. The central station was at Hedeby, in Schleswig. A number were baptized. Twelve boys were bought to be not only rescued from slavery but also to be taught Christianity. This work began in 827. After two years, King Harold was again driven from the country and Ansgar with him. Autbert had been compelled to relinquish the work by sickness.

353. After another two years, during which Ansgar opened a mission in Sweden, he was made Archbishop of Hamburg, in order that he might there have a basis of missionary operations for all Scandinavia. The emperor endowed the mission with the revenues of a rich monastery in West Flanders. Thus equipped Ansgar was beginning again to make good headway in Denmark, when there came an incursion of heathen Danes, Vikings, which completely destroyed the missionary establishment in Hamburg, church building, school and library, including even Ansgar's precious Bible. Bibles were difficult to get in those days. This one had been given him by the emperor. The missionary had not where to lay his head, but was driven from one hiding-place to another. When he turned to the Bishop of Bremen that functionary refused him shelter because he was jealous of the new see of Hamburg, which had been established so near his own. Meantime a new emperor gave away to another the monastery in Flanders. But Ansgar was as devout in adversity as in prosperity. He exclaimed with Job, "The Lord gave, and the Lord hath taken away; blessed be the name of the Lord."

354. After more political changes and the death of the Bishop of Bremen, the sees of Bremen and Hamburg were united with Ansgar in charge. Now for the third time the way opened for the proclamation of the gospel in Denmark. This was in 847. Ansgar at last won Horic, the very king who had driven out Harold and had been a bitter enemy of Christianity. Ansgar did such friendly service in negotiations with the emperor, that Horic became much attached to him and gave him full liberty to prosecute his mission. Many converts were made and a church building was erected at Hedeby, the first in Denmark.

355. One more storm swept over the work. The heathen party arose and Horic was slain, his young grandson Horic being enthroned under a violent pagan regency. But after a little Horic II threw off the regency and gave liberty to propagate Christianity. Now for the fourth time Ansgar set to work with a will and was permitted to see Christianity well planted in Denmark, both in Schleswig and in Jutland.

It was the custom of the times to ascribe miracles to any Christian worker who was eminently useful. The true spirit of Ansgar shines out in his words to those who wished to ascribe miracles to him. "One miracle I would, if worthy, ask the Lord to grant me, and that is that by his grace he would make me a good man."

There was a superstition among the heathen Danes against church bells, lest they cast a Christian spell over the people. It was therefore a great day for the mission when by permission of Horic a church bell rang out for the first time in the land.

356. Ansgar had made a noble beginning. But it took nearly two hundred years after his death in 865 completely to Christianize rugged little Denmark. There were frequent alternations of pagan and Christian rulers. In the first half of the eleventh century Canute the Great was King of England and Denmark. His father, Sweyn, a fierce pagan, had, like the Danes of six hundred years before, conquered all England. But Canute embraced Christianity and sought to introduce it throughout Denmark. By introducing a multitude of English missionaries and stationing them everywhere in the land he practically accomplished his purpose before his death in 1035. It was a generation later, however, in 1060, when the last portion of Denmark, the island of Bornholm, yielded to Christ.

357. It is said that the names of the martyrs of early Christianity in Denmark would fill a volume. We need not be surprised, then, that the first encouragement of modern missions was found there. The first modern missionaries to India and to Greenland were sent out by the King of Denmark. The Moravian missions were befriended there. Since Denmark owed her first missionary and her final missionaries to England it was a fitting thing that she should protect Carey and the first band of English missionaries to India from the hostility of the East India Company.

358. Christianity came into Sweden, as nearly everywhere else, first informally, through the ordinary inter-

course of war and trade. King Bjorn sent word to Germany that there were Christian merchants and captives in his dominion who would like the ministry of Christian priests. The word reached Ansgar at the moment when he was driven from Denmark on the expulsion of Harold. Instead of going southward to safety and comfort, Ansgar took some companions and plunged into the wild North. Crossing the channel between Denmark and Sweden they were overhauled by Norse pirates and stripped of everything. On reaching land they wandered over regions of dismal forest and across lakes which seemed seas. Ansgar's comrades counselled return. But he held them on their way till at last they reached the king. Though they came without the customary presents and entirely destitute, King Bjorn received them kindly and gave them opportunity to preach Christ. They not only ministered to such Christians as they found but were soon instrumental in converting pagans. Herigar, the Governor of Birka, became a Christian and proved to be a staunch defender and promoter of the faith. He immediately built a chapel for the mission.

359. After eighteen months Ansgar went to Germany to secure a strong basis for his various missionary enterprises. In 834 he sent **Gautbert**, a nephew of Bishop Ebo, to Sweden accompanied by **Nithard** and other missionaries. The work prospered so greatly that the heathen were aroused to bitter opposition. At length even Herigar could no longer hold back the tide. A fierce mob broke into the mis-

sion house and murdered Nithard. They manacled Gautbert and sent him out of Sweden. News of this reached Ansgar as he was himself fleeing from the smoking ruins of his Hamburg establishment, laid waste by the Norse marauders.

360. It was seventeen years before circumstances permitted Ansgar to visit Sweden again. As long as the noble Herigar lived he had kept the Christians together. But on his death the cause seemed to be lost. On his second visit Ansgar was not a forlorn suppliant, but had the advantage of ecclesiastical distinction and of an imperial commission. Such outward pomp tended to make an impression on the mind of Olaf, the king. A council was called. One of the Swedish nobles was earnest in advocating that Christianity be given a hearing in the land, as having a God stronger than Thor. The point was carried. Ansgar remained in Sweden two years. Before he left the church in Birka was rebuilt. **Erimbert,** a nephew of the former missionary Gautbert, carried on the work vigorously, assisted by two Danes, **Ansfrid** and **Rimbert.**

361. There was not much more violent opposition, but the mission was not very aggressive for one hundred and thirty years after the days of Ansgar. At the beginning of the eleventh century English missionaries, **Sigfrid**, **Boduff**, **Sigward** and others, entered Sweden. They led King Olaf Skotkonung to Christ and baptized him in 1008. Sigfrid and his comrades succeeded in establishing Christianity to the exclusion of paganism in southern Sweden. The more

inaccessible regions of northern Sweden were not brought to Christ till the next century. At Upsala as late as 1080 Inge, King of Upper Sweden, was mobbed for adhering to Christianity. One of his successors, Eric, who died in 1160, succeeded in bringing all his realm nominally into the fold of Christ.

362. The subjugation of Norway under the banner of the cross is hardly a part of missionary history. It is full of incident and adventure, thrilling to the last degree. But it is more closely allied to the crusades than to missions, except that it resulted, as the crusades did not, in conversion. Three Norwegian kings in the century between A. D. 934 and 1034 brought about the result. They were Hakon the Good, Olaf Tryggvesson and Olaf Haroldson. Hakon had been educated in England, where he became a sincere believer in Christianity. On gaining the throne he kept his religion in the background until he had won the hearty admiration and affection of his people. He gradually brought over priests from England and led his close friends into the faith. Then he assembled a great council, called a Thing, at which he personally pleaded with the people to accept Christianity. But they were not ready, and their spokesman, beginning with strong professions of loyalty, went so far as to make it plain that, unless the king withdrew his proposition, the people would revolt. Finally, through the adroit management of Jarl Sigurd, one of Hakon's most loyal and astute advisers, the king was led to take some small part in a pagan feast. When he made the sign of the cross over it the people were dis-

tressed till Sigurd explained that it was really the sign of Thor's hammer that the king had made. Indignant with himself, Hakon determined to enforce Christianity. Insurrection followed, in which he was slain.

363. After two or three ineffective reigns Olaf Tryggvison, a Viking of Vikings, came to the throne. In his roving life he too had learned Christianity in England, if Christianity it may be called which actuated him. He used all his power and even resorted to tricks to force the people to be baptized. More than once at great assemblies of the Northmen he gave them the choice between being baptized and fighting him.

364. Olaf Haroldson pursued the same policy and practically extirpated idolatry. He drew ecclesiastics largely from England and established them everywhere. The people revolted, accepting Danish rule. But it was so cruel that they reacted toward Olaf and within a year after his death they began to count him a saint. His popular canonization had much to do with firmly fastening Christianity—so-called, at least—in the hearts of the Norwegians.

365. It is an interesting fact that most of what real missionary work was done in the Christianization of Norway was done by Englishmen. As we have seen, this was true to a considerable extent also in Sweden and in Denmark. The people of Scandinavian lands conquered, colonized and gave name to England. They conquered and ruled it again in the time of Sweyn and Canute. Once more in the Norman conquest they poured fresh Norse blood into the old stream.

In England, as Englishmen, the race was spiritualized to some extent and in that form came back to its home-lands to bring the best that it had learned abroad—Christianity.

366. The apostles of the Slavic race were born in Thessalonica, about 775 years after Paul had planted Christianity there. They were two brothers—Constantine, better known as **Cyril** and **Methodius.** Many Slavs had settled in Macedonia. Whether of Slavic extraction or not, these boys grew up with a knowledge of the Slavic tongue as well as of the Greek. Their Christian father, Leon, gave them a careful Christian nurture.

In early youth their lives took on an earnest temper. Their subsequent history proved it to be genuine. In their university careers at Constantinople, Cyril came to be known as the "Philosopher," and Methodius as a painter. The marked ability of Cyril led the Emperor Theophilus to have his own son educated in close companionship with him. High prospects of matrimonial and political preferment were held before him.

367. But the spiritual heritage of the Apostle to the Gentiles was deep in these Macedonian men. A call came for missionaries to the Chazars, a Turanian people living in the Crimea. Cyril and Methodius responded. The king of the Chazars had been beset by both Jews and Mohammedans to give up idolatry. Hence he had sent to Constantinople for light. The missionaries persuaded him and many of his people to accept Christianity.

368. There was another people of Turanian stock,

though largely Slavized, living north of Constantinople --the Bulgarians. They were counted, next to their cousins the Huns, the most terrible of the barbarians. Tacitus had spoken of the Finns, from whom the Bulgarians sprang as a "marvelously savage race," having "neither arms, horses nor household gods; their food is herbage, their clothing skins, their sleeping place the bare ground; their only hope of sustenance rests in their arrows, which from want of iron they point with bones." A few years before the time of which we are speaking, the Eastern Emperor Nicephorus had been barbarously slain by them and his skull had been turned into a drinking bowl. The name of their king has a suitably savage sound, Bogoris. To him and his wild tribesmen Cyril and Methodius determined to go as missionaries. To such people, however, Cyril preached the good message of the Prince of Peace with little effect.

369. Bogoris wanted a gorgeous palace for himself and ordered the artist missionary, Methodius, to paint the walls of the great hall with a picture which would strike terror into every beholder. Methodius, with the gifts of a Byzantine colorist, painted for a higher Master than Bogoris. When the painting was uncovered before the eyes of the rough chieftain and his followers, it fulfilled his specification. It struck terror to all hearts. It was the scene of the last judgment. The king and some of his nobles at once yielded to the supremacy of Christ and were baptized. This was in 861. A pagan party soon made insurrection, but was overcome, and Christianity was permanently established.

370. Pure Slavonic peoples inhabited the lands far to the northwest of Bulgaria in the kingdoms of Moravia and Bohemia. Ratislav, King of Moravia, encouraged the Macedonians to plant Christianity in his realm. They made many converts and founded not a few churches and schools. This work began in 863. Eight years later the Duke of Bohemia, Borziwoi, visited the Moravian king and Methodius took the opportunity to urge on him the religion of Christ. Before leaving the Moravian court, Borziwoi and thirty of his attendants, having received Christ, were baptized. So the stream of Macedonian life poured into Bohemia.

371. Cyril and Methodius found the Slavonic race without a written language. They constructed for it an alphabet based on the Greek. Having made letters for the Slavs, they gave them a literature. They translated the whole Bible into Slavonian and created a liturgy in that tongue. As Max Müller says: "This is still the authorized version of the Bible for the Slavonic race, and to the student of the Slavonic languages it is what Gothic is to the student of German." It is interesting to trace back to the "Alpha, Beta" of Leon's sons in Thessalonica a vast stream of literature a thousand years long, which flows into our own lives with Tourgueneff and Tolstoi.

372. But the great significance of the literary work of Cyril and Methodius is that the Bible and liturgy which they gave to the Slavs of Central Europe in their own tongue became a leading factor in the history of Christendom.

Immediately Latin Christianity fomented bitter opposition to the spread of religion in the Slavonic vernacular. Cyril and Methodius were summoned to Rome. There Cyril died. Methodius made so favorable an impression on the Pope that in spite of the vulgar tongue for the Bible on which he insisted, he was returned to his mission field with the title of Archbishop of Moravia.

The struggle for religion in the Slavonic vernacular was not ended. It was just beginning. Europe immediately rang with one phase of the battle. Hincmar, Archbishop of Rheims; Odo, Bishop of Beauvais; **Æneas of Paris**; and others, shouted themselves hoarse in the insistence that Slavonic Christianity must be utterly Latinized.

373. Agitation against the methods of Methodius became growingly bitter. He was summoned a second time to Rome. Another Pope, John VIII, was in the chair. The brave apostle to the Slavs faced him in long and earnest discussion with arguments from both reason and Scripture. Methodius won the concession that the Moravians might come to God in their mother tongue, and returned to push his mission. But many papists were narrower than the Pope and antagonized seriously the work of Methodius to the end of his days.

374. One of the disciples of Methodius, **Clement,** became a very effective missionary among Bulgarian settlers about Ochrida, in the extreme western portion of Macedonia, on the border of Albania. He not only preached and wrote out simple discourses for

the people to read in their own tongue, but also took great pains in teaching the children. To diffuse education, he carefully trained a company of young men for teachers. He sought to improve the condition of the people by introducing new kinds of fruit trees and to refine their taste by giving them beautiful church architecture and other fine arts.

375. The largest direct service of Cyril and Methodius to the world was in furnishing letters and the Scriptures to Russia. The first living bearers of the Good News to the Russians were men brought in contact with Byzantine Christianity by the vicissitudes of war and trade. The first eminent disciple of Christ in Russia was the Princess **Olga.** She had learned enough of Christianity there to wish to know more. Hence she made a journey to Constantinople. There she was baptized by the patriarch, the emperor standing sponsor. On her return to Russia she endeavored to bring her son, Sviatoslav, to the new faith. But he was too much absorbed in war to care much for religion. He, however, allowed Olga and all who joined her in faith to exercise freedom of conscience in their worship. He even allowed his children to be instructed by her.

376. The grandson of Olga, Vladimir, who became Grand Prince in 980, was for a time a vigorous pagan, even compelling human sacrifices. The story of his adoption of the Christian faith is unique, even in the long and varied history of missions. Mohammedan missionaries came, urging him to adopt their prophet. The reason he gave for not doing so was much more

to their credit than his. As they expounded to him their tenets he exclaimed: "Drink no wine! Drinking is the great delight of the Russians; we can not live without it." Next the Jews living among the Chazars in the Crimea sent their missionaries to Vladimir, trying to persuade him, as their ancestors had tried to persuade their immediate neighbors, to embrace Judaism. They spoke to Vladimir in glowing terms about Jerusalem. But in answer to his questions they had to confess that for their sins they had been dispersed through all lands. He wanted nothing of a religion which had no country. Then came missionaries from the Roman Church and told him about the great God and also about their great Pope. "Return home," he said, "our ancestors did not receive this religion from you." The leaven of Olga was working.

377. Then came a missionary of the Greek Church who was called a "philosopher." He pointed out the errors of his predecessors. Vladimir said that the Jews had told him that both the Romanists and the Greeks worshiped one whom they, the Jews, had crucified. "That is even so," admitted the Greek. "But why was he crucified?" asked the king. This was the missionary's opportunity. He told the story of God's fellowship with us through Christ in suffering. Vladimir was convinced at heart. But the cautious king was determined to be deliberate in this momentous affair. The following year he called his councillors together and laid the question before them. They advised him to send select men to the countries where the different faiths were professed, to see how they

worked in practice, and to bring home a report.

378. This embassy found nothing which impressed them favorably until they came to Constantinople. The wise Emperor Basil secured their attendance at a service in St. Sophia, the most magnificent church building then in existence. It was gorgeous with gold and mosaics in the true Byzantine style. The patriarch wore his most resplendent robes, the choir chanted divinely, innumerable tapers dazzled the eye, the incense intoxicated the senses. When the deacons and sub-deacons, bearing torches, came in procession, wearing white surplices with high wing-like shoulders, and all the vast congregation bowed together in worship, the simple-minded Russians grasped their guides and said: "This is supernatural!" The guides answered: "What! Do you not know that the angels come down from heaven to mingle in our services?" "You are right," said the Russians, "we want no further proof; send us home again." So they brought the report that there was no religion to be considered but the Greek.

379. Still cautious, Vladimir determined to test the matter in his own warlike fashion. He besieged Kherson in the Crimea, vowing that if he took it he would become a Christian. Succeeding in that, he made one more condition. He wrote to the Greek emperor that he would accept his religion provided he would give him his sister in marriage. Princess Anne shrank from the proposal of the barbarian, but for the sake of the conversion of a nation she sacrificed herself. After she had arrived at Kherson Vladimir was finally

baptized (A. D. 988). Two women, Olga and Anne, were the apostles of all the Russias.

380. **Vladimir,** his bride and retinue returned to his capital, Kieff, five hundred miles up the Dnieper. He proclaimed Christianity as the religion of his domain and had the national idol, Perun, overthrown and dragged swiftly across country, while twelve horsemen followed flogging the degraded god to the banks of the river and there tumbled it into the stream. The horrified people held their breath in expectation of some terrible avengement of the sacrilege. But when Perun disappeared over the rapids, paganism was dead in Russia.

Vladimir ordered all the people to assemble at the river to be baptized. So the vast crowds went down into the water, some swimming, some wading up to the neck, some carrying their children in their arms, and were all buried in a wholesale baptism to rise a christened, if not a Christian, nation.

There were no persecutions in Russia. The people followed their monarch. They called him "*Isapostolas,*" equal to an apostle. The people had the Bible in their own tongue, thanks to Cyril and Methodius of a hundred years before, and were able in time to learn something of the Christianity which they were forced to profess in ignorance.

381. The story of the conversion of the other Slavonic tribes, like that of all Eastern Europe, is political and military rather than strictly missionary. But many noble characters with something of the true missionary spirit in them may be seen dimly struggling amid the tumultuous elements of the times.

Among the finest characters in the history of the conversion of Poland were **Dambrowka,** the first wife and **Oda,** the fourth wife, of Duke Mieceslav, in the latter half of the tenth century. Oda had been a nun, but the Roman Church allowed her to marry for the sake of promoting the faith. Later, in 1034, in like manner Prince **Cassimir,** who had entered a Benedictine monastery in Germany, was absolved from his vows that he might assume the throne of Poland which was his by hereditary right.

382. Early in the next century Pomerania submitted to the rule of Poland, promising at the same time to adopt Christianity. But it was difficult to find anyone with sufficient courage to venture as a missionary among the fierce Pomeranians. The Polish bishops absolutely declined to go, but a Spanish friar by the name of **Bernard** offered himself. The barefooted mendicant was an object of profound contempt to the people. When he told them that he was a messenger of the great God they replied that such a being would not send a beggar as his envoy. Bernard was obliged to flee.

383. It was necessary to send a man of personal eminence and attended with the signs of rank and dignity. **Otho,** Bishop of Bamberg, Germany, was prevailed upon to undertake the task. He made two extensive missionary tours through Pomerania with all the pomp available. He was a sincere and earnest man, with great tact and determination. In spite of all his abilities and all his accessories, he nearly lost his life more than once at the hands of the people. By a com-

bination of diplomacy, vigor and devotion he accomplished his purpose. At Pyritz 7,000 candidates were led into the waters of baptism. This was done with more of preparation and decorum than was common in those times in that part of the world. Yet the whole stay at Pyritz was but twenty days. The struggle was more intense and prolonged at Stettin and in some other places.

384. The Wends made a stubborn resistance to Christianity. But their apostle **Vicelin** had gained good headway among them before his death in 1154.

The island of Ruegen, off the German coast of the Baltic Sea, was the last stronghold of paganism in that region. It contained a temple of Svanovit, enshrining a colossal image of that deity. After the conquest of the island by Denmark, **Absolom of Roeskild** with some instructed axe-bearers tore aside the veil of the temple and hewed Svanovit in pieces before the eyes of the horrified populace (A. D. 1168).

Finland and Lapland were not finally subdued to the rule of the faith of Sweden till the last quarter of the thirteenth century, more than four hundred years after Cyril and Methodius began to evangelize the Slavs.

## CHAPTER XXI.

# ICELAND, GREENLAND AND LABRADOR.

385. Iceland a phenomenal country. 386. The first missionaries. 387. King Olaf Tryggvison the great factor in the conversion of Iceland. 388. He swims for missions. 389. His bait catches. 390. The converts save the day. 391. An imported meeting-house. 392. Christianity established in Iceland. 393. Greenland colonized. 394. Leif's visit to Norway. 395. Leif's mission. 396. Christianity in Greenland. 397. Leif's discovery of America. 398. Hans Egede. 399. Gertrude Egede. 400. First missionary work. 401. Good Hope mission. 402. Difficulties. 403. Moravian missions. 404. Missionary women. 405. The first conversions. 406. Results of work. 407. Complete success. 408. Love more efficient than law. 409. Christian Erhard in Labrador. 410. Jens Haven. 411. George III. makes donation to missions. 412. The missionaries. 413. The Privy Council of England makes grant for missions. 414. Features of the work. 415. Results. 416. Ships that were iceberg-proof.

385. Suspended on the Arctic Circle is one of the phenomenal portions of the earth, Iceland; an island of fire and of ice, of volcanoes and of glaciers; counted good for nothing but pasturage, yet unshaded by a single tree. Though six hundred tempestuous miles from the mainland of Europe, every piece of lumber for shelter and all breadstuffs for food must be im-

ported. Extremely poor in material possessions, isolated to the last degree from the rest of the world, and without cities of its own, Iceland has been for a thousand years a land of large intellectual life.

In the early part of this millennium it produced a literature unequaled by that of any other land in those days, a literature of surpassing interest still. The early history of Scandinavia was written not on the mainland but in Iceland. It was written, too, with a wonderful clearness and beauty. The best pictures we have of the thought and life of our Teutonic forefathers come from Iceland. The Eddas give us their religious ideas, the Sagas (stories) their history. At the end of the island's millennium, though without public schools, Iceland has less illiteracy than any other land on earth. Scattered about on lonely farmsteads, or rather cattle and sheep ranches, parents have handed on to children from generation to generation a love of letters. It is not uncommon for the peasants to know, not only their own national poetry and history, but also several European languages. Iceland, even more than England, or than Scandinavia itself, furnishes a demonstration of the tremendous inherent vigor and persistent psychic force of the Northmen stock.

King Harold Hair-fair consolidated the kingdom of Norway and ruled it with such a ruthless hand that many of the old independent nobles emigrated in various directions. Some of them established themselves in what came to be called Normandy and thus became the Norman rulers of England. But hundreds of the more peace-loving, fine-spirited and cultivated families colonized Iceland, going a few at a time, through a considerable period before and after the year 900. There they founded and maintained for four hundred years the only absolutely free republic then in the world. Though hardy and sturdy in the highest degree, they were the portion of the Northmen who preferred industry to piracy and trade to conquest.

386. The migration to Iceland was consecrated with solemn sacrifices to Odin and the other gods of the Norse. It was a hundred years before they were displaced by the true God and his Christ. In 981, an Icelander by the name of **Thorwald** traveling in Saxony and becoming acquainted with Christianity, accepted it with all his heart. He showed his sincerity by persuading **Frederick** the minister who baptized him, to go with him on a mission to Iceland. They labored for five years with some success, but were then compelled by a vote of the Allthing or National Council to leave the island.

One of the good stories told about the work of Frederick gives an interesting episode of missionary life. He pitched his tent near a heathen temple and began to preach to the crowds. The wife of the chief man of the neighborhood was greatly annoyed that a new religion should be preached. So she went into the temple and began to pray with all her might to Thor. It was a question for a while who had the more commanding voice, the lady of the manor or the missionary.

The Icelanders were in frequent communication with their mother country, Norway, and received Christianity mainly through the efforts of King Olaf Tryggvison. He sent **Stefnín,** a native of Iceland, also his own chaplain, **Thangbrand**, a Saxon. The latter was a fighting chaplain, and when the sword of the spirit failed he buckled on the sword of Olaf. Many of the people turned Thangbrand's efforts into a laughing-stock; nevertheless, he made some influential converts.

387. The most decisive influence was exerted by the great personality of Olaf himself. The account as given in the Sagas (stories) of the kings written by Snorri, one of the great Icelandic authors, is so quaint and charming that it must be told in the original account as rendered into English with suitable flavor by Morris and Magnusson. It shows Olaf in a better light than most of his missionary feats. For the conversion of Iceland, he could not depend so much upon force as he did for that of Norway. Hence, we see him using consummate tact in putting himself *en rapport* with the Icelanders through athletic comradeship.

"For that same harvest came out to Nidaros from Iceland Kiartan, the son of Olaf, the son of Hoskuld, and the son also of the daughter of Egil Skallagrimson, which Kiartan hath been called nighabout the likeliest and goodliest man ever begotten in Iceland. There was then also Haldor, son of Gudmund of Maddermead, and Kolbein, son of Thord, Frey's priest, and brother of Burning-Flossi; Sverting also, son of Runolf the priest; these and many others, mighty and unmighty, were all heathen.

"Therewith also were come from Iceland noble men who had taken christening from Thangbrand, to wit, Gizur the White, the son of Teit Ketilbioon's son, whose mother was Alof, daughter of Bodvar the Hersir, son of Viking-Kari; but the brother of Bodvar was Sigurd, father of Eric Biodaskalli, the father of Astrid, mother of King Olaf. Another Icelander hight Hialti, son of Skeggi; he had to wife Vilborg, daughter of Gizur the White. Hialti was a christened man, and King Olaf gave full kindly welcome to father and son-in-law, Gizur and Hialti, and they abode with him.

"Now those Iceland men who were captains of the ships, such of them as were heathen, sought to sail away, when the King was come into the town, for it was told them that the King would christen all men perforce; but the wind was against them, and they were driven back under Nid-holm. These were the captains of ships there: Thorarin Nefiolfson, Hallfred the Skald, son of Ottar, Brand the Bountiful, and Thorliek Brandson. Now it was told King Olaf that there lay certain ships of Icelanders, who were all heathen and would flee away from meeting the King. So he sent men to them forbidding them to stand out to sea, bidding them go lie off the town, and so did they, but unladed not their ships [but they cried a market, and held chaffer by the king's bridges. Thrice in the spring-tide they sought to sail away, but the wind never served, and they lay yet by the bridges.

388. "Now on a fair-weather day many men were a-swimming for their disport; and one man of them far outdid the others in all mastery. Then spake Kiartan with Hallfred the Troublous-skald bidding go try feats of swimming with this man, but he excused himself. Said Kiartan, 'Then shall I try'; and cast his clothes from him therewith, and leapt into the water, and struck out for that man, and caught him by the foot and drew him under. Up they come, and have no word together, but down they go again, and are under water much longer than the first time, and again come up, and hold their peace, and go down again the third time; till Kiartan thought the game all up, but might nowise amend it, and now knew

well the odds of strength betwixt them. So they are under water there until Kiartan is well-nigh spent; then up they come and swim to land. Then asked the Northman what might the Icelander's name be, and Kiartan named himself. Said the other, 'Thou art deft at swimming; hast thou any mastery in other matters?' Said Kiartan, 'Little mastery is this.' The Northman said, 'Why asketh me nought again?' Kiartan answereth: 'Me-seemeth it is not to me who thou art, or in what wise thou art named.' Answered the other: 'I will tell thee then: Here is Olaf Tryggvison.' And therewith he asked him many things of the Iceland men, and lightly Kiartan told him all, and therewith was minded to get him away hastily. But the King said: 'Here is a cloak which I will give thee, Kiartan.' So Kiartan took the cloak, and thanked him wondrous well].

389. "And now was Michælmas come, and the King let hold hightide, and sing mass full gloriously; and thither went the Icelanders, and hearken the fair song, and the voice of the bells. And when they came back to their ships, each man said how the ways of the Christian men liked them, and Kiartan said he was well pleased, but most other mocked at them. And so it went, as saith the saw, Many are the King's ears, and the King was told thereof. So forthwith on that same day he sent a man after Kiartan bidding him come to him; and Kiartan went to the King with certain men, and the King greeted him well. Kiartan was the biggest and goodliest of men and fair-spoken withal. So now when the King and Kiartan had taken and given some few words together, the King bade Kiartan take christening. Kiartan saith that he will not gainsay it, if he shall have the King's friendship therefor; and the King promised him his hearty friendship; and so he and Kiartan strike this bargain between them. The next day was Kiartan christened, and Bolli Thorleikson his kinsman, and all their fellows; and Kiartan and Bolli were guests of the King whiles they wore their white weeds; and the King was full kind to them, and all men accounted them noble men wheresoever they came.

390. "That same harvest came back from Iceland to King

Olaf Thangbrand the mass-priest, and told how that his journey had been none of the smoothest; for that the Icelanders had made scurvy rimes on him, yea and some would slay him. And he said that there was no hope that that land would ever be christened. Hereat was King Olaf so wood wroth that he let blow together all the Iceland men that were in the town, saying withal that he would slay them every one. But Kiartan and Gizur and Hialti, and other such as had taken christening, went to him and said, 'Thou wilt not, King, draw back from that word of thine, whereby thou saidst that no man might do so much to anger thee, but that thou wouldst forgive it him if he cast aside heathendom and let himself be christened. Now will all Iceland men that here are let themselves be christened; and we will devise somewhat whereby the Christian faith shall prevail in Iceland. Here are sons of many mighty men of Iceland, and their fathers will help all they may in the matter. But in sooth Thangbrand fared there as here with thee, dealing ever with masterful ways and man-slaying; and such things men would not bear of him.' So the King got to hearken of these redes, and all men of Iceland that there were, were christened."

391. In the Saga of Howard the Halt, written long before Snorri's Sagas of the Kings, we get a glimpse of the same kind of work by Olaf and of the taking to Iceland of materials for church building.

"But within certain winters heard Howard these tidings, that Earl Hakon was dead, and King Olaf Tryggvison come to the land and gotten to be sole King over Norway, and that he set forth new beliefs and true. So when Howard heard hereof he broke up his household, and fared out with Biargey and Thorhall, his kinsman. They came to King Olaf and he gave them good welcome. There was Howard christened with all his house, and abode there that winter well accounted of by King Olaf. That same winter died Biargey; but the next summer, Howard and Thorhall his kinsman fared out to Iceland. Howard had out with him church-wood exceeding big; he set up house in the nether part of Thorhallsdale, and abode there no long time before he fell sick; then he called to him Thorhall his kinsman and spake, 'Things have come to this, that I am sick with the sickness that will bring me my death; so I will that thou take the goods after me, whereof I wish thee joy; for thou hast served me well and given me good fellowship; thou shall flit thy house to the upper part of Thorhallsdale and there shalt thou build a church, wherein I would be buried.'"

392. In the year 1000, the Allthing of Iceland, after serious discussion, voted to adopt Christianity as the religion of the island, allowing, however, some concessions for a time to the superstitious customs of the people. But in 1016 all compromise was abolished.

The Arctic, and at the same time volcanic, island had one natural advantage over the other northern countries, where nothing was yet known as to baptism except immersion. The Allthing solemnly set apart the pools of certain warm springs as national baptisteries. In these, at last, all the people of Iceland were "buried with Christ by baptism" and "raised" in "the likeness of his resurrection."

393. From Iceland Greenland was discovered and colonized (985). Eric the Red, banished from Iceland, sailed to the inhospitable shores which had been sighted by a previous navigator. Eric said that he thought that colonists would be more apt to come if the country had a pleasant name, so he called it Greenland. That facetious name has stuck to the great trackless, ice-covered peninsula now for nearly a thousand years. But the grim humor of the old Norse outlaw or some other business devices proved effective

and many settlers left Iceland for what was, possibly in fact, a greener land. According to fourteenth century accounts, there were by that time two hundred and eighty Scandinavian settlements in Greenland, with two towns, fourteen churches and a cathedral. But Eric and the first settlers were pagans.

394. The following is the story of their conversion in the Sagas:

"After that sixteen winters had elapsed, from the time when Eric the Red went to colonize Greenland, Leif, Eric's son, sailed out from Greenland to Norway. He arrived in Drontheim in the autumn, when King Olaf Tryggvison was come down from the north, out of Halagoland. Leif put in to Nidaros with his ship, and set out at once to visit the King. King Olaf expounded the faith to him, as he did to other heathen men who came to visit him. It proved easy for the King to persuade Leif, and he was accordingly baptized, together with all of his shipmates. Leif remained throughout the winter with the King, by whom he was well entertained.

395. "Upon one occasion the King came to speech with Leif, and asks him, 'Is it thy purpose to sail to Greenland in the summer?' 'It is my purpose,' said Leif, 'if it be your will.' 'I believe it will be well,' answers the King, 'and thither you shall go upon my errand, to proclaim Christianity there.' Leif replied that the King should decide, but intimated to him his belief that it would be difficult to carry his mission to a successful issue in Greenland. The King replied that he knew of no man who would be better fitted for this undertaking, 'and in thy hands the cause will surely prosper.' 'This can only be,' said Leif, 'if I enjoy the grace of your protection.' Leif put to sea when his ship was ready for the voyage. For a long time he was tossed about upon the ocean, and came upon lands [New England] of which he had previously had no knowledge. There were self-sown wheat fields and vines growing there. There were also those trees there which are called 'mausur' and of all these they took specimens. Some

of the timbers were so large that they were used in building. Leif found men upon a wreck, and took them home with him, and procured quarters for them all during the winter. In this wise he showed his nobleness and goodness, since he introduced Christianity into the country, and saved the men from the wreck; and he was called Leif the Lucky ever after.

396. "Leif landed in Ericsfirth and then went home to Brattahlid; he was well received by every one. He soon proclaimed Christianity throughout the land, and the Catholic faith, and announced King Olaf Tryggvison's messages to the people, telling them how much excellence and how great glory accompanied the faith. Eric was slow in forming the determination to forsake his old belief, but *Thiodhild* embraced the faith promptly, and caused a church to be built at some distance from the house. This building was called Theodhild's Church, and there she and those persons who had accepted Christianity, and they were many, were wont to offer their prayers."

397. Other sagas give more details about Leif's discovery of the New England coast and his return to spend a winter there more than 600 years before the Pilgrims landed. Our present interest is in the fact that the continent of North America was first discovered by a missionary. His mission to Greenland (A. D. 1000) was successful, though it had opposition to meet at first. When all the people were calling Leif the Fortunate because he had fallen in with and rescued a shipwrecked crew in those unfrequented waters, his own father Eric said that the good fortune was offset by the fact that Leif had brought into the country at the same time that trickster the priest. One of Leif's sisters, Freydis, named from the Friday goddess Freya, was a woman of desperate deeds. But in the end all the colony accepted Christianity,

Hans Egede.

which held sway there for four hundred years, with a line of bishops of whom seventeen are known. No account has reached us, only vague hints, of untoward events by which the colony was ultimately destroyed. But everyone who sees the statue of Leif Ericson on the Boston Back-Bay Boulevard, must remember in justice to the facts that discovery was incidental in the career of Eric's son. The main business of that bold figure was carrying the gospel to the heathen.

398. After the last record of the old Norse colony and church in Greenland (1409), three hundred years elapsed without leaving any account of a sound of the gospel over the cold wastes of that land of desolation. Then a young Dane, **Hans Egede,** in his studies at college became acquainted with the stories of the old heroic days as hundreds of others before him had done. But he had the imagination and the wide-reaching altruism to be fired with a longing to renew the work of Leif, the son of Eric, and to minister to any remnant of the old faith which might have survived through nine generations. In his dreams he saw a people with some of the old Norse blood in their veins waiting and watching for a messenger of God to break the silence of the centuries.

Graduated and settled in the little fishing parish of Vaagen, the college ideal clung to him and gained an even deeper hold on his spirit. He devoured every word that he could glean from men who had sailed on whaling expeditions in the Arctic seas. They told him of the terrible condition of the Greenlanders.

399. His wife could not share his desire to go to

that desolate land. His parishioners, who had soon come to love the faithful, devoted young pastor, when they learned of his longing at first protested, then grew angry, and finally thought him deranged. In 1710 he wrote an earnest appeal in behalf of Greenland to his own bishop and to one of the more metropolitan bishops. It took them a whole year to answer and then it was with no more encouragement than was received eighty years later by William Carey from his elders. The fisher-folk of Vaagen came almost to persecute Egede and his family. His vagary, as they thought it, had upset the selfish complacency of the people with their pastor. At this juncture, however, his wife, after much prayer for guidance, came to see the divine call as clearly as he did himself. From this hour on she was his unfailing comrade and his strengthener in every hour of darkness. In spite of the protests of her own mother and of all other hindering friends, **Gertrude Ras Egede** became one of the noblest missionaries in all the annals of our two millenniums.

400. In 1715 Egede published a pamphlet entitled "A Scriptural and Rational Solution and Explanation with Respect to the Objections and Impediments Raised Against the Design of Converting the Heathenish Greenlander." He resigned his pastorate and went to Bergen hoping to enlist merchants in an expedition for trade with Greenland. It was in vain. At last he went to Copenhagen. There some friends of the Danish mission in India, including the king himself, sympathized with Egede's purpose and gave it public indorsement.

There were trying delays even after that. But finally a trading-colonizing-missionary company was organized. After thirteen years of indefatigable toil to that end, Egede set out in the "Hope" for the same shore that Leif the son of Eric had sought seven centuries before.

401. On reaching Greenland in 1721 he found the natives to be no descendants of the old Norsemen, but low, timid, unapproachable Eskimos. In spite of his vanished dream Egede called the new settlement "Good Hope." His children played with the Eskimos and so gradually friendly relations were established. The first convert was baptized three years and a half after his arrival.

Egede had to pick up the language as best he could without helps. He translated some portions of Scripture as soon as possible. It was a difficult undertaking, because the Eskimos lacked a vocabulary, not only for spiritual things, but also for the ordinary thoughts which had been coined into words under such different skies as those of Palestine. How could he render the "Lamb of God which taketh away the sin of the world" to people who had never seen sheep? Egede's greatest work was in laying foundations and opening the door for others, especially the Moravians. Twenty years after the beginning of his mission, when he was in the homeland pleading for it, he said: "We count but between twenty and thirty aged persons and a hundred and odd young ones that have been found capable to receive the holy sacrament of baptism." But he adds: "If amongst ourselves we had no schools nor other pious foundations for the instruction and Christian education of youth and old people, pray what great feats would one or two teachers in a whole country be able to do by once or twice a year, taking a journey throughout the land and preaching a passage sermon?"

402. Some colonists and soldiers of doubtful character were sent to Greenland, who added much to the difficulties of Egede as superintendent of the colony. He was reinforced by only three missionaries, one of whom stayed but a short time. Still the work was making some headway, when a terrible scourge of smallpox was brought to Greenland. The missionaries did all in their power for the wretched and distracted natives. But three thousand of them perished, only eight souls surviving in the vicinity of the station.

After fifteen years in Greenland, Egede's heroic wife laid down her life. The people for whom they had especially toiled were nearly all swept away and the broken-hearted missionary prepared to return to Europe. He gathered the handful of colonists and the remaining natives together and preached to them on this pathetic text: "I said I have labored in vain, I have spent my strength for naught and in vain, yet surely my judgment is with the Lord and my work with my God."

In Copenhagen Hans Egede did useful service to the cause he loved, being put at the head of the missionary training-school there. His son, **Paul Egede,** carried on the Danish mission in Greenland.

403. Three years before the departure of Hans

HERRNHÜT, SAXONY.

Egede from Greenland he welcomed there three Moravian missionaries. Count Zinzendorf, attending the coronation of Christian VI in the capital of Denmark, witnessed the baptism of two Greenland boys whom Egede had sent home. The little church of Moravian refugees on Zinzendorf's estate in Saxony had been in existence but ten years and was without numbers or means. But its heart was stirred by the story of Anthony, the West Indian negro, and at the same time by the story of Greenland's need. When it was known that the Danish Government intended to abandon its mission in Greenland, two or three uneducated day-laborers in Herrnhüt, without resources, felt that they ought to take up the work about to be laid down by the King of Denmark! **Matthew Stach** and his cousin, **Christian Stach;** with **Christian David**, who had felled the first tree in founding Herrnhüt, made up a trio for Greenland. The simplicity of faith which could start on such an expedition without equipment of any kind, educational, financial or ecclesiastical, was either childish or nothing less than sublime; perhaps it was both—was sublimely child-like. The Lutheran friends of missions in Copenhagen were astounded at the situation when the Moravians arrived there. But the unmistakable, unhesitating, Christian devotion on the one side called it out on the other. Count Pless asked the Herrnhütters how they could live after reaching Greenland. They answered that they "would build a house and cultivate a piece of land that they might not be burdensome to any." When he told them that there was no timber in that country with which to build, they said: "Then we will dig a hole in the earth and lodge there." "No," he said, "you shall not be driven to that extremity; take timber with you and build a house." And he gave them the necessary money. Through such friends, the king gave them a cordial letter to Egede and the latter welcomed them with the utmost Christian fraternity. He put them at once in the way of learning the language. They selected a site not far from him on which to build their mission station, which they called New Herrnhüt. They shared with him in the self-forgetful ministry to the natives during the smallpox scourge. When famine stared them in the face and sickness disabled them he and his noble wife cared for them tenderly as if they had been of his own church or his own kindred. On his final departure from Greenland he said to them: "I wish you the Divine blessing and assistance in your call and office and I cherish a lively hope that God will still bring the work in Greenland, which I must now leave full of heaviness, to a glorious issue."

At the end of a year they were reinforced by the arrival from Herrnhüt of **Frederick Boemish and John Beck.** But the following summer no supplies were sent them and they were reduced to dire straits for subsistence. They began the long winter with nothing but a barrel-and-a-half of oatmeal. The natives refused to sell them seals, which the missionaries themselves had no way of catching.

They got along fairly well on shell-fish and train-oil while they could get them, with a little sprinkling of oatmeal. But when they were reduced to seaweed and old tallow candles for food they became greatly debilitated. Only a part of the supplies needed came for the fourth year.

404. It was in the summer of 1736 that the first women were added to the missionary staff, **Madam Stach**, **Matthew's mother**, and his two sisters, **Rosina** and **Anna.** This not only improved the home conditions but also the prospect of efficiency. The young women proved to have more facility in learning the language of the country than their brother or cousin possessed. When the missionaries told the natives that they had come to Greenland to teach them the truth, they replied: "Fine fellows, indeed, to be our teachers! We know very well that you yourselves are ignorant and must learn your lesson of others."

The missionaries made every effort to win the confidence and get near to the hearts of the Greenlanders. Matthew Stach even lived with them in one of their filthy huts for a month at a time. But all to no avail. The savages tried all sorts of serious annoyances to drive the Moravians out of the country. They even stoned them and on one occasion conspired to murder them. It was not until five years had passed that the first decided fruit of the mission appeared. Here is the original record of that thrilling event:

405. "June the 2nd" (write the missionaries) "many Southlanders visited us. Brother Beck at the time was copying a translation of a portion of the Gospels. The heathen being very curious to know the contents of the book, he read a few sentences, and after some conversation with them asked wheth-

er they had an immortal soul, and whither that soul would go after death? Some said, 'Up yonder.' And others, 'Down to the abyss.' Having rectified their notions on this point, he inquired who had made heaven and earth, man and all other things. They reply that they did not know and neither had they heard, but it must certainly be some great and mighty Being. He then gave them an account of the creation of the world, the fall of man and his recovery by Christ.

"In speaking on the redemption of man, the Spirit of God enabled him to enlarge with more than usual energy on the sufferings and death of our Saviour, and in the most pathetic manner to exhort his hearers seriously to consider the vast expense at which Jesus had ransomed their souls, and no longer reject the mercy offered them in the Gospel. He then read to them out of the New Testament, the history of our Saviour's agony in the Garden. Upon this the Lord opened the heart of one of the company, whose name was Kayarnak, who stepping up to the table, in an earnest manner, exclaimed, 'How was that? Tell me that once more, for I too desire to be saved.' These words, the like of which had never before been uttered by a Greenlander, so penetrated the soul of Brother Beck, that with great emotion and enlargement of heart he gave them a general account of the life and death of our Saviour, and of the scheme of salvation through him."

406. Kayarnak proved to be a sincere inquirer. After careful instruction he and others whom he had helped to bring were baptized. From this time on, in spite of many discouragements, the Christian colony at New Herrnhüt grew. By 1748 it numbered one hundred and thirty. Thirty-five were baptized in that one year. The year before the first church building had been erected with frame and boards sent from Europe.

At the end of twenty-five years, a new station was established one hundred miles south of New Herrnhut and called Lichtenfels. Within two years converts

LICHTENAU, SOUTHERN GREENLAND.

were baptized there and many adherents soon gathered about this place. Sixteen years later, a third station was established four hundred miles farther south still, near the southern cape of Greenland. It was not long until there were over two hundred baptized converts in the new station, Lichtenau.

407. The first Moravian missionary to Greenland who had enjoyed the advantage of a liberal education was **Michael Koenigseer,** who came in 1773 to be superintendent of the whole field. Though fifty-one years of age, he was able to acquire the native language as none of his predecessors had been able to do in all the forty years of the mission. He did splendid service until his death in 1786. The year that William Carey arrived in India, **John Soerensen,** in his eightieth year, returned to Europe, having spent forty-nine years as a missionary in Greenland. By the year 1801, the last Greenlander within the immediate field of the Moravians had received baptism. Is there another record of missionary success as complete as this anywhere on earth? It is true that the total population was small, fewer than two thousand souls. On the other hand, it was one of the most groveling, unfeelingly selfish, stolid and stubborn people ever approached by Christianity. It was transformed by the gospel. After conversion, sympathy, kindness, generosity, even to strangers, developed. When an account of the destruction of the Moravian Indian settlement in Ohio at the hands of savage white men and the destitution of the few survivors was read to the Greenlanders' Church, one Eskimo said, "I have a fine

reindeer skin which I will give." Another said, "I have a new pair of reindeer boots which I will send." A third said, "I will send them a seal that they may have something to eat and burn."

408. One of the world-wide lessons taught by the Moravian mission in Greenland the missionaries themselves did not learn for years. Then they had the grace to see their own mistake, frankly to acknowledge it and completely to reverse their method. They began by proclaiming the great God and his rightful requirements of men. It seemed to them that there was no use of preaching much else till this was accepted. But nobody accepted this or cared even to hear about it. It was the story of the Garden of Gethsemane that stirred the first soul. It was found that others were moved in like manner. In 1840 the missionaries became fully convinced that they ought to put to the front the love and sympathy of God as revealed in the suffering Saviour. From that time on the work prospered and became triumphant. Even the hard-hearted Eskimo is not to be hammered to pieces; he is to be melted like his own icebergs, by the omnipotent sunshine.

409. Labrador, though farther south than Greenland, has a more Arctic climate and is inhabited by Eskimos of a more degraded type. **Christian Erhard** had sailed many seas and had been converted at a Moravian mission station in the West Indies. As a mate on a Dutch whaler he had visited New Herrnhüt in Greenland and had learned a little of the Eskimo speech. Some English merchants put him in charge

of a trading expedition for the coast of Labrador in 1752. Four Moravians from the Brethren's settlement at Ziest, in Holland, went with him to found a mission. They landed at Nisbet's Haven and erected a house which they had brought with them, calling the station Hopedale. The trading vessel sailed up the coast. Erhard, going ashore with five of the crew to visit some of the natives, never returned. There were indications found the next year which showed that they had been murdered. The captain was left so short-handed that he returned to Hopedale and took the Moravians on board to help him work the ship back to Europe.

410. Another Moravian, **Jens Haven,** strongly drawn toward the perilous coast of Labrador, made a special study of it. The more he learned of its dangers the more he wanted to go. Zinzendorf advised him to go first to Greenland. Having spent some time in the work at Lichtenfels, he was called to England to inaugurate the work for Labrador. Through the co-operation of Sir Hugh Palliser, Governor of Newfoundland, Haven visited Labrador in 1764 and again the next year, having several of the Brethren with him the second time. But various difficulties made it impossible to establish a permanent mission there until several years later.

411. During this interval, some Labrador natives had been taken to England by the government and treated very kindly by the royal family and others. They were most delighted to meet people who could speak their language, some of the Greenland missionaries.

At length George III granted the Moravians "one hundred acres of land on the coast of Labrador, wherever they pleased to locate themselves, for the purpose of evangelizing the heathen inhabitants." Thus encouraged, Moravians in London and elsewhere organized a company and purchased a ship of a hundred and twenty tons burden to make annual voyages to Labrador in the interest of missions.

412. At last the hopes of Jens Haven were to be realized. In 1770 the Amity made her first voyage. Haven had with him **Lawrence Drachart**, who had been a Danish missionary in Greenland and was proficient in the Eskimo language; also **Steven Jensen.** A clan which had been influenced by Mikhak, one of the Eskimo women, who had been in England, welcomed the missionaries. Having found a suitable opening, they returned to England to make arrangements for the permanent establishment of the mission.

A number of additional missionaries volunteered for the terrible field of Labrador. Haven was married that winter. Two others were married men. There was a physician in the company, and there were a number of artisans, sixteen people in all.

This devoted band landed on the 10th of August, 1771, at the place selected the previous year. They called it Nain. It was about one hundred and fifty miles north of Hopedale, where the unsuccessful start had been made nineteen years before.

413. After a few years, the Privy Council of England granted them a tract of one hundred thousand acres

NAIN, LABRADOR.

for missionary purposes. In 1776 they established a station at Okak, a hundred and fifty miles north of Nain, and in 1782 another as far south, near Old Hopedale, calling it by the same name. Jens Haven was the leader in all these enterprises. We have not space for an account of the thrilling adventures of the Brethren in their journeys over the ice. The following from Haven's journal is a hint as to the trying nature of their work with the natives:

414. "We were forced to creep on all fours through a low passage, several fathoms long, to get into the house; and were glad if we escaped being bitten by the hungry dogs, which take refuge there in cold weather, and which, as they lie in the dark, are often trodden upon by the visitor, who, if he escapes from this misfortune, is compelled to undergo the more disgusting salutation of being licked in the face by these animals, and of crawlings through the filth in which they mingle. Yet this house, notwithstanding our senses of seeing and smelling were wofully offended in such frightful weather, was of equal welcome to us as the greatest palace."

415. The first convert baptized was Kingmingnese, at Okak, the first year of the mission there. This was five years after the beginning of the work in Labrador, the same length of time which had elapsed before the first convert in Greenland. Five years later there were thirty-eight baptized natives at Okak and ten catechumens. From the start, however, the mission exerted a great influence in abating the barbarism of the Eskimos. Large numbers were gradually transformed into at least semi-civilized people.

Mikhak, though friendly and of great service to the mission, did not enter the Christian life. Her husband, Tuglavina, was by far the most able and influential Eskimo in Labrador. From his superior intellectual gifts, he had acquired a vast ascendency over the natives, which he often used wickedly and even murderously. But he would always bear the sharpest rebukes from the fearless Haven. Sometimes he would tremble and weep for shame. At last, after the most careful instruction and cautious waiting, the Moravians received Tuglavina into church fellowship, believing him to be a great example of saving grace. This culminating event in the early Labrador mission took place on Christmas day, 1793, the year in which Carey arrived in India.

416. The mission in Labrador is peculiar in this: It has always been supported by a special organization in London, "The Brethren's Society for the Furtherance of the Gospel."

It has sent its ships—ten different vessels in all—to the dangerous coast of Labrador every year since 1771, without ever having a serious accident. At the time of the Revolutionary War it was captured by a French privateer, but was released without loss. Between the ship which took the first copy of the Septuagint to Rome and the one in which Carey sailed to India uncounted keels cut the sea with missionary messages and messengers. But this charmed Labrador ship seems to have been the only one in our two millenniums devoted exclusively to missions. It, too, engages in trade, but only for the sake of supporting and furthering the gospel.

CHAPTER XXII.

# SPANISH AMERICA.

417. Its extent. 418. Columbus a missionary. 419. His mission. 420. Testamentary proof of interest in missions. 421. Spanish conquests and missions. 422. Las Casas. 423. His work. 424. His wide apostleship. 425. Brazil. 426. Joseph Anchieta. 427. Henry Reichler. 428. Antonio Vieira. 429. Paraguay. 430. Work in Peru. 431. Northern South America. 432. Central America. 433. Mexico. 434. Mexican missionary methods in 1600. 435. Lower California. 436. Florida. 437. New Mexico. 438. Texas. 439. California. 440. An estimate.

417. If one were to travel overland from St. Augustine to San Francisco and sail from there around Cape Horn to St. Augustine, he would have compassed a large fraction of the habitable earth. This was the field of Spanish and Portuguese missions in the New World. This continent and a half they Christianized. It was an extremely faulty Christianity which they brought, but it was all-including and permanent.

If we were to study Romish missions in the New World in the sectarian spirit in which some Roman writers, notably Marshall, have written of all Protestant missions, we might present an appalling array of testimony from the pens of Romanists alone as to the defects of the work and the sins and crimes by which it has been accompanied. But we should be giving no more than half of the truth, and that the half which can bring good to no one. Such a presentation would be most unjust.

418. Was Christopher Columbus a missionary? The motives of human action are seldom, if ever, perfectly simple. They are manifold and mixed. Love to God, love to neighbor, and the basis of the latter, love to self, are motives which ought to hold sway conjointly. It is difficult to be clear as to the proper balance in one's own life and it is impossible to judge surely the life of another; only Omniscience can do that.

It is certain that Christopher Columbus believed that the missionary motive was one of the great actuating motives of his career. From our point of view, Columbus became a sordid and wicked man. But from his point of view, there is no reason to doubt that the following statements, among many more of the same import from his own pen, were made in sincerity:

419. "In consequence of information which I have given your Highnesses respecting the countries of India and of a Prince called Great Can, which in our language signifies King of Kings, how at many times, he and his predecessor had sent to Rome soliciting instructors who might teach him our holy faith, and the holy Father had never granted his request, whereby great numbers of people were lost, believing in idolatry and doctrines of perdition; Your Highnesses, as Catholic Christians, and Princes who love and promote the holy Christian faith, and are enemies of the doctrine of Mahomet, and of all idolatry and heresy, determined to send me, Christopher

COLUMBUS DEPARTING FOR AMERICA.

Columbus, to the above mentioned countries of India, to see the said Princes, people and territories, and to learn their disposition and the proper method of converting them to our holy faith.

"In all these islands there is no difference of physiognomy, of manners, or of language, but they all clearly understand each other—a circumstance very propitious for the realization of what I conceive to be the principal wish of our most serene King, namely, the conversion of these people to the holy faith of Christ, to which, indeed, as far as I can judge, they are very favorable and well disposed."

In the journal of his first voyage Columbus expressed his conviction that Cuba was a part of the country of the Great Khan and that he was near Zayton, China, where we have seen that the medieval missionaries had such a flourishing station. He was enthusiastic about Cuba and said, "I shall labour to make all these people Christians. They will become so readily, because they have no religion nor idolatry."

420. In his will be put the following item:

"I also order Diego, my son, or whosoever may inherit after him, to spare no pains in having and maintaining in the island of Espanola four good professors of theology, to the end and aim of their studying and laboring to convert to our holy faith the inhabitants of the Indies; and in proportion as, by God's will, the revenue of the estate shall increase, in the same degree shall the number of teachers and devout persons increase, who are to strive to make Christians of the natives; in attaining which no expense should be thought of.

"I gave to the subject six or seven years of great anxiety, explaining, to the best of my ability, how great service might be done to our Lord by this undertaking, in promulgating His sacred name and our holy faith among so many nations."

Columbus always delighted to take his first name literally, deeming himself the bearer of Christ to the world. He signed himself, "*Christo ferens.*"

421. There is no reason to doubt that the missionary aim held a high place in the minds of the Spanish discoverers and conquerors who followed Columbus. Though terribly brutal and otherwise immoral they were devoutly religious according to their conception of religion and were bent on propagating the faith. This, which had been a chief motive with which Ferdinand and Isabella were induced to begin the enterprise, continued to be prominent in the whole undertaking. Columbus deeded a portion of his expected estate to the work of recapturing Jerusalem for Christianity. We are not to forget that crusades were counted most pious undertakings. The conquest of Mexico, for instance, in its methods so shocking to all just religious perceptions and so utterly inexcusable in the light of real Christianity, was not without threads of sincere missionary intention woven in with the heartless love of glory and the insatiable greed of gold. Prescott does not go too far when he says:

"There was nothing which the Spanish government had more earnestly at heart than the conversion of the Indians. It forms the constant burden of their instructions, and gave to the military expeditions in this western hemisphere somewhat of the air of a crusade. The cavalier who embarked in them entered fully into these chivalrous and devotional feelings. No doubt was entertained of the efficacy of conversion, however sudden might be the change or however violent the means. The sword was a good argument, when the tongue failed; and the spread of Mahometanism had shown that the seeds sown by the hand of violence, far from perishing in the

COLUMBUS AS ST. CHRISTO-FER.
(From Map of Juan de la Casa, A.D., 1500.)

ground, would spring up and bear fruit to after-time. If this were so in a bad cause, how much more would it be true in a good one?"

422. If there had been nothing better than these occidental crusades, the missionary element in Spanish-American life would be lost out of sight in the overwhelming mass of selfishness and brutality. In the West Indies the natives were enslaved and rapidly exterminated. By a system of assignments Spaniards set apart to themselves not only certain portions of land but also a certain number of natives to each one. The law provided that the Christian faith should be taught to these serfs. That part of the plan was generally ignored, and the natives were simply driven like brute beasts in the work of the fields and mines. To meet this iniquity God raised up one of the most picturesque and brilliant characters in all missionary history, **Bartolomeo de las Casas.** His father had accompanied Columbus in his first voyage. In 1502 young Las Casas, having completed his studies at the University of Salamanca, came to America. Eight years later he was admitted to full priest's orders, being the first priest ordained in America. If all his successors had been equal to him in Christian character and in missionary spirit the New World would have become the "new earth" under the "new heavens" of which Columbus so fondly dreamed and wrote.

423. Las Casas had an assignment of land and aborigines in Cuba. He treated his serfs humanely, but conscience protested. As he was about to preach on a text in the apocryphal book of Ecclesiasticus, ending with "He that taketh away his neighbor's living slay-

eth him; and he that defraudeth the laborer of his hire is a bloodshedder," his conscience was arrested and he was completely converted. The first thing to be done was to give up his Indians. It was not easy to decide to do this—questions of duty are often complicated—chiefly because he feared that they would fall into worse hands and be worked to death, as afterward proved to be the case. But he obviously could not preach against the system of assignments and continue to participate in it himself. There is not space here for the long story of his life and heroic struggle to secure fair treatment for the natives. Again and again he went to Spain and pleaded with successive governments in their behalf. Ferdinand, Cardinal Ximenes the Regent, Charles V and Philip II were all effectually reached by him, in spite of bitter opposition on the part of people interested in the existing state of things. He secured royal decrees and administrative measures for the good of the natives. He was appointed protector of the Indians and gave himself with great devotion to the work of Christianizing, and civilizing them in Cuba, San Domingo, Porto Rico, Venezuela, Nicaragua, Guatemala and Mexico. He was offered a wealthy bishopric in Peru, but declined it, afterward accepting the poor one of Chiapa, Mexico, when he was past seventy years old, in the hope of doing real service to the aborigines there. Las Casas was not alone in his aims. Many missionaries, especially of the Dominican order, which he joined in middle life, warmly co-operated with him. But the lust of gain in the colonists generally thwarted their apostolic and Christ-like toils to a great degree. The splendid vitality of Las Casas kept him in vigorous life to the age of ninety-two. Even so, his death is regarded as "premature" by Arthur Helps, who may be considered his best biographer in English.

424. Las Casas richly deserves the title, "The Apostle of the West Indies." He was also the chief historian of the time in the New World. His writings were the original source of a large part of all current accounts. Some of them exist even yet only in manuscript form. Copies may be seen in the Library of Congress in Washington. Spaniards have naturally been reluctant to allow them to be printed because they paint the discoverers and conquerors in so lurid a light. It is probable that with his own hot temperament and in his burning zeal for the welfare of the aborigines, Las Casas sometimes overcolored the pictures of their oppressors. He had no census statistics, and it is to be hoped that he greatly overestimated the numbers of the natives destroyed. Some of his accounts were published in various European languages, illustrated in some editions with numerous frightful wood-cuts delineating the barbarities perpetrated on the natives. The illustrations, with more or less of the accounts, were freely circulated in Holland to innerve the people in their own struggle against the Spanish yoke.

Columbus was a kind of would-be missionary. Las Casas was a genuine missionary of the most intense type. Like that of all great souls, his work for humanity was wider than he knew. He has been an inspiration to the lovers of liberty and philanthropy in succeeding centuries and in many lands. The following is a copy of the title-page of one of the early English translations of some of his pleas in behalf of the heathen natives of America:

"An Account of the First Voyages and Discoveries Made by the Spaniards in America. Containing The most Exact Relation hitherto published of their unparallell'd Cruelties on the Indians, in the destruction of above Forty Millions of People. With the Propositions offer'd to the King of Spain, to prevent the further Rpin of the West-Indies.

By Don Bartholomew de las Casas, Bishop of Chiapa, who was an Eye-witness of their Cruelties. Illustrated with Cuts. London. M.DC. XC. IX."

425. Mission work in Brazil began near San Salvador in 1549, fifty years after the first occupation of the country by the Portuguese. Though politically a separate country, Portugal is an integral part of the Iberian peninsula and her American colony must be counted as a portion of Spanish America, in some essential respects. The head of the first company of six missionaries was **Manuel de Nobrega.** They soon persuaded many of the natives to live in peace, temperance and monogamy, but found it very difficult to induce them to give up cannibalism. On one occasion they snatched a victim from the hands of the jubilant old women who were just taking him to the fire to be roasted. This daring deed threw the whole region into arms. On another occasion one of the missionaries went among them flogging himself until he was covered with blood and telling them that he did it in order to take upon himself the punishment due to

them for their terrible sin of eating human flesh. This measure proved effective in redeeming one clan. They confessed their sin and enacted severe penalties on themselves in case of its repetition. The missionaries taught some reading, writing and arithmetic and still more music. They found the natives very susceptible to the influence of song. Accordingly not only prayers but also catechism and creed were adapted to music. It seemed to Nobrega that the story of Orpheus was the type of his mission.

426. **Joseph Anchieta** was another Jesuit missionary of heroic and saintly character. There were no text-books when he began to teach the natives Latin, so he wrote out a lesson for each pupil on a separate leaf, sometimes working at this all night. He not only composed for the natives in their own tongue hymns and catechisms but also prepared a grammar and dictionary for the use of missionaries in acquiring the language. He was shoemaker for his brethren, although he went barefooted himself. "I serve as physician and barber, physicking and bleeding the Indians"—his instrument a pocket-knife—"and some of them have recovered under my hands." His biographer describes his work as follows:

"Barefooted, with no other garment than his cassock, his crucifix and rosary round his neck, his pilgrim's staff and his breviary in his hand, and his shoulders laden with the furniture requisite for an altar, Anchieta advanced into the interior of the country. He penetrated virgin forests, swam across streams, climbed the roughest mountains, plunged into the solitude of the plains, confronted savage beasts, and abandoned himself entirely to the care of Providence. All these fatigues, and all these dangers, had God alone for witness; he braved them for no other motive than to conquer souls. As soon as he caught sight of a man, Anchieta quickened his pace; his bleeding feet stain the rocks and sands of the desert, but he still walks onwards. As he approached the savage, he stretched out his arms towards him, and with words of gentleness strove to restrain him beneath the shadow of the Cross, which to him was the standard of peace. Sometimes, when the savages rejected his first overtures, he threw himself at their knees, bathing them with his tears, pressing them to his heart, and striving to gain their confidence by every demonstration of love. At first the savages made small account of this abnegation, but the Jesuit was not discouraged. He made himself their servant, and studied their caprices like a slave; he accompanied them in their wanderings, entered into their familiarity, shared their sufferings, their labors, their pleasures. By degrees he taught them to know God, revealed to them the laws of universal morality, and prepared them for civilization after he had formed them to Christianity."

427. Of another missionary, **Henry Reichler**, a Protestant writer, Clements Markham, says:

"The most heroic devotion could alone have enabled him to face the difficulties which surrounded him. During twelve years he performed forty difficult journeys, through dense forests, or in canoes on rapid and dangerous rivers. He never took any provisions with him, but wandered barefooted and half naked through the tangled underwood, trusting wholly to Providence for support. His efforts were rewarded with success, and having learnt some of the Indian languages, he at last surrounded himself with followers."

The ignorance and barbarism of the Indians formed a slight obstacle to the success of the missions as compared with the selfishness and barbarity of the Portuguese colonists. They enslaved and destroyed the natives relentlessly and hated their friends and protectors, the missionaries, with a hatred so deadly that at last it secured their expulsion from the country.

428. The Las Casas of Brazil was **Antonio Vieira,** court preacher in Lisbon and intimate personal friend and adviser of the royal family. He craved the missionary life and sought to sail without permission to America, in a clandestine way. He was detected and held back by the royal mandate. But at last, after several romantic episodes, he got off to Brazil. He gave himself with intense devotion to work among the natives. He was not only a statesman and a missionary; he was also one of the world's greatest preachers. With consummate tact he secured an invitation from some of the worst of the enslaving colonists to preach to them on the subject. There was a crowded house. He skillfully and passionately lifted them to such a height of moral sensibility that, at a later meeting that very day, they solemnly signed an agreement guaranteeing some semblance of justice to the natives. There was real improvement for a time. But greed was too strong for conscience. He then went to Lisbon in behalf of the Indians. His discourses to king and council, which secured strong measures for Brazil, and his plea with the Jesuit Conclave to be allowed to return to Brazil, in spite of the king's wish to the contrary, read still—even in a translation and to men of another form of religion—like the words of a man who was at the same time a prophet of righteousness and an apostle of grace, inspired to the noblest pitch of Christlikeness. Vieira prevailed and went back from a position of high influence to do the

everyday work of a humble missionary among savages.

In the first seventy-five years of mission work in Brazil, 222 members of the Society of Jesus were sent there, hundreds more later, as well as some from the Franciscan and other orders. They planted so well that a hundred years after their expulsion there remained 800,000 Christian Indians in Brazil.

429. The regions south of Brazil were the scene of still more successful missionary operations. More than 5,000 Spanish missionaries of the Jesuit Company, besides many of other nations and of other orders, gave themselves to heroic service in the vast region between the Parana and Paraguay rivers and the Andes Mountains and southward almost to Cape Horn, between 1586 and 1767.

**Lucas Cavallero**, in his single-hearted devotion to Paraguay, reminds us of Xavier in his work for the Indies. **Manuel de Ortega** might well be called the Apostle of Paraguay, had he not been accompanied and followed by such a number of apostolic men that it seems unjust to name one in preference to half-a-dozen others. Ortega was one of the first. **Cypriano Baraza**, one hundred years later, was one of the foremost. He accomplished great reforms and founded permanent work among the Indians, but was finally murdered by them.

Ortega and his comrades on their way to the field were captured by the English and set adrift in an open boat without adequate provisions or even oars, seven hundred miles from Buenos Ayres. But they reached the port. Then, traveling a thousand miles northeastward across the vast, treeless pampas, they met other Jesuits who had been sent almost as far southward from Peru. Here, in the Upper La Plata basin, they began to subdue the wild and brutal tribes by fearlessness, combined with utmost gentleness. They learned the language, nursed the sick, fed the hungry, overcame unspeakable ignorance and indolence, developing the bands of savages into peaceable, industrious, highly moral communities, fitly called "Reductions." In 1717 there were thirty reductions containing more than 100,000 baptized Indians in one province of Paraguay. Between 1610 and 1768, 702,086 Guaranys, adult and infant, were baptized. They were given letters and the beginning of a literature, along with a practical and diversified industrial education. The following sentences from Robert Southey have special weight when it is remembered that his gifted pen was, in general, hostile to Romanism:

"In every Reduction, not only was the knowledge of reading, writing and arithmetic literally universal, but there were some Indians who were able to read Spanish and Latin as well as their own tongue. Besides carpenters, masons and blacksmiths, they had turners, carvers, printers and gilders; they cast bells and built organs." From roving hunters they became settled agriculturists. "The Indians of the Reductions were a brave and industrious and a comparatively polished people." "The inhabitants for many generations enjoyed a greater exemption from physical and moral evil than any other inhabitants of the globe."

430. Something similar to the missionary work which we have seen going on in the vast valleys of the Amazon and of the La Plata was taking place at the

same time in the smaller territories of Iberian America. The papal sects which furnished the chief missionaries were the Dominican in the West Indies, and the Jesuit in Brazil and Paraguay.

**Francis de Solani**, a Franciscan, has been called the Apostle of Peru. The Dominicans were active there at an early day, especially in educational work. The University of Lima, now known as St. Mark, was established in a convent of their order in the middle of the sixteenth century.

The Augustinian missionaries in Peru included among their number men who had renounced large fortunes in order to give themselves to work for the conversion of the Indians. They were not allowed to receive gold, silver or other valuables from the natives except food. It was hoped that the strong contrast between their conduct in this respect and that of other Spaniards would lead the natives to understand that the missionaries sought only the spiritual welfare of the people. **Vivera** was instrumental in leading one of the Incas, Serai Tupac, to Christ.

The Jesuits established missions in Peru before 1690. **Stanislaus Arlet** writes in 1698 of work among the forest tribes in the mountains:

"We entered the Country of these Barbarians without Arms or Soldiers, accompanied only by Christian Indians (our Guides and Interpreters)." Rapid progress was made not only in nominal conversion but also in real transformation of life.

"Our Arguments against the Plurality of Wives made so strong an Impression on them, that they all (three families excepted) complied with our Arguments and Exhortations against that very prevailing Custom. We have been as successful in reclaiming them from Drunkenness. Some women have already learned to spin and to make Linen Cloth. . . . . As to the other Missions founded hereabouts within these ten years, you are to know, reverend Father, that the Christian Religion is said to make a very great Progress in them, upwards of 40,000 Barbarians having already been baptized. The Churches are thronged with auditors."

431. **Louis Bertrand,** a Dominican, labored with great devotion in New Granada (now Colombia) from 1562 to 1569. His biographer, Byrne, says that "in three years he brought more than 10,000 persons under the sweet yoke of Jesus Christ."

The Jesuit, **Alonzo de Sandobal,** who was sent to Cartagena, Colombia, in 1605 especially to do mission work among the Spaniards, was so impressed with the condition of the Mohammedan and pagan slaves imported from Africa as he saw them landed by ship-loads in Cartagena, that, turning aside from the work to which he had been appointed, he made himself depot-master for the slave ships and their oppressed cargoes. When he was recalled to Peru, **Peter Claver** became his successor. Claver gave himself so completely to the service of the slaves that he was called "The Father of the Negroes." On the arrival of the slave-ships he was at the pier to meet them, to take each slave by the hand, to minister to the sick, to cheer the despondent, to speak of hope; and he proved the sincerity of his words by his deeds of mercy, his absolute devotion. From 1615 to 1654 he made himself the slave of slaves, ministering to them like a tender, self-forgetting mother, stopping at no service, however menial and repulsive. He also carried his work among the natives, penetrating to remote and savage regions.

In Guiana more than one hundred members of the Company of Jesus toiled before 1711.

The most fascinating account of the Jesuits in South America is that which makes up a considerable part of Robert Southey's three sumptuous volumes on the "History of Brazil." In spite of his rank protestantism he thoroughly appreciated these Christlike missionaries and civilizers. Southey as a poet also wrote "A Tale of Paraguay." This narrative poem of some two thousand lines has less literary charm than the prose history. In the preface he affirms that it is founded, though as he hopes not foundered, on fact.

432. In Central America we may take space to mention but one of many missionary achievements. There was a region of most turbulent natives, north of Guatemala. It was called "The Land of War." Las Casas and three other Dominicans succeeded in subduing this region completely by missionary means, having first secured a written pledge from the civil authorities that no Spanish soldier or trader should be allowed to enter that country.

433. The Christian conquest of Mexico was made by a great number of workers, none of whom stand out in great prominence. The Franciscans seem to have done more than any other one sect, with the Dominicans next.

The Augustinians devoted themselves especially to the physical needs of the Indians, building hospitals in connection with their convents. **Alfonso de Veracruz** was a man of great learning and one of the chief founders and teachers of the University of Mexico. He was a champion of the Indians and in opposition to many of his contemporaries he advocated their admission to all the privileges of the church.

**Peter of Ghent,** who refused to accept any rank above that of a lay brother, spent fifty years as a teacher of Mexican Indians in the way of Christianity as he understood it. He not only taught them to abandon Aztec idols in favor of Romish images, he taught them also reading, writing, music, painting, carving and other arts, founding schools as well as churches. The chief ecclesiastic of the country said, "I am not the Archbishop of Mexico, but Brother Peter of Ghent is!"

Before the middle of the 16th century, according to Bishop **Zumarraga,** more than one million Indians had been baptized in Mexico by the Franciscans alone; five hundred heathen temples had been abandoned and twenty thousand idols destroyed.

Mexico soon became a center of missions to the regions beyond. It was from Mexico that a knowledge of Christ was carried to the Ladrone and the Philippine Islands. A great missionary fund was established by devout and wealthy Mexicans, the income of which did good work for generations, until sequestered by the government. Payment on account of it to missions in California has been secured by the intervention of the United States Government.

434. It was difficult for one not a Spaniard to enter Mexico 400 years ago, but Samuel Champlain succeeded in accomplishing the feat about the year 1600, and this is his report of the way in which the natives

were brought to the churches. The account is corroborated by Gage, who smuggled himself into the country thirty-five years after Champlain. Champlain says that the

"Spaniards were constrained to take away the Inquisition, and allow them (the natives) personal liberty, granting them a more mild and tolerable rule of life, to bring them to the knowledge of God and the belief of the holy church; for if they had continued still to chastise them according to the rigor of the said Inquisition, they would have caused them all to die by fire. The system that is now used is, that in every estance (estancia), which are like our villages, there is a priest who regularly instructs them, the said priest having a list of the names and surnames of all the Indians who inhabit the village under his charge.

"There is also an Indian, who is as the fiscal of the village, and he has another and similar list; and on the Sunday, when the priest wishes to say mass, all the said Indians are obliged to present themselves to hear it; and before the priest begins the mass he takes his list and calls them all by their names and surnames; and should any of them be absent, he is marked upon the list, and the mass being said, the priest charges the Indian who serves as fiscal to inquire privately where the defaulters are, and to bring them to the church; in which, being brought before the priest, he asks them the reason why they did not come to the divine service, for which they allege some excuse, if they can find any; and if the excuses are not found to be true or reasonable, the said priest orders the fiscal to give the said defaulters thirty or forty blows with a stick, outside the church, and before all the people."

435. The Californias, Lower and Upper, had been visited by Spaniards, including priests, many times before 1683, when the first mission was opened. The missionary was a German Jesuit, **Eusebius Khuen** (Kino), who had formerly been a professor of mathematics at Ingoldstadt, and a distinguished astronomer

of the fatherland. The mission was not permanently established, however, till 1698, when **M. Picolo** and **John Salvatierra** explored the peninsula for missionary purposes. Before the beginning of 1702 they had established there three missions.

"Each Mission consists of several Villages. A Chapel had been built for the second Mission; but being found too small, we have begun to raise a lofty Church, with Brick Walls, and design to cover it with Timber." . . . With regard to the Missionaries, 'twas with great Pleasure I heard, since my being here [capital of Mexico] that our King Philip V, whom God long preserve, has already provided for them, in a Manner worthy of his Piety and Grandeur; his Majesty, the Instant he was informed of the Progress which the Christian Religion made in these Parts, settling six thousands Crowns a year on our Mission. This will be sufficient to support a great number of Gospel-labourers, who will not fail to come to our assistance."

436. As early as 1544 **Louis Cancer** and other Dominicans were sent by the Spaniards to Florida in a ship fitted out by royal authority for exclusively missionary purposes. But they were driven off by the natives. Fifteen years later a number of Franciscans accompanied Don Tristam de Luna's attempt to found a colony on Pensacola Bay. But the first mission work to be actively established radiated from St. Augustine, being begun in 1566 by **John Roger** and two other Jesuits. They had a school for Indian children in Havana, Cuba. This mission continued for six years, was encouraged by the Pope himself, and had in all eighteen or twenty of the Company of Jesus on the field. They undertook work among the Creeks and Cherokees in the Carolinas and even made an attempt

in Virginia, but finally abandoned this mission. It is a suggestive fact that the two most dauntless of missionary bodies, the Jesuits and the Moravians, have felt justified in withdrawing from unproductive fields.

After an interval of twenty years **John Silva** and eleven other Franciscans in 1592 undertook work from St. Augustine.

Within five years they had six stations and many nominal converts. But a native uprising destroyed the work. In 1601, however, the mission was renewed. In 1617 thirty-five followers of Francis had entered Florida and established twenty stations. The work was extended among the Cherokees and the Apalaches, reaching Georgia as well as Western Florida. Many Christian Indian settlements were formed. But all were scattered by the English, to whom Florida was ceded in 1763.

437. The conversion of the natives of New Mexico from paganism to Romanism had two distinct periods, preceded by some heroic but futile attempts. **Mark of Nice** planted a cross on a hill among the Zunis in 1539. Soon after two other Franciscans, **John de Padilla** and **Louis de Escalona,** attempted to found missions, but were killed by the natives. Forty years later a regular mission was undertaken. But after a few tokens of good the missionaries were killed like their predecessors.

In 1597 a Spanish military post was founded on the Northern Rio Grande and called San Gabriel. The leadership of the missionary part of the undertaking frequently changed at first, but when **Francis de Esco-**

**bar** became the head the work developed great success. He had five co-laborers. By 1608 the Franciscans had baptized 8,000 Indians. Other missionaries reinforced the mission as it rapidly expanded. Within thirty years of the beginning twenty-seven stations had been opened. Some of them had fine church buildings. Many of the natives had been taught to read and write. In spite of all this the natives revolted against the foreign domination, and by 1680 succeeded in driving all the missionaries from the country.

About 1740 mission work was resumed on a large scale and carried on with great and permanent results. As soon as 1748 there were twenty-one stations, nearly all of which have continued ever since to be Roman Catholic centers. Many of the Indians in this region were semi-civilized to start with. By the time of William Carey the natives of New Mexico had been largely won under the banner of the cross.

438. The work of the Spanish missionaries (Franciscans) in Texas was like that in other parts of the Mexican territory. The earliest attempt was made by **Andrew d' Olmos** and **John de Mesa** in 1544. Not much was undertaken, however, till 150 years later. Then work was carried on with considerable success among many tribes. But, unlike that in New Mexico, the results have been almost entirely scattered under United States rule.

439. We have had a glimpse of the beginning of mission work in Lower California. In 1768 the Spanish government withdrew the Jesuit missionaries from that region as from every other. Their place was taken in

Lower California by Franciscans, who were instructed not only to man the old stations, but also to plant new ones in Upper California. So the work began on the Pacific coast of the United States. It was undertaken in a very systematic and thorough-going way. It was to be a military as well as a missionary occupation. Colonists of Christian Indians were also taken and a supply of livestock for the new settlements. The first expedition went partly by land and partly by sea. The leader of the missionary contingent was **Juñiper Serra**.

When he reached San Diego he found that four of the other missionaries, **Crespi, Vizcaino, Parron** and **Gomoz**, had reached that point with another section of the expedition. There these five Franciscans formally opened a mission, July 16, 1769. Within a few years 474 natives had been baptized. They were given some book education and also training in agriculture and in various useful handicrafts. They learned to raise cotton and to manufacture cloth. The California missions were industrial as well as evangelistic.

In 1770 a mission was founded at Monterey. There ten more Franciscans joined Serra. Mission after mission was founded, the one at San Francisco in 1776. When the enthusiastic leader, Serra, died in 1784, ten stations had been opened and about ten thousand Indians christened. The first mission opened by **Palou**, the successor of Serra, was at Santa Barbara in 1786. By the end of the century seventeen mission settlements had been opened. The rule was to leave two missionaries, some live stock and other equipments and a number of Christian Indians at each station. The surrounding natives were gradually drawn to the settlement and there subjected to rigid discipline, which was yet so good and obviously to their advantage that many savages gladly allowed themselves to be tamed. In California as nowhere else the Franciscans followed the methods which had made the Jesuits so successful in their "reductions" in Paraguay.

440. One sad feature of the mission work in Spanish America was the wide-reaching and terrible opposition of the colonists, most of them members of the same church as the missionaries.

Another deplorable feature of the missions was the conflict of the sects among them. These various Roman sects were not only jealous of each other but often bitterly antagonistic even to the extent of thwarting and destroying one another's work.

One of the deep defects of the work was the mass of superstition with which it was encumbered. The devoted missionaries would go without the simplest necessaries of life, but saddle upon their shoulders great packs of paraphernalia for celebrating their mechanical ritual and so tramp through hundreds and thousands of miles of forest and swamp and climb almost impossible Andean heights. Their master superstition was the idea that the rite of baptism has saving efficacy. This has been the master superstition of Christendom. They had it in its most perfect form. They sincerely and passionately believed that a few drops of water on a dying savage, accompanied by the mumbling of the baptismal formula, would make the eternal difference to him between heaven and hell, whatever his life had been. Denser still was the idea that the same ceremony on a new-born babe would make him a Christian, whatever his life might prove to be. The natives were fully equal to the missionaries in believing in the magic power of ceremony. Their first inference in some regions was that baptism was a fatal foreign spell to be avoided if possible. But the missionaries were equal to this critical situation and having moistened the sleeves of their robes beforehand could deftly squeeze out the saving drops unknown to all concerned. Oh, that making Christians of men were so easy a matter! Who would not compass land and sea to christen all mankind?

The deepest defect of all in these missions was the indulgence to a considerable extent of the idea that religion can exist and be genuine without morality. To a certain degree, however, the missionaries were uncompromising in their moral requirements.

Taken as a whole, faulty as the work was, the western hemisphere owes an incalculable debt of gratitude to the missionary zeal which came from the Spanish peninsula between 1492 and 1792, the world-shaping eras of Columbus and of Carey.

CHURCH AT SANTA BARBARA, CALIFORNIA.

CHAPTER XXIII.

# FRENCH AMERICA.

441. Abundant records of these missions. 442. Nova Scotia. 443. Maine. 444. Province of Quebec. 445. Ontario. 446. New York. 447. Michigan and Wisconsin. 448. Illinois. 449. Louisiana. 450. Final outcome.

441. The French missions in North America probably have more abundant records than any other missions in the world. They certainly have the fullest record that ever has been published in the English language. The Jesuit missionaries sent home both formal and informal accounts of their work. Many of these reports were published at the time and aroused great interest in France, calling forth generous contributions for the maintenance of the work. They have been republished from time to time, with the addition of documents previously unpublished. No student can be perfectly contented until he has seen these records for himself. They are to be found in all large libraries. Their last and fullest edition leaves nothing to be desired.

It is published by the Burrows Brothers, Cleveland, O., and is entitled "The Jesuit Relations and Allied Documents, Travels and Explorations of the Jesuit Missionaries in New France, 1610-1791. The original French, Latin and Italian Texts, with English Translations and Notes: Illustrated by Portraits, Maps and Facsimiles. Edited by Reuben Gold Thwaites, Secretary of the State Historical Society of Wisconsin." Sixty-six volumes appeared between 1896 and 1900, bringing out the documents down to 1712. That would be equal to thirty-three volumes, if they were printed in only one language to cover a single century.

This simple but stupendous literary fact brings before the mind, as perhaps nothing else could, the moral magnitude of the French missions in America. They were conducted by well-educated men, men of refinement, in the midst of unspeakable savagery, with a personal devotion and heroism never surpassed. Much of the copious record is not that of missionary work in the strictest sense, but it is all incidental to the work and illustrative of it; and most of it is written by the missionaries themselves in the interests of their enterprise. The works of John G. Shea (R. C.) and of Francis Parkman (Prot.), to say nothing of others, put the substance of the history within reach of the English reading public a generation ago. There is no necessity, therefore, for more than an outline in a work so compact as the present.

442. The first French mission work in America was in the Maritime Provinces of Canada, and was conducted by Jesuits and other Roman Catholic workers. King Henry IV, in the grant to the Protestants, had

stipulated that the natives should be converted to the Roman Church alone. Accordingly, in 1610 the Huguenot proprietors brought a secular priest, **Jesse Flèche,** to Port Royal, Nova Scotia. The first report of his work was written by the hand of a Protestant, Marc Lescarbot, a Paris lawyer, poet and historian. He gives a glowing account of "The Conversion of the Savages who were Baptized in New France during this year 1610." An Indian sagamore, by the name of Memberton, reputed to be one hundred years old, was baptized, with twenty of his people. Lescarbot reports another chief as having come near to the kingdom of God.

A year later two Jesuits arrived, **Pierre Biard** and **Ennemonde Massé.** Three others soon followed. Extensive exploration was made and something of the language learned. But in 1613, being then in the new French colony on Mt. Desert Island, they were killed or carried away at the destruction of the place by the Virginians.

From 1619 to 1624 a party of Franciscans of the rigid Recollet branch toiled in Acadia. Others again of the same order from 1630 to 1633. The Jesuits then took up the work with a central station on Cape Breton Island and prosecuted it intermittently for nearly forty years, when they abandoned the field. About 1673 the Recollets resumed the work and carried it on till all the Micmacs from Cape Gaspé to Nova Scotia were counted Christians.

443. For one hundred and fifty years (1646-1796), though with many interruptions, missions were con-

ducted among the Abenakis, in what is now the State of Maine. **Gabriel Druillettes** was the founder of the mission. The central station was at Norridgewock, on the Kennebec River. Many were won to Christ. But the chronic troubles between the French and the English were naturally acute at this point. In 1688 **James** and **Sabastian Bigot** were on the Kennebec missions and **Peter Thury**, who was not a Jesuit, established a mission on the Penobscot. The Indian converts were devoted to the French, not without reason. After the Peace of Utrecht in 1713, the Governor of Massachusetts urged a Puritan missionary on the Indians. The following reply attributed to them shows the French work in its best light, not only for Maine, but for all the northern country to the Mississippi River. To have a balanced view one would need to keep in mind the fact that French trappers and traders as greedy as the English nearly always preceded the French missionaries, and the fact that from the earliest days there were not wanting English missionaries who were devoted to the Indians:

"When you first came here, you saw me long before the French governors, but neither your predecessors nor your ministers ever spoke to me of prayer or the Great Spirit. They saw my furs, my beaver and moose skins, and of this alone they thought; these alone they sought, and so eagerly that I have not been able to supply them enough. When I had much, they were my friends, and only then. One day my canoe missed the route; I lost my path and wandered a long way at random, until at last I landed near Quebec, in a great village of the Algonquins, where the Black-gowns were teaching. Scarcely had I arrived when one of them came to see me. I was loaded with furs, but the Black-gown of France disdained to look at them; he spoke to me of the Great Spirit, of heaven, of hell, of the prayer, which is the only way to reach heaven. I heard him with pleasure and was so delighted by his words that I remained in the village near him. At last the prayer pleased me and I asked to be instructed; I solicited baptism and received it. Then I returned to the lodges of my tribe and related all that had happened. All envied my happiness and wished to partake it; they, too, went to the Black-gown to be baptized. Thus have the French acted. Had you spoken to me of the prayer as soon as we met I should now be so unhappy as to pray like you, for I could not have told whether your prayer was good or bad. Now I hold to the prayer of the French; I agree to it; I shall be faithful to it, even until the earth is burnt and destroyed. Keep your men, your gold and your ministers; I will go to my French father."

From first to last there were two missionaries to French colonists and twenty to the Indians in Maine. At least eight of these were Jesuits. The most famous was **Sebastian Rale.** He had charge of the work thirty-one years. Most of the others, except Thury, simply made a missionary visit. Rale was killed in border strife by the English and was counted a martyr by the French. In the end most of the Christian Indians migrated to Canada.

A pleasant episode in connection with the French mission in New England was the visit of Druillettes to Boston as an envoy of his government. He was received with great cordiality and hospitality by the Puritans and by the Pilgrims. We are most interested in his meeting at Roxbury with John Eliot, who had just begun his work for Indians. "I arrived at Rosqbray, where the minister, named Master Heliot, who was teaching some savages, received me at his house, because night was overtaking me; he treated me with respect and kindness, and begged me to spend the winter with him."

444. On the St. Lawrence, Champlain introduced missionaries at Quebec in 1615. The first were Recollets, **Denis Jamay, Jean d' Olbeau** and **Joseph le Caron**, with a lay brother, **Pacifigue du Plessis.** They were reinforced four years later by others of the same order. These austere disciples of Francis of Assisi, in their gray robes and shod only with wooden sandals, carried the gospel they had all the way from the lower St. Lawrence to Lake Nipissing. But after ten years they called in the aid of the followers of Ignatius Loyala, whom we have seen doing such effective work in Asia, Africa and South America. For a few years the Recollets and Jesuits conducted the mission jointly, but without marked results. All were carried away by the English in 1629.

In 1632 France gave to the Company of Jesus entire charge of the work. **Paul le Jeune** came as head of the mission. He was accompanied by **Le Noue** and a lay-brother, **Gilbert.** During the annual trade gatherings of natives at Tadousac, Three Rivers and Montreal, as well as Quebec, the missionaries worked with them and then followed them in their wretched wanderings wherever fish and game could be found. One of the most intrepid workers in this way was **Betuex.** At Sillery, four miles from Quebec, a stockaded station was established for the protection of the Algonquin Indians from the Iroquois, and with the hope of leading them from nomadic to agricultural habits.

In 1639 the first women arrived to engage in mission work. There were three Hospital nuns who came to establish a Hotel-Dieux. They opened their first hospital at Sillery. Before long they moved to Quebec into a house provided for them by the Duchesse d'Aguillan. In the same ship came four other women workers, three Ursuline nuns, with Marie de l'Incarnation at their head, accompanied by the foundress of their work in Canada, **Madame de la Peltrie.** The two named were women of most romantic careers. Before many months had gone by both groups of delicate women were nursing a multitude of savages through a terrible scourge of smallpox.

At the mouth of the Saguenay. Tadousac, the Jesuits, under the leadership of **Jean du Quen** established a mission among the Montagnais, which continued from 1640 to 1782. The missionaries followed their nomadic people, enduring unspeakable hardships, through all the vast wilds to Hudson Bay, where a station was opened in 1694. A chief helper in the work from Tadousac was one of the Montagnais converts, **Charles Meiachkwat.** It was through a missionary journey of his that the way was opened for Druillettes in Maine.

In 1641 a missionary settlement was made by the Jesuits at Montreal. The Sulpicians were allowed to take charge of this mission, which was afterward removed to the Lake of the Two Mountains, on the lower part of the Ottawa River.

**Jerome Lalemant** came to Canada as Superior of the Jesuits in 1637. In 1649 he wrote that when he came he had found "but one Christian Huron family, with two or three which composed the Algonquin and Montagnais Church," and that now, after but twelve years, "I leave in it hardly any family—Huron, Algonquin or Montagnais—that is not thoroughly Christianized."

The Indians on the banks of the St. Lawrence, having been driven away by the Iroquois, a mission station was opened for them south of that river, on the Chaudiere, called St. Francis de Sales (1685).

445. The Jesuit mission which had the most of daring adventure and of temporary success, was that to the Hurons, located between Lake Simcoe and the great Georgian Bay of Lake Huron. The Hurons were in race more closely allied to the Iroquois than to the Algonquins. They were less nomadic than the latter, engaged more in agriculture and appeared to be farther on the way to civilization, though still inveterate savages.

The Recollet Franciscan, Le Caron, went among them in 1615. Others of that order during the next ten years did heroic pioneer work, especially **Nicholas Viel**, who was killed by a treacherous Indian as he was nearing Montreal to arrange with the Jesuits for their co-operation.

In 1625, having received some instruction in the Huron language from the Recollets and being guided by one of them, **Jean de Brebeuf** and Le Noue went into the Huron country. Brebeuf was a man of so great physique that it was difficult to induce the Indians to take him in their canoes for the long voyage up the Ottawa river. In most important respects he was for twenty-five years the giant of the mission. He had for coadjutors **Daniel Lalemant, Garnier,** and a full score more of the Company of Jesus, besides many helpers called Donnes, because they gave themselves to the work, and many more French artisans, farmers and workmen employed for the advancement of Christianity among the Hurons. But with all their bravery, patience and tact, they could count in 1640 only one hundred converts out of a population of 16,000 Hurons. Often at imminent peril to themselves, they had baptized a great many dying infants, however, whose "salvation" by that means gave the devoted missionaries sweet satisfaction.

At last, in spite of fierce pagan opposition, the work was beginning to tell, when the Iroquois determined to exterminate their cousins, the Hurons. They did the work with a terrific hand. By 1650, the Hurons as a distinct people were no more, and the most famous mission of the Jesuits in North America was abandoned. Seven of the Company of Jesus had laid down their lives on the Huron altar, including the Titanic missionary, Brebeuf.

446. According to Indian custom, many of the conquered Hurons were incorporated with the conquering tribes of the Five Nations of confederates along the Genesee and the Mohawk. Some of them brought their new-found faith with them and pleaded for the ministrations of the "Black Robes."

**Meantime, Isaac Jogues** (1642) and **Francis Bres-**

**sani** (1644) had been captured by the Iroquois, taken to their country and most inhumanly tortured. These two Jesuits were rescued by the Dutch colonists and sent to Europe. Nothing daunted, they were soon back in America and in 1646 Jogues went as a peace envoy to his former tormentors and a few months later he went among them again to plant a mission. This time they cruelly put him to death. He had borne a sincere and noble witness to Christ among the bloody Mohawks.

Further west, a mission was established among the Onondagas by **Claude Dablon** and **Peter Chaumonot** in 1655, and greatly reinforced the next year. The active influence of Huron Christians helped the work and a number of converts were made. After various ups and down, the French government in Canada lent a strong military hand. A large new mission force was sent. By 1668 there were Jesuits among all the Five Nations. Some distinguished converts were made, Chiefs Assendase, Kryn and Sænrese. Two women who received the name of Catherine were distinguished, Tegakouita, the "Iroquois Saint," and Ganneaktena, the founder of a Christian village. In 1708 the last Jesuit missionary left this region. In a half century there had been some forty missionary priests in Northern New York, most of them Jesuits.

447. On the west shores of the upper great lakes now in Michigan and Wisconsin, there were extensive missions for one hundred and fifty years before 1800. The natives are commonly known by the name of the Ottawas, though many other tribes were included.

JACQUES MARQUETTE.

*G. Trentanove.*

Pioneers celebrated mass at Sault Ste. Marie in 1641 and on the shores of Keweenaw Bay in 1660. A mission settlement was made and a chapel built at La Pointe, western Lake Superior, by **Claude Allouez** in 1665. The record of the first winter's work is characteristic of the early efforts in all the Roman Catholic missions. Eighty infants were baptized and four adults, three of the latter being in danger of death. But Christ was made known to multitudes who had never heard of him. At the end of two years Allouez made the long voyage to Quebec to report to his superior. In two days after making his report, he started back from civilization, taking **Louis Nicholas** with him. Fragments of many tribes gathered around La Pointe. The missionaries proclaimed the faith to representatives of twenty-five different clans. For some thirty years Allouez toiled in all parts of the region which we are now considering. More than any other one man he was its apostle.

He was succeeded in charge of the work at La Pointe by **Jacques (James) Marquette** best known of all the western missionaries, though he was but seven years on the field. He had a gift of tongues. During the year's preparation at Quebec he had acquired a usable knowledge of six Indian dialects. He had also a large endowment of the pioneering instinct as well as unsurpassed devotion. It was in 1669 that he took charge at La Pointe. He proposed to go still farther west among the terrible Sioux. But they declined his overtures and before long attacked and dispersed the Indians from La Pointe. Many of them fled eastward to the straits between Lake Michigan and Lake Huron. The missionary came with them in 1671. The next year a chapel was built on the north shore of the straits, opposite the island of Mackinaw. The new station was named Point St. Ignace, after Ignatius Loyola, the founder of the Jesuits. Five hundred Indians settled about the chapel and came to its services, many of them twice a day. "The minds of the Indians here," wrote Marquette, "are now more mild, tractable and better disposed to receive instruction than in any other part." The people who gave Marquette such satisfaction were largely a remnant of the Hurons. But before long thirteen hundred Ottawas settled at St. Ignace, and work was carried on among them. The mission was closed in 1706 by the hostility of Cadillac, French governor at Detroit. Six years later it was re-opened at Old Mackinaw, on the southern shore of the Strait.

Meantime our old friend Druillettes, whom we met in New England more than twenty years ago, has come to the Sault. By ministry to the sick during an epidemic he has won all hearts. In 1670 a general council of the Indians declared the place to be Christian. The veteran minister was permitted to baptize three hundred in a single year.

While these things were going on at the Sault and at Mackinaw, Allouez had passed through the straits into Lake "Michihiganing" (Michigan) and up Green Bay to a point near its head, where six Frenchmen had a trading-station. There Allouez opened a mission, naming it after the apostle of Asia, St. Francis Xavier. In the spring of 1670 he went up the Fox River, making known to a distressed and harried people the Suffering Saviour. Passing over the portage into the Wisconsin River, he proclaimed Christ to the inhabitants there. No one can read his journals without falling in love with this simple-hearted and sincere missionary. He was in very fact a member of the Company of Jesus. The work among several different tribes in the Green Bay country prospered. **Louis Andre became pastor** at Xavier station, Allouez devoting himself to the people up the Fox River. At Xavier there were before many years five hundred church members.

In 1728 a Jesuit mission was established below Detroit on the Canadian side of the river (Sandwich, Ont.) for the special benefit of remnants of the Hurons. **Armand de la Richardie** was put in charge. He opened a trading post, free from liquor, at which such fair treatment was given that many Indians gathered about in preference to Detroit.

448. Marquette followed Allouez' track over the Fox River portage into the Illinois River and sailed down the latter until he discovered the Mississippi River, June 17, 1673. He followed it down to the Arkansas and then returned by the same route. He found the natives friendly and promised to return to them. He suffered terribly from a wasting disease, but set out in 1674 to keep his promise, going this time by way of the Chicago River. He found it frozen, and, with his two companions, was obliged to spend the winter in a cabin at the mouth of the river. So it came about that the first white resident of Chicago was a

missionary to the heathen. In the spring he completed the journey to the Kaskaskia region. The emaciated paleface told an assembly of two thousand people the story of Jesus. He had kept his word. At the end of a week he started for Green Bay by way of the St. Joseph River and the eastern shore of Lake Michigan. He grew daily weaker. At last he pointed out a bluff near the river, since named for him, as the place of his burial. There his faithful boatmen buried him. It is not unfitting that two hundred and twenty-five years after, this pioneer of the great highways of the West should be remembered in the name of a railway which has a network of tracks over the State of Michigan.

Allouez made three missionary journeys to the Illinois country. But **James Gravier** was the first permanent missionary and did a faithful work for eighteen years (1688-1706). Up to the middle of the eighteenth century thirty-one missionaries labored on the field. By 1721 the Illinois were nearly all Christianized, at least nominally. The chief centers of evangelization were Peoria, Kaskaskia and Tamaroa. There was also a mission on the St. Joseph River near the portage to the Kankakee. For some time in the first quarter of the eighteenth century **John B. Chardon** was the gifted missionary there.

449. Marquette entered Louisiana in 1673. Missions were carried on there by secular priests from the seminary in Quebec and by Jesuits between 1698 and 1714, and by the Jesuits again from 1725 to 1770, the latter coming directly from France by way of New

Orleans. Sixteen missionaries are named in all, five of whom were killed by the Indians. The first two to go were **Anthony Davion** and **Francis de Montigny** who toiled there for fifteen years; but there seem to have been no substantial results.

450. The French missions in Northern America, beginning in 1610, continued to the end of the eighteenth century and onward. The chief activity was within a period of about one hundred years from 1625. Work was done from Nova Scotia to Hudson Bay, the west end of Lake Superior and the mouth of the Mississippi River. The chief activity was within reach of the waterway of the Great Lakes and the St. Lawrence River. More than one hundred and fifty different names are on the roster as given by Shea, not including the central missions on the St. Lawrence. The missionaries were Franciscans, Jesuits, Sulpicians and secular clergy, four-fifths of them being Jesuits. In co-operation were much of the wealth and nobility of France, nearly always the French government, and commonly the traders and colonists. These last were sometimes a severe trial to the missionaries and occasionally hostile, but never to the extent that they were in English and Spanish America. Many have followed Bancroft in the statement that the Jesuits were the first to round every headland and enter every navigable stream in the West, but the records show that the missionaries in all the regions were preceded by the traders. It is to the credit of the French people in America that they were generally a tower of strength to the missionaries.

In results, a nomadic race which is being dispersed and completely subordinated, can not show a monumental outcome. The missionaries themselves had in mind mainly life in another world instead of in this. They believed that baptism would secure the end, consequently the vast majority of all their baptisms were of infants. The mission counted the most successful at the time, was the one to the Ottawas. In 1794 **Gabriel Richard,** a Sulpician, was sent to Detroit by the Bishop of Baltimore, to whose charge that field belonged, with instructions to look after the Indians as well as the colonists. In 1799 he visited Mackinaw, Green Bay, Sault Ste. Marie and other stations of the old missions. He found seven hundred nominal Christians at Mackinaw, but his report to Bishop Carroll said that in all these fields of the old Ottawa mission there had not been a priest for thirty years. Immorality, debauchery and paganism prevailed. Still, on the wide field of French missions in Northern America, the lives of hundreds of men and women were transformed from savagery and made genuine Christian lives, some of them illustrious with grace. The missionaries carried on a large amount of humane, educational and social work. There are in Canada to this day a number of groups of Indians whose ancestors were Christianized more than two hundred years ago.

In ultimate effect, probably the chief value to the world of the French missions in America is the ideal of devotion, discipline and unmeasured heroism which these missions embodied and modestly but minutely recorded. This ideal is dimmed here less than in some other parts of the world by that tendency to suicide, the passion for martyrdom. With only an average number of exceptions, the French missionaries were devoted servants of humanity, true men of God, whose ideal was service to others rather than martyrdom for self.

CHAPTER XXIV.

# ENGLISH AMERICA.

451. Uncollected records. 452. The original intention. 453. "First Fruits." 454. Roger Williams the first missionary. 455. His "Key." 456. What the key unlocked. 457. His long apostolate. 458. Dunster and Harvard. 459. John Eliot. 460. The Mayhews. 461. The Sergeants and Jonathan Edwards. 462. Connecticut. 463. New York. 464. New Jersey. 465. Pennsylvania. 466. Ohio. 467. West Indies calling out the Moravians. 468. Work on the islands.

451. The English missions in North America have never been fully reported. The scanty and scattered records of the work have never been brought together, but are still to be searched for here and there in out-of-the-way places. A little effort in that direction proves that the search thoroughly prosecuted would disclose work every whit as noble in quality and in results as that of the French, whose ample records for the same period fill sixty-six goodly volumes.

452. The Virginia Charter of 1609 and the New England Patent of 1620 contained precisely the same words. "The principal effect which we can desire or expect of this action, is the conversion and reduction of the people in those parts into the true worship of

DEPARTURE OF THE PILGRIMS FROM DELFT HAVEN.
*Charles W. Cope.*

God and Christian religion." Bradford gave among the reasons for the migration of the Pilgrims:

"Lastly (and which was not least), a great hope & inward zeall they had of laying some good foundation, or at least to make some way therunto, for ye propagating & advancing ye gospell of ye kingdom of Christ in those remote parts of ye world; yea, though they should be but even as stepping-stones unto others for ye performing of so great a work."

Winthrop's proposals for a colony were equally full of the missionary purpose. He began by giving "The grounds of settling a plantation in New England" as follows:

"*First,* The ppagacon of the gospell to the Indians. Wherein first the importance of the worke tendinge to the inlargement of the Kingdome of Jesus Christ & winning them out of the snare of the Divell & converting others of them by their meanes."

The Charter of Massachusetts, granted by Charles I. in 1629, shows that England, as truly as Spain, Portugal and France, had for a leading motive Christian missions. After naming certain duties of the officers of the colony, the charter continues:

"and for the directing, ruling and disposing of all other matters and things whereby our said people, inhabitants there, maie be soe religiously, peaceablie and civilly governed, as their good life and orderlie conversacon maie wynn and incite the natives of country to the knowledge and obedience of the onlie true God and Savior of mankind, and the Christian fayth, which, in our roal intencon and the adventurers free profession, is the principale ende of this plantacon."

Similar sentiments are expressed in the charters of other English colonies.

453. The very year that the Massachusetts Charter was granted John Cradock of England called the spe-

cial attention of the colonists to this "principall ende" of their chartered existence. With a single prominent exception they had been slow and scant in missionary activity. They were stirred at last to tell what little they had done. "New England's First Fruits" (1634), is the happy title of the first printed announcement in old England of the missionary and educational work of New England. Missions to the heathen and a college—happy and abiding combination! Thirteen years after the first Pilgrim's foot touched the wild shores of Massachusetts Bay, was soon, perhaps, for a college, but it surely was not too soon for some first fruits from the heathen to whom those shores belonged. The pity is that there was such a meager sheaf, after a round dozen of years. Ten Indians, besides "divers of the Indian Children, Boyes and Girles, we have received into our houses, who are long since civilized, and in subjection to us," are described as having shown some inclination toward Christianity.

The New England fathers were not satisfied to count as converted people who had merely submitted to a few Christian observances. Their standards for nominal admission to the Christian fold were much more exacting than those of the Spaniards and the French. The best that they have to say about most of the ten is to the same effect as the report of the first one at Plymouth: "He could never be gotten from the English, nor from seeking after their God, but died amongst them, leaving some good hopes in their hearts that his soul went to rest." They speak with more confidence of a certain "Blackmore maid, that hath long lived at Dorchester" and of "that famous Indian Wequash, who "is dead, and certainly in heaven; gloriously did the grace of God shine forth in his conversation, a year and a half before his death he knew Christ, he preached Christ up and down, and then suffered Martyrdom for Christ." It was believed that he was poisoned by the Indians because of his faithful preaching of Christ. The convincing proof of his Christianity was that he had become temperate in behavior and in drink, also "putting away all his wives, saving the first, to whom he had most right." Describing his conversion, they say that "some English (well acquainted with his language) did meet him and spent more than halfe the night in conversing with him." The Boston writers did not like to say that it was Roger Williams who was the instrument of the only brilliant missionary success which they could report. But so it appears from his own statement, to be quoted later. According to all accounts he was at that time the only colonist who was well acquainted with the Indian language.

The authors of the "First Fruits" conclude the narrative part with the following reasonable observation:

> "Thus we have given you a little tast of the sprincklings of God's spirit, upon a few Indians, but one may easily imagine, that here are not all that may be produced: for if a very few of us here present, upon very sudden thoughts, have snatcht up only such instances which came at present to hand, you may conceive, that if all in our Plantations (which are farre and wide) should set themselves to bring in the confluence of all their Observations together, much more might be added."

The mission work of New England, like most of that in the first Christian centuries, was done as an essential activity of the Christian life, and not by people who were set apart exclusively for the missionary function.

454. The first man who gave so much attention to the conversion of the native heathen that he can be called a missionary to them, was **Roger Williams.** While assistant pastor at Plymouth (1631-1632) he devoted himself largely to the Indians. He frequently lived with them in their lodges and learned their language so as to use it freely. One of the great causes of the banishment of Williams from Massachusetts was his rigorous insistence that the King of England had no right "to take and give away the lands of other men." He cried aloud as to the King's "injustice in giving the country to his English subjects which belonged to the native Indians." When driven out into the wintry wilderness he found a welcome waiting him among the natives. They sheltered him for more than three months and gladly sold him the land for his new colony.

New England's Prospect, published in London in 1634, says of Williams that he

"in a special good intent of doing good to their (the Indians') soules, hath spent much time in attaining to their language, wherein he is so good a proficient, that he can speake to their understanding, and they to his; much loving and respecting him for his love and counsell. It is hoped (he adds) that he may be an instrument of good amongst them."

This was a dozen years before Eliot had learned to preach to the Indians. The very year that Williams made his settlement at Providence, having been banished from Massachusetts, the authorities of the latter

ROGER WILLIAMS.

had to call him in to help them in making a treaty with the Indians. "Because they could not well make them understand the articles perfectly, [they] agreed to send a copy of them to Mr. Williams, who could best interpret them to them." Sparks says that he "acquired an influence over them [the natives] far superior to that of any other person of his time."

For years all the colonists had to depend on Williams as mediator and interpreter, he being the only man in New England who was adequately acquainted with the Indians and with their language.

455. In 1643 Mr. Williams went to England in the interests of his colony, and published there a book of 224 pages, being an Indian-English vocabulary, or rather phrase-book, and containing other interesting matter about the Indians. Following is the original title-page in full:

# A KEY
into the
# LANGUAGE
of
# AMERICA:
or
An help to the Language of the Natives in that part of America, called NEW ENGLAND.

Together with briefe Obſervations of the Cuſtomes, Manners and Worſhips, &c. of the aforeſaid

## NATIVES,

in Peace and Warre, in Life and Death.

On all which are added Spirituall Obſervations, Generall and Particular by the Authour, of chiefe and speciall uſe (upon all occaſions), to all the Engliſh Inhabiting thoſe parts; yet pleaſant and profitable to the view of all men:

By ROGER WILLIAMS
of Providence in New England.

---

LONDON.
Printed by Gregory Dexter, 1643.

This first document, published to be used in prosecuting missions to the heathen in New England, begins as follows:

"*To my Deare and Welbeloved* Friends *and* Countreymen, *in old and new* England.

"I present you with a *Key*; I have not heard of the like yet framed, since it pleased God to bring that mighty *Continent* of *America* to light; Others of my Countrymen have often, and excellently, and lately written of the *Countrey* (and none that I know beyond the goodnesse and worth of it). This *Key*, respects the *Native Language* of it, and happily may unlocke some *Rarities* concerning the *Natives* themselves, not yet discovered.

"I drew the Materialls in a rude lumpe at Sea, as a private *helpe* to my owne memory, that I might not by my present absence *lightly lose* what I had so *dearely bought* in some few yeares *hardship*, and *charges* among the *Barbarians;* yet being reminded by some, what pitie it were to bury those *Matreialls* in my *Grave* at land or Sea; and withall, remembering how oft I have been importun'd by *worthy friends*, of all sorts, to afford them some helps this way.

"I resolved (by the assistance of *the most High*) to cast those *Materialls* into this *Key, pleasapt and profitable* for All, but specially for my *friends* residing in those parts:

"A little *Key* may open a *Box*, where lies a *bunch* of *Keyes*.

"With this I have entered into the secrets of those *Countries*, where ever *English* dwel about two hundred miles, betweene the *French* and *Dutch* Plantations; for want of this, I know what grosse *mistakes* my selfe and others have run into.

"There is a mixture of this *Lauguage, North* and *South* from the place of my abode, about six hundred miles; yet within the two hundred miles (aforementioned) their *Dialects* doe exceedingly differ; yet not so, but (within that compasse) a man may, by this helpe, converse with *thousands* of *Natives* all over the Countrey; and by such converse it may please the *Father of Mercies* to spread *civiltie* (and in his own most holy season) *Christianitie;* for *one Candle* will light *ten thousand*, and it may please *God* to blesse a *little Leaven* to season the *mightie Lump* of those Peoples and Territories.

"It is expected, that having had so much converse with these *Natives,* I should write some little of them.

"Concerning them (a little to gratifie expectation) I shall touch upon foure Heads:

"First, by what *Names* they are distinguished.

"Secondly, Their *Originall* and *Descent.*

"Thirdly, their *Religion, Manners, Customs, &c.*

"Fourthly, That great *Point* of their *Conversion.*"

456. This Key did, indeed, "open a box where lies a bunch of keyes." When Mr. Williams returned to America he brought a letter to the government of Massachusetts. This letter had the signature of the Earl of Northumberland, Lord Wharton and other members of Parliament. Three of the signers were members of the Commission for Plantations. This letter explained to Massachusetts the reasons for granting a charter to the new neighboring colony, giving as one the deserts of Williams on account of his "great industry and travail in his printed Indian labors. . . . the like whereof (had not been) seen extant from any part of America." It was only a few weeks after the arrival of Williams in Massachusetts with this letter that the interest of that colony was sufficiently aroused to take action for the first time in the direction of Christianizing the natives. The act empowers county courts to "take order from time to time to have them instructed in the knowledge and worship of God." Out of this state action arose the state-paid work of John Eliot.

Another missionary publication of Roger Williams has been lost. At the end of the Key he says: "I have further treated of these natives of New England, and that great point of their Conversion in a little additionall Discourse apart from this."

Mr. Baylie, an English Presbyterian, published a work in 1645, in which he took the Congregationalists of New England to task for their neglect to evangelize the heathen around them. He says that "only Master Williams in the time of his banishment from among them did essay what could be done with those desolate souls." In his own letters Williams speaks of his "soul's desire to do the natives good and to that end to learn their language," and says that "God was pleased to give me a painful, patient spirit to lodge with them in their filthy, smoky holes, (even while I lived at Plymouth and Salem), to gain their tongue." Again, "out of desire to attaine their language, I have run through varieties of intercourses with them, day and night, summer and winter, by land and sea."

In a letter to his friend, Governor John Winthrop, of Connecticut, as early as 1638, he says: "Good news of great hopes the Lord hath sprung up, of many a poor Indian soul inquiring after God. I have convinced hundreds at home and abroad that in point of religion they are all wandering, &c."

The letters of Williams, of which over one hundred and twenty-five have been discovered and printed, are laden with Indian affairs.

457. The next year after Williams had returned from England with the charter for Rhode Island, he moved twenty miles from town, (as far as two hundred miles would be now), into the wilds of the Narraganset country, for the purpose of mission work among the natives, as his latest biographer, Strauss, believes. There he lived for six years, so that many of his letters are

dated from that mission station, with its unmistakably Indian name, Cawcawmsquissick.

The closing paragraphs of Williams' introduction to his "Key" give us a glimpse of his missionary labors, his first convert and his hopes:

"Many solemne discourses I have had with all *sorts of Nations* of them, from one end of the Countrey to another (so farre as opportunity, and the little Language I have could reach).

"I know there is no small preparation in the hearts of Multitudes of them. I know their many solemne *Confessions* to my self and one to another of their lost *wandring Conditions.*

"I know strong *Convictions* upon the *Consciences* of many of them, and their desires uttred that way.

"I know not with how little *Knowledge* and *Grace* of Christ the Lord may save, and therefore neither will *despaire,* nor *report* much.

"But since it hath pleased some of my Worthy *Countrymen* to mention (of late in print) *Wequash,* the *Pequt Captaine.* I shall be bold so farre to second their *Relations,* as to relate mine owne Hopes of Him (though I dare not be so confident as others. Two dayes before his Death, as I past up to Quinnihticut River, it pleased my worthy friend Mr. *Fenwick* (whom I visited at his house in *Say-Brook* Fort at the mouth of that River) to tell me that my old friend *Wequash* lay very sick; I desired to see him, and Himselfe was pleased to be my Guide two mile where *Wequash* lay.

"Amongst other discourse concerning his *sicknesse* and *Death* (in which hee freely bequeathed his son to Mr. Fenwick) I closed with him concerning his *Soule*: Hee told me that some two or three years before he had lodged at my House, where I acquainted him with the *Condition of all Mankind,* & his *Own* in particular, how *God* created *Man* and *All things;* how *Man* fell from *God,* and of his present *enmity* against *God,* and the *wrath* of *God* against *Him* untill Repentance: said he 'Your *words were never out of my heart to this present'*; and said hee *'me much pray to Jesus Christ.'* I told him so did many *English, French* and *Dutch,* who had never turned to *God,* nor loved Him: He replyed in broken English: *'Me so big naughty Heart, me heart all one stone!' Savory expressions* using to breath *from compunct and broken Hearts,* and a sence of *inward hardnesse* and *unbrokennesse.* I had many discourses with him in his Life, but this was the summe of our last parting untill our generall meeting.

"Now because this is the great Inquiry of all men what *Indians* have been converted? what have the English done in those parts? what hopes of the *Indians* receiving the Knowledge of Christ?

"And because to this Question, some put an edge from the boast of the Jesuits in *Canada* and *Maryland,* and especially from the wonderfull conversions made by the Spaniards and Portugalls in the *West-Indies,* besides what I have here written, as also, beside what I have observed in the Chapter of their Religion; I shall further present you with a briefe Additionall discourse concerning this Great Point, being comfortably perswaded that that Father of Spirits, who was graciously pleased to perswade *Japhet* (the Gentiles) to dwell in the Tents of *Shem* (the Jewes) will in his holy season (I hope approaching) perswade, these Gentiles of *America* to partake of the mercies of *Europe,* and then shall bee fulfilled what is written by the Prophet *Malachi,* from the rising of the Sunne in *(Europe)* to the going down of the same (in *America)* my Name shall great among the Gentiles.) So I desire to hope and pray."

For more than forty years Roger Williams continued his apostolic labors among the Indians, making journeys to preach to them when he was an old man. He was not only the first English missionary to the Indians, but it is also true that he has had few, if any, successors showing a more deep and abiding interest in their general welfare. He was not only the foremost "apostle to the Indians" in New England, but he was also, like Vieira in Brazil, and Las Casas in the West Indies, their champion and defender against colonial aggression.

458. The second New Englander to take an active hand in the conversion and education of the Indians was **Henry Dunster,** the first president of Harvard College. It was said of him by Thomas Lechford in 1641: "He hath the platforme and way of conversion of the Natives indifferent right. . . . He will make it good that the way to instruct the Indians must be in their owne language, not English, and that their language may be perfected." During his presidency a new charter was obtained for the college in which he had the object of the school stated to be "the education of the English and Indian youth of this country in knowledge and godliness." Though strenuously opposed in this policy, he was determined that the college should be both a mission-school and a missionary training-school. But the efficient career of Dunster as president of Harvard was cut short by the authorities at the end of fourteen years, because he had become very pronounced and aggressive in his distinctly Baptist views.

459. Soon after the General Court of Massachusetts passed its act for the propagation of the gospel among the Indians, **John Eliot,** pastor at Roxbury, now a part of Boston, began to learn the language of the natives. He had come to the colony in 1631, the same year in which Roger Williams came and began his work among the Indians.

It was in 1646 that Eliot did his first mission

work, preaching to a band of Indians at Nonantum. Having begun, he carried the work on with zeal, as he was able in addition to his pastorate of the church of English colonists. It was largely because of the interest excited in England by Eliot's work that a missionary society was organized and incorporated by Parliament in 1649. "The Society for the Propagation of the Gospel in New England." This first English missionary society was organized one hundred and fifteen years after the formation of the Company of Jesus, and one hundred and forty-eight years before the society inspired by William Carey. Eliot's monumental work was the translation of the Bible (1661-1663) into Indian. In 1666 he published a grammar, twenty-three years after the "Key" by Williams.

In seeking to civilize the nomads, Eliot soon found it desirable to follow the example set by the Jesuits in Paraguay, and to some extent in Canada. He gathered them into Christian villages. He also took pains to raise up native workers. Through these, as well as through his own indefatigable journeys and teachings, the work was extended. His "Brief Narrative of the Progress of the Gospel amongst the Indians in New England in the year 1670," sent to the fostering society in England, describes briefly nine "Praying-Towns," besides those on Martha's Vineyard and Nantucket. At the end of thirty-eight years of toil Eliot had under his immediate care 1,100 converts.

**Daniel Gookin** had been Eliot's principal English helper. A native, **Tackawambit,** succeeded Eliot as pastor of the church at Natick.

460. The Mayhew family, five successive generations of them, did an ideal work for the Indians of Martha's Vineyard and Nantucket Islands during one hundred and sixty years (1646-1806). Thomas Mayhew, Sr., was proprietor and governor of Martha's Vineyard. His son, **Thomas Mayhew, Jr.,** was pastor of the settlement church, and having but a small English congregation, devoted himself largely to work for the natives. Within ten years an Indian church of two hundred and eighty-two members was organized. On his way to England to solicit funds for the mission Thomas Mayhew, Jr., was lost at sea.

His father, **Thomas Mayhew, Sr.,** at once took up the work and learned the Indian language, though he was seventy years of age. "He spared himself no pains in doing his work, often walking twenty miles through the woods in order to preach to or visit these Indians." By 1670 there were three thousand adult Christians on the island.

Before his death Thomas Mayhew, Sr., had associated with himself in his mission work his grandson, **John Mayhew,** (son of Thomas Mayhew, Jr.). He had entire charge of the work for eight years.

He was succeeded by his son, **Experience Mayhew.** This great grandson of Governor Mayhew was in the work more than thirty years. He prepared for the Indian Christians a new version of the Psalms and of the Gospel of St. John.

In "A Brief Account of the State of the Indians on Martha's Vineyard from 1649 to 1720," he says that at the latter date there were left 800 Indians out of the original 1,500 found on the island in 1642. These 800 were in six villages, each one provided with an Indian pastor. He sums up their state of evangelization as follows:

"Tho' there are many Indians on these Islands, who are very negligent as to their Attendance on the Publick Worship of God; yet I know of none, but what do make some Profession of Religion, and will talk soberly, when treated withal about it; having made a trial on some that have been most suspected. And tho' there are among these Indians a great many who are very defective in their Morals; yet there are a considerable number, even of those not yet joined in Church Communion, who live soberly, and Worship God in their Families."

He also published a book of two hundred and seventy-five pages entitled "Indian Converts," giving a sketch of the lives of thirty Indian preachers, and of ninety-eight other notable converts, of whom thirty-nine were women.

This matchless line of missionaries was continued by **Zechariah Mayhew,** son of Experience, who faithfully carried the work for the Indians on into the nineteenth century.

Associated with the Mayhews in mission work for the Indians was **Peter Foulger**, grandfather of Benjamin Franklin. Being an ardent Baptist, Foulger introduced his distinctive views among the Indians. By 1694 a Baptist church was in existence on Martha's Vineyard and another on Nantucket.

One of the Mayhews said of **John Tackamason,** an Indian Baptist pastor: "I had frequent conversation with him while he was in health and sometimes . . . in the time of that long sickness whereof he died; and never, from first to last, saw anything by him that made me any ways suspect the integrity of his heart, but did ever think him to be a godly and discreet man."

Before the year 1700, according to the careful estimate of Dr. W. D. Love, there were 7,000 Christian Indians in New England. There were not that many admitted as communicants under the Puritanic standard; but that many were as fully Christianized as those called Christian Indians under a different standard in, for instance, Canada or Brazil. The work was carried further throughout the eighteenth century.

461. In western Massachusetts among the Berkshire Hills, lived the Housatonic (Over-the-Mountain) Indians. They were led by ministers in the western part of the state, under the patronage of the governor, to ask for a missionary. **John Sergeant, a tutor in** Yale, was appointed in 1734. The scattered Indians were drawn together in a township, Stockbridge, and carefully evangelized and educated. This work developed one of the usual blessings of missions and education. It rose above denominational lines. It was in the hands of Presbyterians and Congregationalists, but Thomas Hollis, the London Baptist philanthropist and the largest early benefactor of Harvard College, pledged the support of twelve scholars in Mr. Sergeant's school. When the missionary died, at the end of fifteen years of service, one hundred and twenty-nine Indians, old and young, had been baptized. There were forty-two communicants.

Two years later (1751) **Jonathan Edwards was** called to take up this work, in conjunction with the pastorate of the church of white people in the same town. Thus it came to pass that one of the greatest intellects that this continent or any other continent has produced, became a missionary to the Indians. He continued in the work for six years, until called to the presidency of Princeton. It hardly seems possible that he could have given much labor to the Indians, for it was during this time that the masterpieces of his writing were produced. It is clear, however, that he had the missionary work at heart. His son, Jonathan, describes the situation in this way:

> "When I was but six years of age my father removed with his family to Stockbridge, which, at that time, was inhabited by Indians almost solely, as there were in the town but twelve families of whites, or Anglo-Americans, and perhaps one hundred and fifty families of Indians. The Indians being the nearest neighbors, I constantly associated with them; their boys were my daily schoolmates and play-fellows. Out of my father's house I seldom heard any language spoken but the Indian. By these means I acquired the knowledge of that language, and a great facility in speaking it. It became more familiar to me than my mother-tongue."

The father's highest ambition for this boy was that he should devote his life to the Indians. He sent the lad when but ten years of age with the Missionary **Gideon Hawley** into the wilds of the west to learn the language of the Oneidas.

In 1775 **John Sergeant, Jr.,** took up the work which his father had begun and Edwards had carried on. He continued in the work at Stockbridge and at New Stockbridge, in New York, whither the Indians migrated, for forty-nine years.

462. Rhode Island and Massachusetts work extended

into Connecticut. Experience Mayhew made more than one missionary tour in that colony, and his interpreter was a grandson of Wequash, whom Roger Williams had brought to Christ. Captain **John Mason** was employed by the "Society for the Propagation of the Gospel" to open a school for the Indians, which he conducted near New London for seven years (1727-1734). Workers from Natick visited the field. In 1733 **Jonathan Barber**, of Springfield, was appointed missionary. The "Great Awakening" of religion under Whitfield, and his specific suggestions, aroused the colonists to a new sense of their obligation to the aborigines.

The most marked mission work in Connecticut was in connection with the "Indian Charity School" in Lebanon. Eleazer Wheelock was appealed to by a poor Indian widow to take her son into his private school. He generously responded. This was in 1743. Others followed. The result was a genuine missionary training-school, which continued at Lebanon for twenty-seven years, when Dr. Wheelock removed it to Hanover, N. H., where it developed into Dartmouth College. Twenty-one Indians from New England, thirty-two from New York, and seven from New Jersey and Pennsylvania attended at Lebanon. Devoted young colonists also were trained there for missions.

Wheelock's first Indian pupil, **Samson Occom**, became the most gifted native missionary that the eighteenth century produced. He was worthy of the elaborate biography which has recently been written by Dr.

W. D. Love. Occom went to England in behalf of the missions to his countrymen, speaking with great acceptance throughout Great Britain. He secured there nearly $50,000 for the work.

463. Occom labored among the Indians in southern New England and finally was instrumental in combining seven settlements of Christian Indians in a migration to the Oneida country, New York, about 1776. He continued with them till his death, which occurred the same year in which Carey's missionary society was organized in England.

The happy name Brotherton was chosen for the new settlement. Not far away was New Stockbridge, to which we have seen that John **Sergeant** came with Stockbridge Indians some ten years later.

About ten years earlier one of the white pupils of the Lebanon training-school, **Samuel Kirkland, had, in the** same region, become an eminent missionary to the Oneidas themselves and to the people of the other Five Nations. In the time of the Revolutionary War, and long afterward, Mr. Kirkland was very useful to both the Iroquois and the Government as a mediator.

In earlier days, beginning in 1641, excellent work had been done among the Indians in this region by **Joannes Megapolenses,** of Albany. He learned to use the Mohawk language freely and received a number of Indians into his church. This staunch Dutch Protestant greatly befriended Isaac Jaques, the Jesuit missionary. In Schenectady earnest work was done and thirty-six Mohawks were church members by 1700.

**Henry Barclay** and other Church of England missionaries did successful work, having two Christian villages with five hundred inhabitants, thirty miles from Albany. In 1741 there were fifty-eight Indian communicants. Two years later only two or three people in the mission remained unbaptized.

The Moravians had a phenomenal work in Dutchess County, New York, between 1740 and 1744. **Christian Henry Rauch** followed two besotted headmen, Tschoop and Shabosh, to their huts. **Tschoop** became a most earnest Christian worker. In 1743 sixty-nine had been baptized at one place, and one hundred and twenty at another. The rum traffic and other wicked relations of the white men with the red men were so interrupted that the colonial authorities were induced to expel the missionaries. Most of the converts went with them to Pennsylvania.

On Long Island **Azariah Horton** did some work among the Shinnecock Indians. **James Davenport,** followed by Horton, preached occasionally to the Montauks on the eastern end of the island. It was here that, connected with the end of Horton's mission, **Samson Occom** began his work, in 1749, as a **school-teacher** and evangelist. He was soon ordained. For twelve years he did here effective, uplifting missionary work.

464. **David Brainerd** began his work among the Indians on the Hudson River, sixteen miles from Stockbridge. But his chief labors were in New Jersey, with missionary tours in Pennsylvania. His greatest service was in promoting the slowly rising tide of interest for missions. The journals of Brainerd were published in part by the Scottish "Society for

Propagating Christian Knowledge," of which he was missionary. The remainder had the advantage of being issued under the great name of Edwards as editor. They were in themselves highly gratifying to the current taste in religion. Though laden with morbid introspection, they were also fragrant with practical devotion to the redemption of those who sat in darkness.

"I spent the evening praying incessantly for divine assistance and that I might not be self-dependent, but still have my whole dependence on God. What I passed through was remarkable and, indeed, inexpressible. All things here below vanished; and there appeared to be nothing of any considerable importance to me but holiness of heart and life and the conversion of the heathen to God."

At a time when his food consisted "mostly of hasty-pudding, boiled corn and bread baked in the ashes and sometimes a little meat and butter," and when his lodging was "a little heap of straw, laid upon some boards a little way from the ground, for it is a log room without any floor," he adds, "and yet my spiritual conflicts and distresses so far exceed all these (and many other uncomfortable circumstances) that I scarce think of them or hardly observe that I am not entertained in the most sumptuous manner." Brainerd died at twenty-nine years of age, after only four years of missionary service and having baptized scarcely two-score converts. But his spirit fired Carey's heart, and "reading the life of Brainerd decided Henry Martyn to become a missionary."

After the death of David Brainerd, his brother **John Brainerd** carried on the work at intervals throughout his life, till 1781.

465. The colony of Pennsylvania, like that of Rhode Island forty-five years before, was established in the true Christian temper toward the natives. In 1682 William Penn and other Friends went entirely unarmed to hold a treaty council with a large body of Indian warriors and chiefs under the elm tree at Shackmaxon. This is the report of Penn's speech:

"The great Spirit, said he, who made you and me, who rules in heaven and earth, who knows the innermost thoughts of man; knows that I and my friends have a hearty desire to live in peace and friendship with the Indians, and to serve them to the utmost of our power. It is not the custom of me and my friends to use weapons of war against our fellow-creatures, and for this reason we have come to you without arms. Our desire is not to do injury and thus provoke the great Spirit, but to do good. We are now met on the broad pathway of good faith and good will, and no advantage will be taken on either side, but all is to be openness, brotherhood and love."

On this basis a treaty was concluded in which the Indians promised that "they would live in love and peace with Onas and his children so long as the sun and moon shall endure." They kept their word. There were no wars with the colony so long as the Friends held the reins of government. Even afterwards, through all the times of bloodshed, the Indians never took the life of a Friend.

At a Quarterly Meeting before long the Friends appointed a number of people "to instruct the natives in the principles of Christianity and the practice of a true Christian life." The Friends carried out the meaning of their beautiful name. They were always the practical, efficient friends of the Indians. They con-

NIKOLAUS LUDWIG.
COUNT VON ZINZENDORF UND POTTENDORF.

tributed large sums of money for the industrial and social betterment of the natives, and broke to them the bread of life. Their missions were of the early Christian type. It was not till near the end of the eighteenth century that they adopted the more formal missionary methods.

The Presbyterian Synod of New York and Philadelphia appointed George Duffield and Charles Beatty to look into the question of missions to the Indians. The latter published in 1768 a "Journal of a Two Months' Tour, With a View of Promoting Religion Among the Frontier Inhabitants of Pennsylvania and of Introducing Christianity Among the Indians to the Westward of the Alegh-geny Mountains." But no permanent work resulted before 1800.

The Moravians were the most active missionaries in Pennsylvania in our period. **Count Zinzendorf** came to America in 1741 and remained a little more than a year. He made three extensive missionary journeys, one in New York and two in Pennsylvania, not only prospecting for permanent work but also preaching through interpreters. His daughter, Countess Benigna, was with him part of the time. He kept his high rank in the background as much as possible, because with both white and red men, it distracted attention from his simple gospel message. He arranged fields and selected twenty missionaries to go to work at once, planning for as many more to begin soon. The work was carried forward vigorously by the ablest men in the Moravian body. **Peter Boehler,** who had studied at the Universities of Jena and Leipsic, and who had been the instrument in London of leading John Wesley into the new religious life, crossed the Atlantic seven times in the interests of the Moravian work in America. Others besides Zinzendorf and Boehler were university men. **Cammerhoff** and Baron **John von Watville** were graduates of Jena, and **Spangenberg** had been a professor at Halle.

Three stations were opened in what is now Carbon County, two in Monroe, one in Lehigh, three in Bradford, two in Venango, and one in Lawrence. Thus the work stretched clear to the western limits of the state. **John Heckwelder** cheerfully sang German missionary hymns amid uncounted perils of the wilderness.

466. The chief apostle of the Indians in Pennsylvania and Ohio was **David Zeisberger.** Six stations were opened in Tuscarawas County, Ohio, two in Coshocton, one in Cuyahoga, one in Erie, and one in Wyandot. In Macomb County, Michigan, there was another and there were three in Canada West. The twenty-seven stations just enumerated were all opened during the missionary activity of Zeisberger (1745-1808). In those west of the Allegheny mountains he was the chief factor. The lives of hundreds of savages, including a number of most wicked tribal headmen, where utterly transformed. For length of service, for purity and singleness of aim and for actual effectiveness no other missionary career in North America approaches that of David Zeisberger.

The worst perils of the Moravian missionaries were not from wild beasts and wild Indians, but from degraded colonists. In 1782 an expedition of 160 armed

Americans under Colonel Williamson, fitted out at Pittsburg, proceeded to Gnadenhütten, a Moravian Indian settlement in Ohio. They took these ever peaceable Christian Indians by surprise as they were gathering their harvest of corn, but assured them that they had come as friends to protect them against hostilities. The Indians entertained them with cordiality and perfect trust. The black-hearted whites, after much pleasant and even pious talk with the Indians, imprisoned them and on the following day deliberately took them one by one, men, women and children, and in cold blood, slaughtered them with the tomahawk and stripped off their scalps. Out of ninety-six Indians but two succeeded in escaping. For cold-blooded, unreasoning brutality, this deed is not matched by the Spaniards in South America, the Dutch in South Africa, or even the Iroquois in the land of the Hurons. The Moravian missions never fully recovered from this blow struck by white men.

467. To complete our survey of missions in America we must return to the region in which we began, the West Indies. The work of the Moravians there was in Danish and English territory and much more akin to that of English America, considered in the present chapter, than to the work considered in the chapter on Spanish America.

As we have gone from one continent to another and from the equator to the poles, we have found the Moravians as active missionaries again and again in the last century of our two millenniums. Their work in the West Indies takes us back to the very beginning of their missionary enterprise.

Count Zinzendorf, the early patron, intimate spiritual brother and adopted leader of the Moravians, had himself drunk at the same fountain of piety in Halle where the early Danish missionary spirit was imbibed. August Francke, the great teacher there, was, perhaps, more than any other one man the forefather of modern missions. Zinzendorf entered into a covenant with a schoolmate, Baron Frederick de Watteville, to establish missions for the heathen, especially for the most neglected. Without thought of its having any connection with his missionary purpose, he invited some religious refugees from persecution in Bohemia to settle on his estate, in 1722. The next year he formed a missionary society with De Watteville and others and sought to forward its objects, but all to no avail. Meantime, the colony on his estate, which had named itself Herrnhüt (the Watch of the Lord) grew and needed his attention. He became convinced that he ought to cast in his lot more completely with them. Visiting Copenhagen to attend the coronation of a new king of Denmark, he heard the story of Anthony, a Negro from St. Thomas, West Indies, as to the degraded condition of the slaves there. On reaching home Zinzendorf related the facts to the Brethren. Anthony himself arrived at Herrnhüt soon after. Out of this sprang the first Moravian mission in 1732, ten years after the establishment of the church-colony, while it still numbered fewer than 400 members.

468. **Loehnard Dober** and Tobias Leupold were two of the Brethren whose hearts were most deeply stirred with a desire to carry the gospel to the West Indies.

JOHN LOEHNARD DOBER.

These humble men, a carpenter and a potter, did not speak of their desire at first. One day they are digging together in the earth. One ventures to hint at his wish. The other quickly responds. See them dropping their tools for a minute and kneeling in prayer. They petitioned the church to let them go. It took the cautious elders a year to consider this proposal, before they could consent to such a momentous experiment. When consent was given, Leupold could not go. **David Nitschmann** took his place. The two young men started, with blessings on their heads and about three dollars each in their pockets. Their baggage was in bundles on their backs. They walked to their port of departure, Copenhagen, 600 miles away. In spite of many obstructions they at last secured passage to St. Thomas, having berth room so small that they could not sit up straight, to say nothing of standing. But all this was nothing; they were ready to be sold into slavery, if need be, in order to reach slaves. Exactly that did not take place. But many of the planters despised and hated them, because they came to enlighten slaves. Before many years, however, one of the proprietors said in the English House of Commons that Moravian slaves were bringing a higher price than others in the market because they were so much more efficient. Forty, then ninety, were baptized. Hundreds followed.

In 1733 work was begun on the Island of St. Croix. One of the converts there, **Cornelius,** purchased his own freedom and became an effective missionary helper for forty-seven years. The only other Danish island was St. Jan, near St. Thomas. Work was begun there in 1741.

In the early days at St. Thomas, Nitschmann having returned to Europe, Dober was employed as watchman on a plantation, for he had to earn his living as best he could. He must have been sometimes extremely lonely and have wondered if he was forgotten at home. One night, near midnight, he beheld two men stalking out of the darkness into the circle of his watch-fire. They proved to be reinforcements from Herrnhüt. The work went on until practically the entire Negro population of the Danish West Indies was **Christianized.**

In the Island of St. Kitts, 100 miles east of St. Croix, a mission was begun in 1777. By the end of the century there were 2,500 converts.

Sixty miles farther east lies Antigua. The work there started in 1756. With severe toil the missionaries earned their bread. **Peter Brown,** from Pennsylvania, labored there with great efficiency for 20 years (1769-89). When he arrived 14 people were counted Christians; when he left, 7,400. In his last year before he broke down with toil 640 were baptized.

Three hundred miles southward is the Island of Barbados and 150 miles further Tobago. Work was begun in the former in 1767 and in the latter by **John Montgomery,** father of the poet, James Montgomery, in 1787.

While we are so near the coast of South America we must notice that there were missions in Surinam from 1735. **Solomon Schumann** came to be called the "Apostle of the Arrawak Indians," so many of them were led by him and his co-workers to trust in Christ. Other races also in Surinam were evangelized.

From St. Thomas, our Moravian starting-point in the West Indies, sailing 600 miles westward we come to Jamaica. The Brethren were invited here in 1754 by planters, some of whom had joined the Moravians in England. But with outward prosperity the spiritual work was less effective than in other islands during our period. Later, thousands were converted till there were nearly twice as many converts there as in any other island.

CHAPTER XXVII

## CONTINUITIES IN MISSIONS.

469. The law of continuity. 470. Racial continuity in missions. 471. Intellectual continuity in missions. 472. Scriptural continuity. 473. This principle held good among Roman Catholics. 474. Importance of other early missionary writings. 475. The permanent significance of a single word. 476. Social continuity. 477. Organic continuity. 478. Continuity unbroken by sectarianism. 479. The deepest line of spiritual continuity.

469. The missions of the two thousand years before the time of William Carey were scattered over the world from Spain to Japan and from Iceland to the Cape of Good Hope, from Nova Scotia to California and from Hudson Bay to Cape Horn. They were conducted by the most widely divergent sects of the children of God. But nothing in either the physical or the spiritual realm is entirely isolated. There are always lines of continuity which give coherence to the whole and show the process of development. To discover the plan of development is to think God's thoughts after Him. Men in the present age are doing this more than it ever has been done before, though some of them are unaware that the mind whose

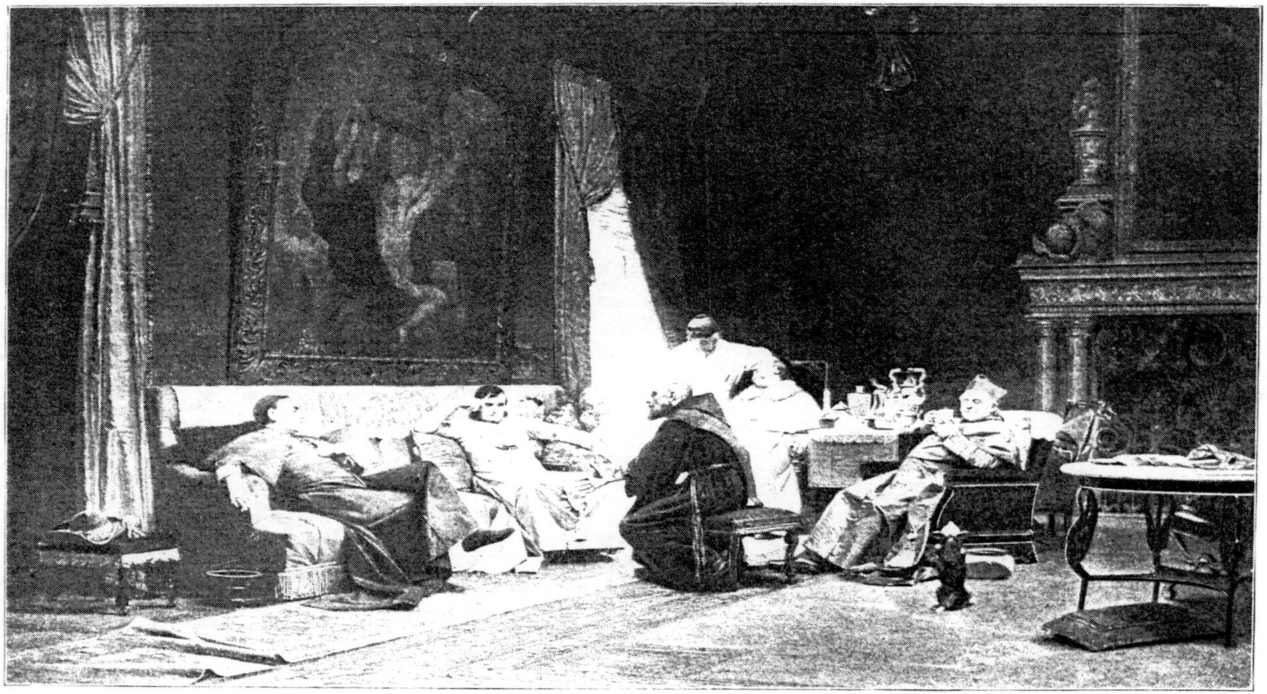

*J. G. Vibert.* THE MISSIONARY'S STORY.

thoughts they are tracing is the mind of God. Annals are no longer counted history. True history is a record of divine evolution.

Concerning a field so extended and so diversified as the one before us it will be possible in the space at command only to note some general outlines of order. We may be sure that if the records had been made and if sufficient attention could be given them not one of the two thousand years would be found devoid of true missionary effort and not one of the efforts could be fully appreciated except as connected with every other one.

470. The basis of all human continuity is racial. The Aryan race has been the missionary race, though only after Semitic initiation. When the dispersed Jews had produced such men as Philo and Paul and, under the inspiration of Jesus, had set religious propagation afoot in the world, the sons of Japheth took up the work and have carried it ever since. Christianity came early and repeatedly in contact with the Mongolian race, winning great numbers. But it never became self-propagative or even self-perpetuating among them. The same is true of the Negro race. Three hundred years before the time of William Carey the Indian race of America began to be infused with Christianity. Thousands were soon enrolled and many a whole tribe was counted as Christianized. But they never did much for the tribes beyond except under Aryan leadership. We must look, then, for all phases of missionary continuity to one or another of the branches of the Aryan stock.

471. The strictly intellectual continuity from first to last has been largely Hellenic. It was the translation of Hebrew thought into Greek which marked the beginning of the propagation of the true religion on a large scale. It was the Hellenistic Jews, both pre-Christian and Christian, who were the first missionaries. The New Testament being written in the Greek language, by that alone to a considerable extent was a rendering of Hebrew ideals into Greek forms. The Epistle to the Hebrews was a most distinct attempt at this made by one of the Alexandrian school of Jews, Hellenist of the Hellenists. The man who wrote more of the New Testament than any other one was himself a Greek. The one who wrote the next largest portion was a Hellenist Jew and directed most of his writing to churches composed of Greeks and Hellenists. The apostle who wrote the third largest portion spent the last thirty years of his life around the eastern shores of the Ægean Sea, a region which was simply a larger Hellas, almost as completely Greek as Greece herself. The prologue of his Gospel is as distinctly a rendering of Hebrew conception into terms of Greek philosophy as were the works of Philo himself. The mental mould which received and reproduced Christianity was Greek. The great ecumenical councils and the battles royal of early Christian philosophy were all Greek. Even in Rome for a long time the church was a Greek church and the Christian writings there were Greek. Whatever language was afterward used there and elsewhere the thought was largely Greek thought. The intellectual conceptions which were car-

ried by the missionaries of the cross to the ends of the earth were indeed from Palestine but were shaped on a mental form which had been evolved in little Hellas.

472. There is one line of missionary continuity which may well be called the backbone of the whole body. It is the line of literature. From the Septuagint rendering of the Sacred Writings on through all the Two Thousand Years the Scriptures and Scripture-filled expositions of Christianity in written or printed form were the spinal column on which all substantial missionary efforts depended for rectitude, permanency and constant nerve supply. We expect this in the work of the Dutch, the Danes, the Puritans and the Moravians. We are not surprised to find it in the records of Tatian, Wulfila, Gregory of Armenia, Columbus, the Si-gnan-fu Nestorian tablet and other accounts of the earlier missions. We have seen that Tatian was converted by the influence which the Old Testament Scriptures gained over his mind. He was the very man to combine the four Gospels of the New Testament into a continuous narrative which was widely used both in the East and in the West. After being lost for centuries copies have recently been found.

In his fascinating address on the relation of the Bible to missions at the Ecumenical Conference in New York Canon Edmonds called attention to the early testimony on this point as follows:

"It is a striking thing that Bible work—the work, that is, of translating and disseminating the Scriptures—began where missions to the heathen began. Its starting point is Antioch.

Listen to St. Chrysostom, the most illustrious name after the Apostolic Age in that great missionary city where many were illustrious, as he comments upon St. John:

"'The doctrine of St. John did not in such sort (as the Philosophers did) vanish away; but the Syrians, Egyptians, Indians, Persians, Ethiopians, and infinite other nations, being barbarous people, translated it into their (mother) tongue, and have learned to be (true) Philosophers.' And King James' translators, who quote this in their 'Address to the Reader,' add a similar passage from Theodoret, next to St. Chrysostom both for antiquity and learning. His words are these: 'Every country that is under the sun is full of these words, and the Hebrew tongue is turned not only into the language of the Grecians, but also of the Romans, and Egyptians, and Persians, and Indians, and Armenians, and Scythians, and Sauromatians, and, briefly, into all the languages that any nation useth.'"

The New Testament itself in large part is simply the missionary writings of the first generation of missionaries. Paul's letters are obviously that. The book of Acts is a history of missions by a missionary helper of Paul. The Gospel by the same author has always been regarded as written especially for the heathen world. The other Gospels, whether for Jew or Gentile, were written to accomplish missionary ends. Even the Apocalypse is plainly addressed to mission churches in Asia Minor. The letters of James and Peter were clearly written for a similar purpose. The last word of the New Testament, John's third letter, was written to tell how to treat missionaries.

The continuity of the spinal cord of sacred writing is perfectly obvious. The Hebrew passed into the Greek, the Greek in the western world into the Latin, and the Latin Vulgate branched into various European versions. There is no straighter stem of the continuous development than our English Bible.

473. We expect the Scriptures to hold a large place in Protestant and in primitive missions. The principle is especially impressive when we note its working in mediæval and Roman Catholic missions. As we saw, one of the great, abiding, services of the Greek Catholic apostles of the Slavs was their creation of an alphabet and translation of the Scriptures, on which the Bible of the Russians and other Slavonic peoples still rests. We found the noble Roman missionary, Monte Corvino, translating portions of Scripture in mediæval China and heard his pathetic appeal for a supply of Christian literature. Let Canon Edmonds tell us how Tatian's Greek *Diatessaron,* Four-Gospels-combined, took a Latin form:

"In the sixth century, and then in the ninth [it] was turned into old Saxon. Under the name of the 'Heliand' it assumed the form of poetry, and was a chief instrument in the conversion of the Saxons whom the severities of Charles the Great had compelled to conform; but whose heart was not won till the 'Heliand' won it. In this form, says Dr. Wace, the gospel lived in the heart of the German people, and in due time produced Luther and the German Bible, thus binding together the second century and the sixteenth, the East and the West. . . .

"Nearly eighty years were to pass before Europe was to stand at the parting of the ways. Twenty editions of the Latin Bible had been printed in Germany alone before Luther was born (Maitland's Dark Ages, p. 469), and in the year that followed the nailing up of the 'Theses' at the door of the church at Wittenberg the fourteenth known issue of a German Bible took place. (October 31, 1517.) All these fourteen issues were large folio Bibles, and were not mere reprints but translations from the Vulgate."

At the very time when the Council of Trent was putting the Bible into the background with Romanists at home, their apostle at the front, Xavier, through his convert and interpreter was translating one of the Gospels into Japanese. Even after that unhappy council the Roman Catholic missionaries everywhere put something in writing for the instruction and upbuilding of converts. Frequently it was fragments of Sacred Scripture, more commonly it was pieces of ritual or creed. But these latter were to a considerable extent based on the facts and even the very words of Scripture. The significant thing is that it was religious literature.

474. Early missionary writings outside of those counted the Sacred Writings played an important part in the propagation of the Gospel. They have gone by the name of "Apologies." To us that term suggests too much of speculation and at the same time of mere defense, to say nothing of its having a savor of deprecating confession. But these writings were for intensely practical ends. They were nobly aggressive. They were missionary documents, tracts and treatises by which heathenism in its popular, also in its philosophical and imperial seats, was boldly attacked. We have seen how Clement and Origen in Egypt, Tertullian, Cyprian and Arnobius in North Africa, Quadratus and Aristides in Athens and Justin and Tatian in Rome, trained their literary guns on paganism. This was being done in other parts of the empire. For instance, Commodianus, who speaks of himself as belonging to

Gaza, wrote a poem casting ridicule on the gods, entitled "Instructions to the Gods of the Heathen." It consists of eighty sections, each one being an acrostic of which the initial letters spell the title of the section. He wrote another poem of 1020 lines, entitled, "An Apologetic Song Against Jews and Gentiles."

There is space in the present summary merely to name some of the early literary missionaries. **Quadratus** and **Miltiades** of Athens, **Ariston** of Pella, **Claudius Apollinaris** of Hierapolis, **Melito** of Sardis, **Theophilus** of Antioch, and **Hermias** all wrote in the second century in advocacy of Christianity, but their writings have been lost. The writings of four other "apologists" of that century have reached us. **Aristides, Justin Martyr, Tatian** and **Athenagoras. Clement, Origen, Tertullian, Cyprian, Commodianus, Minucius Felix** and **Hippolytus** came during the first part of the next century and **Arnobius** at the end of it. We know of at least twenty-nine distinctively "apologetic" writings by these nineteen men between the years 126 and 300, only one of them being later than the year 250. Six of these writings were arguments directed to the Jews, eight were addressed to emperors (two to Hadrian, four to Marcus Aurelius, two to Antoninus Pius), and the other fifteen were intended for such in the heathen world as could be induced to read them. The literary work in missions for 125 years after the year 125 was a mighty force, second only to that of the last half of the first century.

475. It is not only true of the individual that "writing makes the exact man," as the adage has it; writing

is also essential to precision and sureness in the spiritual development of the whole race of men. The most careful writer in the New Testament from a literary point of view, in describing the first mission in Thessalonica speaks of the magistrates of the city by a precise term, "*politarchs.*" Ages afterward scholars hostile to Christianity declared Luke's whole missionary history to be proved untrustworthy by that one word, for there were no such officers known in those days as "*politarchs*" or named by any other writer. But, near the middle of the eighteenth century there was brought to light an ancient Greek inscription containing this word carved in solid stone over the very gateway of Thessalonica through which Paul must have gone when driven away by the action of those "rulers of the city." It was a modern Scotch missionary in Thessalonica, Peter Crosbie, who later rescued that stone and had it sent to the British Museum. Other inscriptions containing this word have been found from time to time until Dr. E. D. Burton has been able to bring together, by the careful and searching work for which he is noted, no fewer than nineteen ancient inscriptions containing this word. He has put them within the reach of all in his "The Politarchs in Macedonia and Elsewhere." That one scientifically exact word of the old Greek medical missionary and historian of missions has put the New Testament itself, of which he wrote so large a part, on a solid rock of demonstration as to its trustworthiness and accuracy.

No intelligent missionaries have expected their work to be abiding except as it has been anchored in let-

POLITARCH INSCRIPTION, VARDAR GATE, THESSALONICA.

ters. From the Apostles on the eastern shores of the Mediterranean to the Franciscans on the western coast of America some expression of Christianity has been put down in black and white to which the eye of the body and the eye of the mind could frequently recur. Though Christ left us no writings, and though none about him which are extant were written for a score of years after his crucifixion, and though Christianity is life, not words, yet it is pre-eminently a literary religion, based on a literature and building a literature. Literature has always been vital to missions. Missions have always been propaganda of culture.

476. The last statement is susceptible of a wide application, even the widest. Missions have everywhere promoted personal refinement and social betterment. In land after land they have initiated a higher civilization. Trade has generally preceded missions and has always followed. But pioneer trade has more often than otherwise debased the natives. In fields most widely separated by space and by the creed of the European visitants we have seen that the missionaries have had more difficulty in counteracting the evil influence of the colonists than in overcoming the inherent degradation of the natives. This is one of the surest disclosures made by a world-wide study of missionary beginnings. In order to uplift communities missions have had to outweigh not only raw barbarism, but also the heavy dross of civilization. Survivals and indurations of barbarism are far more insolvent than the primitive substance. That is why city missions among the slums and missions to the long civ-

ilized portions of Asia are more difficult than missions to the totally uncivilized.

But in spite of their double task missions on all continents have been the effective mainspring to a higher life. This has been especially marked in the history of all the Teutonic peoples. The Franks, the Germans, the Scandinavians and the Anglo-Saxons had their primitive savagery softened and were inspired with the noble, refining ideals which have led them to become what they are by Christian missions. For them to fail now to send this regenerating agency to the portions of humanity which are still destitute would be the colossal instance of ingratitude on our planet. The vital factor in the evolution of society is the growth of altruism, otherism. The essential difference between a savage and a gentleman is that the latter is more gentle, *i. e.*, more considerate of other people. When all men in any place are perfect gentlemen they will pay active attention to the state of all other men in every place so far as they are able. The missionary enterprise is at once the supreme instance and the historic instigation of this temper. It has been somewhat fitfully yet as a whole steadily transforming human society. It is the pioneer of civilization, *i. e.*, of a sense of citizenship; of wider and ever wider relationships with fellow-citizens to take the place of all-absorbing, barbarian selfishness.

477. We are not looking for superficial but for vital continuities, not for those which are formal but for those which are formative. The missionary enterprise has had no continuous, outward organization

except the succession of churches, imaginatively called the Church Universal. A church which does not fail of God's intention for it is a missionary society. But most of the churches through the ages have largely missed this meaning of their existence and have clung only to the selfish side of their purpose, being devoted self-culture clubs. The missionary purpose of the Church has not been held with sufficient intensity and constancy to develop a specialized organism as a vital part of itself. But from time to time it has invented temporary instruments for doing the work. There have been, continuously, two organic elements, however—personal initiative and the contagion of example. While large groups of disciples, called churches, failed to be missionary, between the early age and the time of Carey, individual Christians were fired with the true intention of Christianity, and carried it out by whatever means they found possible. These set others aflame and the holy fire spread. At first there were few formal missionaries. Earnest Christians scattered by business amid the population of the heathen and Jewish world diligently propagated their faith. We are indebted to an enemy for a record of splendid activity. Celsus in the second century sneered at Christianity because it was propagated by shoemakers and fullers, workers in wool and leather, who talked about their doctrines in their workshops.

After the providential agencies which dispersed the Jews and scattered the early Christians the instrumentalities of the missions before Carey might be classified as promiscuous, papal, monastic, mendicant

(Franciscan and Dominican), military, Jesuit, colonial and denominational (Moravian). Each one of these demands at least a whole chapter for mere outline description. The Jesuit and the Moravian are the only ones which have been adequately treated in English as missionary agencies. Each of the other six deserves careful study and a volume of treatment. Here is congenial, pertinent and widely useful work for half-a-dozen of the many educated young ministers whose heart's desire to enter the mission field personally has been providentially thwarted. Concerning one of the most fascinating of them all, the Franciscan order, there is abundance of material already gathered in other languages; one set of twenty volumes in Latin, another of eleven volumes in Italian, the latter devoted distinctively to the missionary work of that wonderful order. Francis of Assisi, the noblest of Roman Catholic missionary inspirers, set a heroic missionary pace himself in the first quarter of the thirteenth century. Before the middle of the sixteenth century there were 120,000 Franciscans scattered throughout the world. They were by no means all missionaries, but multitudes of them were at work in heathen lands. The Recollets and the Capuchins, whose names occasionally appear in missionary history, are branches of the great Franciscan stock. The story of the Jesuits is better known partly because they laid themselves open to just and terrible criticism. But the "Black Robes" were not all black sheep. Many of them were as noble and true missionaries as the Grey Friars or any other brethren. At the time of their suppression in the middle of the eighteenth century they had 275 missionary stations. They are said to have had as many as 13,000 missionaries in the field at one time.

By limitation of space our present study has been confined to missions on the fields with only incidental mention of the sending agencies. But a mere glance at missionary organization shows a real though uneven development. In the early centuries there was no regular organization. Then monasticism became devoted in part to missions. In the West, at least, as we have seen, many monasteries were mainly missionary settlements. Later the mendicant orders took up the work with much more definiteness. Later still, the Company of Jesus carried organization and discipline in missions to the last degree, but not to the highest degree. It was in the last of the twenty centuries under review that the Moravian Brethren brought missionary organization almost to perfection. With them single individualities, with the exception of Zinzendorf, have not stood out in great prominence. It has been more the movement of a whole church. Even the Company of Jesus, with its rigorous and unparalleled subordination of every member to the interests of the order, failed to produce such a uniform level of devotion as that spontaneously reached by the free spirit in the Moravians. There is no other instance on record in any age, even the apostolic age, of a whole church making foreign missions its chief business, in fact, almost its only business. They have done this now for five generations. They, long ago, came to have more members in the churches of their mission fields than in their home-land, as forthputting England has far more people in her colonial possessions than in the mother country. When will all churches learn this grand secret?

478. Apostle means missionary. In this its true sense the apostolic succession has been unbroken. It is too common for those interested in some special group of workers to assume that the good originated with them, when in fact they took it up from others and carried it to some new development. Roman Catholics not only preceded Protestants in time but also led them in zeal. Any one who reads the English and American missionary writings of the seventeenth and eighteenth centuries will discover that Protestants were inspired, sometimes nettled, into evangelizing activity by the Romanists. In 1721 Cotton Mather in Boston published a little book which well illustrates the continuity of missionary effort across all barriers of time, space and creed. Barriers of space and creed were much greater, too, in those days than they are now. It is entitled "India Christiana, a discourse, Delivered unto the Commissioners, for the Propagation of the Gospel among the American Indians, which is Accompanied with several Instruments relating to the Glorious Design of Propagating our Holy Religion in the Eastern as well as the Western, Indies." His own discourse is on "A Joyful Sound reaching to both the Indias." Next is a letter written to Mather by Prof. Francke, of Halle, Germany, the spiritual father of Danish and modern Moravian missions, giv-

ing an enthusiastic account of the Danish mission in India. Then follows a long letter in Latin, with an English translation, which Mather had sent to Ziegenbalg in India, with a reply written by Gründler, a co-laborer of Ziengenbalg. The Puritan says in his letter to the Lutheran:

"Great and Grevious and never enough to be bewailed, has been the scandal given in the Churches of the Reformation; in that so very little, yea, next to nothing, has been done in them, for the Propagation of the Faith . . . while at the same time the Church of Rome, strives, with an Unwearied and Extravagant Labour, to Propagate the Idolatry and Superstition of Antichrist, and advance the Empire of Satan," —with more too virulent for modern ears, followed by—"Their Attempts, how never tired! Their travels, how very tedious! And with what an Ardour are they Ambitious of a Crown, which appears to them a True Martyrdom, and for the Truth."

This is unimpeachable testimony that Protestants were in every sense of the word "provoked to good works" of the missionary kind by the children of Rome. Mather's precious little book ends with "The present Condition of the Indians on Martha's Vineyard, Extracted from an Account of Mr. Experience Mayhew." Though there was a little friction in the connecting links it is a highly significant fact that Germany, New England and India, Jesuit, Lutheran and Puritan, were linked together in one golden missionary chain.

479. The stream of ecclesiastical continuity has been followed down by church history abundantly and superabundantly. It flows through Rome. The continuity of the current of theological thought has been instructively traced by Prof. Allen and others. It

flows through Alexandria. In the historical geography of the Church of Christ there is a third stream, deeper, more vital and spiritual than either of these, which has not often, if ever, been traced continuously in print. It is the stream of evangelizing impulse. Like the current of true thinking it was underground some of the time, but it was never lost. It flows through Thessalonica. This church was more surely of Apostolic origin than that of either Rome or Alexandria. It was unmistakably founded by the Apostle Paul, the foremost primitive missionary. Out of it came the apostles of the Slavonic nations, including Bohemia and Moravia. Out of this portion of the Slavs came Jerome of Prague and John Huss, the reformers, before the Reformation. There were 200,000 evangelical Bohemian Christians when Luther nailed his theses to the door. They suffered everything rather than give up their faith. Out of these came a rescued remnant to settle on Count Zinzendorf's estate as the Moravian Brethren. Out of these came directly the religious culture and life of Schleiermacher to turn the tide of rationalism in Germany. Out of these came also directly the conversion of John Wesley into a source of the mightiest spiritual impulse in England and America. Out of these same Moravian Brethren came the most complete missionary activity which has developed in the first Two Thousand Years of Missions. More still, out of their splendid example and under the religious conditions produced in England by their spiritual child, John Wesley, came the missionary impulse which fired the heart of William

HALL, IN WHICH JOHN HUSS WAS TRIED, CONSTANCE.

Carey and made him the leader in such a new development of missonary enterprise that he has been properly counted the starting-point of the great era of modern missions. He was not unconscious of this principle of continuity, but points it out plainly in his epoch-making document, the "Enquiry into the Obligations of Christians to use means for the Conversion of the Heathens." Section II "contains a short Review of former undertakings for the conversion of the Heathen." He recounts the salient facts of missionary history from the records of Justin Martyr and Irenæus on to his own day, speaking of Augustine and Boniface, Huss and Jerome of Prague, Xavier and Ziegenbalg, Eliot and Brainerd and others. He concludes:

> "But none of the moderns have equalled the Moravian Brethren in this good work; they have sent missions to Greenland, Labrador and several of the West Indian Islands, which have been blessed for good. They have likewise sent to Abyssinia in Africa, but what success they have had I cannot tell. The late Mr. Wesley lately made an effort in the West Indias, and some of their ministers are now laboring amongst the Caribbs and Negroes, and I have seen pleasing accounts of their success."

Carey was received into church membership, licensed to preach and ordained in a chapel at Olney, England. On the opposite side of the village square stood the house in which William Cowper was living, the man who sang for Carey and all England the praises of Moravian missions in nearly one hundred lines of his poem, "Hope." The following are six of these lines:

"See Germany send forth
Her sons to pour it on the farthest north:
Fired with a zeal peculiar, they defy
The rage and vigor of a polar sky,
And plant successfully sweet Sharon's rose
On icy plains, and in eternal snows."

Zinzendorf approaching the West India Islands said to the group of humble Herrnhütters with him on deck, "What will you do on landing if you find that all your brethren who came here months ago to work among the slaves have perished?" They answered, "We will take their places." The Count exclaimed "*Gens æterna*—these Moravians!"

In that memorable saying he spoke a larger truth even than he thought. They had been begotten of generations of ancient Bohemian Brethren—and they of Hussites—and they of Cyril and Methodius—and they of a people from whom the word of the Lord sounded forth not only in Macedonia and Achaia but in every place—and they of a man who counted not his life dear unto himself so that he might testify the gospel of the grace of God—and he on the way to Damascus had been begotten by the spirit of Jesus the Son of God.

*H. L. Robert.* THE PARABLE OF THE SOWER.

# CHRONOLOGICAL TABLE.

### OF MISSIONARY BEGINNINGS AND OTHER PROMINENT EVENTS OF THE WORK.

a—About.
b—Before.
*—Ministry completed.

## BEFORE CHRISTIAN ERA.

586 Hebrew dispersion established.
334 Greek diffusion by Alexander.
a280 Scriptures into Greek begun.
a150 Scriptures into Greek completed.
189 Roman conquest of Syria.
27 Roman Empire established.
a5 Birth of Jesus.

## FIRST CENTURY.

a27 Jesus begins public ministry.
a27 Jesus proclaims his Messiahship to the Samaritans.
a29 Jesus works in Phoenicia.
a30 "The Great Commission."
a30 Gospel in many tongues at Pentecost.
a35 Ethiopia by Candace's Treasurer.
a37 Roman Captain Cornelius converted.
a38 Greeks in Antioch evangelized.
a46 Asia Minor. First foreign mission by Paul and Barnabas.
a51 Macedonia by apostolic band.
a52 Greece by apostolic band.
a52 New Testament Scriptures begun by Paul as a missionary measure.
a62 Rome by Paul.
a64 Crete by apostolic band.

a64 Spain by Paul.
70 Destruction of Jerusalem and localism.
a95 New Testament Scriptures completed by John with letter concerning missionaries.

## SECOND CENTURY.

112 Pliny's report to Trajan.
a125 Literary advocacy of Christianity.
a150 France from Asia Minor.
163* Justin Martyr.
a175 Bardaisan in Edessa.
a185 India by Pantænus.
b200 Scriptures into Syriac.
b200 North Africa.
b200 Austria from Northern Italy.
b200 Britain.
a200 Scriptures into Latin. ("*Itala,*" in North Africa.)

## THIRD CENTURY.

202* Pantænus.
a210 Arabia, Origen in.
220* Clement of Alexandria.
a217 Armenia by Bardaisan.
a230 Rome. Statue of Jesus erected by the Emperor.
b254 Spain. Christianity widespread.
254* Origen.
258* Cyprian.
b270 Scriptures into Coptic.
270* Gregory of New Cæsarea.
b300 Goths by Christian slaves.
a300 Persia.
a300 Roman Empire largely evangelized.

## FOURTH CENTURY.

302 Armenia by Gregory.
313 Imperial sanction of Christianity.

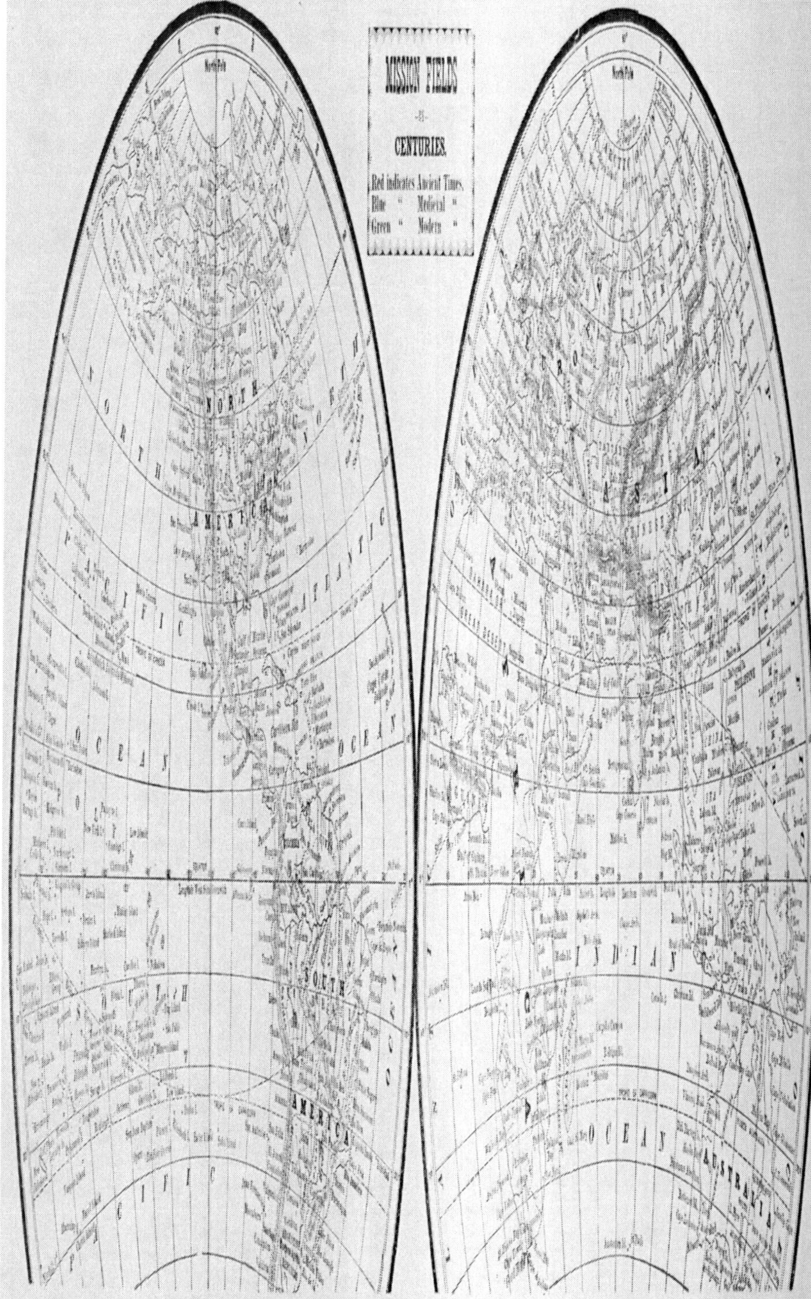
MISSION FIELDS
CENTURIES.
Red indicates Ancient Times.
Blue " Medieval "
Green " Modern "
NORTH
AMERICA
ATLANTIC
OCEAN
SOUTH
AMERICA
ASIA
INDIAN
OCEAN
AUSTRALIA

313 Georgia from Armenia.
314 Suabia and Bavaria.
325 First Ecumenical Council, at Nice.
a330 Abyssinia by Frumentius.
332* Gregory of Armenia.
341 The Goths by Ulfilas.
a350 Scriptures into Abyssinian by (?) Frumentius.
350 Arabia by Greeks.
a375 Scriptures into Gothic by Ulfilas.
381* Ulfilas.
391 Egypt. The Serapeum destroyed.
394 Heathen sacrifices forbidden in Rome by Theodosius.
397* Martin of Tours.
a400 Scotland, Southern, by Ninian.
a400 Scriptures into Latin by Jerome (Vulgate).
a400 Scriptures into Armenian by Mesrob.

## FIFTH CENTURY.

411 Spain, Suevi and Alani.
414 Burgundy.
a431 Ireland by Patrick.
a440 Nestorian advance in Asia.
454 Austria by Severinus.
482* Severinus.
490 Nestorian training-school at Nisibis.
a493* Patrick.
496 France. Clovis baptized.
a500 Franks. First missionary from Ireland, Fridolin.

## SIXTH CENTURY.

529 University of Athens suppressed because of its paganism.
529 Benedictines organized.
a530 Indicopleustes finds Christians in India.
530 Teutonic tribes on the Black Sea.
a536 China by Nestorians. Jaballaha. (?)
a550 Illyria and Mœsia.

a550 Lombards, Northern Italy.
563 Scotland, Northern, by Columba.
563 Scotland, the Picts, by Gildas (?)
a575 Scotland, Southern, by Kentigern.
590 France by Irish (Columbanus).
596 England by Benedictines (Augustine).
597* Columba.
598 England, Ethelbert, King of Kent, baptized.
b600 Scriptures into Georgian.
a600 Germany by the Irish.

## SEVENTH CENTURY.

603* Kentigern.
604* Augustine of England.
604 England, East Saxons.
610 Switzerland by Irish (Gallus).
615* Columbanus.
615 Franconia and Thuringia by Irish (Kilian).
625 England, Northumbria, by Bertha and Paulinus.
a630 Netherlands by Amandus.
630 Croatia.
631 England, East Angles.
634 England, West Saxons.
635 China by Nestorians.
644* Paulinus.
646* Gallus.
650 Mercians.
664 Council of Whitby.
677 Netherlands by English (Wilfrid).
681 England, South Saxons, by Angles (Wilfrid).
696 Bavaria. Duke Theodore II. baptized by Rupert.
a700 Denmark by Willibrord.

## EIGHTH CENTURY.

706 Scriptures into Anglo-Saxon.
709* Wilfrid.
718 Germany by English (Boniface).

719 Scriptures into Arabic.
722 Thuringia and Hesse by Boniface.
724 Destruction of Thor's Oak.
a738* Willibrord.
753 Carinthia by royal influence.
755* Boniface.
772 Germany, Saxony, by arms.
785 Germany, Saxony, Wittekind baptized.
796 The Avars by royal influence.

## NINTH CENTURY.

822 Denmark by Franks (Ansgar).
830 Sweden by Ansgar.
845 Bohemia by Franks.
850 Chazars, Crimea by Greeks (Cyril and Methodius).
b861 Bulgaria by Greeks.
a862 Scriptures into Slavonic by Cyril and Methodius.
863 Moravia by Greeks.
865* Ansgar.
b866 Russia by Greeks.
869* Cyril of Thessalonica.
871 Bohemia by Greeks.
885* Methodius of Thessalonica.
a900 Western Macedonia by Greeks.

## TENTH CENTURY.

912 Normandy. Duke Robert baptized.
934 Norway by royal influence.
950 Hungary by royal influence.
966 Poland by royal influence.
981 Iceland.
988 Russia by royal influence. Vladimir baptized.
998 Faroe and Shetland Islands.
1000 Greenland by Icelanders.
a1000 East Prussia by Dominicans.

## ELEVENTH CENTURY.

a1005 Kerait Tatars by Nestorians.
1008 Sweden. King Olaf baptized.
a1020 Denmark by English.

## TWELFTH CENTURY.

1121 Pomerania.
1139* Otho of Bamberg.
1157 Finland by royal influence.
1168 Island of Rügen.
1184 Livonia.
1190 Teutonic Knights organized.

## THIRTEENTH CENTURY.

1202 Brothers of the Sword organized.
1206 Tatars by Nestorians.
1210 Minor Brothers, "Franciscans," organized.
1216 Brothers Preachers, "Dominicans," organized.
1219 Egypt by Francis of Assisi.
b1225 North Africa by Franciscans.
1226* Francis of Assisi.
1245 Tatars at Karakorum by Franciscans.
1252 Lithuania by arms.
1256 Brothers of St. Augustine, "Augustinians," organized.
b1275 North Africa by Dominicans.
1279 Lapland by royal influence.
1283 Prussia subdued by the military missionary orders.
1292 China by Franciscans.
1292 North Africa by Raymond Lull.
a1300 Tatar Khanates by Franciscans and Dominicans.

## FOURTEENTH CENTURY.

1315* Raymond Lull.
1328* Monte Corvino.
1331* Odoric of Pordenone.
1386 Germany, Lithuania, nominal conversion completed.

## FIFTEENTH CENTURY.

1402 Canary Islands by Franciscans and seculars.
1418 Madeiras.
1432 Azores.
b1460 West Africa by Portuguese.
1460* Henry the Navigator.
1482 Southwest Africa by Portuguese.
1492 Recovery of Spain from the Mohammedans.
1492 Columbus in the West Indies.
1493 West Indies by Dominicans.

## SIXTEENTH CENTURY.

1520 India by Franciscans.
1521 Philippine Islands by Magellan.
1524 Mexico by Franciscans.
1539 New Mexico by Franciscans.
1534 Company of Jesus, "Jesuits," organized.
1542 India by Jesuits (Xavier).
1544 Texas by Franciscans.
1546 Malacca and Amboyna by Xavier.
1549 Brazil by Jesuits.
1549 Japan by Jesuits.
1552* Francis Xavier.
1559 Swedish Association for evangelizing the Lapps.
1566* Las Casas.
1565 Philippine Islands by Augustinians.
1566 Florida by Jesuits.
1586 Paraguay by Jesuits.
1577 Philippine Islands by Franciscans.
1581 Philippine Islands by Dominicans.
1583 China by Jesuits.

## SEVENTEENTH CENTURY.

1610 Nova Scotia by secular priest.
1615 Province of Quebec by Recollet Franciscans.
1615 Ontario by Recollet Franciscans.

1622 *Congregatio de Propaganda Fide* organized in Rome.
1624 East India Islands by Dutch Presbyterians.
1624 Formosa by Dutch Presbyterians.
b1625 Madagascar by Portuguese.
1631 Massachusetts by a Baptist.
1635 West Africa by French Franciscans.
1636 Rhode Island by Baptists.
1641 New York by Dutch Presbyterians.
1641 English Society for Propagation of the Gospel.
1644 French Congregation of the Holy Sacrament organized.
1646 Massachusetts by Congregationalists.
1646 Maine by Jesuits.
1646 New York by Jesuits.
1649 English Society for Propagating the Gospel in New England organized.
1649* Jean de Brebeuf.
1650 Michigan by Jesuits.
a1650 Madagascar by French.
1652* Justus Heurnius.
1652 Africa. Interior by Capuchin Franciscans.
1654 South Africa by Dutch Presbyterians.
b1657 Scriptures into Persian.
1658 Ceylon by Dutch Presbyterians.
1663 Scriptures into Mohican by Eliot.
1665 Wisconsin by Jesuits.
1668 Ladrone Islands.
1669* Johann Adam Schall.
1673 Illinois by Jesuits.
1675* Jacques Marquette.
1681* Gabriel Druillettes.
1682 Pennsylvania by Friends.
1683 Lower California by Jesuits.
1684* Roger Williams.
1697* Antonio Vieira.
1698 Louisiana by secular priests.
1698 English Society for Promoting Christian Knowledge organized.

## EIGHTEENTH CENTURY.

1701 English Society for the Propagation of the Gospel in Foreign Parts organized.
1706 India by Danish-Halle Missionaries.
1707 Tibet by Capuchin Franciscans.
1708 Society in Scotland for Promoting Christian Knowledge organized.
1714 Norwegian Society for Missions organized.
1719* Ziegenbalg.
1721 Greenland by Danes (Hans Egede).
1722 United Brethren, "Moravians," reorganized.
1727 Connecticut by Congregationalists.
a1730 Scriptures into Eskimo by Egede.
1732 West Indies by Moravians.
1733 Greenland by Moravians.
1737 West Africa by Moravians.
1737 South Africa by Moravians.
1740 Pennsylvania by Moravians.
1744 Concert of Prayer for the Conversion of the World.
1745 New Jersey by Presbyterians (Brainerd).
1751 West Africa by the English S. P. G.
1752 Egypt by Moravians.
1758* Hans Egede.
1769 California by Franciscans.
1770 Labrador by Moravians.
1772 Ohio by Moravians.
1780 Cochin China.
1784* George Schmidt.
1792 South Africa by Moravians (permanently).
1792 English Baptist Missionary Society organized under the leadership of William Carey.

# SELECTED BIBLIOGRAPHY.

Two principles have mainly determined the selection; first, special value; second, possible accessibility. With a few important exceptions, books in foreign languages have been excluded. The "list price"—as kindly furnished by the American Baptist Publication Society—is attached to a few books which would be most likely to be procured for private or public libraries in connection with the present course of study. The earliest extant accounts and books which belong in a general way to that class are indicated by the letters "E. E." Books which embody to a good extent such accounts giving the student much first-hand material are marked "E. E. E." The Ante-Nicene Christian Library is designated by "A.-N. L."

## General.

SMITH, G. *Short History of Christian Missions.* Edinb.: T. & T. Clark, 1894. (75 cts.) 238 pp., 155 on our period. By far the best available.

BLISS, E. M. *A Concise History of Missions.* N. Y.: Revell, 1897. (75 cts.)

SCUDDER, MRS. W. W. *Nineteen Centuries of Missions.* N. Y.: Revell, 1899. ($1.00).

HODDER, E. *Conquests of the Cross; A Record of Missionary Work Throughout the World."* 3 vols. N. Y.: Cassell, 1890. ($9.00.) Touches our period occasionally. Graphic.

WINSLOW, M. *Sketch of Missions.* Andover: Flagg & Gould, 1819. Pp. 13-37, Before the Reformation; 38-47, by Roman Catholics; 48-88, by Anglo-Americans; 89-119, by Danes; 120-135, by Moravians.

MILLAR, R. *The History of the Propagation of Chris-*

*tianity and Overthrow of Paganism.* 2 vols. Edinb.: John Mosman & Co., 1723.

KINGSMILL, J. *Missions and Missionaries.* Lon.: Longman, 1853.

GRANT, A. *Past and Prospective Extension of the Gospel by Missions to the Heathen.* Lon.: Rivington, 1845. Bampton Lectures. Chaps. IV, V and VI good rapid survey.

BLUMHARDT, C. G. *Versuch einer Allgemeinen Missionsgeschichte Kirche Christe.* 5 vols. (called 3). Basel: Neukirch, 1828-37. To the Reformation. Fairly complete on the period covered. Has no equal.

MARSHALL, T. W. M. *Christian Missions.* 2 vols. Lon.: Longmans, 1836. Extremely partisan and unfair, but valuable as the only general survey of Roman Catholic missions, though incomplete.

KEANE, A. H. *Man, Past and Present.* Cambridge, Eng.: University Press, 1899. ($3.00.) Conveys latest knowledge as to racial history, traits and religions. Ethnological.

RATZELL, F. *The History of Mankind.* 3 vols. Lon.: Macmillan, 1896. Ethnological.

BRINTON, D. G. *Races and Peoples, Lectures on the Science of Ethnography.* N. Y.: Hodges, 1890.

HAKLUYT SOCIETY "for the purpose of printing . . . the most rare and valuable voyages, travels and geographical records, from an early period of exploratory enterprise." London. Organized 1846. Published 102 vols. up to 1899, many of them invaluable to the student of early missions. A number written by early missionaries themselves. (E.E.)

PINKERTON. *A General Collection of Voyages and Travels in All Parts of the World.* Lon.: Longman, 1808-14. 17 vols. quarto. (E.E.)

CHURCHILL. *Collection of Voyages and Travels.* Lon.: 1732. 6 vols. (E.E.)

BLISS, E. M., Ed. *The Encyclopaedia of Missions.* N. Y.: Funk & Wagnalls, 1891. 2 vols. ($12.00.)

NEWCOMB, H., Ed. *A Cyclopedia of Missions.* N. Y.: Scribner, 1854.

SMITH AND WACE. *Dictionary of Christian Biography.* 4 vols. Bost.: Little, Brown & Co., 1877. ($24.00.) The best of encyclopedic helps on our period.

M'CLINTOCK, J., and STRONG, J. *Cyclopedia of Biblical, Theological and Ecclesiastical Literature.* 10 vols. N. Y.: Harper's, 1867.

ADDIS, W. E., and ARNOLD, T. *A Catholic Dictionary.* Lon.: Paul, Trench, Trübner & Co., 1893. ($2.50.)

McCLURE, E. *Historical Church Atlas.* Lon.: S. P. C. K., 1897. Maps of great value.

NEANDER, A. *History of the Christian Religion and Church.* 6 vols. ($18.00.) Boston: Crocker & Brewster, 1872. Gives considerable space to the spread of Christianity.

KURTZ, J. H. *Church History.* 3 vols. N. Y.: Funk & Wagnalls, 1889. Thorough and concise on the spread of Christianity.

NEWMAN, A. H. *A Manual of Church History.* Phila.: Amer. Bap. Pub. Soc. Vol. I; pp. 639. 1900. ($2.25.)

ALZOG, J. *Manual of Universal Church History.* 3 vols. Cincinnati: Robert Clark & Co., 1876. (R.C.)

DITCHFIELD, P. H. *The National Churches.* 8 vols. Lon.: Wells, Gardner, Darton & Co., 1891-95. Germany, Spain, Ireland, Netherlands, Italy, Scotland, France, America. Early chapters on our period.

WALSH, W. P. *Heroes of the Mission Field.* N. Y.: Whittaker. ($1.00.) Twelve heroes, all of them in our period. Excellent.

## Early.

ROBERTS, A., and DONALDSON, J. *Ante-Nicene Christian Library.* 25 vols. Edinb.: T. & T. Clark, 1867-97. (E.E.) Same, Scribner's, 10 vols. ($40.00.)

SCHAFF, P., and WACE, H. *Select Library of the Nicene and Post-Nicene Fathers of the Christian Church.* 28 vols. N. Y.: Christian Literature Co., 1886-99. (E.E.) Same, Scribner's. ($112.00.)

FARRAR, F. W. *Lives of the Fathers.* 2 vols. N. Y.: Macmillan, 1889. (E.E.E.)

UHLHORN, G. *Conflict of Christianity with Heathenism.* N. Y.: Scribner's, 1879.

MILMAN, H. H. *The History of Christianity from the Birth of Christ to the Abolition of Paganism in the Roman Empire.* 2 vols. N. Y.: Armstrong.

LIGHTFOOT, I. B. *Historical Essays.* N. Y.: Macmillan.

MOXOM, P. S. *From Jerusalem to Nicea. The Church in the First Three Centuries.* Bost.: Roberts, 1895. ($1.50.)

## Medieval.

MACLEAR, G. F. *A History of Christian Missions During the Middle Ages.* Lon.: Macmillan, 1863. 452 pp.

MACLEAR, G. F. *Apostles of Mediæval Europe.* Lon.: Macmillan, 1869. ($1.80.) Abridged and partly rewritten from his *History of Christian Missions During the Middle Ages.*

SMITH, T. *Mediaeval Missions.* Edinb.: T. & T. Clark, 1880. 279 pp.

JARVIS, LUCY C. *The Planting of the Church; a Compendium of Missionary History.* N. Y.: Pott & Co., 1900. ($1.00.) Part I, Pre-Reformation Missions and Missionaries. 152 pp. Good lists of missionaries and movements.

SUMMERS, W. H. *The Rise and Spread of Christianity in Europe.* N. Y.: Revell. (40 cts.)

MERIVALE, C. *The Conversion of the Northern Nations.* N. Y.: Appleton, 1866. Boyle Lectures. VI-VIII directly on the subject. Philosophy of the process. Diffuse.

WYSE, J. *A Thousand Years, or Mission Centers of the Middle Ages.*

NEANDER, A. *Memorials of Christian Life in the Early*

*and Middle Ages.* Lon.: Bohn, 1852. ($1.00.) Part IV, Missions in the Middle Ages.

HARDWICK, CHAS. *A History of the Christian Church. Middle Age.* Lon.: Macmillan, 1874. ($4.20.) Full of the "Growth of the Church." Maps.

SCHAFF, P. *History of the Church.* 6 vols. N. Y.: Scribner's, 1885. ($24.00.) Excellent on Conversion of the Northern and Western Barbarians, pp. 17-142 of Vol. IV.

TRENCH, R. C. *Lectures on Medieval Church History.* N. Y.: Scribner's, 1878. Chapters on the conversion of England, Germany, Monasticism and the Mendicant Orders.

WOODHOUSE, F. C. *The Military Religious Orders of the Middle Ages.* Lon.: Soc. Prom. Christian Knowledge, 1877.

## Mendicant Orders.

SABATIER, P. *Life of St. Francis of Assisi.* N. Y.: Scribner's, 1894.

CIVEZZA, P. M. DA. *Storia Universale delle Missioni Francescane.* Roma, Tibernia; Prato, Guasti; Firenze, Ariana; 1857-1895. 11 vols., 500 to 1,000 pp. each.

ANALECTA FRANCISCANA sive Chronica alique varia documenta at lustariam fratrum minorum spectantra edita a fratribus collegii, S. Bonaventurae adiurantibus aliis aliis patribus eiusdem ordinus. 2 tom Ad Clares Aquas (Quaraacchi) 1885-87. (E.E.)

WADDING, L., and continuations. *Annales Minorum seu trium ordinum a S. Francisco Institutorum.* 25 vols. Rome, 1731-1886. Chief source as to Franciscans. (E.E.E.)

LEON. *Lives of the Saints and Blessed of the Three Orders of St. Francis."* Lon.: Burns & Oates. 4 vols. (8s. 6d. each.)

DRANE, AUGUSTA T. *Life of St. Dominic.* Lon.: Burns & Oates. (3s.)

CURRIER, C. W. *History of Religious Orders.* Boston: Macconnell Bros. & Co., 1896. Pp. 684.

WOODHOUSE, F. C. *Monasticism.* Lon.: Gardner, D. & Co., 1896. 409 pp.

## Jesuits.

LOCKMAN, F. *Travels of the Jesuits Into Various Parts of the World.* Lon.: John Noon, 1743; also Boston: T. Piety, 1762. 2 vols. (E.E.)

*Travels of Several Learned Missionaries of the Society of Jesus.* Lon.: R. Gosling, 1714. 22 letters from India, Indian Archipelago, China and America. (E.E.)

KIP, W. I. *Historical Scenes from the Old Jesuit Missions.* N. Y.: Randolph, 1875. (E.E.)

*Instructive and Curious Epistles of Jesuits.* (E.E.)

McCLEAN, M. H. *Francis Xavier.* Lon.: Paul, Trench, Trübner & Co., 1895. 2 vols. ($2.80.) "The story of St. Francis Xavier's life and work . . . as far as possible in his own words." (E.E.E.)

COLERIDGE, H. J. *The Life and Letters of St. Francis Xavier.* Lon.: Burns & Oates. 2 vols. (10s. 6d.) (E.E.E.)

BONHOURS, D. *The Life of St. Francis Xavier.* Phila.: Eugene Cumminskey, 1841.

CLEMENTS, JAS. *History of the Society of Jesus.* N. Y.: Walsh, 1865. 2 vols. Friendly. 16 sections on missions.

B. N. *The Jesuits.* Lon.: Burns & Oates, 1789. 2 vols. Friendly. Chapters 14, 15, 19, 20, 22, 27, 28, 29 on missions.

NICOLINI, G. B. *History of the Jesuits.* Lon.: Bohn, 1854. Chapter VII, missions. Hostile.

STEINMETZ, A. *History of the Jesuits.* Lon.: Bentley, 1848. 3 vols. Hostile. Unindexed.

## Protestants.

THOMPSON, A. C. *Protestant Missions, Their Rise and Early Progress.* N. Y.: Scribner's, 1894. ($1.75.) Best available for the period covered.

WARNECK, G. *Outline of a History of Protestant Missions from the Reformation to the Present Time.* N. Y.: Revell, 1901. $2.00.

GRAHAM, J. A. *Missionary Expansion Since the Reformation.* N. Y.: Revell, 1899. 244 pp., 45 pp. on our period. Excellent.

STORROW, E. *Protestant Missions in Pagan Lands.* Lon.: Snow & Co., 1888. 191 pp.; 9 pp. on our period.

BROWN, WM. *History of Missions Among the Heathen Since the Reformation.* Phila.: Cols, 1816; 2 vols. 3 vols. 3d edition 1864. Vol. I, pp. 23-34, Dutch; 35-154, English-American; 155-282, Danes; 283-Vol. II, 116, Moravians by countries.

LORD, E. *A Compendious History of the Principal Protestant Missions to the Heathen.* Bost.: Samuel Armstrong, 1813. 2 vols. Pp. 13-60, Introduction, review by centuries; pp. 61-165, The Danish Missions, valuable for its letters from Ziegenbalg and other missionaries.

SMITH, T., and CHOULES, J. O. *Origin and History of Missions.* Bost.: Walker, 1832. 2 vols. folio; 8th edition 1846. Pp. 1-10 by centuries; 41-182 Moravians by countries. Last 7 pp. R. C.

CHARTERIS, A. H. *The Dawn of the Modern Mission.* N. Y.: Armstrong, 1888. 160 pp. on our period.

LEONARD, D. L. *A Hundred Years of Missions.* N. Y.: Funk & Wagnalls, 1895. ($1.50.) Pp. 12-68 on our period.

SMITH, A. M. *Brief History of Evangelical Missions.* Hartford: Robins & Smith, 1844. 37 pp. on our period.

LOVETT, R. *A Primer of Modern British Missions.* N. Y.: Revell. 160 pp.

LAURY, P. A. *A History of Lutheran Missions.* Reading, Pa.: Pilger, 1899. 265 pp., 65 on our period. India, Finland, Greenland.

YONGE, C. M. *Pioneers and Founders.* Lon. and N. Y.: Macmillan, 1871.

CARNE, JOHN. *Lives of Eminent Missionaries.* Lon.: Fisher, 1833. Eliot, Danish and Moravian Missionaries.

CREEGAN, C. C., and GOODNOW, J. A. B. *Great Missionaries of the Church.* N. Y.: Crowell & Co., 1895.

CAMPBELL, J. *Maritime Discovery and Christian Missions.* Lon.: Snow, 1840.

## Moravians.

*Periodical Accounts Relating to the Missions of the Church of the United Brethren Established Among the Heathen.* Lon.: Brethren's Society for the Furtherance of the Gospel. 6 vols. 1790-1814. (E.E.)

HOLMES, J. *Historical Sketches of the Missions of the United Brethren Among the Heathen.* Dublin: Napper, 1818. (E.E.E.)

THOMPSON, A. C. *Moravian Missions, Twelve Lectures.* N. Y.: Scribner's, 1882. ($2.00.) Bibliography, pp. 491-510. Best available for general use.

*Missions-Atlas der Bruder-gemeine.* Seclozen Karten mit Text. Herausgegeben von der Missions direktion der Evangelischen Brüder-Unitat. Herrnhüt. Expedition der Missionsverwaltung, 1895.

HAMILTON, J. T. *The Missionary Manual and Directory of the Unitas Fratrum or the Moravian Church.* Bethlehem, Pa.: Moravian Pub. Office, 1892. 3d edition 60 pp.

SCHWEINITZ, EDM. DE. *Some of the Fathers of the Moravian Church.* Bethlehem: 1882.

SPANGENBERG, A. G. *Life of Count Zinzendorf.* Translated and abridged by Samuel Jackson. Lon.: Sam. Holdsworth, 1858. 511 pp.

CRANZ, D. *The Ancient and Modern History of the Brethren.* Lon.: W. A. Strahan, 1780. Pp. 620. Index.

BOST, A. *History of the Bohemian and Moravian Brethren.* Lon.: Religious Tract Society.

## Chapter I.—Ethnic Movements Missionary.

FISHER, G. P. *The Beginnings of Christianity.* N. Y.: Scribner's, 1893. ($2.50.)

DOELLINGER, J. J. I. *The Gentile and the Jew in the Courts of the Temple of Christ.* Translated by N. Darnell. 2 vols. Lon.: Longman, 1862.

PRESSENSÉ, E. D. *The Ancient World and Christianity.* N. Y.: Armstrong, 1888.

MERIVALE, C. *The Conversion of the Roman Empire.* N. Y.: Appleton, 1865. Boyle Lectures. Heathen thought reaching upward.

SUPER, C. W. *Between Heathenism and Christianity.* A translation of Seneca's De Providentia, Plutarch's, De Sera Numinis Vindicta and other best thoughts of heathenism. (E.E.)

FARRAR, F. W. *Seekers After God.* Seneca, Epictetus and Marcus Aurelius. N. Y.: Macmillan, 1879.

EDKINS, J. *The Early Spread of Religious Ideas, Especially in the Far East.* N. Y.: Revell. 144 pp. (90 cts.)

STORRS, R. S. *The Divine Origin of Christianity Indicated by Its Historical Effects.* N. Y.: Randolph, 1886. (E.E.E.) ($2.00.)

BRACE, C. L. *Gesta Christi; or, A History of Humane Progress Under Christianity.* N. Y.: Armstrong, 1883. ($1.50.)

Standard Church Histories, opening sections.

## Chapter II.—Messianic Race Missionary.

GOODSPEED, G. S. *Israel's Messianic Hope to the Time of Jesus.* N. Y.: Macmillan, 1900. ($1.50.)

YONGE, C. D. *The Works of Philo Judaeus the Contemporary of Josephus Translated from the Greek.* Lon.: Bohn, 1854. 4 vols. (E.E.)

DRUMMOND, JAS. *Philo Judaeus; or, The Jewish-Alexandrian Philosophy in Its Development and Completion.* Lon.: Williams & Norgate, 1888. 2 vols.

BIGG, C. *The Christian Platonists of Alexandria.* Oxford: Clarendon Press, 1896. Bampton Lectures.

LOHR, M. *Der Missionsgedanke in Alten Testament.* Leipzig: Mohr, 1900.

MERIVALE, C. *St. Paul at Rome.* N. Y.: Pott, Young & Co. Chapter I shows influence of the Jews at Rome.

HUDSON. *History of the Jews in Rome.* Lon.: 2d edition, 1884. 394 pp.

SAYCE, A. H. *Early Israel and the Surrounding Nations.* 1889. Lon.: Service & Paton, 1899.

WILLRICH, H. *Juden und Griechen vor der makkäbaischen Erhebung.* Göttingen: Dandenhaeck und Ruprecht, 1895. 176 pp.

## Chapter III.—Messiah Missionary.

*The Twentieth Century New Testament, a Translation Into Modern English, Made from the Original Greek (Westcott and Hort's Text), in Two Parts. Part I—The Five Historical Books.* N. Y.: Revell, 1898. (E.E.) (50 cts.)

STEVENS, W. A. and BURTON, E. D. *Harmony of the Gospels for Historical Study.* Bost.: Silver, Burdett & Co., 1899. (75 cts.) (E.E.)

*The New Testament.* Revised Version by Drs. Hovey, Weston and Broadus. Phila.: Am. Bapt. Pub. Soc. (30 cts.) (E.E.)

RHEES, RUSH. *The Life of Jesus of Nazareth; A Study.* N. Y.: Scribner's Sons, 1900. ($1.25.)

BEACH, H. P. *New Testament Studies in Missions.* N. Y.: The Student Volunteer Movement, 1900.

MATHEWS, S. *A History of New Testament Times in Palestine.* N. Y.: Macmillan, 1899. (75 cts.)

Standard Lives of Christ.

## Chapter IV.—Syria.

BURTON, E. D. *The Records and Letters of the Apostolic Age.* N. Y.: Scribner's, 1895. (E.E.) ($1.50.)

EUSEBIUS and SOZOMEN. *Nicene and Post-Nicene Fathers.* (E.E.E.)

FARRAR, F. W. *The Early Days of Christianity.* N. Y.: Funk & Wagnalls, 1883. (75 cts.)

NEANDER, A. *History of the Planting and Training of the Christian Church.* N. Y.: Sheldon, 1865.

PRESSENSÉ, E. DE. *The Early Years of Christianity.* N. Y.: Scribner's, 1871.

## Chapter V.—Asia Minor.

PLINY THE YOUNGER. *Letters of the Younger Pliny.*

Lon.: Trübner, 1879. Translated by J. D. Lewis. (E.E.)

JUSTIN MARTYR. A.-N. L. (E.E.)

RAMSAY, W. M. *The Church in the Roman Empire Before A. D. 170.* Lon.: Hodder & Stoughton, 1893.

RAMSAY, W. M. *St. Paul the Traveller.* N. Y.: Putnam, 1895. ($3.00.)

TAYLOR, W. M. *Paul the Missionary.* N. Y.: Harper, 1882.

Standard Lives of Paul.

References of preceding chapter.

## Chapter VI.—Persia.

*Syriac Documents.* A.-N. L. (E.E.)

SOZOMEN. *Ecclesiastical History.* N. and P.-N. F. Book II, Chaps. 7-15, on Christianity in Persia. (E.E.E.)

ASSEMANI, G. S. *Bibliotheca Orientalis Clementino-Vaticana, in qua Manuscriptos Codices Syriacos, Arabicas, Persicas, Turcicos, etc. . . . Ex Oriente Conquisitas Comparatas, etc.* Romae Typis Sacrae Congregationes de Propaganda Fide. 1722-1728. 4 vols., quarto, 700 pp. each. (E.E.E.)

GIBBON, E. *The History of the Decline and Fall of the Roman Empire.* Phila.: Porter & Coates. Nestorian Missions, Chapter XLVII.

YEATES, T. *Indian Church History, Syria, Mesopotamia, India and China.* Lon.: Maxwell, 1818. Useful summary of traditions as to Persia.

RAE, G. M. *The Syrian Church in India.* Edinb.: 1892.

ST. CLAIR-TISDALE, W. *The Conversion of Armenia to the Christian Faith.* N. Y.: Revell. ($1.40.)

GREGOR, N. T. *History of Armenia.* Lon.: Heywood, 1897.

MALAN, S. C. *St. Gregory the Illuminator.* Lon.: Rivington, 1868.

ISSAVERDEUS, J. *Armenia and the Armenians.* Venice: Armenian Monastery of St. Lazarus, 1874.

## Chapter VII.—India.

SMITH, G. *The Conversion of India.* N. Y.: Revell. ($1.50.) (E.E.E.)

HAYE, J. W. *Christianity in India.* Lon.: Smith, Elder & Co., 1859.

HOUGH, J. *The History of Christianity in India.* Lon.: Sealey & Burnside, 1839. Also Nisbet, 1849. 5 vols., 600 pp. each. First three previous to 1800.

COSMAS, INDICOPLEUSTES. *Christian Topography.* Lon.: Hakluyt Soc., 1897. (E.E.)

WREDE, F. *St. Thome Christians on the Coast of Malabar.* Asiatic researches. Vol. VII, 1801.

RAE, G. M. *The Syrian Church in India.* Edinb.: 1892.

GIBBON, E. *Roman Empire.* Chapter XLVII on the Nestorians.

JORDANUS, FRIAR. *The Wonders of the East.* 1330. Lon.: Hakluyt Soc., 1863. (E.E.)

D'ORSEY, A. J. D. *Portuguese Discoveries, Dependencies and Missions in Asia and Africa.* 1893. Authorities, pp. 379-384.

MALLESON, G. B. *Akbar and the Rise of the Mughal Empire.* 1896.

ROE, SIR T. *The Embassy to the Court of the Great Mogul.* 1615-19. Lon.: Hakluyt Soc., 1899. 2 vols. (E.E.)

ZIEGENBALG, B., and others. *Thirty-four Conferences Between the Danish Missionaries and the Malabarian Bramans.* Lon.: H. Clements, 1719. (E.E.)

ZIEGENBALG, B., and GRUNDLER, J. E. *Propagation of the Gospel in the East; Being an Account of the Success of Two Danish Missionaries, Lately Sent to the East Indies.* Lon.: Joseph Downing, 1718. Contains also An account of the Malabarians. 58 letters in all. (E.E.)

GRINFIELD, E. W. *Sketches of the Danish Mission on the Coast of Coromandel.* Lon.: Rivington, 1831.

SHERRING, M. A., and STORROW, E. *The History of*

*the Protestant Missions in India,* 1706-1881. Lon.: Relig. Tract Soc., 1884. ($1.50.)

PEARSON, H. *Memoirs of the Rev. Christian Frederick Swartz.* Bost. and Phila.: Perkins, 1835. 411 pp.

STAVORINUS, ADMIRAL. *Voyages.* Translated by Wilcocks. Lon.: 1798. 3 vols. Also in the 11th vol. of Pinkerton's Collection of Voyages and Travels. Lon.: Longman, 1812. (E.E.)

CALLENBACH, J. R. *Justus Heurnius, eene bijdrage tot geschiedenis des Christendanzs in Nederlandsch Oost-Indie.* Nykerk: G. F. Cullenbach, 1897. 368 pp.

BROWN'S *History of Missions,* as to Dutch.

Works on Jesuits.

## Chapters VIII and IX.—China and Tatary.

LEGGE, J. *Christianity in China; Nestorianism, Roman Catholicism and Protestantism.* Lon.: Trübner, 1888. ($1.00.) 65 pp. The Nestorian Monument of Hsi-an Fu, text, translation, notes and a lecture on the monument. (E.E.E.)

YULE, H. *Cathay and the Way Thither; Being a Collection of Medieval Notices of China.* Lon.: Hakluyt Soc., 1866. 2 vols. Invaluable collection of earliest extant accounts, with luminous introduction and annotations. (E.E.E.)

HUC, ABBE. *Christianity in China, Tartary and Thibet.* N. Y.: P. J. Kennedy. ($1.50.) 2 vols. Also Lon.: Longmans, 1857. 3 vols. Next to Yule in value. Embodies many of the earliest extant accounts. (E.E.E.)

MOSHEIM. *Authentic Memoirs of the Christian Church in China.* Edited by R. Gibbings. Dublin: 1862.

POLO, MARCO. *The Book of Sir Marco Polo.* Translated by Henry Yule. Lon.: Murray, 1875. 2 vols. (E.E.)

MENDOZA, JUAN G. DE. Translated by R. Parke. *The Historie of the Great and Mightie Kingdome of China.* Lon.: Wolfe, 1588. Reprinted by Hakluyt Soc., 1853. 2 vols. (E.E.)

LOCKMAN, F. *Travels of the Jesuits Into Various Parts of the World.* Bost.: T. Piety, 1762. 2 vols. Particularly China and East Indies. (E.E.)

D'ORLEANS, P. J., and WITSEN, N. *History of the Two Tartar Conquerors of China.* Hakluyt Soc., Vol. 17. (E.E.)

WILLIAMS, S. W. *The Middle Kingdom.* N. Y.: Scribner's, 1899. ($9.00.) 2 vols. Vol. II, pp. 275-306, our period. Excellent.

JENKINS, ROBERT C. *The Jesuits in China. Attempt at Impartial Judgment.* Lon.: Nutt, 1894. ($2.00.) Controversy on the Chinese Rites examined from the sources by a Protestant, pp. 165.

*Memorie Stariche dell' Eminentiss. Monsignor Cardinale de Taurnon, eposte con monumenti rari ed autentici non piu data alla luce.* Venice: Giuseppe Bettinelli, 1761-62. Eight small 8vo volumes, the original documents of the Chinese Rites controversy. (E.E.)

## Chapter X.—Philippine Islands.

PIGAFETTA, A. *The First Voyage Round the World, Effected in the Years* 1519-22 *by the Chevalier Pigafetta on Board the Squadron of Magellan.* In Pinkerton's Voyages and Travels. Lon.: Longman's, 1812, Vol. II. Also in Hakluyt Series. (E.E.)

ANTONIO DE MORGA. *The Philippine Islands, Moluccas, Siam, Cambodia, Japan and China at the Close of the Sixteenth Century.* Translated by H. E. J. Stanley. Lon.: Hakluyt Society, 1868. Originally published City of Mexico, 1609. Invaluable source as to early missions. (E.E.)

WALTER, R. *A Voyage Round the World in the Years* 1741-44 *by Geo. Anson, Esq., Now Lord Anson.* Lon.: Browne, 1756. Quarto. Same, 16mo. Dublin: Crooks, 1819. (E.E.)

DELGADO, J. J. *Historia General Sacro-Profana, Politica y Natural de las Ilas del Poniente Llamadas Filipinas.* Manila: Juan Atayde, 1892. Vol. I, "Biblioteca Historica Filipina," 943 pp.

INES, F. F. DE S. *Cronica de la Provincia de San Gregario Magno de Religiosas descalzos de N. S. P. San Francisco en Islas Filipinas, China, Japon, etc. Leetor de Sagrada*

*Teologia y Cronista de la misma Provincia en* 1676. Manila: Tipo Lithograpluo de Chofre y Comp., 1892. ($5.95.) Vols. II and III, "Biblioteca Historica Filipina." 712 and 702 pp. (E.E.E.)

EVCMO. *Memoria acerea de las Missiones de las P. P. Augustinos calzados en las Islas Filipinas.* Madrid: Imprenta de Olejandro Gomez Fuentenebro, 1880.

GASPAR. *Conquistas de las ilas Philipinas; temporal y la espiritual par las religiosas orden de san Augustin.* Madrid: Ruiz de Murga, 1698.

FUENTE, V. *Obras del Padre Pedro de Broadeneira, de la Compania de Jesus.* Madrid: Rivadeneyra. Biblioteca de Aulares Espanoles, 1868.

MEDINA, J. T. *Bibliographia Espanola de las Islas Filipinas* (1528-1810). Santiago de Chile: Cervantes, 1897. 666 titles.

MENDOZA, J. G. Two volumes on Missions from the Philippines to China. See literature under China. (E.E.)

CROZET. *Voyage to Tasmania, New Zealand, the Ladrone Islands and the Philippines in the Years* 1771-1772, *Translated by H. Ling Roth.* Lon.: Truelove & Shirley, 1891. Good on the Ladrones (E.E.)

WORCESTER, D. C. *The Philippine Islands and Their People.* N. Y.: Macmillan, 1898. Chap. I.

FOREMAN, JOHN. *The Philippine Islands.* Lon.: Low, Marston & Co. 1899. Chap. VIII.

BUTTERWORTH, H. *The Story of Magellan and the Discovery of the Philippines.* N. Y.: Appleton, 1899. ($1.50.)

BOWRING, SIR JOHN. *A Visit to the Philippine Islands.* Lon.: Smith, Elda & Co., 1859. Chap. XII., "Ecclesiastical Authority."

MEYER, A. B. *The Distribution of the Negritos in the Philippine Islands and Elsewhere.* Dresden: Stengel & Co., 1899. 18 pp. on Philippines.

COLEMAN, A. O. P. *The Friars in the Philippines.* Boston: Marler, Callahan & Co., 1899. A defense of the religious orders. Not thorough. (Paper, 25 cents.)

## Chapter XI.—Japan.

CADDELL, C. M. *History of the Missions in Japan.* N. Y.: P. J. Kennedy.

BROECKAERT, J. *Life of the Blessed Charles Spinola, with a sketch of the Other Japanese Martyrs.* N. Y.: Kennedy, 1899. (45 cents.)

WILBERFORCE, B. A. *Dominican Missions and Martyrs in Japan.* Lon.: Art & Book Co.; also, Catholic Truth Soc., 1897. Pp. 186. (60 cents.)

KENNERS, E. *A Brief Sketch of the Lives and Martyrdom of the Franciscan Saints Canonized by Pope Pius the Ninth.*

NITOBE, I. *The Intercourse Between the U. S. and Japan.* Baltimore: Johns Hopkins Press, 1891.

CHAMBERLIN, B. H. *Things Japanese.* Lon.: Kegen, Paul, Trench, Trübner & Co., 1891.

GRIFFIS, W. E. *The Religions of Japan.* N. Y.: Scribner's, 1895. ($2.00.)

GRIFFIS, W. E. *The Mikado's Empire.* N. Y.: Harper, 1894.

MURRAY, D. *The Story of Japan.* N. Y.: Putnam's, 1894.

CAMPBELL, WM. *An Account of the Missionary Success in the Island of Formosa, Published in London in 1650 and Now Reprinted with Copious Appendices.* Lon.: Trübner, 1889. 2 vols. ($4.00.) (E. E. E.)

## Chapter XII—Egypt and Abyssinia.

CLEMENT and ORIGEN. A-N. L. (E. E.)

NOBLE, F. P. *The Redemption of Africa.* 2 vols. N. Y.: Revell, 1899. ($4.00.) (This and next three on all Africa.)

LYDE, L. W. *A Geography of Africa.* Lon.: A. & C. Black, 1899. 112 pp. Much in little. No maps.

JOHNSTON, H. H. *A History of the Colonization of Africa by Alien Races.* Cambridge, Eng.: University Press, 1899. Pp. 146-8, Concise Summary of Missions Before 1800. Excellent maps.

WHITE, A. S. *The Development of Africa.* Lon.: Philip & Son, 1890.

SHARP, S. *History of Egypt.* Lon.: Bell & Sons, 1876. Vol. II., B. C. 116—A. D. 640.

CHANDLER, R. *Abyssinia, Mythical and Historical.* Lon.: Skeet.

JOHNSTON, C. *Notices of Abyssinia as Historically Connected with Europe, Syria and the Holy Land.* Lon.: Ainsworth, 1845.

## Chapter XIII.—North and West Africa.

CYPRIAN, TERTULLIAN and ARNOBIUS. A-N. L. (E. E.)

POOLE, G. A. *The Life and Times of St. Cyprian.* Lon.: Rivington, 1840.

HEARD, J. B. *Alexandrian and Carthagenian Theology Contrasted.* Edin.: T. & T. Clark, 1893. Hulsean Lectures.

CHURCH CLUB. *History and Teachings of the Early Church.* N. Y.: Young, 1889. Lecture III., "North African Church." Lecture IV., "School of Alexandria."

HOLME, L. R. *The Extinction of the Christian Churches in North Africa.* Lon.: Clay & Sons, 1898.

WHITE, A. S. *Development of Africa.* Lon.: Philip & Son, 1890. Chap. V., Islam and Christianity.

BARNES, L. C. *Shall Islam Rule Africa?* Bost.: Am. Bapt. Missionary Union, 1890.

SMITH, G. *Twelve Pioneer Missionaries.* Lon.: Thomas Nelson & Sons, 1900. Raymond Lull, on our period, pp. 13-38.

BONTIER (B.) and VERRIER (J.). *The Canarian.* Lon:. Hakluyt Soc., 1872. (E. E.)

BEAZLEY, C. R. *Prince Henry the Navigator. The Hero of Portugal and of Modern Discovery.* 1394-1460. *A. D.* N. Y.: Putnams, 1895. (E. E. E.)

AZURARA, G. E. DE. *The Chronicle of the Discovery and Conquest of Guinea.* Lon.: Hakluyt Soc., 1896-1899. 2 vols. Written 1450. (E. E.)

THOMPSON, T. *Memoirs of an English Missionary to the Coast of Guinea, Who Went There for the Sole Purpose of Converting the Negroes.* Lon.: Shepperson & Reynolds, 1788. 30 pp. (E .E.)

TRACY, J. *A Historical Examination of the State of Society in Western Africa, and of the Remedial Influence of Colonization and Missions.* Bost.: Marvin, 1846.

LIVINGSTONE, D. *Missionary Travels and Researches.* 1858. *Expedition to Zambesi.* N. Y.: Harpers, 1866.

COUSINS, W. E. *Madagascar of Today.* N. Y.: Revell. 159 pp. Two paragraphs on our period.

## Chapter XIV.—South Africa.

THEAL, G. M. *History of South Africa.* Lon.: Sonnenschein, 1888. Vols. I. and II. from 1486 to 1795.

M'CARTER, J. *The Dutch Reformed Church in South Africa.* Edin.: 1869.

Literature on Moravian Missions.

## Chapter XV.—Greece and Italy.

BURTON, E. D. *The Records and Letters of the Apostolic Age.* N. Y.: Scribners, 1895. (E. E.) ($1. 50.)

TAFEL. *De Thessalonica ejusque agro Dissertatio Geographica.* Berlin: 1839. (E. E. E.)

BURTON, E. D. *The Politarchs in Macedonia and Elsewhere.* Chic.: Reprinted from the Am. Journal of Theology, July, 1898. (E. E. E.)

TEXIER and PULLAN. *Byzantine Architecture.* Lon.: Day & Son, 1864. Pp. 111-154 on Salonica.

HARE, A. H. *Eighteen Centuries of the Orthodox Greek Church.* Parker & Co., 1889.

FELTON, C. C. *Greece, Ancient and Modern.* Bost.: Ticknor & Fields, 1867.

BIKÉLAS, D. *Seven Essays on Christian Greece.* Alexander Gardner, 1890. 1 vol., pp. 298.

ARISTIDES. A-N. L. (E. E.)

The Standard Lives of Paul.

The same literature as on chapters IV. and V.

REMINGTON, A. R. *The Church in Italy.* Lon.: Gardner, Dalton & Co., 1893.

MERIVALE, C. *St. Paul at Rome.* N. Y.: Pott, Young & Co.

FARRAR, F. W. *Darkness and Dawn, Scenes in the Days of Nero.* N. Y.: Longmans, 1891.

LANCIANI. *Pagan and Christian Rome. Chap. VII.,* Catacombs. Boston: Houghton, Mifflin & Co., 1893.

TACITUS. *Works of, The Oxford Translation Revised.* N. Y.: Harpers, 1895. (E. E.)

JUSTIN MARTYR. A-N. L. (E. E.)

TATIAN. A-N. L. (E. E.)

## Chapter XVI.—Spain and France.

See literature on Medieval period.

MEYRICK, FREDERICK. *The Church in Spain.* Lon.: Gardner, Darton & Co., 1892.

SMITH, R. T. *The Church in France.* Lon.: Gardner, Darton & Co., 1894.

## Chapter XVII.—Britain, Ireland and Scotland.

HADDON (A. W.) and STUBBS (W.). *Councils and Ecclesiastical Documents Relating to Great Britain and Ireland.* Oxford: Clarendon Press, 1896-98. (E.E.)

MACLEAR, G. F. *Conversion of the West. The Celts.* Lon.: S. P. C. K. (80 cents.)

BROWNE, G. F. *The Christian Church in These Islands Before the Coming of Augustine.* Lon.: S. P. C. K., 1894.

HALE, C. *Early Missions to and Within British Islands.*

CATCHCART, WM. *The Ancient British and Irish Churches, Including the Labors of St. Patrick.* Phila.: Am. Baptist Publication Soc., 1894. ($1.50.) (E. E. E.)

TODD, W. G. *The Church of St. Patrick and History of the Ancient Church of Ireland.* Lon.: 1845.

O'LEARY, J. *The Life of St. Patrick.* N. Y.: Kennedy. The writings and the early Lives of Patrick. (E. E.)

GRADWELL, R. *Succat: The Story of Sixty Years of the Life of St. Patrick.* Lon.: Burns & Oates. (5s.) "Monsignor Gradwell has treated his subject from a novel point of view. . . . In the first place, he has chosen a portion only of the life of St. Patrick. Again, he has attempted to exhibit him in the light in which he was seen by his contemporaries."

O'FARRELL, M. J. *A Popular Life of St. Patrick.* N. Y.: Kennedy, 1863. (60 cents.) 380 pp.

CHARLES, MRS. R. *Early Christian Missions of Ireland, Scotland and England.* Lon.: S. P. C. K., 1892.

REEVES, W. *Life of St. Columba, Founder of Hy. Written by Adamnan, Ninth Abbot of That Monastery.* Edin.: Edmonston & Douglas, 1874. Vol. VI. in "The Historians of Scotland." (E. E.)

FORBES, A. P. *Lives of St. Ninian and St. Kentigern, Compiled in the Twelfth Century.* Edin.: Edminston & Douglas, 1874. Vol. V. in "The Historians of Scotland." (E. E.)

LUCKOCK, H. M. *The Church in Scotland.* Lon.: Gardner, Darton & Co., 1893.

## Chapter XVIII.—England.

MASON, A. J. *The Mission of St. Augustine to England According to the Original Documents.* Cambridge: University Press, 1897. 252 pp. (E. E.)

GILES, J. A. *The Miscellaneous Works of Venerable Bede, In the Original Latin, . . . Accompanied by a New English Translation.* Lon.: Whittaker, 1843. 6 vols. (E. E.)

BEDE, THE VENERABLE. *Ecclesiastical History of England,* and *Anglo-Saxon Chronicle.* Lon.: Bell & Sons, 1887. (Bohn.) ($1.50.) (E.E.)

MACLEAR, G. F. *Conversion of the West. The English.* Lon.: S. P. C. K. (80 cents.)

HUNT, WM. *The English Church From Its Foundation to*

*the Norman Conquest.* Lon.: Macmillan, 1899. 444 pp. 222 on our period clear and admirable.

MONTALEMBERT. *The Monks of the West.* Edinb.: Blackwood, 1861. Vols. II.-V.

LINGARD, J. *Antiquities of the Anglo-Saxon Church.* Phila.: Fithian, 1841. Pp. 17-39 Missions to the A-S. Pp. 258-268 Missions of the A-S.

GREEN, J. R. *A Short History of the English People.* N. Y.: Harpers, 1877. ($1.20.)

FREEMAN, E. A. *Old English History.* Lon.: Macmillan, 1890. Chap. VI., "How the English Became Christians."

COLLINS, W. E. *The Beginnings of English Christianity, with Special Reference to the Coming of St. Augustine.* Lon.: Methuen & Co., 1898. 209 pp.

CHARLES, MRS. E. R. *Sketches of Christian Life in England in the Olden Time.* N. Y.: Tibbals & Whiting, 1865. 210 pp. on our period.

## Chapter XIX.—Germanic Regions.

See literature on Medieval period.

BALG, G. H. *The First Germanic Bible Translated from the Greek by the Gothic Bishop Wulfila in the Fourth Century, and Other Remains of the Gothic Literature.* Milwaukee, Wis.: G. H. Balg, 1891. 469 pp., containing a sketch of the life of Wulfila. (E. E.)

SCOTT, C. A. *Ulfilas, the Apostle of the Goths.* 1885.

MERIVALE, C. *Conversion of the West. Continental Teutons.* Lon.: S. P. C. K., 1879. (80 cents.)

BARING-GOULD, S. *The Church of Germany.* Lon.: Gardner, Darton & Co., 1891.

MEYRICK, T. (S. J.) *Life of St. Walburge.* Lon.: Burns & Oates. (2s.)

VAN DYKE, H. *The First Christmas Tree.* Scribners, 1897. ($1. 50.)

DITCHFIELD, P. H. *The Church in the Netherlands.* Lon.: Gardner, Darton & Co., 1893.

MEYRICK, T. (S. J.) *Life of St. Willebrand.* Lon.: Burns & Oates. (2s.)

## Chapter XX.—Scandinavian and Slavonic Regions.

SNORRE STURLASON. *The Heimskringla; or, The Sagas of the Norse Kings.* Translated by S. Laing, annotated by R. B. Anderson.N. Y.: Scribner, 1889. 4 vols. (E. E.)

MACLEAR, G. F. *The Conversion of the West... The Northmen.* Lon.: S. P. C.K. (80 cents.)

DUNHAM, S. A. *History of Denmark, Sweden and Norway.*

CARLYLE, T. *Early Kings of Norway.*

MACLEAR, G. F. *Conversion of the West...The Slavs.* Lon.: S. P. C. K., 1879. (80 cents.)

KRASINSKI, V. *Sketch of the Religious History of the Slavonic Nations.* Edinb.: Johnstone & Hunter, 1851.

LEGER, L. *A History of Austro-Hungary from the Earliest Time to the year* 1889. Translated from the French by Mrs. Beubeck Hill. With preface by E. A. Freeman. Lon. Rivington, 1889. 672 pp.

GINZEL, J. A. *Geschichte der Slavenapostel Cyrill und Method und der Slawischen Liturgie.* Vienna: A. Sshmurleim, 1861.

BONWETSCH, G. W. *Cyrell und Methodius, die Lehrer der Slaven.* Erlangen: 1885.

TOZER, H. F. *The Church and the Eastern Empire.* Lon.: Longmans, 1888. (80 cents.) Chap. VII., Missionary Efforts Among the Slavs.

STANLEY, A. P. *Lectures on the History of the Eastern Church.* N. Y.: Scribners. 1862. Lecture IX., "The Russian Church."

MOURAVIEFF, A. V. *A History of the Church of Russia.* Lon.: Rivington, 1842.

## Chapter XXI.—Arctic Regions.

MORRIS (Wm.) and MAGNUSSON (E.). *The Saga Library.* Lon.: Quaritch, 1891. 5 vols. (E. E.)

REEVES, A. M. *The Finding of Wineland the Good, the*

*History of the Icelandic Discovery of America.* Lon.: Frowde, 1895. (E. E. E.)

PAGE, J. *Amid Greenland Snows: Early Hist. of Arctic Missions.* Revell, 1893. (75 cents.)

EGEDE, H. *A Description of Greenland, with Historical Introduction and Life of the Author.* Lon.: Allman, 1818, 225 pp. (E. E. E.)

VARIOUS. *Modern Apostles of Missionary Byways.* N. Y.: Student Voolunteer Movement, 1899. 40 cents. Hans Egede, by A. C. Thompson, reprinted from his Protestant Missions. 11 pp.

COMMITTEE. *Lives of Missionaries...Greenland, Hans Egede, Matthiew Stach and Their Associates.* Lon.: S. P. C. K.

CRANS, D. *History of Greenland.* Lon.: 1767. 2 vols.

BRIGHTWELL, MISS C. L. *Romance of Modern Missions...A Home in the Land of Snows.* Lon.: R. T. S., 1870.

H. L. L. *Story of Moravian Missions in Greenland and Labrador.* Lon.: 1873.

*History of the Missions of the United Brethren in Labrador,* 1871.

## Chapter XXII.—Spanish America.

WINSOR, J., ed. *Narrative and Critical History of America.* First 5 vols. Bost.: Houghton, Mifflin & Co., 1889. 550 pp. Reliable data as to all America.

BANCROFT, H. H. *The Works Of.* 38 vols. San Francisco: The History Co., 1883-90. All Spanish North America.

COLUMBUS, C. *The First Letter of Christopher Columbus, Announcing the Discovery of America.* Facsimile of Latin and a new translation, by H. W. Haines. Bost.: Published by the Trustees of the Public Library, 1891. (50 cents) (E. E.)

COLUMBUS, C. *Letter to Gabriel Sanchez,* 1493. Bost.: Old South Leaflet, No. 33. (5 cents.) Same letter as preceding. (E. E.)

COLUMBUS, F. *The Discovery of America.* 1571. Bost.: Old South Leaflet, No. 29. (5 cents.) (E. E.)

COLUMBUS, C. *Columbus in Cuba. Journal of First Voyage.* Bost.: Old South Leaflet, No. 102. (5 cents.) (E. E.)

COLUMBUS, C. *Memorial to Ferdinand and Isabella.* Bost.: Old South Leaflet, No. 71. (5 cents.) (E. E.)

FORD, P. L. *Writings of Columbus.* N. Y.: Webster, 1892. (75 cents.) (E. E.)

HELPS, A. *Life of Las Casas.* Lon.: Bell & Daldy, 1868. ($1.00.)

TURON. *Life of Bartholomew Las Casas.* N. Y.: P. O'Shea, 1871.

LAS CASAS. *An Account of the First Voyages and Discoveries Made by Spaniards in America.* (Illustrated.) Lon.: Darby for Brown, 1699. (E. E.)

BENZONI, G. *History of the New World.* Lon.: Hakluyt Soc. Benzoni of Milan visited Spanish America 1541-56. Pp. 160-69 give sad view of the Spanish Christianization. (E. E.)

MARSHALL. *Christian Missions.*

SOUTHEY, R. *History of Brazil.* Lon.: Longman, 1822.

MARKHAM, C. R. *Expeditions Into the Valley of the Amazons,* 1539, 1540, 1639. Lon.: Hakluyt Soc., 1859. 64 pp. of valuable introduction by the editor. Pp. 26-42, best summary of missions for that region. (E. E. E.)

MURATORI. *Relation of the Missions in Paraguay.* Lon.:

CHARLEVOIX, P. F. X. *The History of Paraguay.* Lon.: Lockyer Davis, 1769. 2 vols.

CADDELL, C. M. *History of the Missions in Paraguay.* N. Y.: P. J. Kennedy. (45 cents.)

SOUTHEY, R. *A Tale of Paraguay.* Bost.: Goodrich, 1827.

BYRNE, S. (O. P.) *Sketches of Illustrious Dominicans.* N. Y.: O'Shea, 1884. ($1.00.) Pp. 153. Bertrand of New Granada, Garces of Mexico and Loaysa of Peru.

PETER CLAVER. *A Sketch of His Life and Labors in*

*Behalf of the African Slave.* N. Y.: Christian Press Association, 1895. (20 cents.)

BERNAN, J. H. *Missionary Labors in British Guiana.* Lon.: 1847.

CHINCH, B. G. *Early Missions in Central America.* Am. Catholic Quar., vol. 23, 1898.

BANCROFT, H. H. *History of Central America.* Vols. I. and II., 1501-1800.

CORTES, H. *Account of the City of Mexico.* 1520. Bost.: Old South Leaflet, No. 35. (5 cents.) (E. E.)

CHAMPLAIN, S. *A Voyage to the West Indies and Mexico, in the Years* 1599-1602. Lon.: Hakluyt Soc., 1859. (E. E.)

CLAVIGERO, F. S. (S. J.) *History of Mexico* (to 1521). *Collected from Spanish and Mexican Historians; to Which Are Added Critical Dissertations on the Land, the Animals and the Inhabitants of Mexico.* 2 vols. 1787. (E. E. E.)

*Augustinians in America in the Sixteenth Century.* Currier's "Religious Orders," pp. 669-672. Includes first mission to the Philippines.

PRESCOTT, Wm. H. *Conquest of Mexico.* Phila.: 1861.

DEVACA, C. *Journey to New Mexico,* 1535-36 Bost.: Old South Leaflet, No. 39. (5 cents.) (E. E.)

CORONADO. *Letter to Mendora,* 1540. Bost.: Old South Leaflet, No. 20. (5 cents.) (E. E.)

COUES, E. *On the Trail of a Spanish Pioneer; the Diary and Itinerary of Francisco Garces (Missionary Priest) in His Travels Through Sonora, Arizona and California,* 1775-1776. N. Y.: F. P. Harper, 1900. ($6. 00.) 2 vols. (E. E. E.)

BLACKMAR, F. W. *Spanish Institutions in the Southwest.* Balt.: Johns Hopkins Press, 1891.

POWERS, L. B. *Story of the Old Missions of California.* San Francisco: Wm. Doxey, 1893; also 1897. ($1.25.)

JAMES, G. W. *Old Missions and Mission Indians of California.* Los Angeles: Baumgardt, 1895.

JACKSON, H. H. *Glimpses of Three Coasts.* Bost.: Roberts, 1886. ($1.25.) Pp. 30-77. "Father Junipero and His Work" at Santa Barbara.

THOMAS, P. J. *Founding of the Missions.* California. San Francisco: P. J. Thomas, 1877.

SHEA, J. G. *History of the Catholic Missions Among the Indian Tribes of the United States,* 1529-1854. N. Y.: E. Dungan & Bro., 1855.

## Chapter XXIII.—French America.

THWAITES, R. G. *The Jesuit Relations and Allied Documents.* Cleveland, O.: Burrows Bros., 1896-1900. 66 vols. (E. E.)

BAXTER, J. P. *Pioneers of New France in New England; with Contemporary Letters and Documents.* Albany, N. Y.: Munsell, 1894. (E. E. E.)

PARKMAN, F. *France and England in North America.* Bost.: Little, Brown & Co., 1894. 9 vols. "The Jesuits," 1 vol., ($1.50.)

SHEA, J. G. *History of the Catholic Missions Among the Indians of the U. S.* N. Y.: Edward Dungan & Bro., 1855. ($1.50.)

SHEA, J. G. *Perils of Ocean and Wilderness . . . Gleaned from Early Missionary Annals.* Bost.:Donahoe, 1856.

KIP, W. I. *The Early Jesuit Missions in North America.* N. Y.: Wiley & Putnam, 1846. 321 pp.

CHARLEVOIX, P. F. X. *History and General Description of New France. Translated with notes by J. G. Shea.* N. Y.: F. R. Harper, 1900. 6 vols.

MARTIN, F. (S. J.) *Life of Father Isaac Jogues.* N. Y.: Benziger, 1885. Translated from the French by J. G. Shea. (75 cents.)

HAWLEY, C. *Early Chapters of Cayuga History, Jesuit Missions.* Auburn, N. Y.: Knop & Peck, 1879.

DONOHOE, T. *The Iroquois and The Jesuits.* Buffalo: Catholic Pub. Co., 1895. ($1.00.)

HARRIS, W. R. *History of the Early Missions in Western Canada,* Toronto: Hunter Rose & Co., 1893.

SANFORD. W. B. The Romance of a Jesuit Mission. A Historical Novel. N. Y.: Baker & Taylor Co., 1897. ($1.50.)

MARQUETTE, J. *Father Marquette at Chicago.* Bost.: Old South Leaflet, No. 46. (5 cents.) (E. E.)

SHEA, J. G. *Discovery and Exploration of the Mississippi Valley: with the Original Narratives of Marquette, Alloues, Membre, Hennepin and Anoslase Douay.* N. Y.: Redfield, 1853. (E. E. E.)

VERWYST, C. *Life of Bishop Baraga.* Milwaukee: 1900.

MONETTE, J. W. *History of the Discovery and Settlement of the Valley of the Missisippi by Spain, France and Great Britain; and the Subsequent Occupation, Settlement and Extension of Civil Government by the United States Until 1846.* 2 vols. 1846.

BARTLETT (C. H.) and LYON (R. H.) *La Salle in the Valley of the St. Joseph.* South Bend, Ind.: Tribune Printing Co., 1899.

BROWN, E. O. *Two Missionary Priests at Macinac,* and *Parish Register of the Mission of Michilimackinac.* Chicago: Barnard & Gunthorp, 1889.

## Chapter XXIV.—English America.

WINTHROP, J. *Conclusions for the Plantation in New England.* Bost.: Old South Leaflet, No. 50. (5 cents.) (E. E.)

SHURTLEFF, N. B. *Records of the Governor and Company of the Massachusetts Bay.* Bost.: Wm. White for the Commonwealth, 1853. Vol. I., 1628-1641. (E. E.)

MORTON, T. *Manners and Customs of the Indians.* 1637. Bost.: Old South Leaflet. (5 cents.) (E. E.)

MANY NEW ENGLAND MEN. *"New England's First Fruits in Respect, First, of the Conversion of Some, Conviction of Divers, Preparation of Sundry of the Indians; Second, of the Progress of Learning, in the Colledge at Cambridge in Massachusetts Bay."* Lon.: Henry Overton, 1643. (E.E.)

SHEPARD, T. *The Day-Breaking if Not the Sun-Rising of the Gospell with the Indians in New England.* Lon.: 1647. (E. E.)

MATHER, C. *India Christiana. A Discourse, Delivered Unto the Commissioners, for the Propagation of the Gospel Among the American Indians which is Accompanied with Several Instruments Relating to the Glorious Design of Propagating Our Holy Religion in the Eastern as well as the Western Indies.* Bost.: B. Green, 1721. (E. E. E.)

MATHER, C. *Magnalia Christi Americana; or, Eccliastical History of New England.* 1620-1698. 2 vols. Hartford, Ct.: Andrus, 1820.

BARBER, J. W. *The History and Antiquities of New England, New York, New Jersey and Pennsylvania.* N. Y.: Chas. Allyn & Co., 1856.

SPRAGUE, W. B. *Annals of the American Pulpit.* Vol. I. N. Y.: Carter & Bros., 1866.

DORCHESTER, D. *Christianity in the U. S. From the First Settlement down to* 1887. N. Y.: Hunt & Eaton, 1899.

LOVE, W. D. *Samson Occom.* Bost.: Cong. House, 1900. ($1.50.) (E. E. E.)

COLEMAN, L. *The Church in America.* Lon.: Gardner, Darton & Co., 1895.

BARTLETT, J. R. ed. *Records of the Colony of Rhode Island and Providence Plantations in N. E.,* 1636-1792. Providence, 1856-65. 10 vols. (E.E.)

BARTLETT, J. R. *The Letters of Roger Williams.* Providence: The Narragansett Club, 1874. (E. E.)

WILLIAMS, R. *Letters to Winthrop.* Bost.: Old South Leaflet, No. 54. (5 cents.) (E. E.)

KNOWLES, J. D. *Memoirs of Roger Williams.* Bost.: Lincoln, Edmonds & Co., 1854.

SPARKS, J. *Lives of Roger Williams, Timothy Dwight, and Count Pedoski.* Bost.: Little, Brown & Co., 1845.

GAMMEL, R. W. *Life of Roger Williams.*

ELTON, R. *Life of Roger Williams.* Providence: Whitney, 1853.

MUDGE, Z. A. *Foot-Prints of Roger Williams: a Biography.* N. Y.: Phillips & Hunt, 1871. (75 cents.)

GUILD, R. A. *Roger Williams the Pioneer Missionary to the Indians.* N. Y.: Baptist Home Mission Monthly, 1892. Oct. (10 cents.) (E. E. E.)

STRAUSS, O. S. *Roger Williams, The Pioneer of Religious Liberty.* N. Y.: Century Co., 1894. ($1.25.)

AUSTIN, J. A. *Roger Williams Calendar.* Central Falls, R. I.: E. L. Freeman & Sons, 1897. (E. E.)

ELIOT, SHEPARD, WINSLOW, WHITFIELD, MAYHEW. *Tracts Relating to the Attempts to Convert the Indians.* Collections of the Massachusetts Historical Society. Vol. IV. of the third series. Cambridge: Folsom, 1834. (E. E.)

ELIOT, J. *The Indian Grammar Begun.* Bost.: Old South Leaflet. (5 cents.) (E. E.)

ELIOT, J. *A Brief Narrative of the Progress of the Gospel Among the Indians of New England in the Year 1670.* Bost.: Old South Leaflet. (5 cents.) (E. E.)

MOORE, M. *John Eliot.* Bost.: Bedlington, 1822.

ADAMS, N. *The Life of John Eliot.* Bost.: Mass. Sabb. Assn, 1847.

CAVERLY, R. B. *Life and Labors of John Eliot.* Lowell, Mass.: George M . Eliot, 1881.

WORTHINGTON, E. *John Eliot and the Indian Village at Natick.* Hyde Park, Mass.: Hyde Park Historical Society, 1890.

TOOKER, W. W. *John Eliot's First Indian Teacher and Interpreter, Cockenoi-de-Long Island.* N. Y.: F. P. Harper, 1896.

BYINGTON, E. H. *Puritan as a Colonist and Reformer.* Bost.: Little, Brown & Co., 1899.

MAYHEW, M. *The Conquests and Triumphs of Gracae.* Bost.:1694. (E. E.)

MAYHEW, E. *A Discourse on Men as Reasonable Creat-*

*ures, with a Brief Account of the State of the Indians in Martha's Vineyard from* 1694-1720. (E. E.)

HALLOCK, W. A. *The Venerable Mayhews and the Aboriginal Indians of Martha's Vineyard.* N. Y.: Am. Tract Society, 1874. (40 cents.)

SHERWOOD, J. M. *Memoirs of Rev. David Brainerd.* N. Y.: Funk & Wagnalls, 1884. ($1.50.) (E. E. E.)

PAGE, J. *David Brainerd.* Lon.: Partridge & Co. (75 cents.)

YONGE, C. M. *Pioneers and Founders.* N. Y.: Macmillan, 1871.

WHEELOCK, E. *Narrative of the Original Design, Rise, Progress and Present State of the Indian Charity-school in Lebanon, Conn.* Bost.: Old South Leaflet. (5 cents.) (E. E.)

BEATTY, C. *Journal of a Two Months' Tour for Promoting Religion Among the Frontier Inhabitants of Penna. and Introducing Christianity Among the Indians Westward of the Allegheny Mts. Added Accts. of Attempts to Convert.* Lon.: Davenhill, 1768. (E. E.)

HUMPHREYS, D. *Historical Account of the S. P. G.* Lon.: 1730 Chap. XI. Work for Iroquois Indians. (E. E. E.)

ABORIGINES COMMITTEE. *Some Account of the Conduct of the Relig. Sec. of Friends towards the Indian Tribes.* Lon.: Edward Marsh, 1844.

INDIAN COMMITTEE. *A Brief Sketch of the Efforts of the Relig. Society of Friends to Promote the Civilization and Improvement of the Indians.* Phila.: Friends' Book Store, 1866.

REICHEL, W. C. *Memorials of the Moravian Church.* Phila.: Lippincott, 1870. Vol. I. contains the original accounts of Zinzendorf in America. (E. E.)

LOSKIEL, G. H. *History of the Mission of the United Brethren Among the Indians in North America.* Translated by C. I. Latrobe. Lon.: Breth. Soc. for the Furtherance of the Gospel, 1794.

SCHWEINITZ, E. D. *The Life and Times of David Zeisberger.* Phila.: Lippincott, 1871. (E. E. E.)

HOWELLS, W. D. *Three Villages.* Bost.: Osgood, 1884.

HAZARD, S. *Pennsylvania Archives.* Phila.: Severns, 1854. 12 vols. (E. E.) Read Especially Vols. II., IV. and IX.

BUTTERFIELD, C. W. *Washington-Irvine Correspondence.* Madison, Wis.: Atwood, 1882. (E. E.)

HASSLER, E. W. *Old Westmoreland, a History of Western Pennsylvania During the Revolution."* Pittsburg: Weldin, 1900.

RONDTHALER, E. *Life of John Heckwelder.* Phila.: Townsend Ward, 1847.

*TSCHOOP: The Converted Indian Chief.* (N. B.) Am. S. S. Union.

HECKWELDER, I. *A Narrative of the Mission of the United Brethren Among the Delaware and Mohegan Indians,* 1740-1808. Phila.: McCarty & Davis, 1820.

JAPP, A. H. *Master Missionaries.* Lon.: Fisher Unwin. Fourth Ed.

*Missions of the Church of the United Brethren in the Danish West India Islands.* Lon.: 1832.

BUCHNER, J. H. *The Moravians in Jamaica.* Lon.: Longman, 1854.

## Chapter XXV.—Continuity in Missions.

ALLEN, A. V. C. *Continuity of Christian Thought; a Study of Modern Theology in the Light of Its History.* Bost.: Houghton, Mifflin & Co., 1884. ($2.00.)

HEARD, J. B. *Alexandrian and Carthagenian Theology Contrasted.* Ednb. Clark, 1893.

CRUTWELL, C. T. *A Literary History of Early Christianity.* N. Y.: Scribners, 1893. 2 vols.

DENNIS, J. S. *Christain Missions and Social Progress.* N. Y.: Revell, 1899. 2 vols. ($5.00.) (E. E. E.)

MARTIN, C. *Apostolic and Modern Missions.* N. Y.: Revell, 1898.

LIGHTFOOT, I. B. *Historical Essays.* N. Y.: Macmillan, 1895. Second Essay, "Comparative Progress of Ancient and Modern Missions." Pp. 71-92.

# INDEX OF NAMES AND SUBJECTS.

Figures refer to pages.